RELIGION IN VICTORIAN BRITAIN

VOLUME V
CULTURE AND EMPIRE

RELIGION IN VICTORIAN BRITAIN

VOLUME V
CULTURE AND EMPIRE

EDITED BY
JOHN WOLFFE

AT THE
OPEN UNIVERSITY

MANCHESTER UNIVERSITY PRESS

MANCHESTER AND NEW YORK

IN ASSOCIATION WITH THE
OPEN UNIVERSITY

DISTRIBUTED EXCLUSIVELY IN THE USA AND CANADA
BY ST. MARTIN'S PRESS

Published by Manchester University Press
Oxford Road, Manchester M13 9PL, UK
and Room 400, 175 Fifth Avenue, New York, NY 10010, USA

Distributed exclusively in the USA and Canada by
St. Martin's Press, Inc., 175 Fifth Avenue, New York, NY 10010, USA

British Library cataloguing in publication data
applied for

Library of Congress cataloging in publication data
applied for

ISBN 0 7190 5184 3 *paperback*

This book forms part of an Open University course AA313 *Religion in Victorian Britain*. For information about this course please write to the Student Enquiries Office, The Open University, PO Box 71, Walton Hall, Milton Keynes, MK7 6AG, UK

Typeset by the Open University
Printed in Great Britain
by T. J. International Ltd., Padstow, Cornwall

CONTENTS

PREFACE

This book is the fifth in a series entitled *Religion in Victorian Britain*, published by Manchester University Press in association with the Open University. The first four volumes appeared in 1988 and remain in print. The purpose of this new volume is explained fully in the Introduction. The five volumes form the nucleus of an Open University Course. Volumes I and II, *Traditions* and *Controversies* (edited by Gerald Parsons, 1988), consist of sets of specially written essays covering the major religious denominations and groups of the Victorian period and the issues and controversies between and within them. Volume III, *Sources* (edited by James R. Moore, 1988), is a collection of primary source material from the period, while Volume IV, *Interpretations* (edited by Gerald Parson, 1988), is a collection of recent essays and articles in the field by other writers.

References to other volumes in the series are made in the following style:

RVB, II, 4 (*Religion in Victorian Britain*, Volume II, *Controversies*, chapter 4),

or

RVB, III, 1.2 (*Religion in Victorian Britain*, Volume III, *Sources*, item 1.2).

The authors wish to acknowledge the essential contribution to the development and production of this volume made by other members of the Open University staff. Tim Benton, Dean of Arts, first suggested the project and made it possible; Trevor Herbert, Staff Tutor in Music, gave invaluable advice in relation to Chapter 2. The support provided by Julie Bennett (editor), Tony Coulson (library), Pat Phelps (secretary), Adrian Roberts (course manager) and John Taylor (book trade) has gone far beyond the call of duty.

The authors would also like warmly to thank Professor John Kent for his well-considered and balanced comments on earlier drafts of the chapters. Any deficiencies that remain are their own personal responsiblity.

The authors are all present or former members of the Department of Religious Studies and the Faculty of Arts at the Open University:

Gwilym Beckerlegge, Staff Tutor in Religious Studies

Frances Knight, Temporary Lecturer in Religious Studies (now Lecturer in Christian Theology, University of Wales, Lampeter)

Gerald Parsons, Senior Lecturer in Religious Studies

Terence Thomas, Staff Tutor in Religious Studies (now retired)

John Wolffe, Senior Lecturer in Religious Studies

Recommended Further Reading

Books and articles particularly recommended for further reading are marked with an asterix in the bibliographies at the end of each chapter.

Illustration Sources

The sources for the illustrations reproduced in this book are as follows: front cover, *Punch* 26.9.1857; Introduction, *Punch* 10.10.1857; Ch. 1, *Punch* 26.1.1861; Ch. 2, *Punch* 22.1.1870; Ch. 3, *Queen Victoria Presenting a Bible to an African Ambassador, The British Workman*, 1859. Photo: Mary Evans Picture Library; Ch. 4, *Vanity Fair* 28.11.1874; Ch. 5, *Vanity Fair* 6.2.1875; Ch. 6, title page, *Liverpool Freeman* 8.7.1905. Reproduced by permission of the British Library Board, Fig. 1, Notice for the Liverpool Muslim Institute and Schools, from *Islamic World*, April 1896. Reproduced by permission of Liverpool Libraries and Record Office, Fig. 2, Notice of the Medina Home for Children, from *Islamic World*, April 1896. Reproduced by permission of Liverpool Libraries and Record Office, Fig. 3, Interior view elevation of the lecture hall, Liverpool Muslim Institute (top) and Interior of the lecture hall (bottom), from J. H. McGovern, 'Saracenic architecture', *Islamic World*, April 1896, pp. 366 and 364. Reproduced by permission of Liverpool Libraries and Record Office, Fig. 4, *Mihrab* at the Liverpool Mosque, from J. H. McGovern 'Saracenic architecture', *Islamic World*, April 1896, p. 364. Reproduced by permission of Liverpool Libraries and Record Office, Fig. 5, Mosque at the Oriental Institute, Maybury, Woking (top), *Minbar* or pulpit, Mosque at the Oriental Institute (left) and *Dekké* or reading seat, Mosque at the Oriental Institute (right), from *Illustrated London News*, 9 November 1889, p. 590.

Acknowledgements

Grateful acknowledgement is made to the following sources for permission to reproduce material in this book: Frost, M. (1962) *Historical Companion to Hymns Ancient and Modern*, The Canterbury Press, Norwich/Hymns Ancient and Modern Ltd; Kipling, R. (1920) *Rudyard Kipling's Verse*, Hodder & Stoughton. Reprinted by permission of A. P. Watt Ltd on behalf of the National Trust; Kipling, R. (1923) *Plain Tales From The Hills*, Macmillan. Reprinted by permission of A. P. Watt Ltd on behalf of the National Trust.

Every effort has been made to trace all copyright owners, but if any permission has been inadvertently overlooked, the publishers will be pleased to make the necessary arrangements at the first opportunity.

INTRODUCTION

'O GOD OF BATTLES! STEEL MY SOLDIERS' HEARTS!'

*VICTORIAN RELIGION
IN CONTEXT*

I N May 1857, a seemingly trivial oversight by the British military authorities at Meerut in India had far-reaching consequences. New cartridges issued to native troops had to be coated in grease made up of a mixture of the fat of cows, which were sacred to Hindus, and of pigs, which were unclean to Muslims. Soldiers who felt their religious sensibilities gravely insulted refused to use the new cartridges. They were severely punished and colleagues then mutinied in sympathy. In the ensuing 'Indian Mutiny'[1] the British for some months lost control of much of north central India. There was violence and atrocity on both sides of the armed conflict, and at home the events induced national soul-searching. It was recognized that, as the Conservative leader Benjamin Disraeli put it in the House of Commons, 'The decline and fall of empires are not affairs of greased cartridges', and there was considerable debate about the underlying causes of the crisis (Porter, 1984 edn, pp. 28–30). In a day of 'national fasting and humiliation' on 7 October 1857, numerous church services were held with the purpose of seeking divine forgiveness for national sins and praying for the restoration of British fortunes in the subcontinent (Stanley, 1983). Eventually order was restored, but the implications for the nature of British rule in India, and for attitudes to both empire and religion, were extensive and enduring.[2]

Prominent among the specific ramifications of the Mutiny was a trend towards a reappraisal both of missionary strategy and of attitudes to non-Christian religions. Further connections are suggested by the two *Punch* cartoons relating to the Mutiny, which are reproduced on the cover of this volume and at the beginning of this Introduction. In the 'Popish Organ Nuisance' Cardinal Wiseman in the guise of an organ-grinder is accompanied by a monkey dressed in a garment resembling an ecclesiastical cope. He annoys John Bull, who, preoccupied with events in India, finds the activities of Roman Catholics a tiresome but relatively trivial distraction. Only seven years earlier, though, in the so-called 'Papal Aggression', Roman Catholicism had itself been perceived as presenting a fundamental challenge to Christian Protestant England, of the kind now attributed to the Indian rebels. At the same time, the cartoon points to controversy over changing styles of church worship and music, and specifically to the introduction of organs, perceived in some quarters as 'popish'. 'O God of Battles!' which appeared in *Punch* in the week of the day of 'national fasting and humiliation' strikes a more sombre note. It attributes to Queen Victoria the prayer of her forebear King Henry V on

---

[1] The standard British label for the event reflects the fact that it began as a military mutiny. Indian historians have referred to it as the First War of Indian Independence.

[2] For fuller discussion of the 'Indian Mutiny' see Chapter 3, pp. 122–4.

the eve of Agincourt as portrayed by Shakespeare. The context of the line (from *Henry V*, Act IV, Scene 1) hints that Victoria's resolute intercession is not mere bloodthirstiness, but is linked to an underlying sense of guilt and insecurity analogous to Henry's sense of a need to atone for the death of King Richard II. Victoria is shown embracing her children and surrounded by other women and their families, an image that vividly encapsulates the contemporary perception of women as providing the essential spiritual undergirding of social stability and national greatness even while being themselves insulated from more material and physical struggles. These two cartoons thus not only indicate that if Victorian religion in Britain is to be fully understood it needs to be viewed in an imperial context, but also illustrate a complex web of cultural and political connections with religious life. The essays contained in this volume seek to trace some of these threads, while enhancing understanding of Victorian religion itself.

In 1988, the Open University in collaboration with Manchester University Press published a set of four volumes on *Religion in Victorian Britain*. As Gerald Parsons explained in the Introductions to these volumes, the 'initial and principal aim of the authors' was 'the provision of a coherent and integrated body of material for use by Open University students'. At the same time it was intended that the volumes would provide a more general resource for students of Victorian religion in other institutions.

During the last eight years, these initial expectations have been richly fulfilled. Over that period, several thousand students have studied and successfully completed the Open University course 'Religion in Victorian Britain', using the volumes as core texts. During that period too, the books have been much acclaimed by reviewers, and have proved to be an invaluable resource for undergraduates and senior scholars alike. It would be unwise to claim too much for them, however, for like any work of synthesis they have their own omissions and blind spots. Nevertheless, built as they were on the most recent scholarship of the mid-1980s, they have hitherto well stood the test of time in a field whose essential contours have not changed significantly. Their degree of enduring success is such that the Open University feels every confidence in now producing a fifth volume, which will serve both to expand the existing course and to widen the scope of the set for the benefit of numerous other interested readers.

The first volume in the series, subtitled *Traditions*, primarily reflects a more traditional 'church history' approach to Victorian religion. It contains surveys of the development of Anglicanism, Protestant Nonconformity, Scottish Presbyterianism, Roman Catholicism and Judaism, together with accounts of the clerical renaissance, revivalism, ritualism, freethinking and secularism. It is complemented by the second volume, *Controversies*, which focuses more on the cultural and social dimensions of religion through attention to a series of studies of particular issues and controversies in Victorian religious life. The main ground covered relates to the interactions between religion and working-class life; to changes in the relationships between church, state and society; to the moral dimensions of religious belief; and to the implications of scientific advance and the growth of historical and critical approaches to the Bible. A final chapter also discusses the impact of religions other than Christianity and Judaism, a theme that will receive much more extensive attention in the present volume.

Whereas the material in Volumes I and II was specially written for the series, Volumes III and IV are compilations. Volume III is an edited collection of primary sources for the study of religion in Victorian Britain, whilst Volume IV is a selection of recent studies of aspects of Victorian religion by historians other than those directly responsible for the *Religion in Victorian Britain* series.

This new volume, the fifth in the series, combines elements of Volumes II and III. Part I of the book, which follows this Introduction, contains six essays by five different authors, two of whom, Gerald Parsons and Terence Thomas, also contributed to the earlier volumes. Each author has written as an individual presenting his or her own particular standpoint and approach both to the subject as a whole and to the specific topic of any given essay. The essays accordingly provide an enhanced appreciation of the richness and diversity of Victorian religion. At the same time, the volume has been conceived and written as a collaborative enterprise. The authors have read and commented on each other's work and linkages between the essays have been highlighted and developed. The first three essays on, respectively, gender, church music and foreign missions, have been conceived as introductions to their particular topics, surveying and assessing some of the principal developments during the Victorian period. The remaining three essays, by contrast, adopt a case study approach: two are biographical studies of pivotal but hitherto much misunderstood individuals; the final essay is a pioneering investigation of the presence of Hindus, Muslims, Parsis and Sikhs in Victorian Britain. In all the essays the authors seek to indicate the significance of their subjects in relation to Victorian religious life in general.

Part II of the book contains a compilation of primary sources, selected in the first instance to support, illustrate and develop the arguments of the corresponding essays. The objective is to provide a widening of the scope of Volume III, commensurate with the extension to Volume II offered in the first part of the new volume. As in Volume III, moreover, the opportunity has been taken to reprint a number of important Victorian texts that were hitherto not readily available. It is hoped that the primary sources will suggest to the reader further themes and connections going beyond the scope of the essays themselves.

II

The content of this volume might be collectively characterized as exploring Victorian religion in context, while maintaining a balancing focus on institutional, theological and spiritual developments. Although the range of the original volumes is expanded, the underlying approach remains similar. The choice of specific topics for examination is intended both to reflect and to complement other scholarship on Victorian religion that has appeared since 1988. Accordingly, before turning to highlight some overall themes in our own work, it will be appropriate to survey some of the trends of investigation and interpretation apparent elsewhere. Four aspects of such recent scholarship merit attention.

First, although over the last decade there have been no radical changes in historical interpretation of religion in the Victorian era itself, our knowledge and understanding of the Georgian period that preceded it has been transformed. It was the Victorians who created an enduring caricature of their grandparents as characterized by moral corruption, theological scepticism and spiritual torpor. Now, however, it is increasingly recognized that, although the Georgians, of course, had their fair share of 'sinners' and 'doubters', the eighteenth century as a whole was not so much irreligious as religious in a different way from both the intense, turbulent seventeenth century and the earnest, restless nineteenth. Two much-acclaimed overall surveys of the period (Clark, 1985; Colley, 1992), although differing from each other in many respects, have agreed in emphasizing the centrality of religion to national self-definition and to social and political ideology. Meanwhile, a growing body of detailed scholarship on the Church of England (notably Mather, 1985; 1992; Walsh, Haydon and Taylor, 1993; Nockles, 1994; Smith, 1994) has served substantially to revise the perception that it was sunk in ineffective indolence. Anglicanism, moreover, was central to intellectual and cultural life and, north of the Border, there was parallel engagement between the Church of Scotland and the leading thinkers of the day (Sher, 1985). Even where a more 'pessimistic' approach to eighteenth-century religion continues, there is still a modification of earlier crude stereotypes (Virgin, 1989).

Against this redrawn backdrop the Methodist and Evangelical movements need to be reinterpreted. To an earlier generation of scholarship they appeared to be the counter-cultural exception that proved the rule of general religious decline; they now begin to be seen more as branches growing out of the main trunk of the religious life of the age, albeit eccentric and ultimately disruptive ones (Walsh, 1986; Bebbington, 1989). In particular, the Anglican High Church tradition that had nourished the spirituality and theology of the Wesleys has been shown to have been a continuing force in late Georgian England, and one not so much at odds with Evangelicalism as has been too readily supposed (Mather, 1992; Nockles, 1994, especially pp. 30–2 and 321–3).

Nevertheless, in the long run, the spiritual influence of Evangelicalism, when combined at the end of the eighteenth century with the social consequences of the 'Industrial Revolution' and the political aftermath of the French Revolution, proved to be a powerful solvent of existing religious structures, dominated as they were by the Established Churches. Dissent grew spectacularly between 1790 and 1830, thus precipitating the sense of crisis in church–state relations with which the Victorian era opened. Recognition of this trend is not new (Ward, 1972), but it has in recent years been studied with increased detail and subtlety (Lovegrove, 1988; Smith, 1994; Hempton, 1996a). The most important implication of this work for students of a later period is that the popular culture of early nineteenth-century Britain was not so much irreligious as religious on its own terms. Sometimes popular religiosity meant adherence to organized Dissenting chapels; sometimes it implied a more diffuse assimilation of Evangelical influences; but only rarely was there a complete rejection of a religious view of the world. Indeed, it now becomes possible to argue, with considerable credibility, that in its early phases at least industrialization served to stimulate religion rather than to weaken it (Brown, 1995).

Students of Victorian religion, therefore, need to remind themselves with particular force that the technical beginning of the Victorian age with the death of William IV on 20 June 1837 in itself changed virtually nothing. There has, of course, long been a tendency to apply the epithet 'Victorian' somewhat loosely and to see as foundational to it events, such as the beginning of the Oxford Movement in 1833, and trends, such as the growing influence of distinctively Evangelical values, that significantly predated 1837. Such an approach should be reinforced by the recognition that the religious culture that the Victorians inherited was not so much a still millpond that they stirred up as a fast-flowing river that they diverted. Inevitably, the definition of a distinctively Victorian religious ethos accordingly becomes a more complex and subtle task than it might have appeared in the past.

Second, the reaction reflected in the original volumes in the *Religion in Victorian Britain* series against a 'church history' narrowly focused on theology and institutions has continued, even while much work has still been shaped by the broad structure of the religious traditions of Victorian Britain. Examples of the older style of approach do occur (for example, Hylson-Smith, 1989; Supple-Green, 1990; Hylson-Smith, 1993), but they have become comparatively rare. More characteristic of recent scholarship have been books that have set specific traditions in the wider context of social and cultural history. Thus, the place of grass-roots Anglicanism in the social fabric has been explored (Knight, 1995) and Scottish Baptist churches studied in their local socio-economic context (Bebbington, 1988). Both Methodism in particular and Nonconformity in general have been related to their cultural environment (Hempton, 1996a; Munson, 1991; Watts, 1995). The relationships of Presbyterianism to Scottish identity have been investigated (Walker and Gallagher, 1990; Brown and Fry, 1993) and the social and political history of British Jewry has been surveyed (Alderman, 1992). Even where a scholar's topic of investigation might seem to be narrowly focused on a particular religious tradition, there has often been a revision of previously accepted views of the history of that institution. For example, the nature and chronology of organizational reform in the Church of England has been reinterpreted (Burns, 1990), and a close study of Roman Catholic devotion serves to cast doubt on the hitherto conventional view that there was a clear-cut triumph of the 'Ultramontanes' in the mid nineteenth century (Heimann, 1995).

There has also been a tendency somewhat to diversify our picture of the variety of religious traditions in Victorian Britain and of the inter-relationships between them. Studies of smaller groups such as the Scottish Episcopal Church (Strong, 1995), the Catholic Apostolic Church (Flegg, 1992), the Mormons (Jensen and Thorp, 1989) and the Salvation Army (Horridge, 1993) are important not only for uncovering the intensity of activity and experience to be found in such seeming byways, but also for providing fresh perspectives from which to view the development of the more prominent traditions. For example, given that the Oxford Movement and the Catholic Apostolic Church were both in the first instance products of ferment within the Church of England in the early 1830s, there is surely something to be learned from a comparison of their subsequent histories. Why did the one, arguably, transform the face of the

Church whilst the other rapidly declined into relative marginality? Meanwhile, study of the Mormons provides important wider insights into popular religious cultures.[3]

Some other publications have served to remind us that important currents of strong religious identity could flow across institutionally separated traditions. Two major biographies of John Henry Newman (Ker, 1988; Gilley, 1990) illuminate the career and ideas of a towering personality who in his own life bridged the Anglican and Roman Catholic traditions. Similarly, increasing attention to the history of Protestant Evangelicalism (Bebbington, 1989; Hempton and Hill, 1992; Wolffe, 1995) serves to indicate the links between Scottish and Irish Presbyterianism, English and Welsh Nonconformity, and an important strand within Anglicanism. Nevertheless, as demonstrated by a recent collection of survey essays (Paz, 1995), a traditions-based approach to Victorian religion still has considerable vigour.

Third, the converse of the ongoing reaction against church history has been an increasing acceptance of religion as a central strand in the political, social and cultural history of the period. Several recent monographs have shown how religious influences were fundamental to the calculations, even if not always to the convictions, of politicians of all colours (Parry, 1986; Brent, 1987; Wolffe, 1991; Kerr, 1994). William Ewart Gladstone has, in particular, been reassessed as a statesman for whom religious considerations are now seen as central (Matthew, 1986; 1995; Bebbington, 1993).

The place of religion in the mainstream of intellectual and cultural life has been cogently argued in two solidly documented books (Hilton, 1988; Turner, 1993). Boyd Hilton suggests that Evangelicalism was foundational to the whole ethos of early Victorian Britain. The early part of the period is characterized as an 'age of atonement' in which theological presuppositions about the inherent sinfulness of humanity, the redemptive power of the crucified Christ and the impending judgement of God shaped attitudes to economics, social problems and science alike (Hilton, 1988). Around 1860, Hilton argues, the tenor of theology changed, to stress the incarnation and humanity of Christ rather than his atoning death, and this development too was integrally related to wider intellectual and cultural trends, such as aspirations to build a more harmonious society (*ibid.*, pp. 299–339). In a parallel line of argument,

---

[3] We cannot digress to explore these specific issues in any depth, but we might note how the Oxford Movement sought to transform Anglicanism from within, whereas the Catholic Apostolic Church withdrew from it; and how the Mormons benefited from the insecurities and millennial expectation of the 1840s (Jensen and Thorp, 1989, p. 47).

Frank Turner maintains that in interpreting Victorian ideas and attitudes it is anachronistic to impose a clear-cut distinction between the religious and the secular. Religious ideologies could cloak secular objectives, just as secular ideologies could be pursued with quasi-religious intensity. In a further paradox, Turner suggests that the 'crisis of faith' was a result not of attack on Christianity but of reaction against 'the most fervent religious crusade that the British nation had known since the seventeenth century' (Turner, 1993, pp. 3–37 and 73–100).

One specific implication of such an approach is to reassess and to some extent to downplay the role of science and Charles Darwin in the erosion of traditional Christian orthodoxy. Darwin's life and career have received important re-evaluation (Desmond and Moore, 1991). Meanwhile, other scholars have explored the impact on religion of less immediately obtrusive intellectual currents, notably the influence of positivism and the growth of more critical approaches to history (Cashdollar, 1989; Hinchliff, 1992). Debates on such issues will continue, with ramifications that are now acknowledged to stretch far beyond the relatively confined world of historical theology.

In a similar fashion, religion is perceived as being woven more strongly into the fabric of social history. Several important studies of particular localities have diversified and enhanced our appreciation of the relationship between the churches and social and cultural life at the grass roots, notably those of Nailsworth, Gloucestershire (Urdank, 1990), Croydon (Morris, 1992), Oldham (Smith, 1994) and West Yorkshire (Green, 1996). On one level, work of this kind merely reinforces truisms about the almost infinite diversity of English local experience, and suggests a need for the patient and laborious piecing together of much more of the jigsaw before it becomes possible to speak with confidence about the general picture. Nevertheless, some common themes are suggested. First, religious institutions are shown to have been central to the fabric of society in the areas studied until nearly the end of the nineteenth century. This applies in some localities to working-class as well as to middle-class life: in Nailsworth, Oldham and Keighley (West Yorkshire) alike, there is conclusive evidence that some early Victorian churches were very predominantly working-class institutions. This conclusion is not, of course, inconsistent with the irrefutable evidence that many among the working classes did not attend church, but it does show that the church-going/non-church-going distinction arose *within* the working class and that there was no *inherent* incompatibility between working-class consciousness and religious observance. Second, it is argued that industrialization and urbanization did not in themselves represent insuperable challenges for organized religion: serious problems for the churches came only in the late nineteenth century. The difficulties that then arose are attributed to the rise of alternative power structures in society at local as well as at national level, and to the drift of the churches themselves into an associational rather than experiential conception of religious commitment.[4] This, it is argued, left them very exposed to competition from the alternative forms of leisure and voluntary activity (such as football clubs, trade unions and the Labour Party) which grew up in the late Victorian and Edwardian period and which could also offer a sense of belonging to a social and cultural network.

There is also an increasing sensitivity to the relationships between religious life and the development and differentiation of gender roles, given the indications that well over half those who were members of, or attended, church were women (Green, 1996, pp. 205–9). Religion, it has been argued, was central to the definition of the values and the functions that characterized early Victorian middle-class society. It provided a context 'where women could be valued for their spiritual worth if not their material power, where a "religious career" could give meaning to women's experience and express some of their aspirations' (Davidoff and Hall, 1987, p. 148). Accordingly, it is suggested, the study of religion provides an important springboard for reassessing the place of women in history (Hempton, 1996a, pp. 179–96).

Finally, Victorian religion has over the last decade been viewed in broader geographical perspective. This trend can be viewed as an extension of a process epitomized and assisted by the original four Open University volumes. These constituted a move from a narrow vision of English—or indeed Scottish or Welsh—religion to a wider genuinely British scope of study. Two other recent surveys have adopted a similar approach, also linking the history of religion in Ireland to that in Britain (Wolffe, 1994; Hempton, 1996b). The advantages of studying the so-called United Kingdom in this way lie both in the elucidation of cross-currents of influence, for example in connection with church–state relations, and in the comparative investigation of patterns of development, for instance assessment of the effects of urbanization and industrialization on religious observance.

In a significant body of recent work, comparisons of this kind have been pursued beyond the confines of these islands. In two substantial

---

[4] In other words, people were encouraged to think of themselves as 'religious' primarily because they were members of churches and attended worship more or less regularly, rather than primarily because they had strong personal religious convictions and experiences (for example, an Evangelical conversion).

collections of essays, Evangelicalism has been analysed in transatlantic and, to a lesser extent, in antipodean perspective (Rawlyk and Noll, 1993; Noll, Bebbington and Rawlyk, 1994). Comparison of Catholicism in both its Roman and its Anglican forms with contemporary Catholicism in continental Europe has served to indicate that the British experience was not as distinctive as is all too readily supposed (Franklin, 1987; Tallett and Atkin, 1996). Similarly, the social situation of religion in an urban environment during the nineteenth century has been the subject of studies spanning both the Channel and the Atlantic (McLeod, 1995a; 1995b).

A crucial aspect of the international context of British religion in the nineteenth century was the linkages provided by missions and the Empire. Missionary history has perhaps been particularly slow to move away from the earlier approach, with the Church viewed predominantly as an institution relatively independent of society and culture, and this is certainly still capable of generating works of distinguished scholarship (Stanley, 1992; Walls, 1993). Nevertheless, here too there have been significant steps to set developments in the wider context suggested by work on religion in Britain. For example, the relationship between missions and imperialism has been explored (Stanley, 1990) and the experience of the mission field linked to theological and intellectual changes in this country (Maw, 1990). At the time of writing (late 1996), much creative scholarship in missionary history is under way and further important publications are to be anticipated in the near future.

The overwhelming body of the scholarly activity of the last decade has thus been consistent with the approach adopted in the volumes in the *Religion in Victorian Britain* series. Social historians and church historians now work together, agnostics and committed Christians can find common ground in objective scholarly endeavour (McLeod, 1995c, pp. 751–2). It is in such a spirit that we present our own further contributions to the literature.

III

The specific selection of topics to be covered in the present volume reflects our perception of the needs and interests of Open University students for whom it is primarily intended. It also arises, however, from our awareness of the ongoing process of reappraisal of Victorian religion outlined above, and a consideration of the areas in which we are ourselves best equipped to make a distinctive contribution.

The first chapter constitutes an overview of the relationship of gender to religion in Victorian Britain. This has been a burgeoning field of research over the last decade or so, attracting considerable interest from social historians as well as scholars of religion. The results have been stimulating but hitherto diffuse, so a synthesis is badly needed. The scholarly context of the second chapter, on hymns and church music, is broadly similar. Here too a disciplinary frontier has, as it were, been explored from both sides, while overall appreciation of the subject has remained fragmented. Taken together, these first two chapters can be read both as surveys of their own fields and also as case studies in the interaction of Victorian religion with its social and cultural context. Both authors highlight the formative role of religion, but acknowledge the ways in which it was itself shaped by the surrounding environment.

The third chapter, examining the history of Victorian overseas missions, provides a framework for the three remaining contributions, which consider closely related topics. Running through all these four chapters is a shared awareness that the experience of mission and imperial encounter had profound implications for the outlook and development of religion at home. It was, respectively, the theory and the practice of missions that led Max Müller and John William Colenso to advocate controversial revisions of traditional theology. Moreover, the Empire was not only a vehicle for the export of Christianity, but also a channel for the import of other religions to Britain. Even if such faiths only made a minimal impact at the time, the neglected Victorian phase of the history of their presence in Britain appears in hindsight a significant pointer to the twentieth-century development of British religion. Yet further linkages are suggested by re-reading the first two chapters in the book in conjunction with the last four: missionary endeavour in general and Colenso in particular provided notable stimulus to hymnwriters, whilst the cameos from Charlotte Brontë and Rudyard Kipling that frame Chapter 3 can be read as powerful insights into the definition of gender roles as well as into missionary mentalities. The perceived need to rule an empire and convert the world profoundly shaped the way in which Victorian men and women saw themselves and each other.

A recurrent theme in these studies is awareness of a search for an ultimately elusive security and definition in religious matters. One important implication of the enhanced scholarly understanding of Georgian religion, which was outlined above, is an awareness that there was never any fixed reference point from which Victorian religion developed. Even as the notion of a focused and chronologically specific 'crisis of faith' is undermined, it becomes clearer that the very energy and force of conviction of many Victorians caused them to live in an almost perpetual sense of crisis. Colenso, at least at some periods of his life, provides a striking illustration of this phenomenon.

In offering an even-handed consideration of the situation of men alongside that of women, the first chapter suggests a wider context for the feminist critique of patriarchy. The Victorian urge to define roles, duties and attitudes for *both* sexes was certainly in some respects an oppression of women by men. It also, however, placed a heavy burden on men, who, like their mothers, sisters, wives and daughters, were being expected to conform to narrowly conceived definitions of their role. The equating of Christianity with an idealized domesticity meant that the significant minority, both male and female, for whom circumstances made conformity impossible, were left without accepted alternative frameworks for relating to each other. The likely outcomes were either celibacy or an outright rejection of Christian faith along with the sexual mores attributed to it.

If in relation to gender relations the Victorian urge to achieve definition and security resulted in oppressive consensus, the consequences in the other areas of experience examined in this book were rather different. The pattern is suggested by the development of church music. At least in the early Victorian period all protagonists operated from the assumption that there was one single form of sung worship that would uniquely articulate the devotions of the faithful and prove supremely acceptable to God. Traditional psalm-singing, bands in galleries, choirs in chancels, organs, rousing congregational hymns, Gregorian chant and choral evensong all had their committed advocates and equally earnest opponents. Given that no group had sufficient strength and resources wholly to prevail over the others, the unintended but enduring legacy of contention between them was the diversity of musical styles characteristic of twentieth-century British Christian worship.

For missionaries, too, the quest for certainty and clarity was a powerful motivating force but a longing that was often unfulfilled. Granted that real life figures such as Reginald Heber, Bishop of Calcutta, and James Hudson Taylor of the China Inland Mission might share the courageous innocence of the fictional St John Rivers (in Charlotte Brontë's *Jane Eyre*), the realities of missionary life usually proved more complex. In pre-Mutiny India the desire of the missionaries to overturn idols of 'wood and stone' was always in tension with the awareness of the civil administration (also professedly Christian) that such an outright onslaught on native religion and culture would be bound to produce disastrous instability. The Mutiny itself therefore provoked intense argument as to whether it had been the consequence of over-aggressive Christianization or was a divine judgement for insufficient Christianization. More nuanced middle positions, which appear commonsensical to historians, were unsatisfying for many contemporaries. Nevertheless, the medium-term effect of the cataclysm was to induce considerable questioning of polarized perceptions.

The case studies of Müller and Colenso included in this volume provide examples of such mid-century soul-searching. The controversy aroused in 1860 by Müller's candidacy for the Boden Chair of Sanskrit at Oxford was, indeed, fuelled by remembrance of recent events in the Indian subcontinent. Colenso's rethinking of the missionary position, it is true, occurred in Africa not India, but it is worth noting that it, too, took place in the years immediately before and after the Mutiny. Müller was to remain a somewhat perplexing figure in the eyes of the Victorian religious public. This was not least because, although he remained a supporter of Christian missions, he was very far from being a defender of traditional Christian belief, especially in his convictions that other religions were the work of God, that all religions were 'mere stammerings' (Müller, 1902, Vol. II, p. 491) and that, in the end, people must choose for themselves in their religious beliefs. Colenso, similarly, although a Christian minister and missionary until the end of his life, believed that God's spirit was present in other religions, that certainty was not to be had in this life and that Jesus' message was best summed up as the Fatherhood of God, the Brotherhood of Man and the indwelling of God's spirit in all human beings.

One ultimate response to the insecurities of Victorian Christianity was conversion to another faith, an outcome that, although very unusual, was by no means unknown. Indeed, it is important to emphasize that Hinduism and Islam, at least, were not merely the religions of visiting Asiatic princes, sailors and students, but also attracted indigenous British adherents. Margaret Noble's adoption of Hinduism (see Part II) was the outcome of a lengthy search for the stability of a truth that could be believed with total conviction. A similar process, we might suspect, lay behind the capacity of Abdullah Quilliam's Liverpool Muslim Institute to attract a steady trickle of converts during the 1890s.

On one level such dwelling on the insecurities and search for definition inherent in Victorian religion might appear the mere reiteration of a truism regarding the human condition and the religious response to it. Nevertheless, the point is worth emphasizing because it is all too easily missed by those who allow themselves to be mesmerized by the sheer scale, intensity and exuberance of Victorian religious activity. Moreover, it is arguable that the very achievements and outward confidence of the Victorian religious world made uncertainty less acceptable or tolerable than in an earlier or later age when the expectations focused on religion were rather more limited. It is, for instance, hard to conceive of any Victorian bishop—even Colenso—publishing a book with the title adopted in 1990 by the then Bishop of Durham, *Still Living with Questions* (Jenkins, 1990). Most Victorian religious thinkers instinctively insisted on clear-cut answers or, if these were unobtainable, wandered, as J. H. Newman wrote in the hymn 'Lead, kindly Light':

> O'er moor and fen, o'er crag and torrent, till
> The night is gone.

An inevitable consequence of the urge to achieve definition of a person's own religious position was the stereotyping of those who differed from it. Thus, Robert Gray, Bishop of Capetown, felt impelled to brand Colenso as a heretic, and other Broad and liberal churchmen were liable to be portrayed in similar colours. It was, however, Roman Catholics who were the most obvious and enduring objects of such attitudes, which were not a mere superficial prejudice, but were rooted deep in the religious and cultural psyche of the age (Wolffe, 1991). The illustration on the cover of this volume, together with those on the covers of *Religion in Victorian Britain*, Volumes II and IV, provides graphic documentation of the point. Catholicism was perceived as the antithesis of true religion, sapping the manliness of the nation and undermining it politically through its extra-territorial connections with the papacy. Given the range of religious activity in Victorian Britain that could be exposed to the satirist's eye, the preoccupation of *Punch* cartoonists with effeminate ritualists and scheming Jesuits is very noticeable.

The identification of Britain with Protestantism had been one of the dominating characteristics of eighteenth-century patriotism (Colley, 1992), and it was thus a potent legacy to the Victorian age. Moreover, given that most early overseas missionary activity was promoted by Nonconformists, and by the Evangelical wing of the Church of England, such a world-view was readily and extensively exported to the Empire. During the later Victorian period the association weakened somewhat: the irresistible urge to seek tighter definition of what constituted Protestantism led to fragmentation rather than unity and hence to a gradual loss of credibility. Meanwhile, both in Britain and overseas, Catholicism gained in acceptance and influence. High Church and Roman Catholic missions began to make their presence felt, while in 1900 the success of Elgar's *Dream of Gerontius* indicated that it was now possible for the work of a Catholic to be acknowledged as part of the mainstream of national culture. Nevertheless, in the first quarter of the twentieth century, the partition of Ireland demonstrated the continuing strength of religion as a basis for political and national identification. In a further quarter of a century, India too was to be partitioned between its two major religious groups, an indication that the Victorian tendency to reinforce credal distinctions had potential ramifications far outside Christianity.

There was, however, another side to the coin. Even as the legacy of Victorian religion hardened some social, sectarian and national divisions, it served to bridge others. Religious ideology might stress the subordination of women, but the practical needs of religious organizations, above all in the missionary sphere, gave women opportunities for self-fulfilment that were denied to them in the secular world (Heeney, 1988; Cox, 1992; Gill, 1994). Meanwhile, the sense that the Protestant British nation was accountable to God for its stewardship of the resources and power given to it was certainly a spur to insensitive missionary crusades, but it also served to check the worst excesses of a purely materialistic imperialism. There were Christian preachers willing to acknowledge that the 'Indian Mutiny' might be divine retribution, not only for perceived sins of omission in the failure to Christianize the subcontinent, but also for sins of commission in the 'inordinate, secular, selfish ambition' evident in the conduct of government there (Stanley, 1983, p. 283). It was a similar sense of accountability that led Colenso to denounce the British invasion of Zululand in 1879. In subsequent decades, Christians could not avoid becoming heavily implicated in the sometimes oppressive power structures of the British Empire, but they also played a significant part in fostering the forces that eventually gave rise to the downfall of colonialism. Harriette Colenso, daughter of the bishop, was in the early twentieth century to have a formative influence on the leaders of the movement that was to become the African National Congress (Hofmeyr and Pillay, 1994, pp. 179–80). Also in South Africa, in the 1890s the young M. K. Gandhi acknowledged a substantial indebtedness to the friendship of Christians, even though he found himself unable to accept their creed. Gandhi was especially touched by the readiness of a missionary leader to sustain a warm friendship with him in spite of the crude racism of other whites (Gandhi, 1990 edn, pp. 112–15).

A full exploration of this complex balance sheet would take us far beyond the scope of the present volume. It is possible to present a more unreservedly negative assessment of the record of the missionary movement than that offered here (Kent, 1987, pp. 177–202). What is undeniable, however, is that examination of the imperial and global dimensions of religion in Victorian Britain serves significantly to modify the overall impression founded on investigation of internal developments that 'religious issues and controversies were, by the last two decades of the nineteenth century, well on their way towards a new location somewhere nearer [than hitherto] to the periphery of national life'.[5] It is, indeed, arguable that religion for much of the twentieth century has been relatively marginal to life in much of Britain. However, whatever its checkered and confusing record, it has played a much more central role in the history of many of the parts of the world touched by the Victorians. Moreover, in the last half century, the wheel has in a sense turned full circle, with the migration to Britain of substantial populations from these former colonies. Whether Christian, Hindu, Muslim or Sikh, they have contributed to a substantial reshaping of the contours of religion in this country (Parsons, 1993; 1994). It is hoped that the studies contained in this volume will thus not only increase knowledge of Victorian religion, but also lead to an enhanced understanding of the longstanding sources of powerful currents in contemporary British religious and social life.

BIBLIOGRAPHY

G. Alderman (1992) *Modern British Jewry*, Oxford, Oxford University Press.

D. W. Bebbington (ed.) (1988) *The Baptists in Scotland: A History*, Glasgow, Baptist Union of Scotland.

D. W. Bebbington (1989) *Evangelicalism in Modern Britain: A History from the 1730s to the 1980s*, London, Unwin Hyman.

D. W. Bebbington (1993) *William Ewart Gladstone: Faith and Politics in Victorian Britain*, Grand Rapids, Eerdmans.

R. Brent (1987) *Liberal Anglican Politics*, Oxford, Clarendon Press.

S. Brown and M. Fry (eds.) (1993) *Scotland in the Age of the Disruption*, Edinburgh, Edinburgh University Press.

C. G. Brown (1995) 'The mechanism of religious growth in urban societies' in H. McLeod (ed.) *European Religion in the Age of Great Cities*, pp. 239–62, London, Routledge.

A. Burns (1990), 'The diocesan revival in the Church of England, c1825–1865', unpublished DPhil thesis, University of Oxford.

C. D. Cashdollar (1989) *The Transformation of Theology, 1830–1890: Positivism and Protestant Thought in Britain and America*, Princeton (NJ), Princeton University Press.

J. C. D. Clark (1985) *English Society 1688–1832: Ideology, Social Structure and Political Practice during the Ancien Regime*, Cambridge, Cambridge University Press.

[5] *RVB*, II, Introduction, p. 13.

L. Colley (1992) *Britons: Forging the Nation 1707–1837*, New Haven, Yale University Press.

J. Cox (1992) 'Independent English women in Delhi and Lahore, 1860–1947' in R. W. Davis and R. J. Helmstadter (eds.) *Religion and Irreligion in Victorian Society*, pp. 166–84, London, Routledge.

L. Davidoff and C. Hall (1987) *Family Fortunes: Men and Women of the English Middle Class, 1780–1850*, London, Hutchinson.

A. Desmond and J. Moore (1991) *Darwin*, London, Michael Joseph.

C. G. Flegg (1992) *'Gathered under Apostles': A Study of the Catholic Apostolic Church*, Oxford, Clarendon Press.

R. W. Franklin (1987) *Nineteenth-century Churches: The History of a New Catholicism in Würthemberg, England and France*, New York, Garland.

M. K. Gandhi (1990 edn) *An Autobiography: Or The Story of my Experiments with Truth*, Ahmedabad, Narajivan (first published 1927).

S. Gill (1994) *Women and the Church of England from the Eighteenth Century to the Present*, London, Society for Promoting Christian Knowledge.

S. Gilley (1990) *Newman and His Age*, London, Darton, Longman & Todd.

S. J. D. Green (1996) *Religion in the Age of Decline: Organisation and Experience in Industrial Yorkshire, 1870–1920*, Cambridge, Cambridge University Press.

B. Heeney (1988) *The Women's Movement in the Church of England 1850–1930*, Oxford, Clarendon Press.

M. Heimann (1995) *Catholic Devotion in Victorian England*, Oxford, Clarendon Press.

D. Hempton (1996a) *The Religion of the People: Methodism and Popular Religion c.1750–1900*, London, Routledge.

D. Hempton (1996b) *Religion and Political Culture in Britain and Ireland from the Glorious Revolution to the Decline of Empire*, Cambridge, Cambridge University Press.

D. Hempton and M. Hill (1992) *Evangelical Protestantism in Ulster Society, 1740–1890*, London, Routledge.

B. Hilton (1988) *The Age of Atonement: The Influence of Evangelicalism on Social and Economic Thought, 1795–1865*, Oxford, Clarendon Press.

P. Hinchliff (1992) *God and History: Aspects of British Theology 1875–1914*, Oxford, Clarendon Press.

J. W. Hofmeyr and G. J. Pillay (eds.) (1994) *A History of Christianity in South Africa*, Volume I, Pretoria, HAUM.

G. K. Horridge (1993) *The Salvation Army: Origins and Early Days 1865–1900*, Godalming, Ammonite.

K. Hylson-Smith (1989) *Evangelicals in the Church of England, 1734–1984*, Edinburgh, T & T Clark.

K. Hylson-Smith (1993) *High Churchmanship in the Church of England from the Sixteenth Century to the Late Twentieth Century*, Edinburgh, T & T Clark.

D. E. Jenkins (1990) *Still Living with Questions*, London, SCM.

R. L. Jensen and M. R. Thorp (1989) *Mormons in Early Victorian Britain*, Salt Lake City, University of Utah Press.

J. Kent (1987) *The Unacceptable Face: The Modern Church in the Eyes of the Historian*, London, SCM.

I. Ker (1988) *John Henry Newman: A Biography*, Oxford, Oxford University Press.

D. A. Kerr (1994) *'A Nation of Beggars'? Priests, People and Politics in Famine Ireland*, Oxford, Clarendon Press.

F. Knight (1995) *The Nineteenth-century Church and English Society*, Cambridge, Cambridge University Press.

D. W. Lovegrove (1988) *Established Church, Sectarian People: Itinerancy and the Transformation of English Dissent 1780–1830*, Cambridge, Cambridge University Press.

H. McLeod (1995a) *Piety and Poverty: Working-class Religion in Berlin, London and New York*, New York, Holmes & Meier.

H. McLeod (1995b) *European Religion in the Age of Great Cities 1830–1930*, London, Routledge.

H. McLeod (1995c) Review in *Journal of Ecclesiastical History*, Vol. 46, pp. 751–2.

H. McLeod (1996) *Religion and Society in England 1850–1914*, Basingstoke, Macmillan.

F. C. Mather (1985) 'Georgian churchmanship reconsidered: some variations in Anglican public worship 1714–1830', *Journal of Ecclesiastical History*, Vol. 36, pp. 255–82.

F. C. Mather (1992) *High Church Prophet: Bishop Samuel Horsley (1733–1806) and the Caroline Tradition in the Later Georgian Church*, Oxford, Clarendon Press.

H. C. G. Matthew (1986) *Gladstone 1809–1874*, Oxford, Oxford University Press.

H. C. G. Matthew (1995) *Gladstone 1875–1898*, Oxford, Oxford University Press.

M. Maw (1990) *Visions of India*, Frankfurt am Main, Peter Lang.

J. Morris (1992) *Religion and Urban Change: Croydon 1840–1914*, Woodbridge, Royal Historical Society/Boydell Press.

G. A. Müller (ed.) (1902) *The Life and Letters of the Right Honourable Friedrich Max Müller Edited by his Wife*, 2 vols., New York, London and Bombay, Longmans, Green.

J. Munson (1991) *The Nonconformists: In Search of a Lost Culture*, London, Society for Promoting Christian Knowledge.

P. B.Nockles (1994) *The Oxford Movement in Context: Anglican High Churchmanship, 1760–1857*, Cambridge, Cambridge University Press.

M. A. Noll, D. W. Bebbington and G. A. Rawlyk (eds.) (1994) *Evangelicalism: Comparative Studies of Popular Protestantism in North America, the British Isles, and Beyond, 1700–1990*, New York, Oxford University Press.

J. P. Parry (1986) *Democracy and Religion: Gladstone and the Liberal Party, 1867–1875*, Cambridge, Cambridge University Press.

G. Parsons (ed.) (1993) *The Growth of Religious Diversity: Britain from 1945: Volume I Traditions*, London, Routledge.

G. Parsons (ed.) (1994) *The Growth of Religious Diversity: Britain from 1945: Volume II Issues*, London, Routledge.

D. G. Paz (ed.) (1995) *Nineteenth Century English Religious Traditions: Retrospect and Prospect*, Westport (CT), Greenwood.

B. Porter (1984 edn) *The Lion's Share: A Short History of British Imperialism 1850–1983*, London, Longman (first published 1975).

G. A. Rawlyk and M. A. Noll (eds.) (1993) *Amazing Grace: Evangelicalism in Australia, Britain, Canada and the United States*, Grand Rapids, Baker.

R. B. Sher (1985) *Church and University in the Scottish Enlightenment*, Edinburgh, Edinburgh University Press.

M. Smith (1994) *Religion in Industrial Society: Oldham and Saddleworth 1740–1865*, Oxford, Clarendon Press.

B. Stanley (1983) 'Christian responses to the Indian Mutiny of 1857' in W. J. Sheils (ed.) *The Church and War: Studies in Church History*, Volume 20, pp. 277–89, Oxford, Basil Blackwell.

B. Stanley (1990) *The Bible and the Flag: Protestant Missions and British Imperialism in the Nineteenth and Twentieth Centuries*, Leicester, Apollos.

B. Stanley (1992) *The History of the Baptist Missionary Society*, Edinburgh, T & T Clark.

R. Strong (1995) *Alexander Forbes of Brechin: The First Tractarian Bishop*, Oxford, Clarendon Press.

J. F. Supple-Green (1990) *The Catholic Revival in Yorkshire 1850–1900*, Leeds, Leeds Philosophical Society.

F. Tallett and N. Atkin (1996) *Catholicism in Britain and France Since 1789*, London, Hambledon.

F. M. Turner (1993) *Contesting Cultural Authority: Essays in Victorian Intellectual Life*, Cambridge, Cambridge University Press.

A. M. Urdank (1990) *Religion and Society in a Cotswold Vale: Nailsworth Gloucestershire 1780–1865*, Berkeley and Los Angeles, University of California Press.

P. Virgin (1989) *The Church in an Age of Negligence: Ecclesiastical Structure and the Problems of Church Reform 1700–1840*, Cambridge, James Clarke.

G. Walker and T. Gallagher (eds.) (1990) *Sermons and Battle Hymns: Protestant Popular Culture in Modern Scotland*, Edinburgh, Edinburgh University Press.

A. Walls (1993) 'Missions' in N. M. de S. Cameron (ed.) *Dictionary of Scottish Church History and Theology*, pp. 567–94, Edinburgh, T & T Clark.

J. Walsh (1986) 'Religious societies: Methodist and Evangelical 1738–1800' in W. J. Sheils and D. Wood (eds.) *Voluntary Religion: Studies in Church History*, Volume 23, pp. 279–302, Oxford, Basil Blackwell.

J. Walsh, C. Haydon and S. Taylor (eds.) (1993) *The Church of England c.1689–c.1833: From Toleration to Tractarianism*, Cambridge, Cambridge University Press.

W. R. Ward (1972) *Religion and Society in England 1790–1850*, London, Batsford.

M. R. Watts (1995) *The Dissenters, Vol. II: The Expansion of Evangelical Nonconformity*, Oxford, Clarendon Press.

J. Wolffe (1991) *The Protestant Crusade in Great Britain 1829–1860*, Oxford, Clarendon Press.

J. Wolffe (1994) *God and Greater Britain: Religion and National Life in Britain and Ireland, 1843–1945*, London, Routledge.

J. Wolffe (ed.) (1995) *Evangelical Faith and Public Zeal: Evangelicals and Society in Britain 1780–1980*, London, Society for Promoting Christian Knowledge.

PART I

CHAPTER 1

WE DO NOT FOR ONE MOMENT PRESUME TO SAY WHETHER IT IS RIGHT OR WRONG,—ONLY, IF THIS SORT OF THING IS TO PREVAIL, WHAT'S TO BECOME OF CAPTAIN HEAVYSWELL?

THE CLERICAL BEARD MOVEMENT

'MALE AND FEMALE HE CREATED THEM': MEN, WOMEN AND THE QUESTION OF GENDER

I N 1705, Mary Astell, an Anglican writer and advocate of women's education, pondered the question of whether the study of history was a worthy occupation for a woman. In concluding that the examples of history were rarely edifying, she noted:

> Since the men being the historians, they seldom condescend to record the great and good action of women; and when they take notice of them, 'tis with this wise remark, that such women *acted above their sex*. By which one must suppose they would have their readers understand, that they were not women who did the great actions, but that they were men in petticoats!

(Cited by Johnson, 1983, p. 19)

In this as in many of her other opinions, Astell was some centuries ahead of her time. Her realization that women who did 'great actions' were flouting the conventions of feminine behaviour and would be regarded as 'men in petticoats' was one that became widely accepted in the Victorian period. Furthermore, her recognition that women had been largely written out of conventional historical accounts was not to be fully addressed until the 1980s.

The consideration of such issues arises from the study of gender, which has emerged as a major new line of historical and theological enquiry in the last decade. In this context, 'gender' refers not to the biological differences between the sexes, but to the cultural constructions that create and sustain ideas about appropriate roles for men and women (Gill, 1994, p. 9). Such cultural constructions are in a constant process of redefinition, as the beliefs of a society about what is appropriate for men and women are always undergoing change, even if the rate of change sometimes seems imperceptible.

Gender studies are predicated on the belief that, as the result of a complex variety of social, economic, legal and political pressures and constraints, the experience of men and women has been profoundly different, and that what was or is typical or true in male experience is unlikely to be typical or true for women. The work of feminist historians and theologians has made scholars generally more aware of the limitations of an uncritical acceptance of male experience and values as normative for women.

An example of how this works in practice can be seen in the interest that historians of popular religion in late Victorian Britain have begun to show in the hitherto neglected lives of women of the working class. These women, it appears, were far more likely to be involved in church or chapel than were men (McLeod, 1993, p. 28). Evidence concerning women's religious practice has come from oral history projects, which have pointed to unexpectedly high levels of church-going among the interviewees' mothers in late nineteenth- and early twentieth-century Britain (McLeod, 1986; 1993). These findings have called into question the conclusions of some older studies on the churches and the working class (Wickham, 1957; Inglis, 1963), which tended to use exclusively 'male' evidence to argue for a high level of religious indifference or hostility among working-class society as a whole. By giving proper recognition to a broader spectrum of the available evidence, historians may, as in this case, produce substantial modifications of earlier theses.

Gender history had its origin in feminist enquiries into the 'lost' history of women. In recent years, however, some practitioners have turned their attention to men, with a view to learning more about the cultural construction of masculinity. This chapter concentrates on some of the major themes to emerge from recent explorations of gender and Victorian religion, and considers both the ideological representations and the actuality of the experience of men and women. It begins by examining the centrality of the workplace and the home in shaping Christian and Jewish attitudes about appropriate female and male behaviour. These ideas were disseminated so widely—at least among the middle and upper echelons of society—that they acquired the status of Victorian values rather than simply being binding on the religiously committed. The chapter then considers the shifts in the Christian understanding of femininity, the emergence of 'Christian manliness', the place of single women and the significance of women's education. It concludes by looking at some of the types of church work and ministry that were pursued by Victorian women. The chapter concentrates upon the experience and expectations of the middle classes, because it is there that gender separation was most visibly in operation.

I THE WORKPLACE AND THE HOME

Christian writers in the nineteenth century frequently asserted that it was the Christian religion above all else that had raised woman to her true and honourable status in society. Woman, they believed, was created as the helpmeet of her husband or, in the case of an unmarried woman, of her father or brother. She was spiritually equal with him although socially subordinate. She was to be revered, and not trampled underfoot. It was argued, moreover, that Christianity had rescued women from the abuse and exploitation popularly (but questionably) associated with non-Christian societies—from polygamy, purdah, divorce at the husband's whim and the degradation of being a mere chattel (Gill, 1994). Christian woman was not a doll-like creature who existed solely for her husband's gratification, but a spiritual being with an immortal soul as valuable as that of her husband. It followed that her husband had specific responsibilities towards her: it was his duty by his honest toil to protect and provide for both his wife and his children.

The spiritual significance of the world of work and the domestic realm assumed a critical importance in nineteenth-century Protestant and Jewish attitudes, but seems to have been less consciously articulated in Roman Catholicism. Male employment was viewed not merely as a necessity for economic survival, but as a means through which a man obtained dignity by the demonstration of his independence, his honesty and his competence. These became key attributes in the Victorian understanding of manly virtue. In contrast, the Victorian woman was expected to avoid the workplace in order to be virtuous (unless she had no alternative to avoid destitution). The influential Birmingham Congregationalist John Angell James, writing in 1852, realized that unsupported single women would need to work for a living, but he strongly disapproved of married women doing so:

> In the married state, her sphere of labour, as we shall presently show, is the family; and it belongs to the husband to earn by the sweat of his brow, not only his own bread, but that of the household. In many of the uncivilized tribes, where the ameliorating condition of Christianity is not felt, the woman is the drudge of the family, while the husband lives in lordly sloth. And even in this country, at least in its manufacturing portions, manual labour falls too often, and too heavily, upon married women, greatly to the detriment of their families.
>
> (James, 1852)[1]

Virtually all Christian and Jewish writers of the period would have agreed with James that the only proper realm for a woman was the home, where she was uncontested as queen. James became lyrical as he warmed to this theme: 'There are few terms in the language around which cluster so many blissful associations as that delight of every English heart, the word HOME ... One of the most hallowed, and lovely, and beautiful sights in our world is, woman at home.' George Stringer Bull, in a lecture of about the same date, dwelt much on the 'queenliness' of the ordinary woman at

---

[1] For further examples of James's writing, see *RVB*, III, 3.1.1, pp. 132–4 and 5.1.1, pp. 228–32.

home, extending the metaphor to describe her as 'a real queen in her cottage, nay, her palace' (Bull, 1854, p. 13). This type of rhetoric served to transform the idea of woman from human being into angel. The angel was 'an image wonderfully calculated not only to dissociate love from sex, but to turn love into worship, the worship of purity' (Houghton, 1957, p. 355).

The Victorians' excessive adulation of domesticity, combined with their elevation of the moral value of men's work, was at the heart of much of their distinctive frame of mind. It was an attitude that can be linked with wider changes. Britain's rapid transition from a rural to a predominantly urban and industrial society resulted in new forms of alienation and anxiety. For the first time people were quite likely to find themselves living among virtual strangers. Public institutions and business and commercial enterprises became larger and more complex, with increasing rewards and risks, successes and failures. This environment could be exciting for the successful, but it could also be very frightening. Arthur Helps summed up the mood when he suggested that a statue to Worry be erected in the City of London, 'on which the cunning sculptor should have impressed the marks of haste, anxiety and agitation' (Houghton, 1957, p. 61). Liability was not limited: a businessman who got into debt could be put in gaol by his creditors. An artisan who became too sick to work could end up in the workhouse, separated from his destitute family.

In this hostile environment the home was a retreat from the pressures of the world. Men in particular turned to the family as the source of virtues and emotions that they felt could not be found elsewhere, least of all in business or society. John Ruskin's highly idealized definition of home spoke to a generation: 'This is the true nature of home—it is a place of Peace; the shelter, not only from all injury, but from all terror, doubt and division' (Ruskin, 1865). The religious home, whether Christian or Jewish, had faith at its centre, and women were seen as the guardians of that faith. For agnostics also, the home became a sort of temple. According to Frederic Harrison, at home the family could throw off the trammels of superstition, and learn the sentiment of attachment, reverence and love (Houghton, 1957, p. 347).[2] As traditional beliefs and institutions became questioned or transformed, the Victorians clung to the oldest of all institutions.

The nature of new forms of work may have contributed to this development. The clerk toiling endlessly in his grubby office invested his

---

[2] For Harrison, see *RVB*, II, 10, pp. 226–9 and *RVB*, III, 7.4.1, pp. 449–56.

wife and home with the virtues that perhaps he felt he had forfeited: purity, faith, charity and hope. The fact that men wanted their wives to be religious in a society that remained so clearly obsessed by religion was not in itself surprising; it was sometimes remarked (admittedly by Christian commentators) that even the atheist and the infidel would seek a religious wife in order to ensure a happy home (Johnson, 1983, pp. 39 and 106). On the whole, women seemed willing to be regarded as more 'naturally' spiritual than men, and with greater aptitude for making sense of religion. Among the working classes, it was women who tended to take decisions about their family's religious observance (Cox, 1982, pp. 34–5). Among the middle classes, the alleged greater religiosity of women was attributed to their greater leisure for contemplation, shielded as they were from the knowledge and temptations of the world. Conventional views of feminine faith, gentleness and passivity became subtly interlinked to make women appear more 'naturally' religious. It has been argued that the Victorians' elevation of the family as the paramount social unit served to give women more confidence, but their attempts to extend their influence, by engaging in philanthropic activity in particular, also reinforced the stereotype of women as the more compassionate and self-sacrificing sex (Prochaska, 1980, p. 8).

Marriage and homemaking were presented to women in directly vocational terms, and attempts were made to impress upon young women that in marriage they would fulfil their religious mission, and contribute towards the salvation of themselves and their families. Men, in contrast, were told that they would fulfil their mission by taking an active and constructive part in society, by cultivating piety, sobriety and chastity and, when the time came for them to make a judicious marriage, by assuming a role as head of their household, in the manner recommended by St Paul.

The division of life into public and private spheres, and the elevation of domesticity and family as central to every individual's happiness, marked the beginning of a mentality that remains common in modern Britain. The idealization of home as the safe haven from an impersonal, uncaring world still exerts a strong influence, as does the belief that society's ills would disappear if mothers withdrew from the workplace and concentrated on creating happy homes. This is a legacy of Victorian Britain, not found in the seventeenth and eighteenth centuries, when women often worked in family groups alongside men and children, and lived on a joint income derived from the contributions of all. In these family groups, it was common for a draper's daughter to help in the shop, a farmer's wife to run a dairy, a printer's widow to carry on his business, in addition, of course, to undertaking her domestic responsibilities (Laslett, 1971, pp. 1–2; Davidoff and Hall, 1987, p. 25).

Among the working classes, domesticity had to some extent become aligned with late eighteenth- and early nineteenth-century Evangelicalism in the form of cottage religion. This was based in the home (which was also the workplace), rather than the chapel, and it allowed women to escape the subordinate roles that chapel religion would have assigned them. There was, however, a tension here, and popular Evangelicalism dwelt on two themes which it was not always possible to harmonize. The first was the sanctification of the home; the second was the renunciation of material satisfaction in the pursuit of a spiritual pilgrimage (Valenze, 1985, pp. 28–9). Deborah Valenze has argued that there were distinctive phases in the sectarian Methodism that formed the subject of her investigation. Cottage preaching, in which women took part, flourished during a specific preindustrial phase, when the public and the private converged within the domestic framework of labouring life. By the middle of the nineteenth century, however, cottage religion had been swept into the now respectable Evangelical mainstream. Religion became focused on the chapel rather than the home. Valenze, who is deeply critical of Victorian religion, suggests that this had profound implications:

> The loss of a foundation in cottage and village life meant a loss of a basis of protest. The distinctive theology of popular preachers, rooted in the experience of labouring life, became subsumed under deceptively similar but empty Victorian formulae. Angry and critical asceticism became pious abstinence; cottage solidarity became conservative domesticity. Most revealing of all, female assertiveness became unacceptable. The grievances of women and their families no longer reached the pulpit, but instead were defined in private and personal terms.
>
> (*Ibid.*, p. 11)

Valenze's point about the effects of the increasing institutionalization of Evangelicalism resulting in a new separation between Evangelical men and women may have found an echo in the experience of the middle class as well. Eighteenth-century Evangelical writers like William Cowper and Hannah More had taken it for granted that men as well as women would be active in setting the religious tone of the home. By the 1830s and 1840s, however, Evangelicals tended to assume that men were absent, fully occupied with business in the world, and at work some distance from home. They began to address themselves more exclusively to an all-female audience, advising women on how they should manage themselves, their children and their servants (Davidoff and Hall, 1987, p. 181).

The rapidly expanding middle class learned to identify and define itself by imposing an altered code of behaviour on both its male and its female members. Women whose mothers and grandmothers might have willingly accepted, as part of the natural order of things, employment in agriculture or commerce began to regard the possibility of paid employment for themselves or their daughters as intrinsically shameful. It was a view shared by their husbands, for the ability to support the entire family on the income of the male breadwinner became an important ingredient in the Victorian understanding of 'manliness', and was the essence of middle-class respectability. This naturally put Victorian husbands and fathers under new pressure to achieve much in the separated world of work, with an upward curve of promotion and salary regarded as not merely desirable but essential. The middle-class Victorian wife tended to demonstrate her newly acquired status with the symbolic decision to retire to the sofa with her embroidery, and to employ increasing numbers of domestic servants to maintain her household. The 1860s has been identified as the decade in which women began in large numbers to abandon their earlier domestic tasks, and to make the transition from 'perfect wife to perfect lady' (Tosh, 1991, p. 53). However, whilst this demonstrated social status, it did not guarantee the transmission of religious values. Christian writers sometimes worried about the growing tendency towards inertia in middle-class wives. The Congregationalist Sarah Ellis, who wrote conduct books for women, was particularly concerned with the families of the trading, manufacturing and professional classes who employed between one and four servants. 'False notions of refinement', she believed, were rendering their women 'less influential, less useful, and less happy than they were' (Davidoff and Hall, 1987, pp. 182–3). There was a realization that an empty life was unlikely to bring happiness or fulfilment, and more to the point, nor was it likely to follow the path that led to salvation.

A similarly changing social role resulting in female retirement from the public realm may be discerned in Judaism. In the *shtetls* of Eastern Europe it was not uncommon for the domestic activities of women to include breadwinning, whilst their husbands engaged in spiritual pursuits; the woman might run the family business while her husband 'prayed all day' in the synagogue (Burman, 1986, p. 236). In Britain, however, Anglo-Jewry conformed to the norms of genteel, gentile society. The major separation was between the public realm of the world and the private world of the home, rather than between the sacred sphere occupied by men and the profane sphere occupied by women. Anglicized Jews saw breadwinning as a male responsibility, in which the involvement of women would undermine the social standing of a husband. Following the cue supplied by the British middle classes, prosperous Jews began to employ increasing numbers of domestic servants, thus cutting women off from the religious meaning that the observance of their domestic duties had traditionally supplied. This resulted in a striking inversion of the gender roles traditional in the *shtetl*. Women were no longer seen as material providers but as spiritual helpmeets, and the home took on the characteristics of a sacred haven, rather than a source of worldly distraction (*ibid.*, p. 238). As a result, it tended to be women who assumed responsibility for the transmission of the faith. In a major oral history project that took place in Manchester between 1976 and 1984, many of the interviewees recalled how, although their fathers worked on the Sabbath, their mothers continued to follow tradition and create in the home a special Sabbath atmosphere. They attributed their initial sense of Jewish identity to early memories of the Jewish home, rather than to the synagogue and its practices (*ibid.*, pp. 249–50).

II FEMININITY

Perhaps because men in pre-industrial society were more likely than their nineteenth-century middle-class counterparts to have witnessed their women baking bread or milking cows, they were less inclined to idealize them as frail, innocent, quasi-angelic figures. The transition from activity to passivity that women of the middle classes experienced between the later seventeenth and the early nineteenth centuries was accompanied by a very significant shift in the Protestant understanding of womanhood. Like most such changes, the process was not clear cut, and remnants of the earlier view could still be discerned in the later period. Nevertheless, that the change happened at all illustrates the point made in the introductory paragraphs of this chapter, that definitions of gender are not naturally 'fixed' or 'given', but are continuously being contested at different times and in different places.

The earlier view of womanhood emphasized the disobedience of Eve, and blamed her as the agent through which sin came into the world. Eve the temptress led Adam into iniquity; she fell first. The lesson seemed to be that, despite their supposed spiritual equality, women as a whole posed a danger and a temptation to men, and that they were also morally deficient and sexually insatiable. In order to keep women under control, and to prevent them from posing a danger, they had to be subordinate to the authority of men, and men had to rule over them. Thus, any notion of social equality between the sexes appeared not only anarchic but blasphemous, as it was in flat contradiction to the opening chapters of the Book of Genesis. This rather pessimistic view of women coincided more or less with the teachings of St Augustine and the Early Fathers of the Christian Church. It was a position articulated by Bishop Ken of Bath and Wells in 1682, when he noted that:

> Women are made of a temper, more soft and frail, are more endangered by snares, and temptations, less able to control their passions, and more inclinable to extremes of good, or bad, than Men, and generally speaking, Goodness is a tenderer thing, more hazardous, and brittle in the former, than in the latter, and consequently a firm, steady Virtue is more to be valued in the weaker sex than the Stronger.
>
> (Quoted in Gill, 1994, p. 26)

According to Ken, women were not merely physically weaker than men, but morally weaker as well.

By the nineteenth century, paradoxically, the general tenor of Ken's remarks would have been more likely to have been applied to men than women. It was now men who were regarded as less in control of their passions and more prone to extremes; women were seen as more virtuous and less prone to temptation. Eve herself had become something of a contested figure. For liberal Christians, the advent of biblical criticism was making any appeal to Eve as a woman who had had an actual, historical existence seem problematic. Her memory was nevertheless still invoked by Christians of the more conservative sort, both Anglo-Catholic and Evangelical. In the 1870s, the Anglo-Catholic H. P. Liddon still maintained the traditional stance that the example of Eve indicated that 'woman is more easily led away than man'. In the following decade, the Anglo-Catholic novelist Charlotte Yonge remarked that she had 'no hesitation in declaring my full belief in the inferiority of woman, nor that she brought it upon herself'.[3] Among Evangelicals, the temperance worker Clara Lucas Balfour also appealed to the historicity of Eve when she observed, in 1854, 'We brought all the sin into the world, involving man in the ruin which he was not the first to seek, and it is the least that we can do to offer him a little good now' (Prochaska, 1980, p. 125). Another Evangelical, Charlotte Elizabeth Tonna, also dwelt on the shame of Eve, but with a rather different emphasis. She was swift to remind her

[3] See *RVB*, III, 2.2.2, pp. 95–7.

readers that another woman, Mary, had been chosen by God to bear the redeemer of the world: 'Thus the sex who were lost by giving heed to the deceivableness of Satan, are "saved in child-bearing", so far as they exercise faith, individually, in the Saviour, who by woman was born into the world.' She roundly rejected any notion of woman being more sinful or less spiritual than man (Tonna, 1834/44).

The question of how notions of womanhood shifted from an identification with the voracious Eve figure of the eighteenth century to the virtuous maiden or matron of the Victorian period is a complex one, which defies a simple answer. Leonore Davidoff and Catherine Hall have suggested that the Queen Caroline affair of 1820 'marked a significant moment in terms of public attitudes to marriage and sexuality, an assertion of belief in the unblemished nature of English [*sic*] womanhood, an insistence that femininity meant virtue and honour' (Davidoff and Hall, 1987, p. 155). The Queen Caroline affair might seem a bizarre incident to have had such an effect on public attitudes, but this may indeed be a useful interpretation of the episode, although it should be remembered that the affair was also redolent with political overtones. Caroline was the long-estranged wife of the unpopular George IV. The couple had married for convenience in 1795 when George was Prince of Wales, but had separated almost immediately, and thereafter pursued separate lives and sexual adventures, although George's infidelities were regarded as being more flagrant than Caroline's. On the death of George III in 1820, Caroline decided to return from foreign exile and claim her legal right as queen. George decided to divorce her, but in the ensuing divorce trial it became apparent that public sympathy lay not with him but with Caroline. There were scenes of wild jubilation all over the country when the case against her was dropped. Caroline was cast in the role of an ill-used wife, in need of the support and protection of all good and virtuous men. This combined with a sense of outrage at the double standard of calling her to account, whilst overlooking her husband's well-known infidelities. It could hardly be claimed that she had lived up to the standards of propriety demanded by the Christian establishment, but Caroline nevertheless became something of an icon of domesticity betrayed. Popular opinion considered that a man who had shown himself unfit as a husband was unfit to be a king, the symbolic father of the nation (*ibid.*, pp. 150–5). This in itself was a significant shift, and it contained an important message to men—that true manliness meant honourable and virtuous behaviour, and not promiscuous womanizing. It would appear that ideas concerning womanhood and manliness were to some extent being revised in tandem.

III   CHRISTIAN MANLINESS

This chapter has discussed how the Victorians promoted clearly defined standards of female behaviour and sought to sanction those standards by drawing on religious ideas and references. There was a parallel concern for masculinity. Images of masculinity became just as idealized as those of femininity, exemplified by qualities both physical and moral. The true manly man was brave and honest, self-disciplined and hard working; he was full of robust energy and physical vitality. As the strong, valiant protector of the weak, he was the perfect foil for the feminine female. Indeed the degree of differentiation between the sexes was even reflected in the changes in their physical appearance promoted by Victorian fashions. Delicate complexions, tiny waists, dainty feet and tightly laced, restrictive dresses contrasted with ruddy complexions, strapping chests and well-developed muscles, clothed in practical jackets and trousers (Davidoff and Hall, 1987, pp. 412–14).

Some Christians feared that in emphasizing the supposedly 'natural' predisposition of women for piety and holiness, they ran the risk of presenting Christianity as something that was beneath the notice of men. To make matters worse, it seemed that the strands of Christianity that were becoming the most influential in the second half of the nineteenth century—namely Catholicism in its Roman and Anglican varieties—were particularly insidious in encouraging men to adopt effeminate, unmanly attitudes: 'fastidious, maundering, die-away effeminacy' as Charles Kingsley put it. With its advocacy of clerical celibacy, Catholicism seemed to strike at the heart of manliness. The unprecedented increase in the number of religious communities, in which men and women dedicated themselves to the single life among members of their own sex and sometimes shared their goods in common, seemed to conflict with duty to family, and thus to threaten the stability of society. Advocates of what became known as 'Christian manliness' also felt deeply uncomfortable when they witnessed the trappings of Catholic ritual. Incense, flowers and lace seemed suggestive of the feminine sphere, as did the sight of men in cassocks, surplices and elaborate vestments. It was widely believed that Anglo-Catholicism was the seed-bed of homosexuality (Hilliard, 1982).

To combat the notion that Christianity was only for the feminine or the effeminate, advocates of 'Christian manliness' (or 'muscular Christianity' as it became known by its more hostile detractors) began to search for new ways of presenting the gospel to men; it became implicit that the acceptance of the gospel would make men more manly. Interest in such activities came largely from within the Anglican Broad Church, with some leading proponents also associated with the Christian Socialist movement of 1848–54.[4] Kingsley and Thomas Hughes became the advocates of a manliness that dwelt upon robust energy and courage. They were, however, careful to qualify an excessive emphasis on brute strength by making it clear that tenderness and thoughtfulness for others were also part of the manly character. Hughes noted that 'true manliness is as likely to be found in a weak as in a strong body' (Hughes, 1879, pp. 21–5). Thomas Arnold, Headmaster of Rugby, and Samuel Taylor Coleridge, both founders of the Broad Church tradition, provided a second, slightly more intellectual emphasis which fed this strain of thought. They equated manliness with a departure from childishness, and with maturity, hard work and self-discipline. It was summarized in the slogan 'I act therefore I am', which became the motto of B. F. Westcott, Edward Benson and J. B. Lightfoot, scholars who wished to assume the role of men of action (Newsome, 1961, pp. 195–6).

It was the voices of Kingsley and Hughes that became most clearly associated in the public mind with the promotion of Christian manliness. Kingsley was also a Christian Socialist, and put his creed into action with his sense of outrage at the conditions of many of the very poor. He took practical steps to alleviate their poverty, in one case by trying to improve the water supply to the Jacob's Island district of Bermondsey. This experience supplied some of the settings for his novel *Alton Locke*, which contained harrowing descriptions derived from his observation of working-class life in the 1840s (Chitty, 1974, pp. 130–5). Despite his affinity with the poor, Kingsley was something of a snob, despising in particular the shopkeeping classes whom he judged to be effeminate and unrobust. He adopted the same peculiar criteria when judging the work of fellow writers: 'Kingsley's appreciation of literature was somewhat limited by the fact that he demanded the writer to display "manliness" both in his person and his work, and by "manliness" he usually meant a proficiency in blood sports only attainable by members of the upper classes' (Chitty, 1974, pp. 158–9). Most contemporary authors failed the blood sports test. Kingsley judged Percy Bysshe Shelley to be 'girlish' and despised Ruskin for not sleeping with his wife. After meeting Robert Browning for the first time, Kingsley dismissed him as 'very clever, but low bred and effeminate, a man who fancies that a man can be a poet by profession and do nothing else, a wild mistake' (*ibid.*, p. 159). Kingsley himself had turned to writing to boost the meagre stipend he received as rector of Eversley in Hampshire.

---

[4] See *RVB*, II, 2, pp. 44–6.

Kingsley had a particular loathing for Catholics. Part of this prejudice seems to have stemmed from meeting his future wife, Fanny Grenfell, at a time when she was contemplating joining an Anglican sisterhood at Regent's Park. Kingsley adored Fanny with an ardent passion, and the thought that he had nearly lost her to Dr Pusey, and that she had considered taking a vow of perpetual virginity, distressed him to an inexpressible degree (Vance, 1985, p. 36). He strongly believed in the spiritual significance of sex in marriage, and he developed a near-hysterical horror of celibacy, and of the 'Manichaean' notions that he regarded as having distorted much Christian theology.[5] Kingsley followed his friend F. D. Maurice in stressing the spiritual and symbolic significance of family relations, and accused Catholics of denigrating marriage by implying that celibate Christians were inherently more spiritual than married ones.[6] Kingsley believed that by advocating celibacy Catholics were effectively excluding a large section of the population from the full benefits of Christianity (Vance, 1985, pp. 37–8). The theological question underpinning this was whether or not the ordinary lives and activities of the majority of humanity were religiously significant in themselves. To deny that they were seemed to Kingsley to deny the inherent goodness of creation, and to capitulate to the spirit of Manichaeanism which he so detested. The incarnational theology of Coleridge and Maurice had taught Kingsley that the physical nature of man was redeemed because it had been assumed by Christ.

Kingsley's hostility to Catholic teaching on celibacy boiled over in 1864, when he entered into a public dispute with J. H. Newman, a man whom he had never met, but who had come to symbolize all that he loathed most in the Catholic Church. As an undergraduate at Cambridge, Kingsley had read the Tracts, but their effect had been to make him reject Christianity altogether.[7] Newman could hardly have been more different from Kingsley; he rarely sought out female company, and regarded

---

[5] Manichaeanism derived from the teachings of a third-century Persian sage, Manes (or Mani), who believed that, in a supposedly primeval conflict, light had become trapped in darkness and that the object of religious practice was to release the light imprisoned in the brain. Severe asceticism was advocated in order to promote the process, and as a result the body became disparaged. Manichaean beliefs passed into the Christian tradition via Augustine of Hippo, who was for a time an adherent.

[6] See *RVB*, III, 2.1.3, pp. 84–7 for an example of Kingley's preaching on these themes.

[7] He was later re-converted under the influence of the pious Fanny, who despite her High Church sympathies sent him works of Broad Church theology, including Coleridge's *Aids to Reflection* (Colloms, 1975, p. 52). There appears to be an interesting parallel here with Sarah Frances Bunyon (the wife of John William Colenso), who introduced her future husband to the writings of Coleridge and Maurice at roughly the same date, the mid-1840s (see Chapter 4, section II).

marriages among the Tractarians as a personal betrayal. Kingsley gained no new respect for Newman after his secession to Rome in 1845; indeed he published a piece in *Fraser's Magazine* suggesting that Newman had become morally and intellectually compromised by his conversion (Chitty, 1974, pp. 106–7). It was a similar piece of journalism that provided the catalyst for public controversy, when Kingsley reviewed Volumes VI and VII of James Anthony Froude's *History of England*. The freethinking Froude happened to be Kingsley's brother-in-law; he was also the brother of Newman's much loved but long-dead friend, Richard Hurrell Froude. The volumes under review allowed Kingsley to give free rein to his anti-popish sentiments. He inserted some sentences (quoted below) that cast doubt on Newman's truthfulness and integrity, both qualities crucial to Christian manliness. What mattered to Kingsley, however, was not so much to make a cheap jibe at Newman's alleged lack of manliness, but to question his seemingly Manichaean denial of the incarnational theology that underpinned Kingsley's own ideal of Christian manliness (Vance, 1985, p. 36). Kingsley wrote:

> Truth for its own sake has never been a virtue of the Roman clergy. Father Newman informs us that it need not, and on the whole ought not, to be; that cunning is the weapon which Heaven has given the saints wherewith to withstand the brute male force of the wicked world which marries and is given in marriage.
>
> (Quoted in Chitty, 1974, p. 229)

This was a distortion of a sermon that Newman had preached while still an Anglican in 1844. After a flurry of correspondence, and Kingsley's publication of a hostile pamphlet, Newman responded with what was to become one of the most influential religious works of the nineteenth century, the account of his spiritual odyssey, the *Apologia pro Vita Sua* (Chitty, 1974, pp. 229–37). It was an episode from which Kingsley's reputation was never to recover.

Like Kingsley, Hughes expressed his ideal of manliness in the fiction he wrote. He achieved lasting fame as the author of *Tom Brown's Schooldays* (1857), a phenomenally popular school story (indeed the first in what was to become a phenomenally popular genre) about the rough-and-tumble of school life for an ordinary boy at Rugby, the school that Hughes had himself attended. He followed it with a less well known sequel, *Tom Brown at Oxford* (1861). The main ingredients of *Tom Brown's Schooldays* were friendship, sport, sturdy independence and aggressive patriotism; Tom was a boy who excelled on the sports field rather than in the classroom. Intertwined with the story was a strongly pointed message about the duty of the ordinary young man to protect those who are physically weaker and to stand up to the bullying tyrant. A more directly religious emphasis was not lacking, however. In the second half of the novel, Tom Brown learned to say his prayers and read the Bible. Holy Communion as celebrated in Rugby chapel became a symbol of human interrelatedness and mutual dependence within the family of God. As Norman Vance put it, 'Chapel and cricket pitch can convey the same moral, the importance of unselfishly submitting one's individuality to the service of a common cause' (Vance, 1985, p. 151; see also pp. 143–65).

By the mid-1870s, Hughes had turned his attention away from the worlds of public school and university, and was devoting his attention to the New Testament. It was of concern to Hughes that Jesus himself appeared at times to be subversive of the Victorian understanding of manly behaviour. The gospels portrayed Jesus engaging in such unmasculine activities as washing the feet of his disciples, advocating meekness and turning the other cheek. Such elements might have given rise to the 'gentle Jesus, meek and mild' of the eighteenth-century hymn, but they seemed less acceptable to those schooled in Victorian notions of Christian manliness. Hughes's *The Manliness of Christ* (1879) was an attempt to present Jesus as the incarnation of Victorian Christian manliness, bestriding the scene as a warrior wrestling with an assortment of wicked adversaries (Gay, 1992, p. 104). Hughes was not a skilled biblical exegete in the tradition of Westcott or Lightfoot, and his entry into New Testament scholarship was prompted by a conviction that Christianity was doomed if it could not combat

> The underlying belief in the rising generation that Christianity is really responsible for [the] supposed weakness in its disciples ... The conscience of every man recognizes courage as the foundation of manliness, and manliness as the perfection of human character, and if Christianity runs counter to conscience in this matter, or indeed in any other, Christianity will go to the wall.
>
> (Hughes, 1879, p. 6)

The extent of the success of Kingsley and Hughes in gaining widespread acceptance for their theories is difficult to gauge. Their ideas, blending easily with widely prevalent notions concerning national supremacy and imperial power, became popular in some parts of society, and later they seemed to become discredited. Much about Christian manliness met with the same fate as the rest of Victorian religion: it died in the trenches of World War I. Despite the superficial appeal of war as the ultimate challenge to the manly hero in 1914, 'manliness' turned out to be too naïve a creed to withstand the pressures of modern war (Vance, 1985, p. 202). It was, nevertheless, the creed that, more than any other, caused a generation of young men to enlist almost without question for military service.

Public schools encouraged manliness of the sort that Arnold had fostered at Rugby, and this influence continued into the twentieth century. The exact implications of this, however, may not be as straightforward as they might seem. At first sight, the idea of replacing 'childishness' with 'manliness' had an obvious appeal to schoolmasters intent on instilling maturity into their pupils. So too did the promotion of 'purity' and the discouragement of any leanings towards effeminacy. The sports field was a useful place, not simply to work off youthful energy, but also to develop moral qualities such as courage, fair play and team spirit. Edward Benson, Headmaster of Wellington College and later Archbishop of Canterbury, preaching his farewell sermon to the pupils at Wellington in 1873, summed up the creed succinctly:

> For you will be men. You will seek Purity, that the souls and bodies you offer to those you love and to all-seeing God may be white and unspotted; Truth, that your speech may be simple and clear; Love, that your friendships may be sound and that the brotherhood of men may be to you no shadow.
>
> (Quoted in Newsome, 1961, p. 198)

Questions have been raised, however, about the validity of taking this sort of rhetoric at face value, and about whether the creed of 'manliness' encouraged maturity at all. A recent historian of masculinity, J. A. Mangan, has pointed out that often-repeated sentiments about the virtuous and heroic nature of schoolboys, particularly when uttered by headmasters, may have been mainly for public consumption. He suggested the existence in late Victorian and Edwardian public schools of other dominant codes, which derived little from Christianity:

> What frequently characterized the public schools of this period was an implicit, if not explicit, crude Darwinism encapsulated in simplistic aphorisms: life is conflict, strength comes through struggle and success is the prerogative of the strong. In consequence, conditions in the schools were, to adapt the classic Hobbesian expression, nasty, brutish and for some not short enough. The public school world was often a godless world of cold,

hunger, competition and endurance. There was frequently little kindness and less piety.

(Mangan, 1987, p. 142)

Mangan's arguments about the sheer godlessness of much that went on in public schools would be difficult to refute. He suggests that the dominant and fashionable rhetoric of muscular Christianity may have been adopted as a smokescreen to conceal the full extent to which Darwinism, agnosticism and scepticism had bitten into the consciousness of (even clerical) schoolmasters. As early as 1860, the *Dublin Review* was pointing out the implications of what it described as 'an attempt to keep up the mask of religion'. The aim of creating a boy in the likeness of God had been reduced, the *Review* believed, to 'a mere question of tissues and tendons—to bring out muscle, pluck, self-reliance, independence—the animal man' (quoted in Mangan, 1987, p. 145).

Another recent critic, Jeffrey Richards, has suggested that 'manliness' tended to militate against rather than promote maturity. 'One of the consequences of the official doctrine of manliness with its stress on games, sexual purity and hero-worship was to prolong adolescence well into actual manhood' (Richards, 1987, p. 105). The result was a generation of men who, like Peter Pan (J. M. Barrie's creation of the same period), never quite managed to grow up. Richards suggests that many of the heroes of the Empire, for example Rhodes, Gordon and Kitchener, with their preference for hunting, exploring and warring, contained elements of the boy-man. It was a character-type exemplified by Robert Baden-Powell, the founder of the Boy Scouts. Baden-Powell has been described by Piers Brendon as 'a perennial singing schoolboy, a permanent whistling adolescent, a case of arrested development *con brio*'. Out of an instinctive understanding of boys he created the Boy Scouts. Richards argues that late Victorian 'manly' culture partly re-focused itself on boyishness, with large numbers of men devoting themselves to the training, education and entertainment of boys. J. E. C. Welldon, Headmaster of Harrow and later Bishop of Calcutta, summed up the mood when he wrote with unselfconscious candour in 1895: 'no being perchance is so distinct, none so beautiful or attractive as a noble English boy' (quoted in Richards, 1987, p. 106; see also pp. 104–7).

A further important change in the ethos of late Victorian Christian manliness came in its movement from the Broad Church to the Evangelical mainstream. The Young Men's Christian Association, founded by Nonconformists and conservative Evangelical Anglicans in 1848, had originally sternly eschewed the promotion of physical fitness in favour of

Bible study, prayer and education. By the end of the century, however, it had absorbed the prevailing cult of athleticism, and a gymnasium was to be found at each of its local centres (Vance, 1985, p. 168). The prevalence of ideas about 'a healthy mind in a healthy body' led some Evangelicals to begin to excel at university sports, with cricket and rowing blues volunteering for foreign missions in increasing numbers. Indeed it may well have been these largely forgotten men, rather than Kingsley and Hughes, who gave substance to the term 'muscular Christianity'.

This sturdy mixture of manliness, Evangelicalism and athletic prowess lived on in early twentieth-century Scotland in the person of Eric Liddell, whose memory was revived when he became the subject of a popular film of the 1980s, *Chariots of Fire*. Liddell provoked enormous controversy at the Paris Olympics of 1924 by refusing to run in the 100 metres heats on a Sunday. He changed his event to the 400 metres, and still managed to break a world record and win a gold medal, after which he modestly withdrew to prepare a sermon for the Scottish Presbyterian church in Paris, where he was to preach the following Sunday. In the next year, he departed for missionary work in China, and died in a Japanese internment camp in 1945. Liddell received tremendous popular acclaim among the Protestants of both Scotland and Ulster, but it is significant that the British Olympic Committee was unsympathetic to Liddell's unshakeable Sabbatarian views (*ibid.*, pp. 169–72).

By the early years of the twentieth century, manliness and Christianity were beginning to drift apart, although the separation was not complete: whilst the hugely popular Boy Scout movement became a largely secular organization, the Boys' Brigade retained more of its religious identity. Robert Baden-Powell, despite being the son of the Broad Church Baden-Powell who had contributed to *Essays and Reviews*[8] in 1860, preferred for the Scouts general morality to articulated theology. He was more interested in manliness (or boyishness) than Christianity (Warren, 1987, pp. 199–216). The Boys' Brigade, founded in Glasgow by William Alexander Smith in 1883, was more selfconsciously Christian than the Scouts. Smith saw himself instilling 'manly' forms of religion (a conception he derived from Kingsley and Hughes) into working-class boys between the ages of thirteen and seventeen. The Brigade's overtly Protestant ethos derived in part from Smith's reaction against the allegedly 'effeminate' and 'morbidly introspective' Glaswegian Catholicism. Bible classes featured alongside drill classes in the

[8] See *RVB*, I, 1, p. 40.

timetable.'Here is the whole idea of The Boys' Brigade in a nutshell', wrote Smith in 1891,

> Boys talking to each other in the most perfectly natural way about their Company Bible-Class before all their comrades on the football field! That is the very essence of the Boys' Brigade, for it aims at taking up everything that should enter into healthy Boy-life, and consecrating it all to the service of Christ.

(Quoted in Springhall, 1987, p. 57)

The extent of the Boys' Brigade's success in this respect is difficult to gauge, for it is impossible to know how many Brigade members became religiously committed. John Springhall notes that whereas in 1887–8 almost 80 per cent of Brigade members were regular churchgoers, by 1895–6 the figure had fallen to below 60 per cent, probably reflecting wider recruitment outside Sunday school circles (Springhall, 1987, pp. 52–61).

It is clear that mid-Victorian attempts to ridicule Catholicism as unmanly had not deterred Anglicans who considered themselves to be Catholics from adopting a distinctive style. H. P. Liddon, Vice-principal of the newly founded Cuddesdon Theological College, defended his students against charges of unmanliness and effeminacy in 1858. They might not be prepared to join in every cricket match in the neighbourhood, but they exhibited a different sort of manliness, one that was consistent with the virtue of meekness. 'Our men', wrote Liddon, 'have more control over mere animal spirits and energy than many of their fellow clergy. God forbid that it should be otherwise' (Chadwick, 1954, pp. 93–4). Unsurprisingly, Anglo-Catholics had no difficulty in equating celibacy with manliness. R. W. Church, one of the Oxford Movement's most prominent early historians, defended celibate Tractarians vigorously. Recalling the early days of the Oxford Movement, he remarked: 'To shrink from [celibacy] was a mark of want of strength or intelligence, of an unmanly preference for English home life, of insensibility to the generous devotion and purity of the saints' (Church, 1970 edn, p. 8). In 1867, Cardinal Manning had sounded a more defensive note when he chose to describe Tractarianism (of which he had been part) as a 'vigorous and masculine movement'.[9] In the later Victorian period, celibate clerics became more widely acceptable as truly manly. Flamboyant figures like Father Stanton at St Albans, Holborn, earned respect by being at the front line in the fight against social

---

[9] See *RVB*, III, 2.1.2, pp. 77–8.

injustices. The Broad Church observer C. M. Davies, after witnessing him at work, commented approvingly that there was nothing remotely effeminate about Stanton.[10]

Outside Catholic circles, however, an unmarried man was still seen as less acceptable. By the end of the century, there was increasing public concern about young men of the middle class who possessed the means to marry but preferred to remain bachelors. It was an anxiety that had surfaced first in the late 1860s. It is tempting to speculate about the causes of this apparent rejection of domesticity. Perhaps men had ceased to find the delicate flower that was late Victorian womanhood sufficiently attractive; perhaps they found the prospect of being the sole source of funding for a family that might grow at annual intervals too daunting; perhaps they had become disillusioned with heterosexuality. It could also be that having separated from girls when they went away to school, men in a number of professions found that the separation was perpetuated, and opportunities for mixing with women of their own class were distinctly limited. John Tosh suggests that the heavy and repressive emphasis on 'purity' that this generation of men experienced in childhood made either heterosexual love or the development of a fully realized homosexual identity difficult for them in adulthood. Tosh illustrates his argument by means of the well-documented (if eccentric) Benson family, contrasting the values of Edward Benson, the family's authoritarian and anxious father, with his sons' rejection of domestic life. Three of Benson's sons survived to adulthood, and all favoured life among other men rather than marriage (Tosh, 1991, p. 66; see also pp. 44–68). The pattern in the Benson family seems to have been replicated throughout the middle class, as supposedly eligible bachelors disappeared into all-male communities—public schools, the universities, the armed services and the Empire. 'Freedom from domesticity was a positive manly attribute in a way which had found little parallel among respectable professional men fifty years earlier' (*ibid.*, p. 68). It seemed as if the strategies that the previous generation had adopted to make their sons 'manly' had backfired. The sons had retaliated with a rejection of their parents' values.

IV SINGLE WOMEN AND EDUCATION

As with the attempt to present a particular construction of masculinity, mid-Victorian attempts to present marriage and home as the only valid vocation for a woman were also at risk of backfiring, for they failed to take

[10] See *RVB*, III, 5.3.3, pp. 269–73.

proper account of the reality, which was that many women never married. From the middle of the century, census figures began to reveal three interesting trends. First, females outnumbered males in the birth rate and in the total population—the 1851 figure indicated that overall there were 400,000 more women than men; secondly, 30 per cent of women never married; and thirdly, over half of all women worked for their own subsistence. As the extent to which women were remaining single became clear, the inadequacy was revealed of attempting to elevate the ideal of the Christian family as if it were the universal experience. The schemes suggested for responding to what became unflatteringly known as the 'surplus women problem' reveal much about contemporary views of womanhood. They included encouraging more marriages by lifting the restrictions on military officers and creating land-lease programmes for single men who would promise to marry within six months of taking over the land. It was also suggested that women be encouraged to emigrate to America and the colonies, where there was believed to be a surplus of men (Johnson, 1983, p. 193).

Many women (like many men) remained single by choice. Articulate single women became increasingly peeved by the emphasis on failure that seemed to attach itself to discussion of the 'surplus women problem'. Frances Power Cobbe (a Freethinker from an Evangelical background) put the case for viewing women as individuals in their own right in 1881:

> Here is the root of the misplacement of women, that they have been deemed by men, and have contentedly deemed themselves, to have only a secondary purpose in the order of things. Brigham Young's doctrine that only a woman *sealed* to a man in marriage can possibly be saved, is little more than a carrying out of our British legislator's idea, that women who do not marry (and so do not immediately contribute to the comfort of some particular man) are '*Failures*'. ... Of course there is a sense in which every created being is made for others. Creation is like one of those vast suspension bridges in which every bar and chain tends to support the whole structure. But in *this* sense man is also made for woman, the father for the son, the daughter for the mother, and so on *ad infinitum*. There is no degradation to any, but honour to all, in this view of the solidarity of the family, the State and Humanity. And why? Because every one recognizes that it is only the secondary purpose of each to help the other. The primary *raison d'etre* of every one is his own existence, and only in a secondary sense he exists for others.
>
> (Quoted in Johnson, 1983, pp. 153–4)

Florence Nightingale (an Anglican) had expressed her frustration rather differently thirty years earlier:

> It has become of late the fashion, both of novel and of sermon writers, to cry up 'old maids', to inveigh against regarding marriage as the vocation of all women, to declare that a single life is as happy as a married one, if people would but think so. So is the air as good an element for fish as the water, if they did but know how to live in it. Show us *how* to be single, and we will agree.
>
> (Quoted in Johnson, 1983, p. 173)

Increased opportunities for activity were needed if women were to be liberated from what Nightingale diagnosed as their major problem—having nothing to do.

The education of girls and women had become a matter of increasing interest and importance by the mid nineteenth century. Inappropriate or inadequate education had long been perceived as at the root of female fecklessness, but there had always been the problem of deciding what women were being educated for. If they were being educated for marriage, then an emphasis on the feminine 'accomplishments' thought necessary to attract a husband—music, drawing, fine needlework, perhaps a little French—seemed natural enough. If, however, the purpose was to develop the intellect, and prepare women to be active in society, then rigorous training in the classics and mathematics—the subjects that dominated the university curriculum until the 1870s—might be more appropriate.

There was a common fear of doing physical and mental damage to women by over-educating them, and the most usual Christian response fell somewhere between the advocacy of ephemeral accomplishments and rigorous academic study. The Evangelical educationalist Hannah More, for example, advocated a practical Christian education, which would equip a woman to be a devoted Christian believer and would be a resource upon which she could draw as she grew older.

> To learn how to grow old gracefully is perhaps one of the rarest and most valuable arts which can be taught to a woman. And it must be confessed that it is a severe trial for those women to be called to lay down beauty, who have nothing else to take up.
>
> (Quoted in Johnson, 1983, p. 102)

More despised a concentration on the superficial feminine 'accomplishments', which were designed to attract male admirers. They were froth without substance, and failed to develop women's moral nature or social usefulness. It is, nevertheless, difficult to imagine that More would have had much sympathy with the Anglican educationalists of the mid nineteenth century, who included Frances Buss at the North London Collegiate for Ladies and Dorothea Beale at the Ladies College at Cheltenham. Both institutions helped to set the tone for the extension of public-school academic education to girls, although the realization of that objective was at some distance in the future.

Many Christians and Jews continued to regard the full-blown academic education of a girl as even less desirable than a trivializing one. Scholarship was generally more highly regarded in Judaism than in Christianity, but only in males. Jewish girls who expressed an interest in learning Hebrew or studying the Torah were likely to be rebuffed. Scholarly inclinations were likely to be fostered by early tuition, and to wither away if no tuition was forthcoming. The Manchester oral history project revealed a huge discrepancy between the resources devoted to the religious education of Jewish boys and those devoted to the religious education of Jewish girls. Eighty-eight per cent of the male Jewish immigrants interviewed had received a formal religious education in Manchester, as against 28 per cent of the females (Burman, 1986, p. 243).

To conservative churchmen, the opening of higher education to women, which was beginning in a small way by 1870, spelled the creation of masculine women, who would reject their subordinate role and become domineering. An educated woman would be, in the revealing phrase of J. W. Burgon, Anglican cleric and Fellow of Oriel College Oxford, an 'inconvenient rival'. In a sermon preached in 1871, Burgon continued:

> When, instead of rejoicing in the sacred retirement of her home and the strict privacy of her domestic duties, she is found to be secretly longing for the publicity of print and the notoriety of the platform:—when this, or any approach to this, becomes a common thing,—Woman will too late discover that she has, as far as in her lay, unsexed herself; lost her present unique social position; come to be regarded only as an inferior kind of Man. Man, with all his hardness: Man, without his manliness. She will be no longer a help and consolation. She will inevitably find that she has dethroned *herself*, and degraded *herself*,—to her own heavy harm and loss; to our abiding sorrow and unceasing discomfort.

(Quoted in Johnson, 1983, p. 142)

To some, however, Burgon's sentiments seemed unpleasantly reactionary by 1871, and did not reflect the fact that other Anglican clergy supported initiatives for women's higher education. Seven months after Burgon's sermon, Mary Paley was one of the first five students to enter Newnham College, Cambridge. She was the daughter of a strict Evangelical clergyman, who had not only employed a German governess for her, but had instructed her himself in Latin, Hebrew, Euclid, and English and classical literature (Gill, 1994, p. 115). Emily Davies, first Mistress of Girton College, Cambridge, was the daughter of an Evangelical clergyman, and Elizabeth Wordsworth, first Principal of Lady Margaret Hall, Oxford, was the daughter of a bishop. Given the evident care that some clergy devoted to the education of their daughters, it is perhaps not surprising that out of the 112 women students who were educated at Oxbridge colleges in the period 1869–80 whose backgrounds can be traced, the largest group, thirty-two, was made up of the daughters of Anglican clergy (Sutherland, 1987, p. 101). In London, Queen's College, Harley Street (1848) and the Ladies' College, Bedford Square (1849)—both concerned with the training of governesses—received early support from Anglican clergy including Kingsley, who lectured there briefly in English literature, and Maurice. Freethinkers as well as Anglicans played a prominent part in promoting women's education. Its founder Henry Sidgwick's influence ensured that Newnham was a secular foundation from the beginning, without a college chapel.

V WOMEN, WORK AND MINISTRY

A public rebuttal of Burgon's conservative opinions about the role of women came from another Oxford clergyman, C. J. H. Fletcher, in a sermon preached the following month. Fletcher, like Cobbe, was aware that many women did not marry, and was critical of defining women only in terms of their potential for matrimony and motherhood:

> [A woman] must not ... so plan her life, as that it will seem a failure unless she marry. She must endeavour to find or make some work for herself. If inclination points to some new line of activity, and parents sanction her pursuing it, let her not be discouraged by vulgar sneers or conventional intolerance; let her wed herself to her work, and beautify it by her Womanhood, and she may then rest assured that, so doing, she will not be out of Woman's place.
>
> (Quoted in Johnson, 1983, p. 147)

To underpin these views, Fletcher held a doctrine of the equality of men and women, which derived from his belief in the Incarnation. His understanding of Christ was in sharp contrast with the more or less contemporaneous portrait offered by Hughes, the advocate of Christ's manliness. Fletcher considered that attempts to legitimize female subordination by linking it to the story of Eve had been carried too far:

> Woman's original equality with Man is recovered in Christ. The true ground of her restored dignity is often misrepresented. It does not rest on the fact that the Virgin Mary was the divinely selected instrument of the Incarnation ... Nor is it Woman's elevation in Christ derived from her relation as Wife being (according to S Paul) a sacramental sign of the Church's relation to Christ. Its true cause lies deeper. It is found, first, in this, that Christ's character manifested the womanly virtues—purity, sympathy, gentleness, obedience—which had died out of the world with Woman's degradation. You must never forget that Christ is neither Man nor Woman. He is the divine likeness, the whole humanity. Manhood and Womanhood in one.
>
> (Quoted in Johnson, 1983, p. 144)

The radical Fletcher was not prepared to put any limitation on the types of work that women should be allowed to undertake, and once more his justification was theological:

> What God has fitted them for, they ought to be allowed to do, and what He has fitted them for can only be ascertained by giving them full liberty to follow their bent and choose their work. God has so made us that inclination and fitness for particular work usually go together.
>
> (Quoted in Johnson, 1983, p. 146)

The reality, however, was that women remained severely restricted in the sorts of work that they could undertake, with teaching more or less the only profession open to educated women of the middle class. This was the career followed by the majority of those who attended the new women's colleges. However, even teaching was ruled out for those who felt that they had a place to maintain in society, as it was deemed to give 'a lady rather too much an air of necessity' (Prochaska, 1980, p. 5). A woman who worked for money could be regarded as having invaded the rights of the working classes. Among the middle classes, philanthropy was the vocation that most sprang to mind.

Frank Prochaska has argued that charity work did more than anything else to enlarge the horizons of women in the nineteenth century. A statistical survey of women's work carried out in 1893 by Louisa Hubbard and Angela Burdett-Coutts estimated that about 500,000 women laboured 'continuously and semi-professionally in philanthropy' and another 20,000 supported themselves as 'paid officials' in charitable societies. As Prochaska points out, these figures do not include some 20,000 trained nurses or the 5,000 women in sisterhoods and nunneries who took on work that was essentially philanthropic. There were also many thousands more who worked part time for charity, and who collected money and distributed tracts for the missionary and Bible societies (Prochaska, 1980, pp. 222–5).

For the vast numbers of women who engaged in charity work, the absence of payment was beside the point; what mattered was fulfilment of the religious duty of relieving the sufferings of others. Living as they did with an ever-present sense of the appalling reality of the eternal damnation of the lost, Victorian Christians learned to value their own souls, and also the souls of others. As Prochaska noted in his account of the motivations underlying philanthropy, benevolence was often the product of anxiety: a woman visited the poor not only in anticipation of grace but also in fear of damnation. It was undeniable, however, that many women gained a great deal of satisfaction from their charity work. It served to channel the urge to be useful, recognized, informed and diverted. It enabled some women to be loved, particularly by children. Anne Jemima Clough, who later became the first Principal of Newnham College, noted in her journal after some time spent among the poor: 'The children know me, and speak my name. This was delicious to me, and worth more than a thousand praises' (*ibid.*, pp. 117–25).

Philanthropy was not the preserve of any particular religious tradition; all agreed that it was of the essence of faith to be charitable. There were, however, some differences in emphasis. Evangelical Quakers showed particular commitment to peace causes, Unitarians supported educational charities and Low Church Anglicans promoted tract and Bible societies. Roman Catholics and Jews tended to concentrate exclusively on helping their own people (*ibid.*, pp. 39 and 139). Visiting the homes of the poor was the most popular of all charitable activities. In some parts of London, High Church and Low Church Anglican, Catholic, Methodist, Nonconformist and non-denominational visitors competed against each other in the same districts. Charities proliferated in a society splintered by class and religious allegiance. 'Philanthropic enterprise was, in a sense, *laissez-faire* capitalism turned in on itself' (*ibid.*, p. 106).

Philanthropy was unique in being the only form of church work that was open to women in all denominations. Other activities were likely to be circumscribed as much by the religious ethos of the denomination as by the restrictions imposed by gender. To put it simply, a Roman Catholic woman would not have thought of engaging in an itinerant preaching ministry, any more than a Primitive Methodist would have considered becoming a nun. What, then, were the forms of women's church work and ministry specific to the different traditions?

Female preaching and leadership in worship was mainly associated with Nonconformist revivalism. Once revival gave way to organization and the denomination became immersed in the panoply of a male-led bureaucracy—committees, ordained ministers, theological colleges—female preaching tended to be suppressed. Even the Quakers, whose approach to women's ministry was nothing short of revolutionary by contemporary standards, had disagreements about the proper scope of their activities. Quaker women were encouraged to address female audiences only, and to restrict themselves to other tasks deemed particularly suitable, such as marriage preparation, visiting and the care of widows and orphans. Decisions about policy and doctrine remained firmly under male control, and it was not until 1896 that the Men's Yearly Meeting decided that the most important issues should be discussed at joint sittings of men and women; gradually local Quaker business meetings adopted joint sittings as well. Nevertheless, the Society of Friends did give its women considerable opportunities, and in the early Victorian period women ministers greatly outnumbered men. Elizabeth Isichei, the historian of Victorian Quakerism, suggests that it is 'difficult to imagine any other early Victorian context where the silver eloquence of Elizabeth Fry could ever have found expression' (Isichei, 1970, p. 108; see also pp. 107–10). There is no doubt that Quaker ministry empowered women of eloquence and strong personality.

Female preaching became most widespread with the rise of Methodism, and was an eighteenth- and early nineteenth-century rather than a Victorian phenomenon (Valenze, 1985). In the early years of Methodist revival, there was no official ban to deter female enthusiasts; the priority was on using all available methods and individuals to proclaim the gospel (Hempton and Hill, 1992, p. 133). John Wesley's advice to aspiring female preachers was cautious, but essentially it was no different from that given to men. He advised Alice Cambridge that she should not 'be silent when God commands you to speak', but she should try not to give offence or draw attention to herself. She was also to avoid speaking near another preacher, 'lest you should draw away his hearers' (quoted in Hempton and Hill, 1992, p. 134). However, even if Cambridge's ministry was regarded as essentially supplementary and provisional, it was evidently popular among her hearers. On a tour of Ulster at the beginning of the nineteenth century, she attracted numbers 'amounting to eight or ten thousand persons'.

At the Irish Methodist Conference of 1802, however, it was decreed 'contrary both to Scripture and prudence that *women* should preach or should exhort in public'. Superintendents were directed to refuse a Society Ticket to any woman who preached, with the result that the defiant Cambridge was excluded until Conference decided to re-admit her in 1811. The London Conference of 1803 did not forbid women from preaching, but it strongly discouraged them, recommending that they only speak if there was a shortage of male preachers, and then normally only to women. The official hostility hardened when Wesleyanism fell under the influence of Jabez Bunting from 1814 to 1858 (Johnson, 1983, pp. 87–8). Some women simply defied Conference and continued as before. The best known example was Mary Barritt Taft, who travelled widely in the north of England, strongly supported by her husband, Zechariah Taft, who wrote several tracts defending women's preaching. The consequence of the ban sometimes brought the new rules into disrepute, as when the male followers of the Irish preacher Anne Lutton dressed up in women's clothing in a vain attempt to hear her preach in the 1830s (Hempton and Hill, 1992, p. 134).

The link between revivalism and women's preaching was established once more in the new Methodist denominations, which became offshoots from Wesleyanism in the early nineteenth century. At their outset, both the Primitive Methodists and the Bible Christians gave a prominent place to the ministry of women, and in both denominations the same decline in female participation was noticeable as the years passed. The Bible Christians, for example, listed fourteen female preachers out of thirty at its first conference in 1819. By 1872, however, it had only one woman and 127 men (Johnson, 1983, p. 90).

In the later Victorian period, another revivalist organization, the Salvation Army, adopted the by now familiar strategy of giving an equal place to women. The Salvationists, however, managed to achieve the transition into mainstream denominational life without finding it necessary to silence their female officers. Catherine Booth, wife of the founder of the Salvation Army, had been one of a select body of middle-class women who began a public preaching ministry in the 1860s, prompted by the Second Evangelical Awakening, which had begun with the Ulster Revival of 1859.[11] Women's involvement in 'public prayers and preachings' was among the first of the 'excesses' to be reported in the Ulster revival. It persisted until Dwight Moody's and Ira Sankey's Edinburgh campaign of 1873, which marked the beginning of a new and rather different phase of revivalist Christianity. During Moody's and Sankey's campaigns, women were permitted to address women's meetings only (Anderson, 1969, pp. 470 and 481).

In emphasizing the preaching activities of a very small number of women, it is important not to detract from the informal ministries of thousands of others, who belonged to denominations where women were explicitly forbidden from occupying the pulpit. Most women could not preach in public, but they could convert in private. A fervent Evangelical would never cease to put forward the gospel to all whom she met, distributing tracts to friends, neighbours and strangers alike. Amy Camps, an Anglican who lived in Colchester, devoted her whole life to religion in this way. She began by visiting a school for poor children, supported the Bible Society and visited the inmates of the hospital and the workhouse. She would regularly relay the information gleaned through this work to local clergy and church dignitaries, thus working within rather than independently of church structures. She even persuaded a Colchester vicar to remove from his church the 'idols' (images of the Apostles), which she associated with Tractarianism. In 1842, however, it appeared that her ministry at the local hospital was under threat, with the arrival on the committee of a clergyman who denounced her as the 'preaching and praying woman'. Faced with being excluded from the hospital, Camps appealed for divine guidance and turned to her Bible, which opened at Ecclesiastes, chapter 10, verse 4: 'If the Spirit of the ruler rise up against thee, leave not thy place.' After this, the vicar of her own parish promised to make her a life member of the hospital, and she was not prohibited from her work (Davidoff and Hall, 1987, pp. 141–2). Sarah Martin, 'the Yarmouth prison visitor', functioned as (unpaid) prison chaplain in the town for over twenty years. She too worked with support from local clergy.[12]

Catholicism provided women with rather different opportunities for independent action. In both Anglo-Catholicism and Roman Catholicism, the numbers of women in convents increased dramatically during the

---

[11] See *RVB*, I, 6, pp. 217–18 and *RVB*, III, 5.2.3, pp. 253–8.

[12] See 'Sarah Martin on prison visiting, 1844', Part II, pp. 274–5 for Martin's own account of her activities.

Victorian period. By 1900, there were between 8,000 and 10,000 Roman sisters in some 600 convent houses (O'Brien, 1988, p. 110). As Martha Vicinus noted in respect of Anglican sisters, nuns were involved in 'a complicated picture of institutional subordination and self-determination' (Vicinus, 1985, p. 48). Susan O'Brien has argued that, although they were autonomous in many respects, nuns were also part of a larger body in which institutional power and authority was vested in an all-male hierarchy. They were dependent on maintaining the goodwill of bishops and priests, both for permission to work in any diocese, and for the spiritual and sacramental offices that were necessary for the community. Rather than fulfilling the popular image of retreating into a life of seclusion, many nineteenth-century nuns were required to cope simultaneously with a variety of public and domestic demands. Roman Catholic sisters had to mobilize the necessary finance to build their schools, colleges, orphanages, hospitals and hostels, and subsequently were expected to manage considerable property holdings.

At the same time, unlike most of their male counterparts, women religious undertook a great deal of domestic drudgery. They did their own cleaning and laundry, and that generated by their hospitals and schools, and in some cases they also washed and cleaned for the clergy. In searching for paid work with which to support their communities, most sisters had to rely on the traditional and poorly paid areas of women's employment: embroidery, sewing and laundry work (O'Brien, 1988, p. 116). Most sisterhoods, whether Anglican or Roman, concentrated on active rather than contemplative life, a development that owed much to the strong philanthropic ethos that pervaded Victorian Christianity.

As nuns, religious sisters were able to over-ride the closely constructed gender identity enforced on other women. Nuns had changed their name and their appearance, and they had exchanged family life for community life. Foundresses of religious houses and reverend mothers were undeniably figures of authority, and were expected to exercise leadership without attracting censure for being unwomanly. Cornelia Connelly, the foundress of the Society of the Holy Child Jesus, sought to combine the best feminine and masculine qualities in herself and her sisters. When she wrote the constitution of the Society, she declared that the order should be governed 'with the strength of a Superior and the heart of a mother'. When seeking to encourage sisters who lacked confidence in themselves, she observed: 'We have to learn to make strong women, who while they lose nothing of their sweetness and gentleness, should yet have a masculine force of character and will' (O'Brien, 1988, pp. 136 and 138).

VI CONCLUSION

How then does this discussion of women's ministry relate to the officially sanctioned male and female role models considered earlier? Connelly was unusual among Victorian Christians in believing that women could successfully combine both 'female' and 'male' characteristics within a feminine personality. In contrast, most Christians (and Jews) made a sharp distinction between masculine and feminine virtues and attributes. Such a differentiation between the sexes was a new development. It contributed to a climate in which religion became popularly regarded as solely within the female domain. Women of all denominations were credited with being more naturally 'religious' than men, and were idealized for their supposed purity and spiritual qualities.

The equation of religiosity with femininity (or effeminacy) was regarded in some quarters as disturbing. It led to an attempt to repackage religion for men, in the form of 'Christian manliness'. It was a creed that sought to combine a no-nonsense biblical faith with the cultivation of honour, integrity and a strong, healthy body. It penetrated Victorian culture very successfully, but by the end of the century it was showing signs of losing its nerve. In some circles, 'manliness' became diverted into 'boyishness', implying adolescent immaturity. In others, the fusion of the concepts of 'manliness' and 'Christianity' proved impossible to maintain intact. The Christian manly creed had little to say directly about women, although it made some implicit assumptions. One was that in order to become manly a man must break away from the women who had nurtured him in youth. Once grown into true manliness, however, he should not suppress natural sexual desire, but seek out (and, of course, marry) a woman, who was his natural mate. Kingsley, Hughes and the fictional Tom Brown all married in their early twenties. This expectation proved to be unsustainable when a larger than average proportion of the generation who had been reared on it chose to reject it in the late Victorian period. By the end of the nineteenth century, 'the family' was becoming something of a tarnished icon.

From about the mid nineteenth century, and for a variety of reasons, women were also remaining single in larger numbers. It was this generation of women who looked for new opportunities for usefulness, and who turned to church and secular work in increasing numbers. These women demonstrated that (like their brothers) they were prepared to challenge contemporary notions of what was suitable for their sex, and to run the risk of being pilloried as unfeminine, masculine women. By the end of the Victorian period, although male authority in the Church's hierarchy was as strong as ever, most routine non-priestly work in the Church of England was being done by women. Thousands of women were engaged in district visiting and Sunday school teaching. A significant number were serving the Church full time as nuns, deaconesses, Bible women and teachers in Anglican National Schools. Whilst the Church had become increasingly ready to make use of the talents of women, it was also reducing in significance or abolishing the positions of authority that were traditionally occupied by laymen in each parish—those of parish clerk, churchwarden and vestryman. This was exactly what the advocates of manly Christianity had sought to avoid: the takeover of the Church by clergy and by women, and the gradual exclusion of laymen (Knight, 1995, pp. 195–200).

Finally, to what extent should the question of gender be seen as of central importance in the interpretation of Victorian religion? One point deserves reiteration: 'women are no more a cohesive social entity than men and a shared gender does not in itself produce a common experience' (Hempton and Hill, 1992, p. 131).

Nevertheless, the constructions of both masculinity and femininity were powerful and largely unchallenged in the Victorian period; one reason for their influence was that, in order to become so powerful, they had borrowed from and contributed to contemporary religious culture. Clearly, however, gender needs to be understood alongside social status. The Victorian ideal of femininity had little relevance to a female coal miner or a female docker, although the fact that by the end of the century women had ceased to labour in these occupations reveals something of the understanding of gender held by legislators and employers. As far as the question of gender in religion is concerned, it needs to be considered alongside denominational affiliation, as well as social status. The religious experience of Quakers was shaped differently from that of Catholics, and a female Quaker was likely to find it easier to communicate something of the essence of her religious life to a male Quaker than to a female Catholic, and vice versa. Within most denominations, it could be argued that a more profound distinction existed between layperson and minister than between woman and man. Whilst churches, chapels and synagogues had different expectations of their male and female adherents, the case for a fundamentally different spiritual experience between men and women of the same social class and religious tradition seems not proven.

BIBLIOGRAPHY

O. Anderson (1969) 'Women preachers in mid-Victorian Britain: some reflexions on feminism, popular religion and social change', *Historical Journal*, Vol. 12, pp. 467–84.

G. S. Bull (1854) *'Home,' and How to Make it Happy: A Lecture*, Birmingham.

R. Burman (1986) '"She looketh well to the ways of her household": the changing role of Jewish women in religious life, c.1880–1930' in G. Malmgreen (ed.) *Religion in the Lives of English Women, 1760–1930*, pp. 234–59, London, Croom Helm.

O. Chadwick (1954) *The Founding of Cuddesdon*, Oxford, Oxford University Press.

S. Chitty (1974) *The Beast and the Monk: A Life of Charles Kingsley*, New York, Mason Charter.

R. W. Church (1970 edn) *The Oxford Movement: Twelve Years*, ed. G. Best, London, Rivington (first published London, Macmillan, 1891).

B. Colloms (1975) *Charles Kingsley*, London, Constable.

J. Cox (1982) *The English Churches in a Secular Society: Lambeth 1870–1930*, Oxford, Oxford University Press.

*L. Davidoff and C. Hall (1987) *Family Fortunes: Men and Women of the English Middle Classes, 1780–1850*, London, Hutchinson.

P. Gay (1992) 'The manliness of Christ' in R. W. Davis and R. J. Helmstadter (eds.) *Religion and Irreligion in Victorian Society: Essays in Honor of R. K Webb*, pp. 102–16, London and New York, Routledge.

*S. Gill (1994) *Women and the Church of England From the Eighteenth Century to the Present*, London, Society for Promoting Christian Knowledge.

D. Hempton and M. Hill (1992) *Evangelical Protestantism in Ulster Society 1740–1890*, London and New York, Routledge.

D. Hilliard (1982) 'Un-English and unmanly: Anglo-Catholicism and homosexuality', *Victorian Studies*, Vol. 25, pp. 181–210.

W. Houghton (1957) *The Victorian Frame of Mind 1830–1870*, New Haven (CT), Yale University Press.

T. Hughes (1879) *The Manliness of Christ*, London, Macmillan.

K. S. Inglis (1963) *Churches and the Working Classes in Victorian England*, London, Routledge.

E. Isichei (1970) *Victorian Quakers*, London, Oxford University Press.

J. A. James (1852) *Female Piety; or, the Young Woman's Friend and Guide through Life to Immortality*, Birmingham.

*D. A. Johnson (1983) *Women in English Religion 1700–1925*, New York and Toronto, Edwin Mellon Press.

F. Knight (1995) *The Nineteenth-century Church and English Society*, Cambridge, Cambridge University Press.

P. Laslett (1971) *The World We Have Lost—Further Explored*, 2nd edn, London, Methuen.

H. McLeod (1986) 'New perspectives on Victorian working-class religion: the oral evidence', *Oral History*, Vol. 14, pp. 31–49.

H. McLeod (1993) *Religion and Irreligion in Victorian England: How Secular Was the Working Class?*, Bangor, Headstart History.

J. A. Mangan (1987) 'Social Darwinism and upper-class education in late Victorian and Edwardian England' in Mangan and Walvin (1987), pp. 135–59.

*J. A. Mangan and J. Walvin (1987) *Manliness and Morality: Middle-class Masculinity in Britain and America 1800–1940*, Manchester, Manchester University Press.

D. Newsome (1961) *Godliness and Good Learning: Four Studies on a Victorian Ideal*, London, John Murray.

S. O'Brien (1988) '*Terra incognita:* the nun in nineteenth-century England', *Past and Present*, Vol. 121, pp. 110–40.

F. K. Prochaska (1980) *Women and Philanthropy in Nineteenth-century England*, Oxford, Clarendon Press.

J. Richards (1987) '"Passing the love of women": manly love in Victorian society' in Mangan and Walvin (1987), pp. 92–122.

J. Ruskin (1865) *Sesame and Lilies*, London, Smith, Elder.

J. Springhall (1987) 'Building character in the British boy: the attempt to extend Christian manliness to working-class adolescents, 1880–1914' in Mangan and Walvin (1987), pp. 52–74.

G. Sutherland (1987) 'The movement for the higher education of women: its social and intellectual context in England, *c.* 1840–80' in P. J. Waller (ed.) *Politics and Social Change in Modern Britain*, pp. 91–116, Brighton, Harvester Press.

C. E. Tonna (1834/44) *The Wrongs of Women*, London, W. H. Dalton.

J. Tosh (1991) 'Domesticity and manliness in the Victorian middle class: the family of Edward White Benson' in M. Roper and J. Tosh (eds.) *Manful Assertions: Masculinities in Britain since 1800*, pp. 44–73, London and New York, Routledge.

D. M. Valenze (1985) *Prophetic Sons and Daughters: Female Preaching and Popular Religion in Industrial England*, Princeton (NJ), Princeton University Press.

*N. Vance (1985) *The Sinews of the Spirit: The Ideal of Christian Manliness in Victorian Literature and Religious Thought*, Cambridge, Cambridge University Press.

M. Vicinus (1985) *Independent Women: Work and Community for Single Women 1850–1920*, London, Virago.

A. Warren (1987) 'Popular manliness: Baden-Powell, scouting and the development of manly character' in Mangan and Walvin (1987), pp. 199–219.

CHAPTER 2

INTELLIGENT YOUTH OF COUNTRY TOWN. "AH SAY, BILL, 'ULL THAT BE T' ELIJAH GOIN' OOP I' THAT BIG BOX?!"

MUSIC IN THE MIDLANDS

'PRAISE TO THE HOLIEST IN THE HEIGHT': HYMNS AND CHURCH MUSIC

I N the mid-1850s, the novelist George Eliot visualized with a mixture of nostalgia and patronizing detachment the style of church music prevalent in rural Warwickshire at the beginning of the century:

> And the singing was no mechanical affair of official routine; it had a drama ... Then followed the migration of the clerk to the gallery, where, in company with a bassoon, two key-bugles, a carpenter
> ? understood to have an amazing power of singing 'counter', and two lesser musical stars, he formed the complement of a choir regarded in Shepperton as one of distinguished attraction, occasionally known to draw hearers from the next parish. The innovation of hymn-books was as yet undreamed of; ... for the lyrical taste of the best heads in Shepperton had been formed on Sternhold and Hopkins.[1] But the greatest triumphs of the Shepperton choir were reserved for the Sundays when the slate announced an ANTHEM, with a dignified abstinence from particularization, both words and music lying far beyond the reach of the most ambitious amateur in the congregation: an anthem in which the key-bugles always ran away at a great pace, while the bassoon every now and then boomed a flying shot after them.

(Eliot, 1973 edn, pp. 42–3)

By the time when George Eliot was writing, this style of church music was in marked decline, although it was to linger for some years longer, notably in the West Country. It received further well-known literary commemoration in Thomas Hardy's *Under the Greenwood Tree* (1872).

Another vignette of church music at the beginning of the Victorian era is provided by the experience of the composer Samuel Sebastian Wesley. When organist of Hereford Cathedral in the early 1830s, he found that nearly all the men in the choir were habitually absent and that he was accordingly largely dependent on boys' voices for the performance of the services and anthems. Undeterred, he composed 'Blessed be the God and Father', an anthem originally designed to be sung by trebles and a solo bass. A decade and a half later most of the men in the cathedral choir were still superannuated, non-resident, in poor health or 'not efficient' (Chappell, 1977, pp. 25–6).

The situation was already changing, however, and by the end of the Victorian era it had been transformed. Cathedral choirs had developed high standards of musical professionalism and were performing a repertoire enhanced by the contributions of two generations of

[1] A 1562 edition of the metrical psalms, on which see below, p. 61.

competent indigenous composers, such as S. S. Wesley, John Stainer and Charles Villiers Stanford. In parish churches, harmoniums or organs and surpliced choirs in the chancels had replaced the bands in the galleries as described by George Eliot. Hymns were still a relative novelty in early nineteenth-century worship, but by the time of Queen Victoria's death (1901) they were a staple part of services in almost all Christian denominations, and a central focus of the religion experienced by the laity.

These developments can be variously portrayed, as a trend from chaos to order, from impiety to devotion, from amateurism to professionalism or, less positively, from spontaneity to control, from rich diversity to monochrome uniformity, from popularity to élitism. In seeking to analyse them we must try to suspend the kind of prejudice that passes for historical judgement, and endeavour to trace the course of change in an objective manner. We shall turn first to examine the growth of the hymn as a central feature of Victorian religion, then consider the distinctively Victorian version of that form of choral music perceived by a later age as reflecting an immemorial continuous tradition, and finally survey the wider cultural context of church music.

I HYMNS AND VICTORIAN RELIGIOUS CONSCIOUSNESS

In a generic sense, hymns are as old as the Christian Church itself: St Paul exhorted the Ephesians to address 'one another with psalms and hymns and spiritual songs' (Ephesians 5:19); St Augustine defined them as 'the praise of God in song' (Drain, 1989, p. 24). Both words and music are intrinsic features of the hymn as we know it: vernacular verse written for congregational singing in devotion and worship. In Britain it was primarily an eighteenth-century development. In Germany the Protestant Reformation of the sixteenth century had been associated with extensive hymn-singing under the leadership of Martin Luther. In Britain, on the other hand, as in other countries influenced by the more austere Protestantism of John Calvin, there was a suspicion of any texts not directly derived from Scripture. Accordingly, for the first two centuries after the Reformation, sung worship was dominated by metrical psalms, rhyming versions of the biblical text. A familiar example that survives in modern hymnbooks is 'All people that on earth do dwell', dating from 1561 and based on Psalm 100. Although the verse of seventeenth-century poets, notably George Herbert, John Milton and John Bunyan, was much later to be adopted for hymns, it had initially been intended only for private devotion and was not set to music.

From the later seventeenth century, attitudes began slowly to change. In England Calvinist orthodoxy was relaxed, and revised texts of the metrical psalms were produced, with the objective of improving literary quality, even at the price of adhering more loosely to the biblical texts. There was also a movement towards the use of verse for singing biblical texts other than the psalms, of which a notably enduring and successful example was 'While shepherds watched their flocks by night' (1700). However, even in the early nineteenth century, as George Eliot's account indicates, the adoption of such innovations was by no means universal and uncontested. Development was even slower in Scotland, where in 1741 the General Assembly of the Church set up a committee to collect paraphrases (songs based on scriptural texts other than the psalms), but these were not generally published and circulated until 1781 (Cameron, 1993, pp. 643–4).

Meanwhile, Isaac Watts (1674–1748), an Independent (Congregational) minister, published works between 1705 and 1719 that constituted a clear move away from exclusive insistence on biblically derived texts, although the title of his *Psalms of David Imitated in the Language of the New Testament* (1719) provided a nod towards the older tradition. A similar trend was apparent in the work of his younger contemporary, Philip Doddridge (1702–51), also an Independent, whose hymns were first published posthumously in 1755. Thus, during the eighteenth century, Old Dissent, and Independents in particular, acquired an extensive repertoire of hymns (Sadie, 1980, Vol. 8, p. 848).

It was, however, the Evangelical Revival that placed hymns firmly at the centre of worship. Writers such as William Williams Pantycelyn (1717–91) and, above all, Charles Wesley (1707–88) produced hymns that could authentically articulate the experience and aspirations of relatively impoverished and poorly educated people. Thus, Williams's greatest hymn, 'Arglwydd arwain trwy'r anialwch' (1745), translated into English as 'Guide me, O Thou great Jehovah' (1771), applied biblical imagery in a manner that gave comfort and purpose to the eighteenth-century spiritual pilgrim. Charles Wesley wrote over 6,000 hymns, which gave Methodists ample scope to celebrate collectively their deliverance from sin and fear of hell, and their assurance of salvation:

No condemnation now I dread;
Jesus, and all in Him is mine!

(Wesley, 1821 edn, p. 197)

In the hands of Charles and John Wesley, hymn-singing became, for the first time, not merely a routine part of worship but a means of stirring up spiritual fervour, and even of drawing in converts attracted by lively music and intense language (Sadie, 1980, Vol. 8, p. 849). The practice was warmly encouraged by John Wesley, who in 1780 published a compilation entitled *Hymns for the Use of the People called Methodists*, which became a basic resource. The link between revivalism and hymn-singing was reinforced in the early nineteenth century. Lorenzo Dow's *A Collection of Spiritual Songs used at the Group Meetings in the Great Revival in the United States of America* (1806) was reprinted in England and formed the basis for collections made by Hugh Bourne and used by the emerging Primitive Methodist Connexion, which he led. These songs 'expressed religious ecstasy with rough vigour', and were accessible to and powerful among the largely working-class constituency of early Primitive Methodism (Kent, 1978, pp. 63–4). The strong association that thus developed between hymns, popular revivalism and religious dissent caused them to be regarded with suspicion among more conservative elements in the Established Churches.

The Evangelical hymn-writing impulse nevertheless also extended to the Church of England. It was expressed notably by Augustus Toplady, whose 'Rock of ages' was first published in 1775, and John Newton and William Cowper, whose fruitful collaboration resulted in the *Olney Hymns* of 1779. There was, however, an ambiguity as to whether hymns should be used in church services: when Toplady published a collection of his work in 1776 he entitled it *Psalms for Public and Private Worship*; Newton and Cowper originally envisaged that their hymns would be used in weekday meetings rather than on Sundays (Drain, 1989, p. 80). Nevertheless, during the next few decades, hymns were increasingly introduced into Sunday worship by Evangelicals, particularly in Yorkshire where their presence was strongest. In 1820, the legality of the practice was put to the test when a Sheffield incumbent, Thomas Cotterill, was taken to court by disgruntled parishioners who opposed the innovation. After a confusing judgement, which indicated that whilst hymns were technically illegal they had been legitimated by custom, the Archbishop of York, Vernon Harcourt, publicly sanctioned their use.

The Archbishop of York's decision in the Cotterill case effectively opened the door fully to the use of hymns in the public worship of the Church of England. Although hymn-singing was initially associated particularly with the Evangelical party in the Church, it was then rapidly adopted by all strands of Anglicanism. Poems by the leaders of the Oxford Movement, such as several in the collection in John Keble's *Christian Year* (1827) and J. H. Newman's 'Lead, kindly Light' (1833), were originally written as expressions of private devotion, but within a few decades had acquired tunes and prominent places in the hymnbooks. John Mason Neale, in reflection of the Tractarians' preoccupation with the medieval church, translated and adapted numerous Latin hymns for Anglican congregations.

In the Roman Catholic Church, too, hymns rapidly gained ground. In 1852, the convert Frederick William Faber acknowledged the appeal to the English poor, including Catholics, of Charles Wesley's, Newton's and Cowper's hymns. He sought to counteract the doctrinal influence of such Protestant hymns by his own composition of 'some simple and original hymns for singing' (Faber, 1852, p. v). These had a considerable popularity, associated with the Catholic revivalism of the mid-Victorian years.[2]

Even in Scotland the progress of the hymn was inexorable, although it was retarded somewhat by traditionalist Calvinist opposition. Thus, metrical psalms and paraphrases remained dominant for a generation longer than in England, but hymns were generally adopted during the third quarter of the nineteenth century (Cameron, 1993, p. 421). Only a minority of conservatives stood out against the trend, but these few proved irreconcilable and metrical psalmody has survived throughout the twentieth century among the smaller Presbyterian churches, notably in the Gaelic-speaking West Highlands and Western Isles.

The general triumph of the hymn during the Victorian period is well illustrated by Table 1, which shows the number of hymnals recorded in the British Library catalogue as published up to 1940.

Table 1

Date	No. of hymnals*	Date	No. of hymnals
Before 1740	8	1841–1860	363
1741–1760	37	1861–1880	411
1761–1780	51	1881–1900	208
1781–1800	58	1901–1920	129
1801–1820	119	1921–1940	99
1821–1840	188		

*Including second and subsequent editions, but not duplicate copies.

[2] See *RVB*, I, 6, pp. 223–6.

The first upward surge in hymn publication occurred with the Evangelical Revival in the mid-eighteenth century, and this was reinforced by the revivalism of the 1790s and early 1800s. This trend was confirmed by the official sanction given to hymns in the Church of England in 1820, but this decision appears to have been not so much an opening of the floodgates as an acceptance of the inevitable. The first half of Queen Victoria's reign saw the publication of a profusion of hymnals that reflected the enterprise of particular individuals or the needs of specific churches and localities. Subsequently, there was a trend towards compilations that could command wider acceptance, a process initiated with the publication of the first edition of *Hymns Ancient and Modern* in 1860. This gradually came to dominate the Anglican market. Methodism was distinctive in already having John Wesley's widely accepted compilation of 1780, but other Nonconformist denominations followed the trend in the later Victorian era, notably with the *Baptist Hymnary* (1879) and the *Congregational Church Hymnal* (1887) (Temperley, 1981, pp. 158–62). A Welsh language hymnbook, *Llyfr Tonau ac Emynau* (The Book of Hymns and Tunes) appeared in 1869 and a second volume was added in 1879 (Luff, 1990, p. 191). The major Scottish Presbyterian churches each acquired their own hymnbooks between the 1850s and the 1870s. In the Free Church the trend was vigorously resisted, notably by the conservative Calvinist James Begg, but even there hymnbooks were published in 1872 and 1881 (Murray, 1984, pp. 89–90). By 1885, the 'battle of psalms versus hymns' was judged to be 'pretty well over' (Curwen, 1885, p. 81). In the 1890s, the Scottish churches joined together with the Presbyterian Church in Ireland to authorize *The Church Hymnary*, first published in 1898. Older Scottish Reformed traditions were reflected in the publication of the *Metrical Psalter* in the following year (Cheyne, 1983, p. 101). The success of such official and semi-official compilations weakened the market for more freelance collections, publications of which accordingly tailed off towards the end of the century. However, although by the late Victorian period hymnody had become an institutionalized part of the worship of all the major Christian churches, scope for innovation and popular appeal remained, most notably in the songs brought across the Atlantic by the revivalist Ira Sankey in the 1870s, and the rousing choruses associated with the Salvation Army. In the 1890s, it was estimated that a total of two million hymnbooks was sold every year (Stead, 1895, p. 6).

There can be little dispute about the popularity and success of hymns as an almost universal expression of Christian worship during the Victorian era. They thus provide a valuable source for understanding the

* by definition psalms cannot be of Christmas

religious consciousness and outlook of the period. At the outset, however, an important distinction needs to be made between the hymn as originally written, to be understood in the context of the life and career of its author, and the hymn as taken up by the wider church and community, set to music, perhaps adapted in response to theological sensitivities or to permit easier singing, and then included in compilations. The study of both aspects of hymns raises important questions and provides revealing evidence of their role in this period, but the two aspects should not be confused by attributing to an author, perhaps long dead, the state of mind experienced by a congregation singing his or her hymn.

The distinction can be illustrated by reference to one of the most famous of all 'Victorian' hymns, Henry Francis Lyte's (1793–1847) 'Abide with me', probably written shortly before its author's death in 1847 (Maxwell-Lyte, 1947). However, it has been suggested that, technically, the hymn was not Victorian at all, having possibly been written much earlier in Lyte's life, in response to the death of a friend in 1820 (Bradley, 1989, p. 9). If we are interested in the hymn as a reflection of Lyte's own outlook and of the moderate Anglican Evangelicalism of which he was a prominent representative, the question of when the hymn was written is of considerable importance. Lines such as:

Swift to its close ebbs out life's little day;
Earth's joys grow dim, its glories pass away;

read differently if they are taken to have been written by a healthy man in his mid-twenties just embarking on his clerical career, from the impression they convey if they are thought to have been written by a man in his mid-fifties who knew himself to be terminally ill. Are they evidence of a young man's poignant perception of the fragility and transience of human life, or of a dying man's courageous resignation and powerful Christian faith? However, if we are interested not in Lyte's own development, but in the states of mind of congregations who have sung 'Abide with me', the circumstances of its composition pale into irrelevance. We need to consider rather the reasons why three of the original eight verses were dropped when the hymn was included in *Hymns Ancient and Modern* in 1860; to assess the impact of William Henry Monk's tune 'Eventide', also written in 1860; and to reflect on the various contexts in which the hymn has been used: in evening services, at funerals, in private devotion and, in the twentieth century, at the FA Cup Final. Ultimately, the success of the hymn is rooted in language that has a universality which can simultaneously encapsulate the insecurities of the young and the regretful longings of the old and the bereaved (Drain, 1989, pp. 314–15 and 328–9; Garland, n.d.).

Three brief case studies will serve to illustrate the personal background to some popular Victorian hymns, and also indicate unexpected affinities between hymnwriters, which were to be heightened by the processes of compilation and mediation to the public. A first example is provided by Horatius Bonar (1808–89), the most prominent Scottish hymnwriter of the period, who was ordained as parish minister of Kelso, Roxburghshire, in the year of Queen Victoria's accession (1837). After the Disruption in 1843 he became a leading member of the Free Church, moving to be minister of the Chalmers Memorial Church in Edinburgh in 1866, where, ironically, there was considerable resistance in his own congregation to the introduction of hymns. He served as Moderator of the General Assembly in 1883. In addition to hymns, he published numerous devotional works, some of which were bestsellers (Cameron, 1993, pp. 84–5; Gibb, 1989; Gordon, 1991, pp. 111–47).

Bonar was thus a writer broadly representative of the Scottish Presbyterianism of his day. Some of its starker theological emphases are apparent in his hymns. He had a strong sense of sin and guilt and a clearly evangelical view of the atonement:

> I lay my sins on Jesus
> The spotless lamb of God;
> He bears them all, and frees us
> From the accursed load.
> I bring my guilt to Jesus,
> To wash my crimson stains
> White in His blood most precious
> Till not a spot remains.
>
> (*The Church Hymnary*, 1898, No. 194)

Bonar was also a convinced premillennialist, expecting the imminent second advent of Christ, and taking a gloomy view of the state of the world and the Church in the meantime:

> The serpent's brood increase;
> The powers of hell grow bold;
> The conflict thickens; faith is low,
> And love is waxing cold.
> How long, O Lord our God,
> Holy and true and good?
> Wilt Thou not judge Thy suffering Church
> Her sighs and tears and blood?
> Come, then, Lord Jesus come!
>
> (*Ibid.*, No. 112)

He also reflected and stimulated the devotional and liturgical changes in his church during the Victorian era, notably in his widely used Communion hymn, written in 1855, which was symptomatic of increasing emphasis within Scottish Presbyterianism on the importance of the sacrament:[3]

> Here would I feed upon the bread of God,
> Here drink with Thee the royal wine of heaven;
> Here would I lay aside each earthly load,
> Here taste afresh the calm of sin forgiven.
>
> (*Ibid.*, No. 415)

Despite its Presbyterian origins, this hymn eventually found its way into the characteristically Anglican *Hymns Ancient and Modern*, albeit shorn of the line in which Bonar made clear his firmly Protestant doctrine of the sacrament: 'Too soon we rise; the symbols disappear' (Frost, 1962, p. 357).

In an intriguing counterpoint to the evident activity and success of his life, many of Bonar's hymns are suffused with a tone of weariness, of longing for rest and, eventually, for death and for heaven. Their style is well illustrated by the opening lines of his most popular and enduring work, first published in 1846:

> I heard the voice of Jesus say
> 'Come unto Me and rest;
> Lay down, thou weary one, lay down
> Thy head upon My breast'.
>
> (*The Church Hymnary*, 1898, No. 172)

A second example of a Victorian hymnwriter, Frederick William Faber (1814–63), was an equally central figure but in a very different Christian tradition. He was brought up an Anglican and ordained in 1837, but converted to the Roman Catholic Church in 1846, becoming a leading force in the development of the London Oratory. He played a crucial role in popularizing Ultramontane devotion in England.[4] Faber's distinctively Catholic convictions were extensively expressed in his hymns, for instance in the following addressed to 'Mary, the Flower of God':

> O Flower of Grace! divinest Flower!
> God's light thy life, God's love thy dower!
> That all alone with virgin ray
> Dost make in heaven eternal May,

---

[3] See *RVB*, I, 3, p. 135.

[4] See *RVB*, I, 4, pp. 159–60.

Sweet falls the peerless dignity
Of God's eternal choice on thee!
Mother dearest! Mother fairest!
Maiden purest! Maiden rarest!
Help of earth and joy of heaven!
Love and praise to thee be given,
Blissful Mother! Blissful Maiden!

(Faber, 1852, pp. 67–8)

He also expressed his fervent identification with his adopted faith in terms defiant of the suspicions of his Protestant contemporaries:

Faith of our Fathers! Living still
In spite of dungeon, fire and sword:
Oh how our hearts beat high with joy
Whene'er we hear that glorious word:
Faith of our Fathers! Holy Faith!
We will be true to thee till death!

...

Faith of our Fathers! Mary's prayers
Shall win our country back to thee;
And through the truth that comes from God
England shall then indeed be free.
Faith of our Fathers! Holy Faith!
We will be true to thee till death!

(*Ibid.*, pp. 135–6)

Nevertheless, although located at the opposite ecclesiastical pole from Bonar, Faber showed some affinities with the Scottish writer. Bonar's sense of the majesty and power of God, implicit in his hymns on the second coming, but explicit elsewhere in his writing (see, for example, hymns Nos. 10 and 126 in *The Church Hymnary*, 1898) was replicated in Faber's lines:

My God! How wonderful Thou art,
Thy majesty how bright,
How beautiful Thy mercy seat
In depths of burning light!

(*Ibid.*, p. 3)

Also strongly apparent in Faber's writing was the sense of the Christian life as a wearisome journey, although both his tradition and his personality imbued his language with a heightened sentimentalism:

> Far, far away, like bells at evening pealing,
> The voice of Jesus sounds o'er land and sea,
> And laden souls, by thousands meekly stealing,
> Kind Shepherd, turn their weary steps to thee.
> Angels of Jesus, angels of light,
> Singing to welcome the pilgrims of the night!
>
> (Frost, 1962, p. 328)

Such weariness with the present world and longing for the life to come has been identified as a widespread characteristic of Victorian hymns (Tamke, 1978, pp. 42–4).

In further resemblance to Bonar, Faber found his work rapidly co-opted into the Anglican canon represented by *Hymns Ancient and Modern*, although, also like Bonar's work, it did not escape mutilation. His Good Friday hymn 'O come and mourn with me awhile' was radically shortened, allusions to Mary removed, and its perceived excessive emotionalism toned down, notably by changing 'Love' to 'Lord' in the repeated refrain, 'Jesus, our Love, is crucified' (Drain, 1989, pp. 331–6).

A final case study, representative both of the Church of England and of the important contribution to Victorian hymnody made by women, is provided by Frances Ridley Havergal (1836–79). She was a daughter of William Henry Havergal, who himself made an important contribution to Victorian church music through his work on psalm chants, and she inherited her father's musical gifts. Although a highly educated and able woman, who never married, she did not have any career apart from her literary work and personal evangelistic activity, a significant contrast with the two male examples surveyed above. Her spirituality was characteristically evangelical, with a long period of inward striving culminating in teenage conversion, and this was reinforced much later, in 1873, by an experience which she referred to as her 'consecration' (Havergal, 1881, pp. 26–40 and 124–33; Gordon, 1991, pp. 188–200). This development identified her with the Holiness or Keswick movement within Evangelicalism,[5] which enthusiastically adopted her hymns. Havergal's work was particularly strongly rooted in her own religious experience: she wrote in 1870 that 'I need to have *felt* a theme and *lived into it* before I can write about it' (F. R. Havergal Papers 7520/2, Worcestershire County Record Office).

As in Bonar's hymns, in those of Havergal there was frequent reference to the cross and atonement:

[5] See *RVB*, II, 1, pp. 30–2.

> Jesus, Master, whose I am
> Purchased, Thine alone to be,
> By Thy blood, O spotless Lamb,
> Shed so willingly for me;
> Let my heart be all Thine own;
> Let me live to Thee alone.
>
> (*The Church Hymnary*, 1898, No. 247)

However, the tone was appreciably softer than Bonar's, expressing too her sense of intense personal commitment to Jesus. Here, as in Faber's devotion to Mary, it seems that the sublimated sexuality of the celibate was reinforcing the attitude of worship. In contrast, however, to both Bonar and Faber, there was little weariness apparent in Havergal's long march with Christ:

> True-hearted, whole-hearted, faithful and loyal,
> King of our lives, by Thy grace we will be!
> Under Thy standard exalted and royal,
> Strong in Thy strength, we will battle for Thee.
>
> (*Ibid.*, No. 257)

Do such words, we might wonder, hide the frustration of a woman for whom the 'battle' must often have seemed to have been at second hand, set against the exhaustion of men for whom it was very much an everyday reality? Havergal shared Bonar's expectation of the second coming of Christ and of heaven, but her perception of the state of the world and the Church in the meantime was a less gloomy one:

> Thou art coming; we are waiting
> With a hope that cannot fail,
> Asking not the day or hour,
> Resting on Thy word of power,
> Anchored safe within the veil.
> Time appointed may be long,
> But the vision must be sure;
> Certainty shall make us strong
> Joyful patience can endure.
>
> (*Ibid.*, No. 113)

Paradoxically, when Havergal was at her most intense and personal her underlying devotional aspirations sounded strikingly similar to those of Bonar and Faber. Her most famous hymn, written in 1874, expressing her sense of consecration, can interestingly be compared with their writing:

Havergal:

Take my life, and let it be
Consecrated, Lord, to Thee;
Take my moments and my days,
Let them flow in ceaseless praise.

(Frost, 1962, p. 331)

Bonar:

Fill Thou my life, O Lord my God,
In every part with praise
That my whole being may proclaim
Thy being and Thy ways.

(*Ibid.*, p. 337)

Faber:

For Thou to me art all in all
My honour and my wealth,
My heart's desire, my body's strength,
My soul's eternal health.

(Faber, 1852, p. 6)

Common to all three writers was a powerful sense of the reality and presence of God, which drew them into expressions of total commitment of life and worship. Herein perhaps was the most profound reason for the appeal of their hymns to Victorian Christians in a manner that transcended ecclesiastical and theological difference.

Indeed, a tendency to revise theologically suspect sentiments notwithstanding, hymnbooks could provide a notable island of calm amidst the storms between and within different Christian traditions. Even in the 1860s, the compilers of *Hymns Ancient and Modern* included two items by Bonar and seven by Faber, among a relatively limited selection of contemporary hymns (Drain, 1989, pp. 134 and 253–4; Frost, 1962). In the Preface to his 1856 collection of *Hymns of Faith and Hope*, Bonar stated that: 'They belong to no church or sect. They are not the expressions of one man's or one party's faith and hope: but are meant to speak what may be thought and spoken by all to whom the Church's ancient faith and hope are dear.'

When Havergal's hymns became widely popular among Evangelicals in the early 1870s, some were selected for inclusion in the 1875 revision of *Hymns Ancient and Modern*, a decision that evidently gave her great satisfaction because she was uneasy with appearing too exclusively identified with one party in the Church of England (Drain, 1989, pp. 134–5). A similarly broadminded spirit was evident in the attitudes of the compilers of the Presbyterian *Church Hymnary* of 1898. Although, as might be anticipated, Bonar was particularly well represented, with seventeen hymns, there were also eight by Faber and twelve by Havergal. In one of the selected hymns, Faber himself had written:

> But we make His love too narrow
> By false limits of our own;
> And we magnify His strictness
> With a zeal He will not own.

> (*The Church Hymnary*, 1898, No. 165)

Given that so much of the history of religion in Victorian Britain often appears to hinge on contention and division, it is salutary to remind ourselves that sentiments of this kind too were being widely disseminated and expressed in worship.

When the three hymnwriters given as examples are set in a wider context, some other characteristics of Victorian hymns are worth highlighting. The motif of weariness and longing for paradise was particularly fully developed in the revivalist songs popularized by Sankey in the 1870s. These propagated the idea of the hereafter, not only as a place of ultimate spiritual fulfilment, but also as one of relatively down-to-earth reunion with loved ones (Kent, 1978, pp. 224–5). The following example illustrates their tone:

> There's a land that is fairer than day,
> And by faith we can see it afar,
> For the Father waits over the way,
> To prepare us a dwelling-place there.
> In the sweet by and by
> We shall meet on that beautiful shore;
> In the sweet by and by
> We shall meet on that beautiful shore.

> (Sankey, n.d., No. 9)

This theme, however, was balanced, as in Havergal's hymns, with a more positive sense of the Christian life in this world as a crusade to be waged energetically. To some extent this attitude reflected the tendency of evangelicals in particular to highlight the strand in Christian tradition that dwelt on a sense of siege from a hostile world. This outlook was famously expressed in the hymn by Philip Bliss, extensively used by Sankey, 'Hold the fort!' (Kent, 1978, p. 218).[6] The genre was further extended, especially at a popular level, by American imports such as Julia Ward Howe's 'Mine eyes have seen the glory of the coming of the Lord' (Stead, 1895, p. 23), and by the songs of the Salvation Army.

The theme of Christian warfare and the use of military motifs are good examples of the tendency of many Victorian hymns to draw upon both religious and secular influences and in so doing probably to generate confusion in the consciousness of those who sang them. When, in 1866, Samuel John Stone wrote of the Church:

> 'Mid toil and tribulation
> And tumult of her war

he had very specifically in mind the contemporary ecclesiastical conflict in South Africa between Bishop Colenso of Natal and Bishop Gray of Capetown, the latter of whom Stone strongly supported (Frost, 1962, p. 283; Rogal, 1978, p. 25).[7] Similarly, Sabine Baring-Gould's 'Onward Christian soldiers', written in 1864, the year in which the case of *Essays and Reviews* was considered by the Privy Council, was in the first instance a vigorous defence of traditional orthodoxy in the face of theological questioning and popular unbelief. This outlook is most apparent in a verse in Baring-Gould's original text:

> What the saints established
> That I hold for true
> What the saints believed
> That believe I too
> Long as earth endureth
> Men that faith will hold, —
> Kingdoms, nations, empires,
> In destruction rolled.

> (Rogal, 1978, p. 30)

Simultaneously, however, the Christian warfare theme also reflected a secular trend of fascination with matters military, stimulated initially in the 1850s and the 1860s by the Crimean War, the 'Indian Mutiny' and the American Civil War, and symbiotically sustained by the imperial enthusiasm of the last quarter of the century (Anderson, 1971, pp. 69–71). Other notable examples of hymns employing a military theme are William

---

[6] See *RVB*, III, 5.3.4, p. 277.

[7] On Colenso, see Chapter 4.

Walsham How's 'Soldiers of the Cross, arise' (1854) and his 'For all the saints who from their labours rest' (1864) (Adey, 1988, p. 205; Frost, 1962, pp. 307 and 409–10). Even though Baring-Gould and Walsham How wrote of spiritual battles, it is likely that some of those who sang their hymns chose to see them as a legitimation of earthly warfare. Indeed, this tendency is apparent in the hymnbooks themselves. Charles Wesley's 'Soldiers of Christ arise' was adapted and abridged with the effect of emphasizing the more material aspects of the Christian's struggle (Adey, 1988, pp. 203–5 and 220–1) and Baring-Gould's ringing affirmation of orthodoxy, quoted above, dropped out of the version of 'Onward Christian soldiers' that was normally sung (Rogal, 1978, p. 30).

A parallel tendency was apparent in missionary hymns. Writers who dwelt on the Christian imperative to proclaim the gospel in other lands might have had an exclusively spiritual purpose in mind, but their language almost inevitably could also be taken as an affirmation of British superiority and national glory. Such must have been the effect, if not the intent, when in 1897 Queen Victoria chose John Ellerton's missionary hymn of 1870 for her Diamond Jubilee service:

> We thank Thee that Thy Church unsleeping
> While earth rolls onward into light,
> Through all the world her watch is keeping,
> And rests not now by day or night.
>
> (Tamke, 1978, pp. 131–2)

Even if, as the last stanza of the hymn acknowledges, 'earth's proud empires' do 'pass away', the link between the universal church and the 'empire on which the sun never set' was inescapable. Such a linkage was also implicit in Arthur Campbell Ainger's 'God is working his purpose out' (1894):

> March we forth in the strength of God with the
>   banner of Christ unfurled,
> That the light of the glorious Gospel of truth may shine
>   throughout the world.
> Fight we the fight with sorrow and sin, to set
>   their captives free,
> That the earth may be filled with the glory of God as the
>   waters cover the sea.
>
> (Frost, 1962, p. 290)

It was left to Rudyard Kipling, who stood somewhat outside the mainstream of Christianity, to write a hymn, also in the Diamond Jubilee year, that drew on the language of the Old Testament to provide a prophetic reminder of the dangers of spiritual pride and the fragility of national glory:

> Far-called our navies melt away
> On dune and headland sinks the fire;
> Lo, all our pomp of yesterday
> Is one with Nineveh and Tyre!
> Judge of the nations, spare us yet,
> Lest we forget, lest we forget.
>
> (Kipling, 1920, Vol. 2, p. 118; Tamke, 1978, pp. 136–7)[8]

By contrast, some other aspects of Victorian life made curiously little impact on the awareness of hymnwriters. In particular, there was an almost total failure to engage with the day-to-day realities of life, at least that of the lower classes, in an increasingly industrialized and urbanized society. Cecil Frances Alexander's 'All things bright and beautiful' (1848) has been much criticized for its seemingly complacent endorsement of social inequality, and for children in the urban slums the following stanza must have seemed particularly remote from their experience:

> The tall trees in the greenwood,
> The meadows where we play,
> The rushes by the water
> We gather every day.
>
> (Frost, 1962, p. 369)

Faber, for his part, visualized the angels singing, not seemingly in the streets of the city, but 'o'er earth's green fields and ocean's wave-beat shore' (Frost, 1962, p. 328). A hymn by Bonar did acknowledge the challenge and the excitement offered by the city, but coupled it with nostalgia for a rural idyll (Bonar, 1866, pp. 185–7). Images of work, if manual at all, were drawn from agriculture (*The Church Hymnary*, 1898, No. 261), and Walsham How's 'faithful warriors' apparently had opportunity to contemplate the view as 'The golden evening brightens in the west' (Frost, 1962, p. 409). Harvest hymns expressed a similar state of mind, and were increasingly numerous and popular in later Victorian Britain. Such pastoral allusions might be defended as building on the evident rural nostalgia and pastoral romanticism of urban congregations, but they must have reinforced an image of Christianity as escapist and

---

[8] For further discussion of the changing context of missionary hymns, see Chapter 3. Links between hymns, patriotism and imperialism are discussed in more detail in Wolffe, 1989, pp. 192–4 and Wolffe, 1994, pp. 213–15. See also Adey, 1988, pp. 196–221.

removed from everyday life.[9] The only city to receive significant attention in Victorian hymns was the heavenly Jerusalem, but even here there was a blindness to William Blake's searching question, posed in the first decade of the nineteenth century:

> And was Jerusalem builded here
> Among these dark satanic mills?

(Drain, 1989, pp. 439–52)

Blake's 'Jerusalem' did not enter the hymnbooks until the twentieth century, and did so then with a tune provided by the agnostic Hubert Parry, which located it much more in a culture of patriotic celebration than one of religious devotion and aspiration.

The rural escapism apparent in Victorian hymns was one aspect of a wider social and cultural conservatism. The social unrest of the early nineteenth century produced a number of hymns that offered a more or less explicit Christian critique of contemporary social structures. Notable examples are James Montgomery's 'Hail to the Lord's anointed' (1821) and Ebenezer Elliot's 'When wilt Thou save the people?' (1832). Such critical voices were to recur in the early twentieth century, for instance in Henry Scott Holland's 'Judge eternal, throned in splendour' (1902) and G. K. Chesterton's 'O God of earth and altar' (1906). In the intervening Victorian era, however, hymns that alluded to temporal suffering and inequality tended either to seek to deflect resentment by focusing on prospects for transformed life beyond death, or to address symptoms rather than causes through exhortation to almsgiving and social service (Tamke, 1978, pp. 91–120).

The analysis in this section of the chapter has concentrated up to this point on the texts of hymns and their authors, but we turn now to the wider set of issues identified above (pp. 65–6) relating to the reception and use of hymns in church and outside it. It must be emphasized that, at least in the earlier part of the Victorian period, worship would have been dominated by older metrical psalms and hymns, rather than by contemporary works. The natural time-lag between composition, wide diffusion and general familiarity that occurs in relation to almost any literary innovation was especially apparent in the case of hymns, because of the tendency to conservatism and clinging to the familiar evident in the worship of most congregations (Eliot, 1973 edn, p. 47). Thus, in a sample

---

[9] A further illustration of a preoccupation with nature in Victorian hymns is provided by Thomas Lynch's controversial collection *The Rivulet* (1855), on which see *RVB*, I, 2, pp. 103–4.

of 140 hymnals published between the mid eighteenth and early twentieth centuries, all but twenty of the hymns most frequently included had been written before 1800, and all but four of them before 1830 (Adey, 1988, pp. 72–3 and 255). In the original 1860 edition of *Hymns Ancient and Modern*, only 96 (36 per cent) of the hymns were nineteenth century (Drain, 1989, p. 254). In the 1870s, the work of the Wesleys still dominated Methodist hymn-singing (Ashby, 1961, pp. 80–2). In the Church of England at least the tendency to draw on the past rather than the present was accentuated by the substantial numbers of translated Latin hymns, and to a lesser extent German ones, included in *Hymns Ancient and Modern*. The use of medieval hymns, which was promoted particularly by Neale, reflected the wider Tractarian and Romantic agenda of seeking a return to a pristine pre-Reformation Christianity, and was a counterpart to the activities of A. W. Pugin and the ecclesiologists in the field of architecture.

Nevertheless, especially in the last third of the nineteenth century, more contemporary hymns rapidly gained ground. Some, such as those of Havergal, appear to have acquired almost instant popularity, whilst others were given an assured place by inclusion in compilations. The 1875 edition of *Hymns Ancient and Modern* showed a very marked increase in the number of nineteenth-century hymns, to 53 per cent (Drain, 1989, p. 254).

In 1898, of 625 hymns in *The Church Hymnary*, 312 were still in copyright, which meant that they were by living or recently deceased authors. Now, a century later, we need to make a leap of the imagination to realize that hymns and tunes that to us seem part of the fabric of church life would for Victorian congregations have seemed relative innovations. For example, what might be considered as the 'traditional' overture to the English Christmas, 'Once in royal David's city', was written by Cecil Frances Alexander only in 1848.

The experience of hymn-singing is, of course, a product of the tune as well as the words, and the musical contribution of the Victorians in the sphere of hymns was even more decisive and extensive than their literary one. Of the tunes in *The Church Hymnary*, 470, or more than three-quarters, were in copyright on first publication. Many of them were the work of a relatively small number of recent English composers, notably Joseph Barnby (1838–96), John Bacchus Dykes (1823–76), Henry Gauntlett (1805–76), William Henry Monk (1823–89), Henry Smart (1813–79), John Stainer (1840–1901), Arthur Sullivan (1842–1900) and Samuel Sebastian Wesley (1810–76). The life spans of these men point to a period of compositional activity extending from the 1840s to the 1870s, although continuing with diminished intensity until the end of the century. Up to these mid-century decades, hymns and metrical psalms had not necessarily been generally associated with any particular tunes: when they were sung, words and music would be selected from different books. This could lead to a degree of disjuncture, as was evident at Doncaster Parish Church in the later eighteenth century when the organist was merely told which tune to play without prior knowledge of the words being used. Naturally, it was impossible for him to vary the musical texture or dynamics to reflect the text (Temperley, 1979, p. 215). No doubt this was an extreme case, but a lack of clear linkages between tune and words would obviously have made it more difficult for hymns to lodge in the memories of those who sang them. Moreover, when Victorian composers wrote tunes designed for specific words, they had an opportunity to intensify the mood of the texts. This is the case, for example, in Monk's 'Eventide' written for 'Abide with me', Dykes's 'Vox dilecti' for 'I heard the voice of Jesus say' or Sullivan's 'St Gertrude' for 'Onward Christian soldiers'. It was in such partnerships of words and music that the characteristic styles of Victorian hymnody were created.

Before we discuss Victorian hymn tunes further, some brief reference to earlier musical styles is required. Metrical psalm tunes and paraphrases had a steady, regular rhythm and a tune that covered only a small compass of notes, as is illustrated by familiar examples such as 'Old hundredth' ('All people that on earth do dwell') and 'Winchester old' ('While shepherds watched'). In striking contrast to this kind of tune, early Methodists sang hymns to much more florid music, which reflected aspects of some popular secular music of the time. There could be several notes to a single syllable, a much wider compass and a tendency to repeat words and phrases to fill out the tune. A good example, which survived the efforts of later reformers, is 'Helmsley' ('Lo, He comes with clouds descending'). However, Methodist tunes were themselves simpler than the contemporary musical styles of church bands, who used so-called 'fuging' tunes. These usually consisted of two sections, in the second of which there was extensive repetition of the text and the vocal parts sang different portions of this at the same time. It was this kind of music that John Wesley had in mind when he attacked 'complex tunes which it is impossible to sing with devotion' and which have 'no more of religion ... than a Lancashire hornpipe' (Temperley, 1979, p. 209; Routley, 1957, p. 96). Such music was also inappropriate for an ordinary, unrehearsed congregation. It was the genius of the Methodists to find a musical idiom that was sufficiently popular and lively to engender hearty singing, while still being consistent with a genuine and intense religious devotion.

Although the style was despised by the Victorian musical establishment, it undoubtedly had a continuing popular appeal, and an echo of it can be found in much later Nonconformist hymn tunes, such as those of Josiah Booth (1852–1930).

In music, as in texts, the Tractarians sought to restore the medieval era, but, while purists used plainsong settings, and their agenda was reflected in *Hymns Ancient and Modern*, this style of music never gained more than a limited acceptance with congregations (Temperley, 1979, p. 273). More popular, probably, was the use of German chorale tunes such as 'Nun Danket' ('Now thank we all our God') and the writing of new tunes in a style evidently inspired by the austerity and simplicity of the metrical psalms, such as S. S. Wesley's 'Aurelia' ('The Church's one foundation'). By the 1860s, however, Victorian Anglican hymnody was developing its own distinctive style, epitomized by the work of Dykes, Monk and Barnby. It reflected the influence of Mendelssohn, whereas the earlier Methodist style owed much to Handel, and was characterized by flowing melodies and lush harmonies. Well-known examples of the latter style, in addition to those noted previously, include Barnby's 'Cloisters' ('Lord of our life and God of our salvation'), Dykes's 'St Drostane' ('Ride on, ride on in majesty') and Monk's 'All things bright and beautiful'. Such music is calculated to stir a response in the worshipper that is more one of contemplative devotion than of the fervent joy and praise associated with Methodist hymnody.

Despite their Anglican origins and character, words and tunes of this kind became widely diffused in British religious life by the end of the Victorian age. As the contents of *The Church Hymnary* indicate, they were readily accepted in Scotland, where the absence of a strong indigenous hymn-writing tradition, once the metrical psalms had been discarded, meant there could be little resistance to an English takeover. Sir John Stainer, formerly organist of St Paul's Cathedral, was even recruited as musical editor. Tunes of Scottish origin, such as 'Martyrdom' ('O God of Bethel') and 'Crimond' ('The Lord's my shepherd'), were rare survivors in Victorian and post-Victorian hymnbooks, although they continued to be used for the singing of metrical psalms.

English and Welsh Nonconformity, with their distinctive traditions of hymn-singing, drawn both from Watts and Doddridge and from the Evangelical Revival, were more resistant to Anglican influence. This was to be expected because the general triumph of the hymn in Victorian Britain was itself a reflection of the wider transformations in religious life stemming from Evangelicalism and Nonconformity. It was true that a limited affinity with Anglican styles was apparent in English Nonconformity, particularly among the more conventionally cultured and socially aspiring groups, notably the Congregationalists and the Unitarians (Routley, 1957, p. 131; Adey, 1988, pp. 38–9). Nevertheless, the dominant style of music, as of texts, was significantly different among the minority of staunchly Evangelical Anglicans who stood out against the use of *Hymns Ancient and Modern* (Routley, 1957, pp. 130–1). That difference is apparent even in the work of Henry Gauntlett, who stood in something of a middle position between Anglican and Nonconformist styles, having spent the crucial decade of 1852–61 as organist at the Congregational Union Chapel, Islington. His tunes, such as 'Irby' ('Once in royal David's city') and 'University College' ('Oft in danger, oft in woe'), have a noticeably more hearty, congregational tone when compared with those of Dykes and Barnby. More centrally characteristic of Victorian Nonconformity and Anglican Evangelicalism, however, were robust, rousing tunes such as the American import, 'Morning light' ('Stand up, stand up for Jesus') and Josiah Booth's 'True-hearted', written for Havergal's eponymous hymn. Welsh Nonconformity, particularly well insulated from Anglican influences, maintained its own distinctive idioms, with music characterized by dramatic intensity and almost hypnotic melodies, as illustrated by 'St Denio' ('Immortal, invisible, God only wise') and 'Cwm Rhondda' ('Guide me, O Thou great Jehovah'). The latter tune, having been written in 1903, is testimony to the survival of this Welsh tradition right through the Victorian era. An important stimulus and source of enhanced musical respectability was provided by the work of Joseph Parry (1841–1903), first professor of music in the University of Wales. He was himself the composer of over 400 hymn tunes, notably 'Aberystwyth' ('Jesu, lover of my soul'/'Saviour when in dust to Thee') (Routley, 1957, pp. 160–4; Temperley, 1981, pp. 164–5).[10]

The tunes associated with revival hymns share the characteristics of Nonconformist hymnody, but in an accentuated form. They had a fervency and simplicity designed to appeal to the uneducated, in a style that has been described as 'the folk-song of the music-hall' (Routley, 1957, p. 132). Musically, they had a crude rhythm and straightforward melody, intended for singing by a wholly untrained congregation. Examples include Philip Bliss's 'Hold the fort' and 'Daniel's band', both of which were taken up by Sankey and Moody, and in softer, more sentimental vein, 'Safe in the arms of Jesus'. Such characteristics were shared by the music of the Salvation Army, of which a contemporary critic remarked that it

[10] Welsh-language hymnody is a major subject in its own right, which, as a non-Welsh speaker, I am unable to examine in detail. Luff, 1990, is a useful introduction in English, although primarily concerned with an earlier period.

'defies our standards of criticism; but for all that it may be serving its special end' (Curwen, 1885, p. 31). Moreover, in an intriguing meeting in musical terms of the ecclesiastical extremes, a similar style was also apparent in Roman Catholic revivalist hymnody, where Faber's emotional words were set to 'weak, sugary' tunes (Temperley, 1981, p. 167) in the popular *Crown of Jesus* hymnal of 1864, compiled by Henry F. Hemy. In nineteenth-century Catholic worship, hymns were not used at the Mass, but they did form an important feature of evangelistic services and of Benediction, a rite that gained great popularity during the period (Routley, 1957, p. 151; Temperley, 1981, p. 167; Heimann, 1995, p. 45–58).

The assorted musical styles associated with hymns give indications of their differing functions in the worship of the various Christian traditions. In High and Broad Church Anglicanism, hymns were essentially ancillary to the liturgy, which remained the central expression of congregational worship. Care was taken to select hymns to reflect the seasons of the Church's year, a choice assisted by the organization of *Hymns Ancient and Modern*. Accordingly, for congregations in such churches, hymn-singing expressed not so much intense personal devotion as a sense of ordered, stable and respectable spirituality, undergirded by an awareness of conformity to the secular middle-class musical and literary taste of the time. A further development of this pattern, originating in the late Victorian era but acquiring considerable popularity in the twentieth century, was the carol service at Christmas. This ritual linked together the nostalgic recovery of folk carols with the use of Christmas hymns whose sentiments were more in conformity with orthodox clerical sensibilities. The 'Nine Lessons and Carols' format was pioneered by Edward White Benson, first as Bishop of Truro in a temporary cathedral from 1878, and then at Addington Parish Church after his move to become Archbishop of Canterbury in 1883. The rite was to be adopted at King's College, Cambridge, after World War I (Routley, 1958, pp. 228–30).

Among Evangelicals and Nonconformists, on the other hand, the hymns were themselves a more pivotal focus of worship. They were likely to be chosen to reflect and reinforce the teaching of the sermon rather than to supplement the liturgy. Hymnbooks were thus arranged on the basis of theological themes rather than the liturgical round. In this respect, the Scottish *Church Hymnary*, despite the Anglican derivation of much of its contents, conformed to the Nonconformist model. The more vigorously participatory style of the music would have reinforced the sense that in singing such hymns a congregation was collectively reaffirming its central convictions in a manner analogous to the recitation of the creed in the Anglican liturgy.

Whether Anglican or Nonconformist, revivalist or Roman Catholic, there is no doubting the success of hymns as a widespread popular expression of Victorian piety. They stood at the interface of religious and secular culture and themselves became part of the folk tradition. It was claimed in 1895 that 'the songs of the English-speaking people are for the most part hymns' (Stead, 1895, p. 21). Hymns would be sung even by the normally unchurched and could lodge firmly in the consciousness even of those who repudiated their sentiments (Davies, 1876, p. 178; Burnett, 1982, p. 94). They could also become a spur to personal and family devotion, as in the home of a Northamptonshire stonemason in the mid nineteenth century where a child was powerfully impressed by his mother's singing of one of Doddridge's hymns (Burnett, 1982, p. 83). Even as the diversity and divisions of Victorian religion are reflected in hymnody, hymns are also important evidence of extensive common ground and cross-fertilization between the traditions, and of the pervasiveness of religion both among the educated and in popular culture of the period. D. H. Lawrence was later to recall that, despite his subsequent rejection of Christian dogma, the hymns he had learned as a child still meant 'almost more than the finest poetry' to him. They provided him with a dimension of wonder and mystery otherwise lacking in prosaic, educated adult life (Lawrence, 1930, pp. 155–63). It is evidence such as this that has led one scholar to conclude that 'If there has been a "common religion" in England in the last hundred years it has been based not on doctrine but on the popular hymns' (Obelkevich, 1987, p. 554).

II THE REINVENTION OF CHURCH MUSIC

George Eliot's account of a pre-Victorian church choir, with which this chapter opened, provides significant insights into the style of music prevalent in many English rural churches up to the middle of the nineteenth century. The choir was located in the gallery, probably at the west end of the church and so without the visually prominent function in worship characteristic of the later Victorian and twentieth-century Anglican choir. At 'Shepperton' (probably the childhood home of Mary Ann Evans (George Eliot), Chilvers Coton in Warwickshire) the instrumentalists would have given a lively, but rather secular, tone to the worship. There would have been no organ. It seems that, in the anthems above all, the choir was not leading the worship of the congregation but was showing off its own musical virtuosity, while others present merely listened.

Elsewhere provision differed, but was to be equally unacceptable to Victorian reformers. In the towns organs were more common than in the country, but were by no means universal. Singing would be led from the gallery by a choir formed either of one of the religious societies of young men that flourished in the early eighteenth century, or of children from a local charity school. In either case, the choir was effectively selected on the basis of criteria other than musical ability. Nevertheless, the very existence of such a choir tended to be a disincentive to the remainder of the congregation to participate in the singing (Temperley, 1979, pp. 124–40). The cathedrals and collegiate foundations, with their endowed choral foundations, might have had higher pretensions, but were plagued by absenteeism, lack of training, poor organization and limited repertoires. At St Paul's in 1813 there was a chorister of seven years' standing who 'could neither play a bar of music nor read at sight'; at the same cathedral in 1834 Evensong was held up for ten minutes while the choice of anthem was discussed (Barrett, 1974, pp. 19 and 31). At Rochester throughout the 1780s the choir recycled a mere two service settings and seven anthems (Rainbow, 1970, p. 244).

Meanwhile, in churches lacking any choir, organ or band, the parish clerk (precentor in Scotland) alone led the singing. Initially, he would have 'lined out' the metrical psalms, singing each line which was then repeated by the congregation, but this practice fell into disuse during the eighteenth century, except in Scotland. Here it still flourished after a fashion, as is evident from the following account of a service at Rothiemurchus in the early nineteenth century:

> the precentor ... then rose and calling aloud the tune ... began himself a recitative of the first line on the keynote, [and the tune] was taken up and repeated by the congregation; line by line he continued in the same fashion, thus doubling the length of the *exercise*—for really to some it was no play—serious severe screaming quite beyond the natural pitch of the voice, a wandering search after the air by many who never caught it, a flourish of difficult execution and plenty of the *tremolo* lately come into fashion.

(Quoted in Patrick, 1949, p. 141)

Elsewhere, lining out gave way to solo singing by the clerk, or to a complete lapse in attempts to provide music in services (Temperley, 1979, pp. 88–90 and 138–9).

There is, however, a danger in assessing pre-Victorian church music too much through the eyes and ears of its Victorian critics. In some respects, there had been significant improvement during the eighteenth century, and, at their best, rural church bands and charity school choirs could achieve high standards of performance. John Wesley was very favourably impressed by the singing of a church choir in Aberdeenshire in 1761 where the local laird, Sir Archibald Grant, promoted significant improvements which set a standard for the rest of Scotland (Cameron, 1993, p. 614; Patrick, 1949, pp. 149–63). That the style of Georgian church music was not to the taste of a later age should not obscure its appeal to and success for its own generation. Moreover, the English church bands became important popular village institutions and were a focus of loyalty to the church. Victorian parsons who sought to disband them were liable to drive their members off into Dissent (Gammon, 1981, pp. 79–80). Even the much-maligned cathedrals had their enthusiasts in unexpected quarters, as is apparent from the following account of Evensong at York Minster in 1769 from the leading Evangelical, William Richardson:

> The gloom of the evening, the rows of candles fixed upon the pillars in the Nave and Transept, the lighting of the Chancel, the two distant candles, glimmering like stars at a distance upon the Altar, the sound of the Organ, the voices of the Choir, raised up, with the pealing of the Organ in the chaunts, services, and anthem, had an amazing effect upon my spirits, as I walked to and fro in the Nave ... I was greatly affected.
>
> (Quoted in Temperley, 1977, p. 11)

In the early nineteenth century, there were similarly positive reactions to choral services at Norwich Cathedral and at King's College, Cambridge (Rainbow, 1970, pp. 207–8 and 244–5). Richardson's comments indicate that such a response was liable to be a broad aesthetic and religious one, owing as much to the environment as to a critical assessment of the musical standards, but even if choral worship only succeeded in relation to such criteria it could be argued that it was fulfilling its essential function.

Nevertheless, during the nineteenth century the progress of reform gradually gathered momentum. Three overlapping phases can be identified, which mirrored trends in British religious life in general and in the Church of England in particular.

In the first phase, from the 1790s to the 1830s, the initiative was taken by the Evangelicals. As we have seen (above, pp. 63–4), it was in these decades that hymns gained acceptance in the Church of England, reflecting the Evangelical preference for worship that could directly engage the emotions and commitment of the congregation. An important centre of innovation was in York, where, as perpetual curate of St Michael le Belfrey, Richardson had a new organ installed at the early date of 1784 and promoted congregational participation in the singing of psalms and hymns. Jonathan Gray, a local amateur musician and also an Evangelical, pioneered chanting of canticles and psalms in parish churches. The practice appears to have been quite extensively adopted in the York area by the 1820s and came eventually to replace metrical psalmody as the 'traditional' Anglican form of worship. Gray and Richardson aimed to involve the whole congregation in the singing, other than those 'totally without a voice or ear for music', and even the tone deaf were encouraged in 'join in heart and affection' (Temperley, 1977, p. 13). Similar developments occurred around 1800 in other Yorkshire towns where Evangelicals were strong, notably Doncaster and Bradford (Temperley, 1979, pp. 215–17), but wider diffusion was probably initially limited. In George Eliot's 'Shepperton' around 1830, innovation in church music was still associated with Evangelical 'methodistical' influence (Eliot, 1973 edn, p. 47). Evangelical leadership was also apparent in Scotland where musical development in the 1820s was centred on St George's, Edinburgh, under the ministry of Andrew Thomson (Patrick, 1949, pp. 195–6).

In the second phase, from the 1830s to the 1860s, the initiative passed to High Churchmen. Despite their theological differences with the Evangelicals, the Tractarians shared with them an anxiety to promote general participation in sung worship. Significant early examples of Tractarian clergy who encouraged congregational chanting are Walter Kerr Hamilton (later Precentor and eventually Bishop of Salisbury) at St Peter-in-the-East, Oxford, during the later 1830s, and, from 1839, Frederick Oakeley at the Margaret Chapel in London. Hamilton and Oakeley, however, differed from the Evangelicals in preferring Gregorian chants to Anglican ones, a reflection of the characteristic Tractarian endeavour to restore an idealized Christian antiquity. A central figure in diffusing such ideas and practice was Thomas Helmore, who in 1842 was appointed Vice-principal and Precentor of the recently founded teacher training College of St Mark, Chelsea. Helmore taught the students, only a minority of whom had particular musical ability, to sing unaccompanied daily choral services in the college chapel. On completing their training and becoming teachers at Anglican National Schools all over the country, the students would be well placed to promote musical reform in the parishes. Meanwhile, Thomas's younger brother Frederick developed an energetic career as an itinerant choirmaster, travelling widely on short-term engagements during which he introduced Tractarian musical ideals into churches from Kent to Perthshire. Further momentum was provided by the Society for Promoting Church Music, founded in 1845, and its journal the *Parish Choir*, which began publication in 1846 (Temperley, 1979, pp. 253–62; Rainbow, 1971, pp. 58–139).

Meanwhile, a distinct sequence of development was promoted by more conservative non-Tractarian High Churchmen, focusing particularly on Leeds Parish Church. Here a surpliced and professional choir had been introduced in 1818. After Walter Farquhar Hook became vicar in 1838 and had the church rebuilt in 1841, he made provision for a daily sung service, securing from 1842 the services as organist of the leading church musician of the day, S. S. Wesley. In the rebuilt church the choir was placed in a prominent position between the congregation and the sanctuary, which was then innovatory in a parish church, but was subsequently to become customary. Hook was much influenced by John Jebb, an Irish High Churchman who advocated the use of Anglican rather than Gregorian chant. The latter was perceived as both musically impoverishing and theologically suspect because of its associations with Roman Catholicism. In further contrast to the Tractarians, Jebb argued that services should normally be sung by the choir alone to ensure satisfactory musical standards (Rainbow, 1970, pp. 28–36). This view was shared by S. S. Wesley, who argued that members of a congregation freed of the need to concentrate on singing themselves would be able to cultivate a deeper attitude of genuinely spiritual worship (Wesley, 1961 edn, pp. 33–4). A second early model for the performance of the full choral service was provided by the opening in 1856 of St Michael's College, Tenbury, by Frederick Ouseley, a clergyman who was also a composer in his own right.

During this period, reform occurred in spite of the cathedrals rather than because of them. The Ecclesiastical Duties and Revenues Act of 1840 took financial resources away from the cathedrals to support needs elsewhere in the Church and thus left them with reduced means to spend on choirs and organs. In the late 1840s, the choir of Christ Church, Oxford, was described as 'miserably deficient', and it was around this time that the boys of St Paul's choir found themselves singing the 'Hallelujah Chorus' with only one tenor and one bass present as the organist valiantly attempted to cover up the lack of men's voices. At Durham in the 1850s, the precentor complained that he had 'no means whatever of obtaining the attendance of any single member [of the choir] at a practice, on any occasion, save by begging it as a *personal favour*' (Rainbow, 1970, pp. 203 and 287; Barrett, 1974, p. 22). It is revealing that in 1842 S. S. Wesley had regarded it as a positive career move to leave Exeter Cathedral in favour of Leeds Parish Church (Chappell, 1977, p. 43).

During the final phase, from the 1860s to the end of the century, the trend in favour of reform became general, and lost its association with particular church parties and theological standpoints. By the 1870s, it was acknowledged that 'A due regard for the artistic element in worship is no longer regarded as symptomatic of advanced opinions' (Davies, 1876, pp. 429–30). Indeed, the driving force could now be characterized in more broadly cultural and social terms. The prosperous professional middle class who formed the backbone of most Anglican congregations wanted a form of worship that was differentiated both from the earnestness of Dissent and the perceived indecorum of old-style church bands and singers (Temperley, 1979, pp. 276–7). They were, therefore, natural allies for the clergy who, even if lacking clear-cut Evangelical or High Church motives for change, were still drawn to arrangements that seemed to reflect their own enhanced sense of professionalism and dignity while giving them increased control over all the details of worship. A further natural ally was an increasingly self-conscious body of professional church musicians, whose training and background ensured conformity to conventional, mainstream musical taste. Increasing material prosperity made it possible for ordinary parish churches to employ salaried organists and choirmasters, even if in some cases musical aspirations ran ahead of the financial means to support them (Temperley, 1979, pp. 281–3; Davies, 1876, p. 269).

The forms of worship and music that came to dominate the later Victorian Church of England were those that are perceived as 'traditionally' Anglican a century later. There was a surpliced choir made up of men and boys, which processed into the service with the clergy and sat in the chancel. Instrumentalists were replaced by organs, although in poorer churches or those without competent organists there was often an intermediate phase with a barrel organ or a harmonium. The choir tended to dominate the singing. The congregation might join fully in the hymns, but would struggle with the psalm chants, and remain silent if a more competent or ambitious choir attempted anthems and choral settings of the canticles. The composer Monk once remarked that 'the better the choir singing in any church, the worse will be the congregational singing' (quoted in Curwen, 1885, p. 83). The general pattern thus owed a lot to the conservative High Church model set by Hook and S. S. Wesley at Leeds Parish Church in the 1840s. On the other hand, the secure position of hymns and the attempts at congregational chanting also reflected Evangelical priorities (Temperley, 1979, p. 277). An indication of the wide acceptance of this style of worship by the 1880s is provided by a staunchly Evangelical newspaper, *The Rock,* which in May 1882 published a 'Centigrade Ritualometer' intended to measure the extent to which a church had deviated from commitment to 'Scriptural Truth' (zero on the scale) and moved towards Roman Catholicism (100 on the scale). It is striking that most musical innovations were seen as relatively innocuous: a surpliced choir rated 2, chanted amens 4 and a processional hymn 6. These developments were collectively classified as 'aesthetic'. Even *Hymns Ancient and Modern* (16) and choral services (22) were still in the temperate or 'churchy' zone (*The Rock*, 12 May 1882). Tractarian attempts to secure the general use of Gregorian chant were, on the other hand, defeated by a combination of the disdain of musicians, the theological suspicion of the clergy and the musical incompetence of congregations. At the peak of its popularity in 1875, this style of worship was being used in 19.6 per cent of London churches, but the proportion dropped significantly within a few years (Temperley, 1979, p. 273). Gregorian chant rated a torrid 'ritualistic' 58 on the Centigrade Ritualometer.

During the last third of the century, the cathedrals at last began to make up lost ground. A landmark date in this respect was the appointment of John Stainer as organist of St Paul's Cathedral in 1872. Able musicians, notably S. S. Wesley, had held cathedral appointments before, but Stainer was distinguished by possessing both musical attainments of a high order and good organizational abilities and interpersonal skills. He established a strong partnership with the Dean, R. W. Church, and gained complete control of the hitherto disorderly choir (Rainbow, 1970, pp. 287–9). An account of a choristers' practice in 1884 indicates that conditions had been transformed from the days when it was seemingly possible for a choirboy not even to be able to read music properly and for most of the men to absent themselves from services:

> the discipline is perfect ... The boys work with a will. The scene is animated, for most of them beat time as they sing ... The voice exercises last about ten minutes. Then the boys sit and questions are asked and instruction given, on musical notation and theory ... Continual singing has made the boys such good readers that they seldom try a new piece more than three times before it is heard at the cathedral ... The men belonging to the choir, eighteen in number, attend a rehearsal with the boys once a week.

(Quoted in Barrett, 1974, pp. 24–5)

The strength of vested interests in choirs meant that improvements elsewhere were patchy and protracted: for instance, an incompetent or absentee choirman could not be dismissed and it was necessary to wait, sometimes for decades, for him to resign or die. Nevertheless, the general trend in the late Victorian period was to follow the example of St Paul's with better treatment and training of choristers, tighter discipline of the adult singers and a gradual advance in musical standards (Barrett, 1974, pp. 25–37). Arguably, however, it was only in the early twentieth century that the cathedrals decisively re-established their musical leadership over the parish churches.

The period after 1860 also saw the choral repertory become much more distinctively Victorian. Up to the middle of the century, eighteenth-century works by now unknown and little-regarded composers had tended to predominate. To some extent this situation reflected the normal delays in cultural diffusion that we have already noted in relation to hymns, but conservatism had been accentuated both by the inertia of the cathedrals and by an explicit musical antiquarianism. William Crotch (1775–1847), the dominant figure in the musical establishment at the time of Queen Victoria's accession, held that the model for all church music should be what he called the 'sublime' style, at its peak in the polyphony of the sixteenth and seventeenth centuries. Standards of composition had, in his view, declined markedly since then; novelty was to be deplored, and contemporary composers could do no better than imitate the style of the remote past (Gatens, 1986, pp. 65–6). This tendency to make a virtue out of lack of originality transmitted itself to much younger men, notably Frederick Ouseley (1825–89) (*ibid.*, p. 151), whose musical conservatism was reinforced by the theological antiquarianism of the Tractarians.

Nevertheless, even in the earlier nineteenth century there were English composers who were receptive to more recent influences, such as that of Mozart and, later, Mendelssohn. These pioneers included Thomas Attwood (1765–1838) and his pupils T. A. Walmisley (1814–56) and John Goss (1800–80). It was, though, S. S. Wesley who proved to be the only English composer of his generation capable of creating a distinctive style of his own: Romantic in ethos, and with a sensitivity to biblical texts that gave his anthems a satisfying coherence and devotional power. Unfortunately, he wrote relatively little. As a result, the dominant contribution to the later Victorian choral repertoire was made by younger, and arguably lesser, composers, of whom the most prominent were Stainer and Barnby. Their characteristic style is hard to describe without using subjective and value-laden terms such as 'sentimental', although certain technical qualities can be identified. An important but not defining feature is the use of colourful harmonies with subtle dissonances, which are employed in a predominantly homophonic texture. (Homophony implies either a close similarity in the rhythms of simultaneously sounding parts—as is the case in hymns—or a clear distinction between melody and accompaniment.) In addition, there is a tendency towards regular and balanced phrase lengths. Many of the features are also reflected in secular vocal music, such as the Victorian partsong.

Further stylistic change was apparent in the last two decades of the century, with the advent of the composers associated with the English 'musical renaissance': Hubert Parry (1848–1918), Charles Villiers Stanford (1852–1924) and Edward Elgar (1857–1934). It was Stanford, the least well known of the three in terms of general musical history, who made the most substantial contribution to the church music repertoire, producing numerous service settings in a style that showed the influence of Brahms. The widespread adoption of more recent music in parish churches was greatly assisted by the publication of contemporary works as supplements to the *Musical Times*, and by Novello's Parish Choir Book, a series that began publication in 1866 (Temperley, 1979, pp. 286–90).

Despite the ascendancy of the High Anglican choral model of church music during the later Victorian period, the alternative Evangelical model of more vigorous and active congregational participation was not wholly eclipsed. At St Pancras in the 1860s, 1870s and 1880s, there was no choir other than 'a few children in charity attire', but large congregations joined in singing of the hymns and chanting of the canticles (Temperley, 1979, pp. 274–5). Worship of this kind was relatively unusual in the Church of England, but it was more widely adopted in the Nonconformist and Scottish Presbyterian Churches. The task of training congregations was greatly assisted by the tonic sol-fa method, which made it possible for people to gain rudimentary musical skill and understanding while avoiding the hurdle of reading traditional stave notation. This system was pioneered in the 1840s by John Hullah in England and Thomas Mainzer in Scotland and widely diffused by John Curwen (1816–80), himself a Congregationalist minister. Chapels such as King's Weigh House (London), Union Chapel, Islington and Lozells (Birmingham) were acclaimed for the standards of musical attainment evident among their congregations. Moreover, singing was not limited to hymns but extended to canticles and simple anthems as well, as is apparent from the contents of the *Congregational Church Hymnal* of 1887. Thus, some aspects of the Anglican model were attractive to Nonconformists, even while exclusive surpliced choirs were rejected. A similar but somewhat slower trend towards participation by the congregation was apparent in the more plebeian Baptist denomination (Curwen, 1885, pp. 64–70; Temperley, 1981, pp. 158–62).

Nevertheless, the progress of organs and choirs was inexorable. In Scotland, where in 1807 the use of organs had been declared by the Presbytery of Glasgow to be 'contrary to the law and constitution of our Established Church', they were only introduced after considerable controversy, with singing remaining unaccompanied in the meantime. William Lindsay Alexander, a leading Congregational minister, advocated the use of organs in 1848 (Alexander, 1848, pp. 327–30). Dissenters began to introduce them from the 1850s, but they were not authorized in the Church of Scotland until 1866 and in the Free Church not until 1883. However, once legitimized they rapidly became the norm, and choirs also became widespread (Cameron, 1993, pp. 614 and 616). Even among Methodists, there were by the end of the century complaints 'of a departure from the simplicity and bare spirituality of Wesley's services, of a lack of warmth in the congregation, and a disposition to hand over the singing to a choir' (quoted in Temperley, 1981, p. 164). Meanwhile, in the 1870s, Sankey depended on massed choirs to back up his solo voice and to draw his audiences into participation: a century earlier Charles and John Wesley had needed no such assistance to get their people to sing.

The Roman Catholic Church followed a distinctive but interconnected pattern of development. In the early part of the nineteenth century, the embassy chapels in London had provided some of the finest church music in the capital, and the Portuguese chapel in particular drew Protestants as well as Catholics to hear the singing of Haydn and Mozart Masses. Samuel Wesley (1766–1837), son of Charles and father of Samuel Sebastian, was drawn to Catholicism for aesthetic reasons and composed Mass settings and motets. It is intriguing to speculate as to whether his son's distinctive style owed anything to this mediation of Catholic influence. Subsequently, the growing confidence of Catholics in the early Victorian years was associated with heightened musical aspirations both in London and in some provincial centres, notably York and Birmingham. The use of 'hired musicians' and of elaborate settings incurred the wrath of Pugin, who, zealous for musical as well as architectural purity, called for a reversion to plainsong (Young, 1995, pp. 31–67). More significant in restraining the development of Catholic music was the mid-century Irish influx, which left the Church with few resources to invest in such relative luxuries as choirs. Meanwhile, Father Faber's hymns appealed to lower-class Catholic musical and devotional tastes. From the 1860s, there were attempts to introduce male choirs on the Anglican pattern into Catholic churches. This movement was led by

Cardinal Manning, who, as an Anglican, had been one of the leaders of the choral revival in his former church (Rainbow, 1970, p. 136). These developments reached their culmination with the establishment of a professional choir at Westminster Cathedral when it was opened in 1901. Catholic church music, of course, differed from Anglican in that it was centred on the liturgy of the Mass rather than those of Matins and Evensong, and there was also a more marked and enduring prejudice against contemporary music (Temperley, 1981, pp. 210–13). Nevertheless, it is noteworthy that in the 1870s and 1880s the musical life of St George's Church in Worcester made an important contribution to nourishing the talent of the young Elgar. Several of his early works, notably 'Salve regina' (1876) and 'Ecce sacerdos magnus' (1888) were written for Catholic worship.

The reinvention of English church music during the Victorian era was in general, despite significant denominational and local variation, predominantly an Anglican affair, an Anglicanism moreover that in this respect even exported itself to Scotland. It was Anglicans who set the pace and whom Nonconformists, Presbyterians and Roman Catholics aspired to emulate. This conclusion is the more striking when we recall that in other respects the Church of England's social and political influence appeared to grow weaker during the period. Nevertheless, the case of church music reflects a wider cultural trend, which is also illustrated by the widespread adoption of Anglican architectural models during the later nineteenth century. The paradox is heightened when we reflect that the model of church music adopted was initially defined by conservative, non-Tractarian High Churchmen, a group otherwise seen as largely driven into marginality by the later Victorian period. The diffusion of this model was not, however, achieved without considerable latent tensions: between innovation and conservatism; between Protestant and Catholic theological assumptions; between congregational participation and choral exclusiveness; between church music as artistic performance and as an act of devotion; between sacred and secular influences. In these as in so many other respects the diversity and flexibility of the Victorian church was both a strength and a weakness.

III RELIGION AND VICTORIAN MUSICAL CULTURE

In the concluding section of the chapter, we want to widen the focus to examine not merely church music in the narrow sense of the term, but also the wider relationships between musical and religious life. A potentially very long agenda opens up, and it is impossible to address this fully in the space available. However, some brief general observations can be made.

It is immediately apparent that religious music did not exist in an hermetically sealed cultural bubble: the imprint of secular influences extended from the English theatre music of the eighteenth century, through the great continental Romantic composers, to the partsongs that resembled many Victorian hymn tunes. Few composers specialized exclusively in church music. Most, such as S. S. Wesley, Stainer and Stanford, wrote secular music as well, even if their religious music is now much the better known. Conversely, later Victorian composers now primarily associated with secular music, for instance Sullivan, Hubert Parry and Elgar, also made extensive contributions to the church music repertoire. Cross-fertilization was therefore inevitable, and although ecclesiastical purists might lament the intrusion of the idiom of the concert hall and the theatre into the church, the traffic was by no means all one way. There is, for example, an inescapably hymn-like resonance about some of the choruses in Gilbert and Sullivan's operettas.

There was, moreover, substantial middle ground. In large part this was provided by hymns, which, as we have seen, frequently lodged in the consciousness and culture even of those who had loosened their ties with institutional religion. General William Booth recognized that by setting some Salvation Army hymns to existing popular secular tunes he could enhance their appeal: he said that he enjoyed 'robbing the Devil of his choice tunes' (Tamke, 1978, p. 35; Davies, 1962, p. 169). Conversely, the popularity among soldiers in World War I of singing blasphemous or obscene words to familiar hymn tunes suggests that the impact of the music of Victorian Christianity was widespread, even if its theology and spirituality were not assimilated outside a committed minority (Mews, 1992, p. 469).

A further important musical point of contact between the secular and religious worlds was provided by oratorios, sacred cantatas and other works based on biblical or devotional texts. Music of this kind was liable to be regarded with suspicion by churchmen because it was seen as devaluing Christianity by turning it into entertainment, but its appeal was unquestionable. Handel's oratorios, above all *The Messiah*, enjoyed enormous popularity in Victorian England, being performed not only on a massive scale in new London venues such as the Crystal Palace and the Royal Albert Hall, but also by the numerous local choral societies which became a prominent feature of provincial cultural life. Second only to the success of Handel's works was that of Mendelssohn's *Elijah*, first performed at the Birmingham Festival in 1846. The *Musical World* judged the composer to have 'combined the passionate expression of the dramatic with the solemnity and grandeur of the Church music' (quoted in Werner, 1965, p. 18). The extensive popular appeal of this work is satirically illustrated in the *Punch* cartoon on the first page of this chapter. Mendelssohn strongly influenced a generation of now largely forgotten indigenous composers, such as William Sterndale Bennett (1816–75) and George Alexander Macfarren (1813–87), who added extensively to the repertoire of similar works (Temperley, 1981, pp. 219–23). The young Sullivan established his reputation with compositions of this kind, notably the *Festival Te Deum* (1872), celebrating the Prince of Wales's recovery from typhoid, and *The Light of the World* (1873) (Jacobs, 1984, pp. 75–6).

Consideration of two late Victorian works, Stainer's *Crucifixion* and Elgar's *Dream of Gerontius*, will serve to sum up the development of church music in the period and its relationship to the wider cultural world. *The Crucifixion*, the work of John Stainer, then organist of St Paul's Cathedral, was first performed at Marylebone Parish Church on 24 February 1887. It was subtitled 'A Meditation on the Sacred Passion of the Holy Redeemer' and was a setting of a libretto by W. J. Sparrow Simpson based on the events of Good Friday. The work was designed for use by parish church choirs, with tenor and bass solo voices, and with the choral items interspersed by hymns to be sung by the whole congregation. Consistent with this intention, the accompaniment requires only an organ of relatively modest specifications, such as would by that date have become standard in Anglican churches. The aspirations were thus primarily devotional rather than musical, and as a result the work has attracted the disdain of musical critics on account of its perceived triviality and sentimentality. In terms of its contribution to worship, however, it enjoyed great success. It was widely and easily performed, and later Victorian congregations appreciated the tuneful and straightforward music, linked to a devotion that sought to humanize the Passion narratives (Charlton, 1984, pp. 146–55). It thus reflected a number of theological trends characteristic of the period, including a move away from emphasis upon the judgement of God and from a substitutionary understanding of the doctrine of the atonement towards an emphasis upon the doctrine of the incarnation, the humanity of Jesus and the fatherhood of God.[11]

If *The Crucifixion* popularized music in the cause of religion, *The Dream of Gerontius* by Edward Elgar, first performed at the Birmingham Festival on 3 October 1900, pointed towards the popularization of religion in the cause of music. To some extent it reflected the intense

[11] For fuller discussion of this shift in theological emphasis in the context of later Victorian attitudes to the Bible and biblical criticism, see *RVB*, II, 11, pp. 254–5.

spiritual commitment of the then closing Victorian age. It was a setting of words from a poem by J. H. Newman, written in 1865 and containing two of the best-known hymn texts of the period, 'Firmly I believe and truly' and 'Praise to the Holiest in the height'. There were thus links to the hymn-singing tradition derived from the Evangelical Revival: Newman himself was an ex-Evangelical and the poem had come to the attention of Elgar as to many of his contemporaries through its association with the eccentric Evangelical and national hero, General Gordon of Khartoum (Anderson, 1993, p. 211). At the same time, *Gerontius* owed much to the Catholic tradition, to which Newman had converted, and in which Elgar himself had been born and brought up. Edwardian ecclesiastics of a more Protestant disposition might find this combination of influences unacceptable (Young, 1995, pp. 127–33), but the fact that it could occur at all shows that there were deep cross-currents in the development of Victorian religion, which transcended the interdenominational conflicts of the age. Moreover, the subject of the work, the death and afterlife of a Christian, reflected a theme that, as we have seen, was widespread in Victorian hymns of all traditions. On one level, therefore, the work can be read as a weaving together of the threads of the piety and church music of the preceding decades. The Roman Catholic Bishop of Birmingham hailed it as 'a triumph of faith' (*ibid.*, p. 121).

There were, though, other important dimensions to *Gerontius*. Elgar himself did not see it as church music, at least not in the narrow sense:

> Look here: I imagined Gerontius to be a man like us not a priest or a saint, but a *sinner,* a repentant one of course but still no end of a *worldly man* in his life, & now brought to book. Therefore I've not filled the part with Church tunes & rubbish but a good healthy full-blooded romantic, remembered worldliness, so to speak. It is, I imagine, much more difficult to tear one's self away from a well to do world than from a cloister.

(Quoted in Young, 1995, p. 118)

The work indeed found its natural home in the concert hall rather than the church. Successful performance required the resources of a full orchestra and a large professional choir. The music was of a quality such that it established Elgar's reputation as a leading composer in the mainstream of European culture, and ensured the continuing popularity of *Gerontius* for musical reasons among those who might view its theological sentiments with caution or scepticism.

In juxtaposing *The Crucifixion* with *The Dream of Gerontius* it is possible to gain revealing insights into both the achievements and the limitations of Victorian church music. *The Crucifixion* can be seen as a realization of the hopes of some early Victorian reformers. It provided music that was spiritually elevating while being accessible to ordinary churchgoers, who could actively participate themselves through singing the hymns. On the other hand, it was found wanting on strictly musical criteria. By contrast, *Gerontius* was an acclaimed musical masterpiece, but despite its religious subject-matter it had no conceivable liturgical function and offered no scope for participation by the congregation, whose members were thus, even if seated in church, effectively reduced to the status of a mere audience. Even the hymn texts were professionalized, with 'Firmly I believe and truly' being sung by a tenor solo and 'Praise to the Holiest' in a complex, large-scale choral setting. A few months after the first performance of *The Dream of Gerontius,* Queen Victoria was dead. It is therefore appropriate that the evocation of heaven contained in the work serves as an apotheosis of Victorian church music itself, with the indication that, even as some aspirations were magnificently fulfilled, others remained elusive.

BIBLIOGRAPHY

L. Adey (1988) *Class and Idol in the English Hymn,* Vancouver, University of British Columbia Press.

W. L. Alexander (1848) 'Lectures on the public psalmody of the church', *Scottish Congregational Magazine* (New Series), Vol. 8.

O. Anderson (1971) 'The growth of Christian militarism in mid-Victorian Britain', *English Historical Review,* Vol. 86, pp. 46–72.

R. Anderson (1993) *Elgar,* London, J. M. Dent.

M. K. Ashby (1961) *Joseph Ashby of Tysoe, 1859–1919,* Cambridge, Cambridge University Press.

*P. Barrett (1974) 'English cathedral choirs in the nineteenth century', *Journal of Ecclesiastical History,* Vol. 25, pp. 15–37.

H. Bonar (1866) *Hymns of Faith and Hope,* London, James Nisbet.

I. Bradley (ed.) (1989) *The Penguin Book of Hymns,* Harmondsworth, Viking.

J. Burnett (1982) *Destiny Obscure: Autobiographies of Childhood, Education and Family from the 1820s to the 1920s,* London, Allen Lane.

N. M. de S. Cameron (ed.) (1993) *Dictionary of Scottish Church History and Theology,* Edinburgh, T & T Clark.

P. Chappell (1977) *Dr. S. S. Wesley: Portrait of a Victorian Musician,* Great Wakering, Mayhew-McCrimmon.

P. Charlton (1984) *John Stainer and the Musical Life of Victorian Britain,* Newton Abbot, David & Charles.

A. C. Cheyne (1983) *The Transforming of the Kirk: Victorian Scotland's Religious Revolution,* Edinburgh, St Andrew Press.

The Church Hymnary (1898) Edinburgh, Henry Frowde.

J. S. Curwen (1885) *Studies in Worship Music*, No. 2, London, J. Curwen.

G. M. Davies (1876) *Orthodox London: Or, Phases of Religious Life in the Church of England*, 2nd edn, London, Tinsley.

H. Davies (1962) *Worship and Theology in England from Newman to Martineau, 1850–1900*, Princeton (NJ), Princeton University Press.

*S. Drain (1989) *The Anglican Church in Nineteenth-century Britain: Hymns Ancient and Modern (1850–1875)*, Lampeter, Edwin Mellon Press.

G. Eliot (1973 edn) *Scenes of Clerical Life*, ed. D. Lodge, Harmondsworth, Penguin (first published 1858).

F. W. Faber (1852) *Jesus and Mary: or Catholic Hymns for Singing and Reading*, London, Richardson.

*M. Frost (1962) *Historical Companion to Hymns Ancient and Modern*, London, William Clowes.

*V. Gammon (1981) '"Babylonian performances": the rise and suppression of popular church music, 1660–1870' in E. Yeo and S. Yeo (eds.) *Popular Culture and Class Conflict, 1590–1914*, pp. 62–88, Brighton, Harvester.

H. J. Garland (n.d.) *Henry Francis Lyte and the Story of Abide with Me*, Manchester, Torch.

*W. J. Gatens (1986) *Victorian Cathedral Music in Theory and Practice*, Cambridge, Cambridge University Press.

G. L. Gibb (1989) *Horatius Bonar and his Hymns*, Edinburgh, St Catherine's Argyle Church.

J. M. Gordon (1991) *Evangelical Spirituality From the Wesleys to John Stott*, London, Society for Promoting Christian Knowledge.

M. V. G. Havergal (1881) *Memorials of Frances Ridley Havergal*, London, James Nisbet.

M. Heimann (1995) *Catholic Devotion in Victorian England*, Oxford, Clarendon Press.

A. Jacobs (1984) *Arthur Sullivan: A Victorian Musician*, Oxford, Oxford University Press.

*J. Kent (1978) *Holding the Fort: Studies in Victorian Revivalism*, London, Epworth Press.

R. Kipling (1920) *Rudyard Kipling's Verse*, 2 vols., London, Hodder & Stoughton.

D. H. Lawrence (1930) *Assorted Articles*, London, Martin Secker.

A. Luff (1990) *Welsh Hymns and their Tunes: Their Background and Place in Welsh History and Culture*, London, Stainer & Bell.

W. Maxwell-Lyte (1947) 'A famous hymn', *The Times*, 1 November 1947.

S. Mews (1992) 'Music and religion in the First World War' in D. Wood (ed.) *The Church and the Arts: Studies in Church History*, Volume 28, pp. 465–75, Oxford, Blackwell.

D. Murray (1984) 'Disruption to union' in *Studies in the History of Worship in Scotland*, pp. 79–95, Edinburgh, T & T Clark.

*J. Obelkevich (1987) 'Music and religion in the nineteenth century' in J. Obelkevich, L. Roper and R. Samuel (eds.) *Disciplines of Faith: Studies in Religion, Politics and Patriarchy*, pp. 550–65, London, Routledge & Kegan Paul.

M. Patrick (1949) *Four Centuries of Scottish Psalmody*, London, Oxford University Press.

*B. Rainbow (1970) *The Choral Revival in the Anglican Church 1839–1872*, London, Barrie & Jenkins.

S. J. Rogal (1978) '"Onward Christian soldiers": a re-examination', *The Hymn*, Vol. 39, pp. 23–30.

*E. Routley (1957) *The Music of Christian Hymnody*, London, Independent Press.

E. Routley (1958) *The English Carol*, London, Herbert Jenkins.

S. Sadie (ed.) (1980) *The New Grove Dictionary of Music and Musicians*, 20 vols., London, Macmillan.

I. D. Sankey (n.d.) *Sacred Songs and Solos*, London, Morgan & Scott.

W. T. Stead (1895) *Hymns that Have Helped*, London, The Masterpiece Library.

*S. S. Tamke (1978) *Make a Joyful Noise unto the Lord: Hymns as a Reflection of Victorian Social Attitudes*, Athens (OH), Ohio University Press.

N. Temperley (1977) *Jonathan Gray and Church Music in York, 1770–1840*, York, Borthwick Institute.

*N. Temperley (1979) *The Music of the English Parish Church*, Volume 1, Cambridge, Cambridge University Press.

*N. Temperley (ed.) (1981) *The Romantic Age 1800–1914*, London, Athlone Press.

J. R. Watson (1981) *The Victorian Hymn*, Durham, University of Durham.

J. Werner (1965) *Mendelssohn's 'Elijah'*, London, Chappell.

J. Wesley (1821 edn) *A Collection of Hymns for the Use of the People called Methodists*, London, Thomas Cordeux (first published 1780).

S. S. Wesley (1961 edn) *A Few Words on Cathedral Music*, London, Hinrichsen (first published 1849).

J. Wolffe (1989) 'Evangelicalism in mid-nineteenth-century England' in R. Samuel (ed.) *Patriotism: The Making and Unmaking of British National Identity: Volume 1 History and Politics*, pp. 188–200, London, Routledge.

J. Wolffe (1994) *God and Greater Britain: Religion and National Life in Britain and Ireland, 1843–1945*, London, Routledge.

P. M. Young (1995) *Elgar, Newman and the Dream of Gerontius in the Tradition of English Catholicism*, Aldershot, Scolar.

CHAPTER 3

QUEEN VICTORIA PRESENTING A BIBLE TO AN AFRICAN
AMBASSADOR

FOREIGN MISSIONS AND MISSIONARIES IN VICTORIAN BRITAIN

N the closing chapters of *Jane Eyre*, after the heroine of the novel has been through many traumatic experiences, Charlotte Brontë inflicts yet another trial on the hapless Jane. Faced with a life-threatening situation, she finds herself on the doorstep of an Evangelical clergyman of the Church of England. Jane survives and discovers that she is not merely an heiress of some quite considerable means but also a cousin of her clerical saviour, St John E. Rivers (the 'E' standing for Eyre). After recovering her composure and her status in life, she then has to cope with the Reverend Mr Rivers, who has already revealed that he is destined for a missionary life in India, pressing suit on her to become his wife and 'helpmeet', and 'fellow-labourer' in the task he has set himself.

The task is described in very dramatic terms. He has, he says, through this 'vocation', this 'great work', this

> foundation laid on earth for a mansion in heaven ... hopes of being numbered in the band who have merged all ambitions in the glorious one of bettering their race—of carrying knowledge into the realms of ignorance—of substituting peace for war, freedom for bondage, religion for superstition, the hope of heaven for the fear of hell.
>
> (Brontë, 1966 edn, pp. 399–400)

Jane had her own perceptions of what being a missionary involved. She thought Mr Rivers strong but cold. As she sat in the parlour of the house she shared with him and his sisters she reflected:

> This parlour is not his sphere, the Himalayan ridge, or Caffre bush, even the plague-cursed Guinea Coast swamp, would suit him better ... It is in scenes of strife and danger—where courage is proved, and energy exercised, and fortitude tasked—that he will speak and move, the leader and superior. A merry child would have the advantage of him on this hearth. He is right to choose a missionary career—I see it now.
>
> (*Ibid.*, p. 419)

Jane for her part, in response to his proposal of marriage, still pining for Mr Rochester and somewhat appalled at the loveless marriage she is being explicitly offered, at first turns down his proposal, then under the most intense pressure agrees a compromise of accompanying him as a 'sister' or 'deacon', which in turn appalls Mr Rivers, and finally she rejects his proposal completely (*ibid.*, pp. 426–35).

Brontë wrote *Jane Eyre* in 1846–7. In the section of the novel relating to the events referred to above there is a suggestion that the events took place around 1809. The problems of dating the story accurately are, apparently, insoluble. At least we can be sure that by 1847 the idea of someone becoming a missionary in India was sufficiently common for it to feature quite prominently in a novel. There was nothing unusual in a man, especially an Evangelical, deciding that he had such a vocation. It was less usual, this early in the century, for an Anglican, Evangelical clergyman to decide that he had such a vocation. It would be quite usual for a man, a missionary, to take his wife to India to be his helpmeet. It was much more unusual for a single woman to go as a missionary in her own right at this time. The reasons for following a vocation to be a missionary in India as given by St John Rivers match what we know of many of the men who answered this call in the early part of the nineteenth century, and Jane's perceptions of what was demanded of a missionary, and her reference to 'the leader and superior', were also not far from the real thing.

In this chapter, some account of the missionary movements of the nineteenth century in general will be given, but such movements will be illustrated mainly by reference to India. India was one of the key areas of missionary work in the period and therefore we can learn a great deal about the topic by looking at this one area of operations. Not that it is at all easy, in spite of such a wealth of documentation regarding what went on, to arrive always at definite conclusions. As with many other aspects of the study of history, including the history of religions, interpretation of evidence and ideological bias often affect the writing of the history.

I SETTING THE SCENE

In his massive history of the expansion of Christianity over 1900 years (Latourette, 1938–45), Kenneth Scott Latourette referred to the nineteenth century as the 'great century'. Of the seven volumes of his history, three volumes are devoted to this one period. Yet one has to be careful in accepting his description too easily. It is true that at the end of the century there were, according to some statistics, over 17,000 missionaries working in countries not their own, of whom just over 9,000 came from Britain and Ireland, with the vast majority of the rest from the United States of America (Stanley, 1990, p. 83). The number of foreign missionaries from Britain and Ireland equalled the number of accountants or architects in employment in these countries. There were half as many missionaries as there were Anglican priests and three times as many missionaries as Roman Catholic clergy in Britain and Ireland. The British missionary societies and agencies spent annually £2,000,000, equivalent to 2 per cent of government expenditure, and as much as the total salaries of the entire civil service. These are astonishing figures by any comparison and are partly the reason for Latourette's description of the century (Porter, 1992, p. 372). They are an illustration of the heightened religiosity of the churches in Britain during this period. However, it is worth noting that the same period saw a comparative decline in organized religion in Britain relative to the general growth of the overall population.

Care in accepting Latourette's description is required because these figures were reached only at the end of the century and were reached only after a massive surge from about 1880. Before that date, missionaries were comparatively few, as is illustrated by the statistics for one of the most active societies over the whole century. These provide a striking picture and an interesting insight into Brontë's references to St John Rivers's ambitions and Jane Eyre's response. Between 1800 and 1809, the Church Missionary Society (CMS), the most likely vehicle for St John Rivers's ambitions, had only two recruits. (Recruits were those who were accepted out of those who offered their services.) The next decade saw an increase to 28 recruits, the following decade to 80 and in the 1830s there were 104 recruits. The 1840s saw a decline to 76, but the really significant rises were in the following decades: to 250 in the 1880s and a big leap to 671 from 1890 to 1899 (Stanley, 1990, p. 80).

If we look at the breakdown between numbers of male and female recruits, we see an equally interesting range of statistics. There were no female recruits until 1820. Thereafter, decennial totals varied from five to nine until 1880 when the decade produced no recruits. The following decade, however (1890–9), produced 315 (*ibid.*). So, although the figures quoted for missionaries and funding in 1899 are, indeed, extraordinary, they do not reflect the position during the rest of the century. In fact, the numbers are even more remarkable for the final decade of the nineteenth century given the low figures preceding 1880. Therefore, we must be careful about calling it the 'great century'. Rather it was the 'great last twenty years' of the century and the trend continued into the twentieth century up to the outbreak of World War I.

The upward trend throughout the century was not consistent and there were periods of peaks and troughs. There are some reasons to suggest that the peaks had some links with imperial expansion, although not exclusively so. At times certain events in the mission field, like the martyrdom of John Williams in the South Seas, news of which arrived in 1839, suggest peaks (Stanley, 1990, p. 78). For instance, another peak relates to the decision of the CMS to open wider the doors of recruitment to single women in 1887 (*ibid.*, p. 81). However, certain peaks in recruitment were contemporary with the opening up of areas of Africa, especially East Africa with the opening of the Suez Canal in 1869. The last two decades of the nineteenth century and the early twentieth century saw a period of 'high imperialism' and the relationship between imperial expansion and missionary expansion cannot be totally coincidental. There must be some consequential relationship—but more of that later.

We have to go back before the Victorian period to obtain a clear picture of the development of missions. Until the 1790s, foreign missionary activity was rather sporadic and not very extensive in geographical range. There were chaplains overseas serving the spiritual needs of expatriate employees of commercial organizations such as the East India Company. (In looking at the history of clergy overseas there is a need always to distinguish between chaplains and missionaries.) But how were these chaplains and missionaries recruited and supported?

The Society for the Propagation of the Gospel in Foreign Parts (SPG) was formed in 1701 to provide spiritual support in plantations, colonies and factories 'beyond the Seas' (*ibid.*, p. 55). Its work involved, primarily, the chaplains just referred to. It was financially supported by the state until 1825 when it 'underwent a remarkable transformation from a colonial church society financed by parliamentary grants and royal letters' (*ibid.*, p. 61) to become a voluntary organization, which took over the support of missionaries hitherto supported by the Society for Promoting Christian Knowledge (SPCK). The SPCK was formed in 1699 and was and is best known for the publication of religious works and for teaching the rudiments of the Christian faith. However, the Society was possibly the first Anglican organization to support missionaries in the special sense of the word. In a very ecumenical spirit, it supported from 1728 a number of Danish Lutheran missionaries in Tranquebar in South India.

What eventually became the CMS, a voluntary Evangelical society in the Church of England, was formed in 1799. The CMS had, at first, a policy of recruiting only ordained clergymen. The consequence was that very few men from Britain were recruited in its early years. Hence the suggestion that St John Rivers was rather unusual for his time. Of the first twenty-four CMS missionaries, only three were English, and of the remainder seventeen were recruited from Germany. In addition to the limitations imposed by its policy of recruiting only clerics, the CMS experienced the problem of receiving only lukewarm support from the bishops of the Church of England. As the respectability of the Society grew, so did episcopal support, and the number of clerical recruits gradually increased, so that between 1820 and 1829 eighty men were recruited.

In the earliest days of missionary enthusiasm, this very enthusiasm, arising out of the Evangelical Revival, made the societies suspect in the minds of many people, including the bishops of the Church of England just referred to. This is, perhaps, more clearly demonstrated when we turn to look at societies formed in Nonconformist circles, which somewhat predated the CMS. The history of missions in the Victorian period finds its origins in the activity of certain prominent men who were the products of the Evangelical Revival.

Thomas Coke, deputed by John Wesley to develop Methodist presence in the West Indies and America, published a *Plan of the Society for the Establishment of Missions among the Heathens* in 1783. He appointed the first missionaries to the West Indies in late 1786 and early 1787, resulting in a Methodist membership of 6,570 by 1793. Over a period of years he attempted to get the Methodist Church to respond to his arguments for missions, and when this failed he set out to form his own support groups. He succeeded mainly by his own persuasive efforts. It was not until 1818 that the Methodist Conference brought these voluntary support groups together in the national Wesleyan Methodist Missionary Society. Eventually every member of the Methodist Church automatically became a member of the Missionary Society.

The other major name, even eclipsing Coke, at least in prevailing missiology, is that of William Carey (1761–1834), shoemaker and Baptist minister. In 1792, he published *An Enquiry into the Obligation of Christians to use Means for the Conversion of the Heathen*. He reminded his readers of the gospel report of Jesus Christ's commission to 'preach the gospel to every creature'. He argued that this commission applied to all Christians at all times. Contrary to the dominant Calvinism of the time, according to which men and women were predestined to election or perdition and therefore could not be converted by human effort, he dramatically called on his contemporaries to 'expect great things from God' and 'attempt great things for God'.

In October 1792, what became known as the Baptist Missionary Society (BMS) was formed. This was the first missionary organization created by the Evangelical Revival. Not only was it the first missionary organization but was really the first true missionary society, and the notion of societies to carry on mission work was one of the most significant developments in religion in the Anglicized world in the nineteenth century.

Carey and his family set out for India the following year and settled in Bengal. Although idealist in many ways he was also a pragmatist, and not long after his arrival took employment as a foreman in an indigo factory, a trade that over 100 years later became a focus for one of Mahatma Gandhi's protests against the operation of the British Raj. On hearing of his taking up this work the BMS wrote a letter 'full of serious and affectionate caution' (Stanley, 1990, p. 72). This was not a full-time job and for nine months of the year he was able to devote himself to the study of oriental languages. This study led to some of Carey's most enduring legacies to India. After experiencing disappointment in his attempts to convert Indians directly—it took him and his colleagues seven years to achieve their first convert—he turned to education as a means to the same end.

As missions developed in India, the question of education loomed large. That education should feature so prominently in early and continuing missionary work is an interesting matter of discussion. It has been maintained that the emphasis on education shows the influence of the European Enlightenment on Evangelicals, who, otherwise, had nothing to thank the Enlightenment for, with its considerable attack on religion generally (Stanley, 1990, p. 62; Willmer, 1962). Within the missionary movement in general, and within India in particular, the subject of education became itself an object of debate. Carey's approach to the matter was to enable Indians to study their own religion and culture, whereby he hoped to undermine the Indians' confidence in their own culture. The other approach looked to the educating of Indians in western culture and ideas through the English language. The earliest exponent of this approach was Alexander Duff, a Scottish missionary to whom we shall return later.

Carey was joined in 1799 at Serampore in Bengal by two fellow Baptists, Joshua Marshman and William Ward. For the next twenty years and more, the three of them set a pattern for missionary work emulated in other parts of India. They set themselves to learning Indian languages and translating the Christian Scriptures into these languages. They also set up mission schools. Carey himself was responsible for the idea of Serampore College, founded in 1818, which exists still, awarding degrees through affiliated colleges throughout India. He also founded the Agricultural Society of India in 1820 and for his botanical studies was made a Fellow of the Linnaean Society in 1823 (Bebbington, 1990). He and his colleagues, furthermore, translated Hindu sacred classics into English, including the Hindu epic, the *Ramayana*. Their purpose in translating this Hindu material was to demonstrate the superiority of

Christian literature and to prepare Christians for the task of evangelizing the Hindus, on the principle of 'know thine enemy'. They rejoiced in the fact that income from the sale of the *Ramayana* funded their translations of the Bible into Indian languages. Ironically, the education and published works introduced by Carey, his colleagues and others who followed their example largely only served to educate Hindus to defend their religion better, thereby helping to launch a Hindu renaissance (a general movement of intellectuals who projected Hinduism as a reformed religion of the nineteenth century), and eventually to provide the intellectual resources for the challenging of the whole concept of the British Raj and domination of India.

Other missionary societies followed. In 1795, what became the London Missionary Society (LMS) was formed. This society was deliberately established to cover a variety of dissenting bodies and committed itself to a 'fundamental principle that our design is not to send Presbyterianism, Independency, Episcopacy or any other form of church government ... but the glorious gospel of the blessed God to the heathen' (Walls, 1990b, p. 571). Although the LMS did, at first, attract recruits from a number of denominations, including the Church of Scotland but excluding the Church of England, it very soon became and remained virtually a Congregationalist society, not least because the other denominations began to set up their own societies. The LMS quickly developed, and within months of its formation had sent more than thirty missionaries to the Pacific Ocean area. The attraction of this area for prospective missionaries was based on the publication of the reports of Captain James Cook's voyages to the Pacific. Carey confessed that it was these reports that first 'engaged my mind to think of missions'. John Williams, one of the earliest missionary martyrs, was sent out by the LMS. His death, unusual in that he was killed by local inhabitants, was not an isolated death. Many of the earliest LMS missionaries quickly died. They showed themselves inept in meeting the physical as well as the mental challenges of their new environment and enterprise. Later the LMS took on the responsibility for training those they sent out as missionaries.

Evangelicals in Scotland also tried to get the missionary impulse moving, but with only moderate success at first. A society was formed in Glasgow in 1796 and was followed shortly after by the Scottish Missionary Society. Local groups were formed and found the outlet for their enthusiasm and finance through the LMS. In 1796, an Evangelical, John Erskine, tried to involve the General Assembly of the Church of Scotland. He failed because of the strength of Moderate opinion, which regarded the new-found Evangelical enthusiasm as rather threatening generally and representative of a form of political radicalism. It was not until 1824 that the Church of Scotland formed its own missionary organization. In 1843, the Church of Scotland was rent apart by the 'Disruption' and the formation of the Free Church. All the missionaries in the Church of Scotland left to join the Free Church, so the Church of Scotland had to start recruiting all over again.[1]

One of the most formidable characters in the original organization of the Church of Scotland was the first missionary it commissioned, Alexander Duff (1806–78). Mention has already been made of the difference between his approach to education and that of Carey. Duff arrived in India in 1830 to begin a missionary programme of education through the medium of English. His basic attitude, reminiscent of Enlightenment philosophy, was that truth is a unity. Thus, the teaching of science, philosophy and Christian doctrine belonged together and combined they would undermine the beliefs of Hinduism. He was not building on entirely barren ground. There were already young Indian intellectuals who were questioning traditional thought and turning for new ideas to western rationalism. In 1835, the East India Company decided that its administration should be carried on in English, thus replacing Sanskrit and Persian. This meant there was an immediate need for the education that Duff was providing in Calcutta and later in Madras. Duff initiated a tradition of school and higher education provided by Scottish missionaries, which maintains its influence still in major Indian cities. Madras Christian College has been the *alma mater* of many prominent Indian intellectuals, the most prominent of whom was Sarvepalli Radhakrishnan, former Oxford professor, philosopher and President of India. Radhakrishnan is a symbol of what these Scottish colleges achieved. The majority of their students were always non-Christian. Hinduism did not crumble as Duff hoped. Indeed he, probably, like Carey, helped inadvertently in training men like Radhakrishnan to build the Hindu renaissance, and very few converts to Christianity were made.

A relatively late entrant into the missionary field was the Universities' Mission to Central Africa (UMCA), formed in 1859. The immediate catalyst for its formation was a speech given in the Senate House of the University of Cambridge in December 1857 by David Livingstone (1813–73). The UMCA was a High Church missionary organization, similar to the SPG, with which it amalgamated in the second half of the twentieth century. Both societies have been referred to as examples of

---

[1] See *RVB*, II, 5, pp. 108–23.

'the new and aggressive Anglo-Catholicism nurtured by the Oxford Movement', examples of High Churchmen who had earlier jumped 'onto the missionary bandwagon' (Stanley, 1990, p. 61). Stanley goes on to say in a somewhat questionable vein: 'the SPG and the UMCA remained strange children in a movement whose attitudes and assumptions remained essentially evangelical throughout most, if not all, of the nineteenth century' (*ibid.*). In this particular interpretation of history these and other High Church Anglican missionary organizations are excluded on the grounds, presumably, that they are not Protestant. Such an assumption is understandable in the context of the Church of England, in that, whilst the Church derives ultimately from the Protestant Reformation, and the evangelicals within the Church would have been proud to be known as Protestants, some High Church Anglicans wished to revert to pre-Reformation Catholicism. However, the assumption still unfairly marginalizes the significant contribution, not only of High Church organizations, but also of the Roman Catholic missionary orders that came on the scene in the second half of the nineteenth century. The irony concerning the formation of the UMCA is that the person who immediately inspired the founders, Livingstone, was himself a Scottish missionary of the LMS. A person further removed from the image of a High Church Anglican can hardly be imagined.

In his speech in the University of Cambridge, Livingstone coined a phrase that was handed down in subsequent missiology: 'I go back to Africa to try to make an open path for commerce and Christianity.' That phrase 'commerce and Christianity' has been around ever since and has provided ammunition for the detractors of Christian missions and been an embarrassment to their defenders. A more detailed consideration of this debate follows below. The immediate result of the speech was the newly formed UMCA's first major endeavour, an expedition to the River Zambezi in 1860–2, an attempt to combine 'legitimate commerce in the hands of Christian men ... [as] the perfect partner of missionary activity'. This met with such disastrous results, however, that it was never attempted again by the UMCA (Stanley, 1990, pp. 73–4).

The organizations mentioned above were some of the major missionary organizations in Britain and Ireland. They were a mixture of voluntary societies and official church organizations. They operated in many parts of the world: in India, China, Africa and the West Indies. The expansion of activity continued. Many other societies were formed, some of them specializing in work for certain groups of people, such as women (the so-called zenana missions in India) and others specializing in certain areas of the globe. For example, in China the China Inland Mission, formed in 1865 under the leadership of James Hudson Taylor, was important. In Africa, from 1866, the Mill Hill Fathers, a Roman Catholic order, was prominent. In South America, the South American Missionary Society operated from the 1870s. In north-east India the missionary arm of the Calvinistic Methodist or Presbyterian Church in Wales, following the arrival of its first missionary in 1841, produced quite remarkable results among peoples whose cultural distinctiveness was threatened by the commercial ambitions of plains Hindus migrating north.

Missionary organizations were also formed in other western countries, such as Denmark, Switzerland, Germany and, of course, the United States of America. American missionaries went to the Pacific, as in James Mitchener's graphic portrayal in his novel *Hawaii* (1959), and in 1813 they arrived in Bombay. Their main work only began in 1833 after the renewal of the East India Company's charter in that year effected changes to allow this. Together the organizations added up to a massive operation, which gave rise to the figures quoted earlier.

II   HISTORICAL AND MISSIOLOGICAL DISCUSSION POINTS

In analysing the historical facts that were the result of the missionary efforts of the nineteenth century, a number of issues have caused debate. These issues are approached from various perspectives and the same historical evidence is interpreted in a variety of ways. Because the missionary work was carried on in a period of British commercial and political expansion, consideration of the issues mainly involves answering the basic question: 'What was the relationship between the missionary expansion and British imperial expansion?'

The question needs to be addressed from four perspectives, that is, the operation of Christianity in respect of:

(i)   conversion,

(ii) colonialism,

(iii) commerce,

(iv) culture or civilization.

(The fourth point is sometimes divided into fourth and fifth points.) All these areas of discussion, although separated out in the above list, are closely intertwined and constantly overlap. There is no clear delineation at any point in this list. Although the question of religious conversion might be thought to be clearly separated, in fact, as we shall see, not even this area is as clear cut as we might think.

Christianity and Conversion

Given that the main religious impulse behind the missionary movements of the Victorian period lay in the Evangelical Revival of the eighteenth century, it is not surprising to learn that the desire to convert people of various geographical and cultural backgrounds to Christianity was very much to the fore in missionary policy and effort.

One major effect of the Evangelical Revival was to bring about a change in the dominant Protestant theology of the previous period, namely the belief in Calvinistic predestination and salvation of the elect few. Under the prevailing Calvinism there had been not only no need to work for the conversion of those who were not in the way of salvation but such work would be seen as either fruitless or even contrary to the will of God. It was the power of the Revival that modified, and then in large measure overthrew, out and out Calvinism, and established the belief that through the power of the Holy Spirit unregenerate people could be brought to faith through repentance for past sins and a commitment to faith in the saving power of the Cross of Christ. This kind of attitude was the driving force of the Evangelical Revival and led to the conversion of many people.[2]

In considering the transition from such preaching in Britain to preaching in countries 'beyond the Seas', we must pause to think why, if there was still so much work to be done in Britain for the salvation of souls, there eventually became such a rush to save the souls of peoples of other nations? There is no clear answer to the question. It is an especially intriguing question when we recall that in the earlier stages of the foreign missionary enterprise it was men, and very occasionally women, of the so-called 'lower orders' who offered themselves and were sent to foreign lands. Gradually, as the nineteenth century advanced and foreign missionary work became more 'respectable', the complexion of the missionaries changed. Research into the records of the LMS shows that even later in the century (1845–80), there was still a significant proportion, about 20 per cent, of skilled working-class candidates (Oddie, 1974, p. 62). This is not surprising in view of the fact that in the initial call for volunteers the LMS appeal was for 'Godly men who understand mechanic arts'.

In the period just referred to, the LMS chose 106 men to work in India. Papers relating to 71 men remain available, among whom 64 give their previous occupation. Of these, 11 were students or student teachers. Of the rest, one-quarter were in skilled working-class occupations:

[2] See *RVB*, I, 9, p. 216.

harness-maker, joiner's toolmaker, printer. A slightly larger percentage were engaged in occupations that would rank them as the lower ranks of the middle class: clerks in offices and banks, drapery assistants. Less than one-third could be classed as professional: qualified chemists, a fair number of teachers, including one who described himself as 'Tutor in school, then professor in Bombay'.

As to why these men wanted to take the gospel abroad, they claimed to have been influenced by sermons, lectures and publications such as the biographies of missionaries and such works as J. Williams's *A Narrative of Missionary Enterprises in the South Sea Islands* (1837). Their motives were varied, but one or two stood out above the rest. Many of them were grateful for the blessings they had received through religion and therefore wanted to show this gratitude. For example, W. Johnson wrote: 'As I have found pardon & peace through the gospel, I desire that others may know this gospel & obtain deliverance from the degradation of misery of sin' (Oddie, 1974, p. 66). Many wanted to glorify God through their efforts. The most commonly expressed motivation was the need to obey Christ's command to preach the gospel to every creature: 'I feel as if this command were addressed especially to me & directing me to go hence among the Heathen' (*ibid.*). But why the heathen in far off countries? Were there not heathen at home in Britain? The answer one person gave to this question was: 'To work at home with such a strong conviction within me would be to work with a burdened conscience' (*ibid.*, p. 67). Maybe, but it still does not explain fully why the conscience would be burdened.

Oddie suggests that the expression that the needs of the foreign mission field were greater than those at home 'was not only because they recognised the paucity of labourers overseas, but because many of them continued to share in the sentiments of the well-known hymn sung on missionary occasions: "o'er heathen lands afar thick darkness broodeth yet"' (*ibid.*). Unfavourable descriptions of Hinduism and other non-Christian religions continued to play an important part in stimulating missionary enterprise during the middle of the nineteenth century. In 1848 we find the following statement: 'the harrowing accounts of the deplorable state of the Heathen, which I had read and heard first excited within me the ardent wish to attempt with God's aid, the amelioration of their wretched condition' (*ibid.*). Even though as the century advanced some of the candidates admitted to having read the works of Monier Williams and Max Müller in the late 1880s,[3] we still find someone

---

[3] See *RVB*, II, 13.

influenced by 'accounts of the degradation & the cruelty, the superstition, ignorance and above all the death-like apathy of those among whom I might be going' (*ibid.*).

It is noticeable how often the word 'heathen' occurred in the statements we have looked at, and this from only a very small sample. Those who inhabited the countries and continents to which the missionaries went were almost invariably identified as 'heathen'. These heathen were lost in the darkness of unbelief, the darkness of the separation from the worship of the one true God. It is probable that, for the most part, those who viewed the heathen in this fashion also believed that they were eternally lost, that they 'perished in eternal perdition'. There were those, occasionally, who were not prepared to declare outright that the heathen were inevitably lost and destined for perdition but even these, who claimed to be among the 'enlightened', felt that they had to assume that the heathen were lost. It is not too difficult to see that if any doubts were ever entertained as to whether the heathen were destined for perdition the cutting edge of missionary preaching would be blunted. Indeed this is something that began to happen in the late nineteenth century and became even more prevalent in the twentieth century. The more liberal the missionary became the less successful the mission seemed to become.

In viewing the future and the goals of missionary endeavour 'two parallel theological developments' (Stanley, 1990, p. 75) affected the ways in which the goals were understood. The two approaches have been labelled 'postmillenial' and 'premillenial'. The 'millenial' element refers to biblical, apocalyptic expectation of a thousand year era of the triumph of the Christian gospel on earth. The triumph was linked by those in the missionary movement to missionary endeavour. The postmillenialists, the position adopted by the majority of missionaries up until about 1880, thought that missionary success would hasten the millennium and were therefore full of expectation and optimism in the founding of a new creation, a transformed world, through the conversion of humanity to the religion of Christ. As we shall see below, the postmillenialist understanding was itself transformed as the nineteenth century progressed. The premillenialists, however, expected cataclysmic divine intervention in history before the millennium could be established. They accordingly were concerned to prepare those who could be converted, those who could be 'saved', not in order to transform the world, but so that when the catastrophe of evil that was expected finally erupted and destroyed the world as it existed, there would be at least some souls who were there to inherit what was left of the universe and keep it for God.

The contrast between the two theological positions has been summed up as follows:

> Those evangelicals who began to move in a liberal direction in their doctrines of the atonement, the authority of Scripture and eternal punishment retained the postmillennial hope but in an increasingly diluted form. The expectation of social transformation was no longer tied so explicitly to the process of personal conversion, and began to be understood more loosely in terms of the spread of Christian civilization and idealism ... Postmillenialism without the cutting edge of Puritan theology degenerated all too easily into a facile creed of liberal imperialism.
>
> Other sections of evangelicalism moved in a contrary theological direction ... This alternative Christian view of history [the premillenial] posited that the moral and spiritual state of the world would actually get worse before the cataclysmic intervention of the second coming [of Christ]. The mission of the church, therefore, was not to transform human society into the kingdom of God, but to rescue individuals from an increasingly evil world, and hasten the return of Christ by a policy of rapid evangelistic expansion. Christ could not return until every nation had had an opportunity of responding to the gospel.
>
> (Stanley, 1990, pp. 75–6)

Stanley clearly thinks that what happened historically was unfortunate. He contrasts the 'cutting edge of Puritan theology' with degeneration into 'a facile creed of liberal imperialism'. It is unfortunate that this subject is dealt with in such a judgemental fashion. It is not as if the 'cutting edge of Puritan theology' ceased to exist. It persisted even into the twentieth century among certain groups and missionary organizations. What is referred to as the 'facile creed of liberal imperialism' was regarded by many as the only way to proceed towards the emancipation of those to whom the missionaries went. Some missionaries were aware that their task as persons concerned for the welfare of those with whom they came into contact was not merely to convert but also to elevate, and in this respect the structures of Indian tradition and British imperial policy were antithetical to the true emancipation of millions of Indians. This 'liberal imperialism' often turned into 'radical anti-imperialism' and produced many of the social and political leaders of the future India and African countries.

We have already reminded ourselves of one popular hymn. Here is another by someone who worked, and died in 1826, in India, Bishop Reginald Heber. He went out to India to be Bishop of Calcutta in 1823.

> From Greenland's icy mountains,
>   From India's coral strand,
> Where Afric's sunny fountains
>   Roll down their golden sand,
> From many an ancient river,
>   From many a palmy plain,
> They call us to deliver
>   Their land from error's chain
>
> What though the spicy breezes
>   Blow soft o'er Java's isle,
> Though every prospect pleases
>   And only man is vile:
> In vain with lavish kindness
>   The gifts of God are strown;
> The heathen in his blindness
>   Bows down to wood and stone.

The hymn goes on to say what Christians have to do to remedy this situation where this beautiful creation, the gift of God, is being trampled on by heathen humans, 'men benighted' as the hymn later describes them. Such sentiments seem shocking to a later politically correct age in which different religions exist in much closer proximity, but are fundamental to understanding the missionary motivation of certain sections of the overall movement until well into the twentieth century.

In the nineteenth century, all that has just been said was justification enough to leave Britain and go to India, Africa or wherever and convert the 'benighted', make them Christian, baptize them according to what was believed to be Christ's command. And the missionaries met with some success. Slowly, at first, some of those they went to responded and were converted, but never many. Not even at the height of missionary endeavour were there many converted. Even where they were converted, certainly in India, the converts came from the lower economic, social orders. In India the phenomenon of mass conversions was experienced at different times, but these movements were never among the top three classes of Hindus—the priestly (Brahmin), military and trading castes—but always among the lowest castes and usually among the outcasts. Some more statistics provide a picture: 'Between 1789 and 1858, 559 missionaries went to India from the thirteen main Protestant [including presumably the American] societies working there ... It was calculated in

1860 that there were 112,000 Protestant Christians in India' (Williams, 1994, p. 389). If that total referred only to converts, this would give an average of about 1,600 converts a year. However, when the inclusion of families and the effects of births and deaths are taken into account, the average figure is considerably less. If the figures are accurate, and there is no guarantee that they are, it may be thought that this was an expensive endeavour in terms of return on expenditure. Not that the missionaries would have thought in this way. For them the joy in heaven over one sinner who repents would have provided them with quite a different balance sheet.

As the century wore on the 'convert the heathen' motivation diminished, although the number of missionaries in absolute terms increased. Studies in Hinduism and Islam, and to some extent Buddhism, obviously had their effect. The work of Monier Williams and Max Müller almost certainly influenced some prominent missionaries such as J. N. Farquhar (1861–1929), who popularized the notion that Christianity was the fulfilment of the hopes of Hindus and adherents of other religions. The objections of people like F. D. Maurice, much earlier in the century, to the traditional doctrines of eternal hell were also bound to have had an effect. During the late nineteenth century 'candidates [for the LMS] were not only less inclined to state a belief in the doctrine of everlasting punishment, but in a number of cases questioned its validity' (Oddie, 1974, p. 69). In 1882, a candidate writes: 'I shall interest myself in the social conditions of the people, & with increasing knowledge of their wants, try to improve their mode of living & if I can do something towards relieving or lessening their bodily ailments I shall not fail to do so' (*ibid.*, p. 70).

This last statement is in line with the developments that took place generally in missionary work, the move to 'a facile creed of liberal imperialism' (see above). There was an increase in overall missionary numbers, which is explained by the fact that the evangelists were added to increasingly by doctors, medical workers and teachers, although the number of straightforward gospel evangelists did not diminish. More and more, missionary work became associated in the minds of people with new hospitals, dispensaries, schools and colleges. A more realistic view of the prospect of conversions took over and missionary work was increasingly viewed as humanitarian work, even civilizing work, to which we shall look in a moment.

However, as with all human design, individual missionary motivations could be mixed and were not wholly to do with the desire to carry out the will of God. It is not unreasonable to expect that prospective missionaries had what we might call more selfish motivations too. This might help to answer the question 'Why to India, not to Liverpool or Manchester?', bearing in mind, of course, that there were 'home missions' operating in British cities. The question might have been answered truthfully: 'It does not sound nearly so romantic or exciting.' Or, perhaps very near the mark for some candidates: 'Who would offer me free training as a minister or a teacher to go to Manchester?' In 1861, one candidate responded that 'he had been sorely tempted by the prospect of increased "opportunities for study"; but then, he added, he had discovered other higher and more worthy motives!' (Oddie, 1974, p. 71). It is not inconceivable either that certain candidates offered themselves from a desire to enhance their personal status. One such candidate acknowledged that being a missionary was an 'honourable and dignified position'. An Indian Christian, writing in 1889, said of the missionary: 'He moves on the most intimate terms with the Collector or Doctor or Engineer of the station; and receives the same homage from the natives, which they ungrudgingly give to the Collector Sahib and those who move in his circle' (*ibid.*).

This aspect of being a missionary leads us to look at the missionary movement generally from other perspectives, more particularly at the relationship between Christianity and colonialism.

Christianity and Colonialism

There has never been any doubt in the minds of historians and missiologists that there has been an integral link between much missionary work and colonialism. Not all missionary work can be addressed in this way because there have been areas, such as Latin America, where the missionaries have gone without the benefit of political power. There is considerable disagreement, however, among historians and missiologists as to the precise form of the relationship between Christianity and colonialism, and, one might add, imperialism. The issue revolves around whether Christian missionary societies and organizations in Britain were dependent on British colonial power in order to achieve their missionary aims or whether it just happened that the missionary movement coincided with British political expansionism.

On the one hand, it is argued that it is 'well-nigh impossible to establish any plausible connection between the revival of the Protestant missionary conscience and ... trends in British colonial policy ... The only adequate explanation of the origins of the missionary societies is in terms of theological changes which were quite autonomous of developments in imperial history' (Stanley, 1990, p. 59). The assumption underlying this view is that the Evangelical Revival was an other-worldly event and bore no relationship whatsoever to the social, political and economic tendencies of the time. This assumption has been challenged, and it can be demonstrated that the Revival occurred to a large extent among classes of people for whom economic, social and political progress was of real importance (Potter, 1974, ch. 1). It is argued that it is too simplistic to see the Revival as a value-free, autonomous movement independent of the social, economic and political powers of the time. Whatever the strengths of the various arguments, knowing the way that human movements actually work, whether religious or not, it must be simplistic to try to isolate the Evangelical Revival from its cultural and social context. One does not need to be an opponent of religion to recognize that religions are not, can never be, totally autonomous from the cultural forces of their time.

It could still be correct to say, however, that many of those influenced by the Evangelical Revival who were in the forefront of the missionary enterprise from the late eighteenth century onwards were not looking for political success by Britain abroad to further their missionary ideals. Indeed it has to be realized that what turned out to be eventually a large British Empire was itself the product of political expediency as much as of imperial design. In 1883, it was said: 'We seem, as it were, to have conquered and peopled half the world in a fit of absence of mind' (quoted in Stanley, 1990, p. 45). There were times when the powers that be in London were very keen for Britain not to be involved in political expansion and there is truth in the view that it was only as Britain found that it could not successfully trade unless it took over political power that the Empire grew to the extent it did. In that case it is a corollary that British missionary designs were not based on British imperial aims. However, even that statement must be accepted with caution.

One of the confusing things about British colonial expansion in India is that the story is tied up with a primarily commercial venture, namely the East India Company. The Company had an interesting history. It received a charter from Elizabeth I in 1600 and was given a monopoly of trade between Britain and the Far East. In the eighteenth century, it effectively was given rule of a large part of India. Political power was in the hands of the Company in India and a committee responsible to Parliament in London. Following the so-called 'Indian Mutiny' in 1857, the Crown took control of the government of British India; the India Act of 1858 abolished the Company.

Ever since societies began to send missionaries to the Indian subcontinent there has been controversy over the role of the East India Company. In 1793, in the debate in Parliament over the renewal of the

Company's charter, the leading Evangelical William Wilberforce and Charles Grant, an official of the Company, tried to introduce a 'pious clause' into the charter, which would require the Company to finance schoolmasters and missionaries. The matter was hotly debated. Some of the participants in the debate make interesting reading. Charles James Fox, a leading Whig, saw 'all systems of proselytisation as wrong in themselves, and as productive of political mischief'. The Bishop of London saw 'considerable difficulty in adopting a measure ... of propagating the Christian religion among the natives'. The Archbishop of Canterbury was concerned that Englishmen should enjoy the 'comforts' of religion but 'would not attempt to convert the natives to Christianity unless they were disposed to embrace it'. The Company for its part was happy to accept a clause that spoke of a 'bounden duty to provide for the religious and moral welfare of the inhabitants of India' but as already said drew the line at being required to finance missionaries. Wilberforce was forced to withdraw his 'pious clause' (Carson, 1990, p. 172).

Wilberforce and his friends accused the Company of being 'inimical' to Christianity. This accusation has stuck, and religious writers to this day continue to maintain that the Company 'was hostile to missionary effort' (Neill, 1964, p. 232). However, recent historical research provides an alternative perspective. At least sixty years before the Wilberforce clause, the Company had approved missionary work and had provided financial support. It is true that the Company had expelled some missionaries in the late eighteenth century as undesirables. The Company was cautious on two fronts: it did not wish to offend the Indians among whom it had to operate, and on whom it depended for recruiting employees and setting up trading contacts, and it did not want supposedly enthusiastic Christians and possible political radicals disrupting the life of the areas in which the Company operated. In the 1793 debate, the Company had maintained that the Hindu religion was immutable, that Government-supported missionaries would give the wrong signals to Indians—that they were about to be forcibly converted—and that financially the whole project would be too expensive. It must be remembered that the Company never made a great profit and was often on the verge of insolvency.

The Company believed itself to be acting in a way that was consonant with its role as an arm of government. To have discretion to allow missionaries to operate in its territories, which it did, was one thing, to have to pay for the upkeep of missionaries, which had been in the past a matter of voluntary contribution, including contributions by Company officers, was another (Carson, l990, p. 173). It was only likely to offend the local population. This was a fear that was not exaggerated. There is strong reason to believe that two insurrections, mutinies by company troops, in Vellore in 1806 and the 'Indian Mutiny' of 1857, were in part the result of native troops believing that they were the target of Christian missionary efforts, and that there was a real fear of forceful conversion.

The main point to be made in this historical dispute is that, contrary to Evangelical propaganda at the time and in subsequent historical writing, the Company was not antithetical to Christian missionaries being present in its territories, provided they observed certain standards of behaviour. Given the Company's protectiveness towards the indigenous religions and the caution exercised towards missionaries, this could be interpreted by missionaries as antipathy towards them. Furthermore, the Company not only did not intervene in matters that westerners considered immoral among Hindus, such as the practice of widow self-immolation (*sati*), it actually profited from the religious practices of Hindus. The Company, in exercising virtual political control over considerable areas of India, decided, according to the practices of the previous Maratha rulers, to take over control of pilgrim taxes, which were levied in order to provide support for the temples visited. In controlling these taxes the Company also added revenue to its coffers. The Company's complicity in matters of Hindu morality and religious practice caused offence to Christians working in India and in the British Parliament. Eventually *sati* was abolished in certain territories, following a more successful campaign in Parliament when the Company's charter came up for renewal in 1813. This time the Evangelicals won a modest victory:

> Temple tax was abandoned, and later administrations felt free to intervene against certain Indian religious customs such as *sati* ... Bishops were appointed, and the system of government chaplains reformed and enlarged. Missions were, with occasional exceptions, unhindered, and often favoured. But anything approaching an official mission to India was carefully avoided. This attitude towards missions remained characteristic of government policy throughout the nineteenth century.
>
> (Walls, 1990a, p. 560)

This historical dispute has been summed up as follows: 'The early relationship between Protestant missions and East India Company rule was ... ambiguous. If it was not characterised by the open conflict which subsequent Christian literature tended to imply, neither can it fairly be described as anything approaching a partnership or conspiracy' (Stanley, 1990, p. 100). It does seem that one of the main features of the relationship between missions and colonial power in India was that the Evangelicals did not want to be associated with colonial power directly but did want political favours to give them an advantage in their conversion programmes. It has been a feature of much missionary activity in the nineteenth century and later that missionaries think that the governments of their home countries should in some way favour their attempts at conversion on the grounds that their governments are supposed to be Christian and therefore should be oriented towards turning the world Christian. Governments have other agenda. It could be said that governments showed more respect for the culture and religion of nations and peoples with whom they had to deal than did Christian missionaries, although possibly because this made for good political and trade relations. The missionary response might be that that showed the weakness of Christian commitment among governments. For the governments it might be said that they were more humanistic than the missionaries, at least outwardly and in the case of religion, whilst at times being quite brutal in enforcing their laws.

All these matters came to a head with the event referred to in British history as the 'Indian Mutiny' or the Sepoy Rebellion. Recent Indian historians sometimes refer to the event as the First War of Indian Independence. It shocked the British establishment in India and in Britain. The Mutiny involved soldiers, sepoys, in the British Indian army. The causes were complex, the result of insensitivity by the British authorities who carried on a vigorous programme of the westernization of India. Minor kingdoms were annexed, railways were built, telegraph services introduced and western-style universities set up. All these modernizing activities were viewed with suspicion and superstition. The activity of missionaries was interpreted as further British effort to change the character of India. Although the British authorities did not formally support missionaries, the fact that they allowed missionaries to operate was sufficient to create suspicion. Hindus and Muslims alike suspected British intentions and a tense situation was created over a number of years. In 1857, new Enfield rifles were supplied to the soldiers. The cartridges required greasing. The material provided consisted of cows' or pigs' fat. The animal grease offended the sensibilities of both Hindus and Muslims. 'The mistake was genuine, the cartridges were withdrawn, explanations were offered, but the flashpoint had been reached. The conviction ran like wildfire that there was a plot against the old cultures; the Mutiny followed' (Spear, 1975 edn, p. 141).

The Mutiny broke out on 10 May 1857 at Meerut. The next day Delhi had been taken by the mutineers. Military action followed in various cities on the Gangetic plain. Much of the rest of India remained aloof, whilst the Sikhs of the Punjab threw in their lot with the British, but the cities of Kanpur and Lucknow were besieged. Many British soldiers and their wives and children died in the action. According to one account, 1,500 'English' lives were lost. Vicious slaughter was instigated by both sides and the reprisals by the British authorities afterwards were often brutal. Although the activity of missionaries was a factor in the events leading to the Mutiny, not many missionaries appear to have suffered. According to the records of the time, 'thirty-eight missionaries, chaplains, and members of their families died in the course of the outbreak. About twenty Indian Christian victims are recorded, but here there is less certainty about the numbers, which may have been far greater than is suggested by the record' (Neill, 1964, pp. 279–80).

The British establishment was severely shocked. As a consequence of the Mutiny, various political actions took place. British administration was tightened up, more Indians were brought into decision-making bodies, more British recruited for the Indian Army, and the East India Company, already a rather moribund organization even before the Mutiny, was wound up. Queen Victoria made a proclamation designed to calm what now became more clearly her Indian subjects. British missionaries in India objected to the religious freedoms for all Hindus, Muslims and other religionists contained in the proclamation. The proclamation said, among other things, 'we do strictly charge and enjoin all those who may be in authority under us, that they abstain from all interference with the religious belief, or worship, of any of our subjects on pain of our severest displeasure'. One missionary interpreted this statement to mean that British administrators were restricted from interfering in activities that Christians would consider idolatrous or in some way objectionable. (Previous administrations had, for instance, outlawed the practice of *sati*.) The statement, according to this missionary,

> interferes with [the administrators'] Christian liberty, their personal duty, appointed and enforced by a higher Master than any human government; and amidst opportunities of usefulness greater than any that are enjoyed in England, it puts a gag upon their tongue, and a handcuff on their arm. Hoping to save the native, it really persecutes the Christian.

(Mullens, 1859, p. 12)

Obviously, strongly held attitudes can breed bizarre logic.

Evangelicals believed that the killing and humiliation were an expression of the wrath of God on the British authorities for not pursuing the conversion of India more assiduously. A day of 'national fasting and humiliation' was observed on 7 October 1857, a date that, it is suggested, 'marked the beginning of a shift in public opinion. On 7 October, pulpits of every ecclesiastical and theological complexion hammered home the message that only a Christian policy could save India' (Stanley, 1983, p. 85). The British government, however, in the person of Queen Victoria, believed that the missionary agenda might have been one of the causes of the Mutiny. At least that is one way of understanding the statement on the freedom of religion in the royal proclamation. Much as missionaries like Joseph Mullens might have desired a more robust Christian response from the Queen, generally they appear to have moved closer to the government of India, which replaced East India Company rule. In the latter half of the nineteenth century, the dominant Christian view of British rule in India was that India had been granted to Britain by God and therefore it was the duty of the British to work for the conversion of India. There was more sympathy among the ruling authorities for the missionary view as a response to the ferocity of the Mutiny and the memories of women and children who were killed.

Perhaps the position in the last quarter of the nineteenth century is best summed up by quoting from two sources. The first is an official statement made by the CMS, an Evangelical missionary society of the Church of England which, as the century progressed, moved closer to the centre of the English establishment, and the second an unofficial statement from the CMS's periodical, the *Church Missionary Intelligencer*. The CMS, officially, longed 'that the English speaking race may have the honour of leading the way in a policy of Christian Imperialism, which shall have no other object than to bring nearer the fulfilment of the divine promise that the kingdom of this world is to become the Kingdom of our Lord and Christ'. The *Intelligencer* in 1860 (Vol. 11, p. 151) affirmed that: 'All recent events in India have urged upon us this lesson ... that if we would rule in peace over the heathen entrusted to our charge, we must give to them the Gospel' (quoted in Stanley, 1990, p. 103). According to a recent Evangelical historian:

> The picture, then, is of qualified missionary support for imperialism. Yet, though qualified, the overall identification made 'a powerful moral impact'; and although it often sought to control and alleviate the harsher aspects of imperialism and was inspired by a genuine concern for the welfare of the people who were, or were

likely to be, oppressed, it is difficult to avoid the conclusion that the connection altered missionary attitudes, and the way missionaries were generally perceived, significantly.

(Williams, 1994, p. 398)

Christianity and Commerce

We have seen how close was the relationship between missionaries and government in India, but it is clear that in the case of Christianity and commerce missionaries were also close to the main organization of commerce in India. However, the link between Christianity and commerce is not, perhaps, as clearly seen in the Indian context as it is in the African.

Livingstone's reference to 'commerce and Christianity' at the University of Cambridge in 1857 has been described as 'the fatal ambiguity vitiating the Victorian sense of mission—the propagation of the gospel had been coupled quite unashamedly with the pursuit of British commercial expansion' (Stanley, 1990, p. 70). The full story is not as bad as it may seem, however. It is true that in places where British political influence did not extend the missionaries sometimes followed the traders. But the relationship was never an easy one in such situations. The traders often were exploitative and the missionaries often had to try to defend the local population from depredation and worse at the hands of the traders. Film caricatures of drunken and lascivious European traders in African outposts are, unfortunately, not always an exaggeration. It is also true that, in certain areas of Africa where slave traders operated and thereby contributed to the local economy, missionaries often tried to introduce other methods of trading in order to provide an alternative economy to that of slave trading. It has been claimed, with some justification, that '"Commerce and Christianity" was an anti-slavery ideology' (*ibid.*, p. 71). There were specific examples of leading Evangelicals, such as the members of the Clapham Sect, who actually went about setting up trading companies. Such a one was the Sierra Leone Company, formed in 1790, at a very early time in the history of this missionary period.

It has been argued that missionary involvement in commerce was again, like involvement in education, an implication of the European Enlightenment. There was an assumption that economics, politics and religion formed a whole approach to human affairs. The conjunction of commerce and Christianity was seen as having considerable virtue, but if commerce appeared in an ungodly way then it was to be opposed. It was the firm conviction of many who prosecuted the missionary approach in the nineteenth century that Christianity and commerce were good bedfellows provided only that Christianity was the dominant partner. This is clearly seen in another statement by Livingstone:

> Commerce has the effect of speedily letting the tribes [in Africa] see their mutual dependence. It breaks up the sullen isolation of heathenism. It is so far good. But Christianity alone reaches the very centre of the wants of Africa and the world. The Arabs or Moors are great in commerce, but few will say that they are as amiable as the uncivilized negroes in consequence. You will see I appreciate the effects of commerce much, but those of Christianity much more.
>
> (Schapera, 1961, pp. 301–2; quoted in Stanley, 1990, p. 73)

This interpretation of the link between Christianity and commerce has been identified as the 'providential' explanation of the phenomenon. It has been argued that the 'corner-stone' of the 'intellectual structure' of the kind of evangelicalism that argued the Christian approach to commerce 'was the doctrine of providence. God was the supreme governor of the universe' (Stanley, 1983, p. 72). According to this view, this 'theological and ideological background ... enabled early Victorian Christians to regard the association of commerce and Christianity as such a natural and harmonious alliance' (*ibid.*). Furthermore,

> all the operations of providence were directed towards the end that the earth should be full of the knowledge of the Lord. Human history was the story of the divine preoccupation with the furtherance of the gospel of salvation. God directed all human affairs with this one supreme goal in view.
>
> (*Ibid.*, pp. 72–3)

And, of course, 'all human affairs' included the commercial. According to this interpretation, the action of the missionaries is to be understood almost purely in terms of the religious motivation, the evangelical drive, the drive to achieve a religious, Christian outcome, of those who were the participants in these historical, missionary events. No external or non-religious motivation or proposed outcome is acknowledged and the religious explanation is primary. It may be partly informed, although to a very limited extent, by other contemporary intellectual ideas.

This interpretation of the missionary action has been criticized and a different interpretation offered. The criticism is that too much emphasis has been placed on 'the degree of autonomy to be attributed to ideas, and the primacy of theological or intellectual beliefs in determining the pattern of missionary action ... in writing about late nineteenth-century missionary motivation' (Porter, 1985, p. 598). There is even a serious question mark raised against the too easy assumption that Christianity was a constant accompaniment of commerce. It is argued that, whilst there is some evidence to support the providentialist view of the relationship between commerce and Christianity, there is much stronger evidence to support a view that commerce was seen as acting independently from Christianity as a missionary evangelical force. The main thrust in introducing Christianity to other countries and cultures, it is maintained, was more often based on a motivation to civilize rather than simply to convert, and that different emphases arose from changes in social developments in Britain over the period of missionary endeavour in the nineteenth century. Beginning from the early part of the nineteenth century it has been argued that:

> By 1800, there were few who took an uncritical or broadly tolerant view of non-European societies, fewer still who admired their achievements. The duty of benevolence was enjoined on both religious and secular grounds: its fulfilment necessitated the civilization of the peoples of Africa and Asia ... British law, commerce, good government, literature, education were all it seemed for export.
>
> (*Ibid.*, pp. 599–600)

In considering the contrasting merits of the 'providentialist' and 'civilizationist' views of the relationship between Christianity and commerce there is a balance to be achieved by recognizing that both interpretations are valid at different times and in different places during the nineteenth century. There is evidence that some earlier missionary views were antithetical to commerce, hence the BMS's concern about Carey's involvement in the indigo trade (see p.107 above). There is clear evidence to the contrary in Livingstone's view that Christianity and commerce could work hand in hand. There is also evidence that some missionaries saw the need to establish commerce themselves as a way of emancipating the people they hoped to convert. Towards the end of the period under consideration the pendulum had swung away from too close an association between Christianity and commerce, and a negative perception of commerce took over in evangelical circles. The conclusion of one of the participants in this debate is that: 'Missionary attitudes to commerce were thus the result of an interplay between the Enlightenment conviction that sound commerce would promote liberty and even religion, and the distinctively evangelical emphasis that Christianity alone was the key to health and happiness in society' (Stanley, 1990, pp. 72–3).

Christianity and Culture (or Civilization)

If there is one area in which the legacy of nineteenth-century missions still causes problems for the churches set up in various lands as a result of that activity it is in the area of Christianity's impact on culture, or the Christian notion of civilization.

What we find today in India, for instance, in cities, towns and villages, are remnants of the Gothic revival, which is so much part of the physical expansion of religion in Britain during the nineteenth century. An example is the church of St Paul's, Pune (or Poona), dating from 1867. Apart from one architectural feature the building was indistinguishable in design from hundreds of Anglican and some Nonconformist churches built in Britain during the same historical period. As the *Deccan Herald* (a local Pune newspaper) of 6 March 1867 reported: 'This structure is of the early English style of Gothic architecture' (Jadhav, 1967, p. 28). At the ceremony of laying the foundation-stone by Sir Bartle Frere, Governor of Bombay, in 1863, the Reverend Mr Gell is reported in the *Poona Observer* of 1 September 1863 to have said:

> The plans now adopted have been the result of mature delibera-
> tions in which Your Excellency, and the Commander-in-Chief, have
> with kind interest personally taken part and we feel every hope that
> the church now to be commenced, will prove the superior
> adaptability of Christian architecture, to the necessities of an
> Indian Climate.
>
> (*Ibid.*, p. 26)

The 'adaptability' must be a reference to one architectural feature which stands out as a concession to the Indian climate, namely the number of doors along each side of the church that can be left open to catch whatever breeze may stir during the hot season. The church building was designed by the Reverend Mr Gell himself and was intended for 'the increasingly important non-official and Eurasian community for whom insufficient accommodation could be afforded in St. Mary's Church' (*ibid.*). This was the other Anglican church built in the military cantonment area, consecrated by Bishop Heber, the author of the hymn 'From Greenland's icy mountains', in 1825 and 'primarily devoted to [the] military' (*ibid.*). Both churches still stand and serve the English-speaking Christian community of Pune. In both cases nothing is more designed to set Christianity apart, in a way undesired by many contemporary Christians in India, than this architectural heritage.

Missionaries working in the western India state of Maharashtra communicated through the medium of Marathi, the language of 36 millions of the population of the state. A teacher of Marathi in a college of Pune University was once heard to say, in a lighter moment in rather an intense language course, that there were three kinds of Marathi: *deshiya*, that is, the Marathi of the Deccan plateau, *konkanastha*, the Marathi of the coastal plain south of Bombay, and missionary Marathi. The teacher was referring to the standard of Marathi spoken by missionaries but also to the standard of the translation of the Bible into that language. Monier Williams referred to this translation in 1861 and thought it could be improved by better knowledge of Sanskrit. Although there were singular exceptions—the Urdu translation of the Bible was always rated highly—reference to poor translation of the Scriptures stands as an example of the cultural gap between Christianity and the Indian.

Although there were exceptional missionaries, especially in the late nineteenth century, who adopted a tolerant attitude towards the cultural phenomena they encountered in India and elsewhere, generally speaking missionary attitudes were of the negative kind:

> There can be little dispute that, for most of the nineteenth century, British Christians believed that the missionary was called to propagate the imagined benefits of Western civilization alongside the Christian message. It was assumed that the poor, benighted 'heathen' were in a condition of massive cultural deprivation, which the gospel alone could remedy. At present they were shockingly different from civilized Europeans; in years to come, when gospel power had done its work, those differences would be largely eliminated. However, this fundamental theological conviction that Christianity would exert a standardizing influence on other peoples was in practice modified, to a greater or lesser extent, by the impact of actual experience of other societies.

(Stanley, 1990, pp. 157–8)

The same author goes on to list four 'prior assumptions' in the minds of British missionaries, which informed their actions and responses to what they saw when they arrived in such countries as India. The first was 'that the cultures which missionaries were penetrating were in no sense religiously neutral—rather they were under the control of the Evil One' (*ibid.*, p. 161). A sign of this was the participation of Hindus in idolatrous practices. Secondly, it was supposed 'that nineteenth-century Britain constituted a model of Christian culture and society' (*ibid.*). Thirdly, the 'confidence of British Christians in the essential benevolence of their own culture rested ... on the implicit faith in human progress which was one of the legacies of the Enlightenment to Christian thought' (*ibid.*). The fourth assumption was that what the missionaries had to offer in the way of civilizing activities actually worked. They had evidence from such places as Sierra Leone, where there had been a rapid growth of the Church among the erstwhile slaves (*ibid.*, p. 162).

Compared with some other areas of missionary activity, India presented a different prospect. Whereas in Africa and in the South Seas the local people appeared to be 'primitive' with no written works and, as the missionaries saw it, little or no morals either, India presented the missionaries with an agglomeration of sophisticated beliefs, coherent structured religious practices and a morality that was strict in many ways, although in some respects repugnant to westerners. Such practices as *sati*, and other forms of self-immolation and, in some temples, animal sacrifices, offended Christian sensibilities. The most offensive aspect of Hinduism was probably what the missionaries knew as 'idolatry'.

So-called idolatry was particularly anathema to Protestant, Evangelical Christians. In part the Protestant Reformation had been the reform of the Church in respect of statues and images such as those of the Virgin Mary and other saints. Missionaries who read Monier Williams and Max Müller would have been encouraged in their view of idolatry. Williams could speak of certain forms of Hinduism as 'grotesque forms of idolatry, and the most degrading varieties of superstition'. In the writings of Max Müller, for 'idolatry' read 'fetish'. Fetishism, according to Max Müller, was 'the superstitious veneration felt and testified for mere rubbish' (Max Müller, 1882, p. 65). We obtain a picture of Max Müller's evaluation of religion in his discussion of progress or evolution and retrogression in religion. 'The Hindus,' he maintains, 'who, thousands of years ago, had reached in the Upanishads the loftiest heights of philosophy, are now in some places sunk into a grovelling worship of cows and monkeys' (*ibid.*, p. 69). Max Müller was, of course, raised as a Lutheran Protestant and not only did he abhor what he described as fetishism, he considered the study of such a phenomenon as not worthy of scholars of the science of religion. Missionaries wrote to him to express their gratitude for his scholarship in their struggle to convert the Hindu.

That which western Christianity, especially Protestant Christianity, deems to be idolatry can be viewed in an entirely different light. The use of images, or icons, grew out of an attempt to visualize the invisible, to create a way through what is finite in order to reach the infinite. This sacramental or iconic impulse is present in most forms of religion. Even in religious traditions in which the iconic is formally abjured, we can still find language or abstract expressions that are in essence iconic. A clear expression of the iconic use of a material object is the use of the Bible, both verbally and physically, in much of Protestant Christianity. Of course, in the Hindu context the feelings of missionaries were exacerbated by the hideousness of what they saw: idols with elephant heads and human bodies, or monkey heads and human bodies, eight-armed human figures, female figures riding bulls and killing lions, more abstract objects that were horribly reminiscent, as they were meant to be, of male and female genitalia. They abhorred what they saw and the practices associated with the veneration of images confirmed their worst fears about the evil that they were called to eradicate. However, as the century wore on there were those under the influence of such as Monier Williams, who could write dispassionately on the Hindu view of images, who came to a more rational understanding of what the dynamics of the veneration of images were.

There is no question that the missionaries' attitudes towards the objects of their evangelization was often racist. In West Africa the first African bishop, Samuel Crowther, found that Anglican white missionaries refused to acknowledge his leadership and split the local mission. A missionary in the Sudan confided to his diary that he had come to the bitter conclusion that 'we can trust nothing with a black skin on it'. In these matters the missionaries in many ways reflected the mores of their age and civilization. After all, the slavery of oppressed ethnic groups was only abolished legally in 1833. Up until the period of the European Enlightenment, the Christian world had, apparently, seen nothing contradictory in embracing the gospel and approving the institution of slavery.

It was quite late in the century before a significant shift occurred in the appreciation of African or Indian cultures. The growth in the study of other religions did have the effect of enhancing the western and hence the missionary view of other cultures.[4]

III CONCLUSION

There is no question that the missionary aspect of British religion during the Victorian period was very substantial and presents a complex picture. Only a small portion of the whole has been looked at here. References have been made to foreign missionary work in every quarter of the globe

---

[4] See *RVB*, II, 13.

and by many nations of the Christian West. It is important, nevertheless, to keep a sense of proportion. Some of the statistics presented in this chapter may appear quite impressive, but missionary endeavour was always no more than the interest of comparatively few of the members of British churches. There were always those who objected to missionary work, especially to missionary fervour. This was particularly true in the Church of England early in the nineteenth century, but a remnant of this kind persisted throughout the Victorian period. At the other end of the spectrum there were those who were fanatical about missionary work and gave prodigally of their substance and their lives to the missionary cause. It is a salutary experience to visit old cemeteries in India and see the resting places of hundreds of people, women and children as well as the men who normally ran things, and to see the young ages recorded on the tombstones. However, the vast majority of members of the British churches were indifferent to missionary work, seeing their Christian obligation more in terms of the maintenance of the status quo, politically, socially and religiously.

Small though the effort was in overall terms, the effect was not inconsiderable and the presence of churches of various kinds in all the countries of the world stand as a testimony that not all the grain fell on stony ground. Out of this missionary endeavour came the ecumenical movement, born in countries like India, which worked to overcome the denominational difference that divided Christians, sometimes very bitterly, and based on old western Christian divisions. This movement led in turn to the establishment of the World Council of Churches, which in the late twentieth century is involved socially and politically in many parts of the world. The aid programmes in Third World countries have been especially important.

It will have been obvious that the whole missionary enterprise was a mixture of strong faith, courage, folly, mixed motivations. Missionaries were, after all, human beings, and were subject to the strengths and weaknesses of being human. Since most of this chapter has been concerned with India, perhaps a word from India will sum up the ambivalence that some commentators recognize in the sum total of missionary activity.

Let us end with something from Rudyard Kipling, having begun with Charlotte Brontë. In 1886, Kipling was twenty-one years of age and working as a reporter on the *Civil and Military Gazette* in Lahore (now in Pakistan). He began to write short stories drawn from his experiences of the British Raj. The stories were later published in book form. In the first of his *Plain Tales from the Hills* (1888), Kipling tells the tale of 'Lispeth', a girl born to a Hill-man and his wife who when their crops had failed became Christians and had their daughter baptized Elizabeth. Her parents died when she was still a child and she grew up in a Mission in the home of a Chaplain and his wife. She grew tall and beautiful and eventually fell in love with an Englishman who feigned to love her back and when he went away swore that he would return to marry her. He never did. After Lispeth had pined for some months the Chaplain's wife eventually told her that it was never intended that the Englishman should return to marry her, that it was 'an excuse to keep you quiet, child'. 'Then you have lied to me,' said Lispeth, 'you and he?' The Chaplain's wife made no reply. Lispeth immediately left the Mission and returned dressed in Hill-woman's dress, saying 'I am going back to my own people ... You have killed Lispeth.' She returned to her folk, where she was married to a woodcutter 'who beat her after the manner of *paharis*'. '"There is no law whereby you can account for the vagaries of the heathen," said the Chaplain's wife, "and I believe that Lispeth was always at heart an infidel."' The narrator muses: 'Seeing she had been taken into the Church of England at the mature age of five weeks, this statement does not do credit to the Chaplain's wife' (Kipling, 1923 edn, p. 8).

Kipling prefaces his tales with short poems, presumably written by himself since they bear no other name. The preface to the tale of Lispeth reads as follows:

> Look, you have cast out Love! What Gods are these
> You bid me please?
> The Three in One, the One in Three? Not so!
> To my own gods I go.
> It may be they shall give me greater ease
> Than your cold Christ and tangled Trinities.

(*Ibid.*, p. 1)

The poem is entitled 'The Convert'!

BIBLIOGRAPHY

D. W. Bebbington (1990) 'William Carey' in Dowley (1990), p. 572.

C. Brontë (1966 edn) *Jane Eyre*, ed. Q. D. Leavis, Harmondsworth, Penguin Books (first published 1847).

P. Carson (1990) 'An imperial dilemma: the propagation of Christianity in early colonial India', *Journal of Imperial and Commonwealth History*, Vol. 18, pp. 169–90.

*T. Dowley (ed.) (1990) *The History of Christianity* (A Lion Handbook), Tring, Lion Publishing (first published 1977).

B. Jadhav (1967) '100 Years of St. Paul's Church, Poona' in *St. Paul's Church Poona: 1867–1967, Centenary Souvenir*, pp. 24–43.

R. Kipling (1923 edn) *Plain Tales from the Hills*, London, Macmillan (first published 1888).

*K. S. Latourette (1938–45) A *History of the Expansion of Christianity*, 7 vols., London, Eyre & Spottiswoode.

J. Mullens (1859) *The Queen's Government and the Religions of India*, London, Ward.

F. Max Müller (1882) *Lectures on the Origin and Growth of Religion*, London, Longmans, Green.

J. Mitchener (1959) *Hawaii*, New York, Random House.

*S. Neill (1964) A *History of Christian Missions*, Harmondsworth, Penguin Books.

G. A. Oddie (1974) 'India and missionary motives, c. 1850–1900', *Journal of Ecclesiastical History*, Vol. 25, pp. 61–74.

A. Porter (1985) '"Commerce and Christianity": the rise and fall of the nineteenth-century missionary slogan', *Historical Journal*, Vol. 28, pp. 597–621.

A. Porter (1992) 'Religion and Empire: British expansion in the long nineteenth century, 1780–1914', *Journal of Imperial and Commonwealth History*, Vol. 20, pp. 370–90.

S. C. Potter (1974) *The Social Origins and Recruitment of English Protestant Missionaries in the Nineteenth Century*, PhD thesis, University of London.

I. Schapera (ed.) (1961) *Livingstone's Missionary Correspondence 1841–1856*, London, Chatto & Windus.

P. Spear (1975 edn) A *History of India 2*, Harmondsworth, Penguin Books (first published 1965).

*B. Stanley (1983) '"Commerce and Christianity": providence theory, the missionary movement, and the imperialism of free trade', *Historical Journal*, Vol. 26, pp. 71–94.

B. Stanley (1990) *The Bible and the Flag: Protestant Missions and British Imperialism in the Nineteenth and Twentieth Centuries*, Leicester, Apollos.

A. F. Walls (1990a) 'Outposts of Empire' in Dowley (1990), pp. 557–70.

A. F. Walls (1990b) 'Societies for mission' in Dowley (1990), pp. 571–6.

A. F. Walls (1990c) 'David Livingstone' in Dowley (1990), pp. 564–5.

*C. P. Williams (1994) 'British religion and the wider world: mission and Empire, 1800–1940' in S. Gilley and W. J. Shiels, A *History of Religion in Britain*, ch. 20, Oxford, Blackwell.

J. Williams (1837) A *Narrative of Missionary Enterprises in the South Sea Islands*, London.

H. Willmer (1962) 'Evangelicalism 1785 to 1835', Hulsean Prize Essay, University of Cambridge.

CHAPTER 4

MEN OF THE DAY. NO. 92. THE RIGHT REV. JOHN
WILLIAM COLENSO, D.D., BISHOP OF NATAL

'... he desires to live in charity with all men, and is yet
fated to find himself engaged in conflicts which those
only can avoid who are content to stand by and see
Truth despised, and Justice trodden underfoot'.

RETHINKING THE MISSIONARY POSITION: BISHOP COLENSO OF NATAL

AT a special service early on the morning of 7 January 1866, in the cathedral church of St Peter's in Pietermaritzburg, Natal, the Dean, the Reverend J. R. Green, read out a 'sentence of greater excommunication' passed by the Bishop of Cape Town, Robert Gray, then the senior bishop in the Anglican Church in southern Africa. The sentence proclaimed that the man excommunicated was separated

> ... from the Communion of the Church of Christ, so long as he shall obstinately and impertinently persist in his heresy and claim to exercise the office of a Bishop within the Province of Cape Town. And we do hereby make known to the faithful in Christ, that, being thus excluded from all communion with the Church, he is, according to our Lord's command, and in conformity with the provisions of the Thirty-third of the Articles of Religion, 'to be taken of the whole multitude of the faithful as a heathen man and publican'.
>
> (Quoted in Guy, 1983a, pp. 157–8)

In a pastoral letter to the clergy and laity of the Diocese of Natal, to supplement and explain the excommunication, Bishop Gray added that:

> The heresies into which Dr Colenso has fallen are no light or common errors. They touch the very life and being of the Christian Church, overthrow the faith of Christendom. It is not merely the distinctive teaching of the Church of England that he has impugned. He has assailed those fundamental truths of our common Christianity, which are equally cherished by the Churches of the East and the West, and by every sect and denomination of Protestant Christians. It is with Christianity itself, as a revelation from God, that he is at war.
>
> (*Ibid.*)

The man thus excommunicated was John William Colenso, the Anglican Bishop of Natal, at once ecclesiastical leader of the Anglicans among the white settlers of colonial Natal, head of the Church of England mission to the black population of Natal and Zululand, and brother Bishop Robert Gray of Cape Town. Even in the context of the highly charged and bitter controversies of the Victorian Church of England, the solemn excommunication of one bishop by another was a dramatic and extraordinary event. How then did it come to pass that in mid-Victorian colonial southern Africa, far away—or so it would seem—from the passionate turmoils of the Victorian Church of England, just such an event should occur, in a diocese on the missionary frontier of the Church?

Most accounts of the Colenso affair present the controversy as, essentially, either a chapter in the history of Victorian biblical criticism and the furore surrounding mid-Victorian Broad Church theology, or an incident in the changing relationship between church and state in Victorian England.[1] There is, however, another and quite different dimension to the story of John William Colenso and his 'heresies'. That other story focuses primarily not upon the theological and constitutional controversies of the Church of England but, rather, upon the missionary origins and the pastoral and evangelistic context of Colenso's pilgrimage into theological liberalism and consequent conflict with his church. It is this second and less often recounted history with which the present chapter is concerned.

I THE MAKING OF A MISSIONARY

John William Colenso was born at St Austell in Cornwall on 24 January 1814. Although of Nonconformist background, his family had joined the Church of England in 1827 and by 1830 John William was already helping the local parish priest in his pastoral work and considering ordination into the ministry of the Church of England. The young Colenso has been described as intense and precocious and as having an evangelical faith characterized by a grim concern with the fate of the souls of those to whom he ministered in helping the local priest (Guy, 1983a, pp. 4–5). In 1832 Colenso entered St John's College, Cambridge, and secured academic success in 1836 as that year's second best student in Mathematics in the whole of the University. Elected a fellow of St John's, he was ordained in 1839 and also took up a teaching post at Harrow School, only to suffer financial hardship when his house burned down. In order to pay the resulting debts, he returned to his Fellowship at St John's and, as well as being a tutor, became a highly successful writer of school arithmetic textbooks.

In matters of faith and belief, Colenso remained, thus far, a somewhat austere and evangelical Low Churchman. In the early 1840s, however, this began to change. In 1842 he met Sarah Frances Bunyon, two years younger than himself and the daughter of a London insurance broker. They quickly became engaged and were eventually married in January

---

[1] As, for example, in *RVB*, I, 1, pp. 43 and 62–3; and in *RVB*, II, 4, pp. 99–101 and *RVB*, II, 11, pp. 245–6.

1846, by which time Colenso had accepted appointment as Rector of the parish of Forncett St Mary's in Norfolk. Frances (as Sarah Frances Bunyon was commonly called) was not only to be a deeply committed partner to Colenso during the rest of his life, eventually outliving him by ten years, but was also an intriguing figure in her own right. Moreover, she was a crucial influence in the development of Colenso's religious beliefs, faith and theology. Also brought up an evangelical, by her mid-twenties Frances Bunyon had rejected evangelicalism, finding the basis of her subsequent faith in the writings and thought of Samuel Taylor Coleridge and F. D. Maurice. Within months of meeting Colenso, Frances had introduced him to the writings and ideas of both Coleridge and Maurice. Through family contacts, she was also instrumental in introducing Colenso to Maurice himself. John Colenso and Frances Bunyon thus became members of Maurice's theological circle in the early 1840s and Colenso and Maurice struck up a close friendship. Maurice in due course conducted the marriage of John Colenso and Frances Bunyon in 1846 (Guy, 1983a, pp. 3–4, 12–14 and 24–33; Rees, 1958, pp. 17–20 and 25–30).

For Colenso, the introduction to the religious and theological ideas of Coleridge and Maurice was fundamental, both for his own faith and for his subsequent career. He found a new and liberating breadth in the religious and theological outlook to which his fiancée introduced him. In particular, he found in Coleridge a liberation from reading the Bible in a literal way and from a faith based on miracles, signs, rational 'evidences' and intellectual 'proofs'. Instead, Coleridge presented the possibility of a faith based upon experience; an understanding of Christianity as a life and a living process rather than a philosophy or set of beliefs. In Maurice, meanwhile, Colenso found an emphasis on God as loving Father rather than stern Judge and a consequent rejection of the ideas of both eternal punishment and substitutionary atonement in favour of a belief in the universal redemption of humanity. He also found the conviction that, since God was present in all humanity, therefore God's spirit and witness were already present in some way in all cultures and societies, both Christian and non-Christian (Guy, 1983a, pp. 23–9).

The Colensos remained at Forncett St Mary's for seven years, until 1853, immersed in the work of parochial ministry and also steadily developing an interest in missionary work overseas. John Colenso had been attracted to such work from as early as 1839 after hearing a sermon on behalf of the Society for the Propagation of the Gospel in Foreign Parts (SPG) by the future Bishop of Oxford, Samuel Wilberforce. During the years at Forncett St Mary's, Colenso accordingly acted as local organizing secretary for the SPG and edited two of its journals, *The Church in the Colonies* and the *Monthly Record.* In 1847, meanwhile, Frances Colenso's sister Harriette and her husband sailed for Borneo as missionaries, under the auspices of the Church Missionary Society, he eventually becoming Bishop of Labuan (Guy, 1983a, p. 33; Rees, 1958, pp. 32–3). It was not until 1852, however, that an opportunity occurred for the Colensos to act upon their own missionary ambitions.

In 1852, Bishop Robert Gray of Cape Town was in England seeking suitable candidates for the newly created South African bishoprics of Grahamstown and Natal. When he visited the diocese of Norwich, Colenso was recommended to him as a possible appointee and Gray duly offered Colenso the post of first Bishop of Natal. After a period to consider the offer, Colenso accepted in April 1853 and on 30 November that year was duly consecrated in Lambeth parish church as the first Bishop of Natal. At the consecration he was formally presented to the Archbishop of Canterbury by Gray, and by Gray's close episcopal friend, Samuel Wilberforce, by now Bishop of Oxford. The formal presentation of Colenso by Gray and Wilberforce—both of whom were theologically traditional and conservative High Churchmen—was a moment pregnant with both irony and pathos. Within thirteen years Gray was to excommunicate Colenso for his alleged theological heresies and Wilberforce was to be one of the most vociferous opponents of Colenso among the English bishops.

The events of 1853, moreover, become somewhat perplexing when viewed in relation to the appearance of Colenso's first theological work—a collection of sermons published in October 1853, after he had accepted the see of Natal, but before his consecration. Colenso's *Village Sermons* contained eight sermons preached at Forncett St Mary's and one—on the singularly relevant subject of missionary teaching—preached at Great St Mary's, Cambridge, in March 1853. The book was dedicated to Colenso's friend and mentor F. D. Maurice. In particular, he applauded Maurice for his teaching that Christ died for all, not just for some, and that God loved all '... the poor dark heathens of Africa, as well as ... the far more highly privileged, and, therefore, also far more highly accountable, Christians of England—and that we all belong, not to the Devil, but to CHRIST, though we are not yet baptized into Him' (Colenso, 1853, p. viii).

In the sermon on missionary teaching, Colenso showed that he already understood the missionary vocation in distinctively Maurician terms. The missionary, Colenso argued, should not begin with 'words of terror on his lips' seeking to tell the unconverted 'heathen' of 'the dreadful hell, which their sins of ignorance have deserved' and 'into which their forefathers have already passed'. Rather, the missionary should begin with 'the voice of comfort and love' and should be willing to discover God's witness already present in the hearts of the unconverted as well as proclaiming the message of Christ to them:

> I believe that, by thus meeting the heathen, half way, as it were, upon the grounds of our common humanity, and with the recollection that that humanity is now blessed and redeemed in Christ—that we are all redeemed, not accursed creatures ... we may look for far greater success in missionary labours, and far more of stability in the converts that may be made, than by seeking to make all things new to them—to uproot altogether their old religion, scoffing at the things which they hold most sacred ... which alone have stood to them, for so many years long, as the representatives of the spiritual world.
>
> (Colenso, 1853, pp. 141–2)

Thus did Colenso, bishop designate of Natal, make clear the essentially Broad Church and Maurician nature of his theology and his conception of the missionary task. He did so, moreover, at a time when Maurice's views were already the subject of fierce controversy and when Maurice was on the way to dismissal from his chair at King's College London because of the unorthodoxy of his theological opinions.[2] Nor did Colenso's espousal of such unorthodoxy go unremarked. Both Evangelical and High Church newspapers protested at this expression of liberal theological opinion by a soon-to-be missionary bishop. The Evangelical *Record* attacked Colenso's theology fiercely, whilst the *Church and State Gazette* asked pointedly:

> ... if Professor Maurice be dismissed for his teaching, what then is to become of Dr. Colenso, the newly-appointed Bishop of Natal, who declares in his recently published volume of sermons that, if he knows much of Christianity, almost all his knowledge is owing to the teaching to which he listened at the feet of the Professor?
>
> (Quoted in Guy, 1983a, p. 43)

There remains the puzzle, therefore, of why Gray and Wilberforce were still willing to present Colenso for consecration despite his theologically liberal views, of which—given the publication of *Village Sermons* and the reactions of the theologically conservative press—both bishops must

---

[2] For the controversy over Maurice's views and its place within Victorian Anglican theological controversy, see *RVB* I, 1, pp. 39–40.

surely have been aware. If Gray was troubled by such theology, why did he not withdraw his offer of the bishopric of Natal? Gray's biography does not address the question (Gray, 1876, Vol. 1, p. 371). It may have been that the sheer shortage of candidates for the new dioceses was too great to allow Gray the luxury of such a course of action. Or he may have assumed that Colenso would abandon his unorthodox theological ideas once safely installed in Natal and engaged with the realities and demands of the missionary task. If so, Gray could not have been more wrong. Whatever the explanation, however, it did little credit to Gray and Wilberforce that they presented for consecration a man whose theological unorthodoxy was already a matter of public knowledge, only subsequently to complain bitterly of his theological 'weakness' and 'heresy' and to excommunicate him—but in December 1853, all that lay in the future.

II   THE SEEDS OF CONTROVERSY

The newly consecrated Bishop Colenso paid his first visit to Natal during early 1854. He spent ten weeks travelling through the immense diocese for which he was to be responsible, learning as much as he could as quickly as he could about both the white settler community and the much larger black population. He then returned to England and spent much of 1854 raising funds for his new diocese and its missionary needs. He also published an account of his visit—*Ten Weeks in Natal: a journal of a first tour of visitation among the colonists and Zulu Kafirs of Natal* (Colenso, 1855)—the proceeds of which went towards the fund-raising. The Colenso family, together with the rest of the mission party, eventually left for Natal in March 1855, arriving in late May at what was to become the bishop's residence, 'Bishopstowe', together with a combined mission station and mission school known as 'Ekukhanyeni' (the 'Place of light') outside Pietermaritzburg.

From the outset, Colenso found himself immersed in controversy, a state of affairs that continued until the end of his life. Why was this so? Like most history, the history of Colenso and his controversies has been written, for the most part, by the winners—and Colenso ended, emphatically, on the losing side. Consequently, the conventional explanation of the controversies that surrounded him during his years in Natal emphasizes *his* alleged personal failings—most notably an alleged combination of unbending stubbornness and naïvity, in turn combined with an enthusiasm for controversy and a sceptical, doubting temperament unsuited to the task of being either a bishop or a missionary, let alone both. These failings—it is then argued—caused Colenso to pursue eccentric and unorthodox theological views in a blunt and unimaginative manner and thus led inexorably to his excommunication.[3] This is a convenient explanation for those historians for whom Colenso—more than a century after his death—still continues to raise irksome and stubbornly intractable theological issues. It is also, however, rather less than convincing. A more credible explanation is to be found in the complex and highly combustible combination of circumstances—theological, ecclesiastical and political as well as personal—that existed in Natal in the 1850s, 60s and 70s.

Colenso went to Natal as a missionary bishop who had already moved from evangelicalism to a Broad Church, 'Maurician' faith and theology. In particular, he already questioned the traditional doctrines of eternal punishment and substitutionary atonement, and he firmly believed that God's witness was present somewhere within the culture and traditions of those to whom he was to be a missionary. He went to a colony at that time on the edge of the empire, to be both bishop of the existing (but small) white Anglican church among the settlers in Natal and missionary bishop to the black population—a dual role fraught with potential tensions. The settlers were characteristically independent-minded frontier individualists, suspicious of a bishop who might try to assume an English 'establishment' status and leadership in 'their' colony. Colenso, moreover, took to his role as missionary bishop a conviction that God was already present somewhere within African culture. As a result of this belief, although he was a Christian paternalist who believed that British culture constituted a 'civilized' Christian 'norm' and that it was Britain's role to bring both Christianity and education to the indigenous population of Africa, he nevertheless insisted also that both African culture and society and the African population were to be treated with respect, not merely exploited and abused. For Colenso, British colonial expansion was, above all, a sacred trust and duty. This, however, was a view of African culture and the status of the black population not generally shared by the white

---

[3] For a summary and critique of such conventional interpretations, see Guy, 1983a, especially pp. 54–5, 58–61, 79–80 and 174–89. For influential accounts of Colenso that contain conventional negative assumptions and stereotypes even when seeking to acknowledge more positive aspects of his career and character, see Hinchliff, 1962, 1963 and 1964, and Chadwick, 1972. For an example of the continuing dismissal of Colenso in general histories of Victorian Anglicanism, see Gilley, 1994, p. 303. On the particular question of Colenso's alleged bluntness and insensitivity it is also worth asking why *his* repeated insistence on seeking plain answers to the issues he raised should so often be judged a fault, whilst the propensity of his opponents (including his fellow bishops) to denounce him as, variously, 'heretical', 'blasphemous', 'abominable', 'blind', 'ignorant', 'half-informed' or even an 'instrument of Satan' is more usually passed over or implicitly regarded as no more than the understandable expression of an outraged orthodoxy. For the above list of epithets for Colenso, see Deist, 1984, p. 107.

settlers of Natal (Guy, 1983a, pp. 47–51; 1991, pp. 189–91; Edgecombe, 1980, pp. 15–16).

In addition to these sources of potential conflict, however, there were then added the theological tensions and controversies of the Victorian Church of England. Although it was only the 1850s, and although it was some thousands of miles away from Oxford and England, by the time Colenso reached Natal the theological parties and battle lines of the Church of England had already got there before him. A substantial part of the laity in his new diocese was staunchly Protestant and Evangelical. Some of the clergy in his diocese, however—including most notably J. R. Green, previously appointed as 'Rural Dean' of Natal by Bishop Gray of Cape Town and in due course to read out Gray's excommunication of Colenso in 1866—were equally staunch Tractarians. Robert Gray, himself, was a traditional and conservative High Churchman, also now influenced by the Oxford Movement and determined that the Church of England in southern Africa over which he presided would be firmly under his episcopal control and authority and not compromised—as the Church of England itself appeared to be after the Gorham Judgement—by interference from the secular state and its courts.[4]

It was indeed a combustible mixture and Colenso duly found himself embroiled in controversy from the very beginning of his time in Natal. Thus, by 1856 the predominantly Evangelical laity of Durban had come to perceive Colenso to be a High Churchman of potentially tyrannical temperament—their grounds for this included Colenso's willingness to allow his clergy to wear a surplice when preaching; his exclusion of non-communicants from voting in parish vestry meetings; and his insistence upon regular offertory collections to avoid financial dependence upon private pew-rents. They therefore accused him of being 'Tractarian' and 'Papistical' and burnt him in effigy in the market square in Durban, accompanied by banners proclaiming 'No Popery' and 'Down with the Bishop'. At the other end of the theological spectrum, meanwhile, Colenso found himself in conflict with genuine Tractarians among his clergy, including, in particular, Dean Green at Pietermaritzburg. By them Colenso stood accused of unorthodoxy in his teaching on the nature of the presence of Christ in the Eucharist. Colenso's staunchly Protestant stance offended Green's equally staunchly Tractarian insistence upon a Catholic interpretation of the sacraments. In 1858, Green wrote to Bishop Gray at Cape Town formally accusing Colenso of heresy (Hinchliff, 1963,

---

[4] For the Gorham Judgement and its significance for the Victorian Church of England, see *RVB*, I, 1, pp. 37–8 and *RVB*, II, 4, pp. 96–8.

pp. 49–50 and 82–3; 1964, pp. 69–74; Guy, 1983a, pp. 56–8; Brain, 1984, pp. 384–6).

On this occasion Gray rejected the charge of heresy, but already he was himself showing irritation with Colenso. In particular, Gray apparently became impatient with what he saw as undue frankness in Colenso's letters to him. Gray, it seems, expected more respect and less bluntness from a bishop he had appointed and whom he saw as his subordinate. Colenso, for his part, was already frustrated that Gray—far away in Cape Town—seemed to expect him to expend great energy and effort on accommodating the theological prejudices and predilections of his clergy and laity in Natal. Colenso, however, believed that his priority should be the time-consuming business of learning the Zulu language and preparing a translation of the Bible into Zulu. Gray, he thought, had little idea how demanding this missionary task was (Guy, 1983a, pp. 59–61 and 66).

Within four years of Colenso beginning his work in Natal, therefore, the foundations were already laid for the major conflict with Gray that was to occupy the 1860s and attract the attention not just of the Church in southern Africa but of the whole Church of England—and, indeed, of the Victorian press and public as well. That controversy, however, had its origins not in the squabbles over churchmanship of the High Church clergy and Low Church laity of white settler Natal, but in Colenso's missionary work among the Zulu and the impact of this upon his own, already liberal, theology. From the very beginning of his engagement with the missionary dimension of his work as Bishop of Natal, Colenso's already liberal theological views and the demands of presenting Christianity to the Zulu worked creatively upon each other. His liberal theological outlook caused him to see existing missionary work from an unconventional perspective, whilst the demands and challenges of the missionary context, once viewed from such a perspective, then acted as a further catalyst to his theological liberalism.

This process of mutual interaction was clear even in the published accounts of Colenso's preliminary visit to Natal in early 1854. In both *Ten Weeks in Natal* and a shorter pamphlet, *Church Missions among the Heathen in the Diocese of Natal* (1854), Colenso not only gave a description of the colony, its landscape and people, but also expressed ideas about missionary work and its relationship with the culture and religion of the indigenous black population of Natal which were subsequently to involve him in the two major controversies of his life and to determine the course of his career. From the outset, Colenso was deeply critical of the existing missionary preaching and practice that he found in southern

Africa. In particular, he was appalled by the prevalence of a traditional understanding of hell and eternal punishment within the preaching of the majority of the missionaries at work in the colony. To teach the African population that eternal torment was the divinely appointed fate of the unconverted was, Colenso protested, '... utterly contrary to the whole spirit of the Gospel, as obscuring the Grace of God, and perverting His Message of Love and "Goodwill to man", and operating, with most injurious and deadening effect, both on those who teach, and on those who are taught' (Colenso, 1855, p. 253).

It was not only the matter of hell that concerned Colenso, however. He was also exercised by the general repudiation of African culture and religion, of which missionary teaching on eternal punishment and the necessity of conversion was but a part. Where conventional missionary thinking—and white settler attitudes in general—found among the African population only 'superstition', 'immorality', 'irreligion', and an alleged incapacity for either honesty or hard work, Colenso, with his conviction that God was at work within all human societies and cultures, found both moral and religious awareness. For example, he remarked specifically upon the Zulu consciousness of good and evil and right and wrong, and upon the love of family exhibited within Zulu society. The Zulu, Colenso asserted, were 'a spirited and manly people', 'affectionate' and 'docile', and 'in moral character, singularly honest and truthful' (Colenso, quoted in Edgecombe, 1982, p. 2). Moreover, Colenso went further and observed that the Zulu were at present, '... almost wholly free from habits of drunkenness, and, in their intercourse with Europeans, they shrink with abhorrence from some other vices, which have tended so fearfully, in many of our colonies, to the destruction of the native races'.

As for the religious perceptions of the Zulu, far from having no God—as many contemporary white commentators asserted—Colenso reported that they

> ... have certainly two distinct names in their own tongue for the Supreme Being, and very expressive names, namely, un-Kulunkulu, the Great-Great-One, = the Almighty; and un-Velinqange, the First Out-Comer, = the First Essence of Existence. They spoke of Him repeatedly to me, and quite of their own accord, as the Maker of all things and all men.
>
> (Quoted in Edgecombe, 1982, p. 2)

They also now, moreover, devised a name for Colenso himself, as bishop, calling him 'Sobantu' (meaning 'Father of the People') a name '... entirely of their own invention, and constructed out of the notions which they have formed of the Bishop's duties from what they have been told about them' (quoted in Edgecombe, 1982, p. 6).

In *Ten Weeks in Natal* Colenso also issued his first protest against the standard missionary practice of insisting that, in order to be baptized, polygamists who wished to convert to Christianity must separate from all but one of their wives—thereby causing the disruption of the familial life of the Zulu concerned and, potentially, destitution for the wives thus abandoned. Although he opposed polygamy itself as both unchristian and uncivilized—and thus maintained that male converts who were not married should marry only one wife—Colenso nevertheless argued that existing polygamists who converted should not be required to separate from any of their wives, thus avoiding the broken relationships and social dislocation which would otherwise occur (Colenso, 1855, pp. 139–41; Guy, 1983a, pp. 49 and 73–4; Brain, 1984, p. 384).

The publication of such views immediately brought Colenso into conflict with the majority of the missionaries already at work in Natal, as well as with the settler community in general, which resented his rejection of its own profoundly negative stereotype of the indigenous African population and his insistence upon the duties and responsibilities implicit in colonialism. The missionary community objected, in particular, to Colenso's repudiation of its preaching on the necessity of conversion and the prospect of eternal punishment for the unconverted and to his willingness to baptize polygamists—a decision which conservative Victorian missionaries not only found 'unscriptural', but which also provoked some of their deepest moral beliefs and sexual prejudices. Even in the matter of the names to be used for God, however, Colenso excited opposition. Other missionaries objected to Colenso's proposal to use the Zulu names for God in his preaching and his translations of the Bible and liturgy on the grounds that this would result in the continuing currency of 'pagan' concepts and their new association with the Christian God. Better, such missionaries argued, to use a completely different word, without any traditional pagan overtones, thus emphasizing the completeness of the cultural and religious break at the point of conversion. Colenso, by contrast, proposed to tell the Zulu that their names for God were excellent and that Christian missionaries would now teach them more about this God (Colenso, 1855, p. 134).[5]

[5] On the matter of the most appropriate translation for God, Colenso's view eventually prevailed, 'Nkulunkulu' becoming an established usage. On the issue of polygamy, however, Colenso's views were never to secure official approval, despite his publication, in 1861, of a closely argued ninety-four-page long *Letter to His Grace the Archbishop of Canterbury, upon the question of the proper treatment of cases of polygamy, as found already existing in converts from heathenism.*

From the earliest years of his episcopacy, therefore, Colenso not only advocated ideas and practices that were to culminate in the major controversies of the 1860s and 70s, but also found himself engaged in controversy on several fronts at once. Despite this, indeed perhaps even because of it, Colenso devoted much of his time and energy in the later 1850s to the demanding tasks of continuing to learn the Zulu language, compiling dictionaries and grammars of Zulu, and translating the Bible, Prayer Book and other materials into that language—in the process, it may be added, securing an enduring place in the history of Zulu literature and linguistics (Guy, 1983a, pp. 65–6). And as he did so, he became increasingly convinced of the rightness of his original protest against the crudely and uncompromisingly stark preaching presented to the Zulu by most missionaries. The version of Christianity proclaimed by most of the missionaries at work in Natal, Colenso increasingly believed, was not only immoral because of its emphasis on the wrath, anger and judgement of God, instead of on God's love and compassion, but also evangelistically ineffective because its wrathful severity was itself a barrier to the conversion of 'heathens' whose own moral sense revolted against such teaching. 'The great drawback here', Colenso wrote in 1859, 'is that the country is already saturated with a corruption of Christianity, and the natives have acquired such a view of the character of God and of the Gospel as keeps them back from desiring to have a much closer acquaintance with it' (quoted in Cox, 1888, Vol. 1, p. 119).

By the early 1860s, Colenso felt obliged to present a more thorough and systematic statement of his thinking on these matters. The resulting publications caused no little furore.

III RESISTING THE 'CORRUPTION OF CHRISTIANITY': 'HERESY' AS MISSIONARY VOCATION

In 1861, Colenso published a commentary on Paul's letter to the Romans. Significantly, it was entitled *St Paul's Epistle to the Romans: newly translated and explained from a missionary point of view*, and, as the dedication of the book made clear, the missionary context was, indeed, crucial:

> The teaching of the great Apostle to the Gentiles is here applied to some questions which daily arise in Missionary labours among the heathen, more directly than is usual with those commentators, who have not been engaged personally in such work, but have written from a very different point of view, in the midst of a state of advanced civilization and settled Christianity.
>
> (Colenso, 1861b, unnumbered page)

In particular, Colenso returned to the questions of hell, eternal punishment and atonement. Looking back to his days as a parish priest at Forncett St Mary's, and to his *Village Sermons* of 1853, Colenso recalled that at that time he did still believe in eternal punishment

> ... as far as that can be called belief which, in fact, was no more than acquiesence, in common, I imagine, with very many of my brother clergy, in the ordinary statements of the subject, without having ever deeply studied the question, probably with a shrinking dread of examining it, and without having ever ventured formally to write or preach a Sermon on the subject, and pursue it, in thought and word, to all its consequences. There are many, who, as I did myself in those days, would assert the dogma as a part of their 'Creed', and now and then, in a single sentence of a Sermon, utter a few words in accordance with it, but who have never set themselves down to face the question, and deliver their own souls upon it to their flocks, fully and unreservedly. For my own part, I admit, I acquiesced in it, seeing *some* reasons for assuming it to be true, knowing that the mass of my clerical brethren assented to it with myself, and contenting myself with making some reference to it now and then, in my ministrations, without caring to dwell deliberately upon it, and considering what might be urged against it.
>
> (*Ibid.*, p. 197)

Now, however, after some years as a missionary, during which time both the explicit preaching of his fellow missionaries and the questions of his own converts had forced him to 'dwell deliberately' upon this doctrine and consider both its consequences and what might, indeed, be urged against it, Colenso found himself obliged to declare that he could '... no longer maintain, or give utterance to, the doctrine of the endlessness of "future punishments"' (*ibid.*).

Such a doctrine, Colenso argued, contained too many contradictions, contravened too many aspects of ordinary moral sense, and offended against that God-given awareness of righteousnesss, truth and love which the Spirit of God 'has written upon our hearts'. If God was a righteous judge, knowing all, how could a sharp line be drawn between the saved and the damned when in practice the moral character of human beings showed infinite shades, the good always having some evil in them and the evil some seeds of good? And what of the prospect and possibility of moral and spiritual development beyond this life? Was it to be supposed that the child who died in infancy either remained thus for eternity or alternatively expanded at once to the full potential of which it was capable? Scripture, Colenso asserted, did not answer this question, but analogy with nature argued for a gradual process of growth and progress—and if this were so for infants then why might it not also be a possibility for all? The Christian, however, Colenso affirmed, might at least be certain that when the Spirit of God in the heart thus prompted the questioning of doctrines traditionally taught by the Church, the moral instincts should be given priority:

> ... any interpretation of Scripture, which contradicts that sense of right which God Himself, our Father, has given us, to be a witness for His own perfect excellences, must be set aside, as having no right to crush down, as with an iron heel, into silence the indignant remonstrance of our whole spiritual being. And it cannot be denied that there is such a remonstrance ... against the dogma, ... as usually understood, of 'Endless Punishment'. This dogma makes no distinction between those who have done things worthy of many stripes and those who have done things worthy of few, between the profligate sensualist and the ill-trained child.
>
> (*Ibid.*, p. 210)

The Epistle to the Romans, moreover, Colenso argued, was itself 'one of the strongest possible protests against such a notion'. Nor, he asserted, did the New Testament support another 'dogma of modern theology', namely that '... our Lord died for our sins, in the sense of dying *instead of* us, dying *in our place*, or dying so as to *bear the punishment* or *penalty* of our sins' (*ibid.*, p. 115). The 'common modern dogma' to this effect, Colenso suggested, had probably arisen from '... following the English Version [of Paul's letter] without due attention to the Greek original' (*ibid.*, p. 116).

It was precisely in his missionary encounter with the Zulu, moreover, that Colenso found himself brought face to face with these matters—not least because the Zulu provided an example of the human conscience at odds with traditional Christian teaching:

> Such questions as these have been brought again and again before my mind in the intimate converse which I have had, as a Missionary, with Christian converts and Heathens. To teach the truths of our holy religion to intelligent adult natives, who have the simplicity of children, but withal, the earnestness and thoughtfulness of men,—to whom these things are new and startling, whose minds are not prepared by long familiarity to acquiesce in, if not to receive, them,—is a sifting process for the opinions of any teacher,

who feels the deep moral obligation of answering truly, and faithfully, and unreservedly, his fellow-man looking up at him for light and guidance, and asking, 'Are you sure of this?', 'Do you know this to be true?', 'Do you really believe that?' The state of everlasting torment after death, of all impenitent sinners and unbelievers, including the whole heathen world, as many teach, is naturally so amazing and overwhelming an object of contemplation to them, and one so prominently put forward in the case of those who have been under certain missionary training, that it quite shuts out the cardinal doctrines of the Gospel, the Fatherly relation to us of the Faithful Creator. The conscience, healthy, though but imperfectly enlightened, does not answer to such denunciations of indiscriminate wrath, and cannot, therefore, appreciate what is represented as Redeeming Love, offering a way of escape.

(*Ibid.*, p. 218)

Colenso's commentary on Paul's letter to the Romans brought together a cluster of issues which were to remain central to the religious and theological controversies in which he was to be engaged for the rest of his life. First, there was his abiding conviction of the essentially loving and Fatherly nature of God—and hence a passionate concern to ensure that the character of this God should not be obscured or compromised by association with morally dubious or repugnant doctrines. Second, there was his insistence upon the priority of the witness of God's spirit in the heart of the individual over the claims of either biblical text or the teaching of the Church. Third, there was the vital influence of the missionary context, the demands of which provided the catalyst for Colenso's own thinking, making him address directly and thoroughly issues which he had hitherto avoided. Finally, there was the moral duty, once these issues were addressed, to answer the questions thus raised in a plain, honest and unequivocal manner.

When, in mid-1861, Bishop Gray of Cape Town read the commentary on Paul's letter—a copy of which Colenso had sent him—he at once asked Colenso to withdraw the work and suppress it. Colenso replied that he could not do so: for one thing the book was already in the process of being published in England as well as in Natal, and in any case he could not conceal '... what appears to be the truth from fear of consequences' (quoted in Guy, 1983a, p. 106). Moreover, by this time Colenso was already engaged in the preparation of a second and potentially even more radical work examining the first six books of the Bible in the light of modern biblical scholarship, geological discoveries, and—again—the simple but penetrating questioning of a Zulu convert who asked of the story of the Flood and Noah's Ark, 'Is all this true?' (Colenso, 1862, p. vii). Colenso was also about to return to England, partly to seek renewed support for his missionary efforts at Ekukhanyeni, but now in addition to confront the issues already raised by his commentary and those shortly to be raised by his forthcoming study of the opening books of the Bible.

The Colenso family duly arrived in England at the end of July 1862. By this time Bishop Gray was already in England, having decided to place the matter of Colenso's commentary in the hands of the Archbishop of Canterbury and the English bishops. In this he was actively supported by Samuel Wilberforce, to whom Gray had written in 1861, immediately after reading Colenso's commentary on Romans, accusing Colenso of publishing '... the most objectionable views, and entirely substituting a new scheme for the received version of Christianity' (quoted in Guy, 1983a, p. 112). Gray and Wilberforce tried to dissuade Colenso from publishing his additional work on biblical criticism, but without success. Colenso, meanwhile, sought the opinions of other theological liberals within the Church of England. He received sympathy for his ideas and aims, but also caution and hesitation over his approach. Both Benjamin Jowett and A. P. Stanley expressed caution over the tone of the first draft of the work on biblical criticism when Colenso showed it to them—Stanley in particular arguing that Colenso should try to make it read '... more like a defence, and less like an attack', advice which led Colenso to try to 'soften' the tone before publication (Guy, 1983a, pp. 117–18). For both the Colensos, however, the most painful and distressing response was that of F. D. Maurice. Expecting the support of their one-time mentor, John and Frances Colenso were shocked—as she recalled in a letter years later—to hear Maurice say that '... if he [Maurice] could not believe that Moses wrote the Pentateuch, he could not believe in God at all, or in the powers of the world to come'. Maurice's advice was simply: 'Suppress your book and resign your bishopric' (Rees, 1958, pp. 395–6).

In his own mind and conscience, however, Colenso had already confronted not only the question of whether or not to resign, but also the question of how to present his critical views on the opening books of the Bible. Thus he wrote in September 1861 to Wilhelm Bleek—a respected specialist in Bantu philology at Cape Town, son of a professor of theology at Bonn, and a close friend of Colenso since they had travelled to South Africa on the same ship in 1855—explaining that:

> My *present* idea is *not* to resign my office—but to print my 'Notes on the Pentateuch' which tear the whole story to pieces in such a way,

that (as far as I can see) no *reasoning* man can refuse to follow; and then to challenge the Church of England upon the question, whether it will maintain as Sacred Truth a palpable falsehood.

(Quoted in Guy, 1983a, p. 107)

Colenso added to this that he was by no means clear, yet, that he was in contravention of any of the Church's laws, and also that he would wait to see if an answer could be given to his forthcoming book—'... and most thankful should I be if an effectual and complete one could be given'. At heart, however, he felt that nothing less than 'a complete Revolution' in English religious life was needed. Colenso thus placed his trust in the plain statement of the truth, believing that his case would either be accepted or clearly refuted.

In October 1862—with the controversy over *Essays and Reviews* still at its height—the first part of *The Pentateuch and Book of Joshua Critically Examined* was published. The book examined the story of the Israelites in the wilderness after leaving Egypt and focused especially upon the practical implications of the numbers said to have left Egypt in the Exodus. Colenso showed the impossibility of many of the numbers stated in the biblical text. He demonstrated the practical impossibility of the fulfilment of ritual and sacrificial requirements if the numbers were taken literally. He showed the many contradictions that must follow if the text were regarded as, in all respects, historically true and accurate (Colenso, 1862, especially chs. 2, 6, 9–12 and 14; Rogerson, 1984, pp. 221–3). It was, he insisted, not a matter of speculation but 'a simple question of facts' and one, moreover, upon which he made a point of appealing, in particular, to the laity of the Church of England (Colenso, 1862, pp. xx and xxxv–vi). He also explained that the origins of this book, like his commentary on Romans, lay in his missionary and evangelistic work among the Zulu, which had forced him to confront what he had previously avoided. Occupied in the translation of the Bible into Zulu, he explained that he had debated with the Zulu,

> ... so as not only to avail myself freely of their criticisms, but to appreciate fully their objections and difficulties. Thus, however, it has happened that I have been brought again face to face with questions, which caused me some uneasiness in former days, but with respect to which I was then enabled to satisfy my mind sufficiently for practical purposes, and I had fondly hoped to have laid the ghosts of them at last for ever. Engrossed with parochial and other work in England, I did what, probably, many other clergymen have done under similar circumstances,—I contented myself with

silencing, by means of specious explanations, which are given in most commentaries, the ordinary objections against the historical character of the early portions of the Old Testament, and settled down into a willing acquiesence in the general truth of the narrative, whatever difficulties might still hang about particular parts of it. In short, the doctrinal and devotional portions of the Bible were what were needed most in parochial duty. And, if a passage of the Old Testament formed at any time the subject of a sermon, it was easy to draw from it practical lessons of daily life, without examining closely into the historical truth of the narrative.

(*Ibid.*, pp. vi–vii)

In Natal, however, Colenso continued, he had been brought face to face with these very questions. Translating the story of the flood, he had been asked by a Zulu:

Is all this true? Do you really believe that all this happened thus,—that all the beasts, and birds, and creeping things, upon the earth, large and small, from hot countries and cold, came thus in pairs, and entered into the ark with Noah? And did Noah gather food for them *all* ... My heart answered in the words of the Prophet, 'Shall a man speak lies in the Name of the Lord?' Zech. xiii.3. I dared not do so. My own knowledge of some branches of science, of Geology in particular, had been much increased since I left England; and I now knew for certain, on geological grounds, a fact, of which I had only had misgivings before, viz. that a *Universal Deluge*, such as the Bible manifestly speaks of, could not possibly have taken place in the way described in the Book of Genesis Knowing this, I felt that I dared not, as a servant of the God of Truth, urge my brother man to believe that, which I did not myself believe, which I knew to be untrue, as a matter-of-fact, historical narrative.

(*Ibid.*, pp. vii–viii)[6]

---

[6] The reference to the increase in his knowledge of geology reflects Colenso's reading on scientific matters in order to prepare a reader of *First Lessons in Science* for use in the mission school at Ekukhanyeni. The works which he read included Charles Lyell's *Elementary Geology*. Subsequently, Lyell was to be one of Colenso's staunchest supporters, and Frances Colenso was to correspond regularly from Natal with both Mary Lyell, who actively associated herself with her husband's geological work, and with Mary's sister, Katherine, who married Charles Lyell's brother and who was a keen botanist and friend of J. D. Hooker, the curator of Kew Gardens, himself another of Colenso's scientific supporters.

As he had anticipated, Colenso quickly found himself the centre of controversy. Along with the furore in the press, the bishops of the Church of England met and advised the SPG to withhold the funds out of which Colenso paid his clergy in Natal. They also wrote to Colenso, declining to enter into debate over the handling of the biblical text, but asserting that there was inconsistency between his opinions and his office as a bishop, which was causing scandal and distress within the church. They therefore urged him to examine his conscience and resign. Colenso declined on the grounds that he did not believe himself to be either legally or morally wrong. The overwhelming majority of the bishops then published inhibitions preventing Colenso from preaching in any churches within their dioceses. Individual bishops—including Wilberforce and the Archbishop of Canterbury, Longley—also dismissed Colenso's arguments as, variously, rash, feeble, trite, puerile and merely repetitions of objections already frequently refuted (Guy, 1983a, pp. 131 and 136). A second line of attack relied upon ridicule. Colenso was portrayed as the naïve mathematician who added up the numbers in the Bible and suffered a crisis of faith because the sums did not work. Similarly, much was made of the bishop who was converted by the heathen to whom *he* had gone as a missionary. Nor was such polemic and satire left to the popular press. No less a figure than Matthew Arnold also poured scorn upon Colenso's first volume, mocking both its alleged obsession with arithmetical problems and its attempt to place such issues openly before the laity—the majority of whom, Arnold clearly believed, were not equipped to judge such matters (*ibid.*, pp. 134–5 and 186–7).[7]

Colenso, meanwhile, continued with his biblical studies, publishing three more parts of *The Pentateuch and Book of Joshua Critically Examined* during 1863. In these volumes Colenso presented a detailed scholarly interpretation of the biblical texts with which he was concerned, examining complex issues of textual interpretation and seeking to show the various strands of material which had been woven together and subsequently attributed to Moses and Joshua. In Part 4, however, which examined the first eleven chapters of the Book of Genesis, he also addressed head-on the Zulu question that had led him to embark upon

[7] The novelist Anthony Trollope, who supported Colenso, attempted to reverse the satirical trend by publishing 'The Zulu in London', an account of an imagined visit by a Christian Zulu to an Evangelical rally in London. The Zulu visitor is shocked by the intolerance shown towards 'his' bishop's views, by the absence of debate, by the assertion of the truth of every word of the Old Testament, and by the call to the clergy to keep such 'doubtful questions' from their 'poor ignorant flocks' (Trollope, 1865, reprinted in apRoberts, 1974, pp. 51–60). For the ambiguities and anxieties in Arnold's attack on Colenso, in addition to Guy, cited above, see Ridge, 1994, pp. 24–6.

his investigation of the opening books of the Bible. In dealing with the story of the Flood and Noah's Ark, Colenso once more deployed the relentlessly devastating rational criticism that he had previously applied to the numbers of Israelites said to have been in the wilderness. How was the ark inhabited with all the different creatures? How much food was needed for all the animals? How did Noah and his family cope everyday with feeding them all and cleaning them out? How were the needs of animals from hot and cold climates simultaneously accommodated? How did the animals get from Mount Ararat to their subsequent habitats—especially in the case of flightless birds such as the dodo of Mauritius and the apteryx of New Zealand (Colenso, 1863c, pp. 176–210; Rogerson, 1984, pp. 226–7)?

As each part of *The Pentateuch* was published, Colenso also included a substantial preface in which he answered critics of the previous volumes and reiterated his aims in writing. For example, in the preface to the second part, he repeated that he had deliberately written for the 'thoughtful and intelligent laity', believing that without their support it would be impossible to overcome the restraints on freedom of thought and speech in the Church of England. He also asserted that many of the clergy shared his own disbelief in the literal truth of many aspects of the early books of the Bible but kept back their views from the laity—a point implicitly conceded by his critics when they complained that much of what Colenso had said in his first volume had long been familiar to students of theology. He therefore issued a particular challenge to his fellow bishops who judged and condemned him, calling on them to '... answer my arguments by a book ... and not to seek to put them down by sneers, by mere declamation from the pulpit or the platform, or by sending a brief excommunication to the Times' (Colenso, 1863a, pp. xxxiv–v). Then, in the preface to Part 3, Colenso sharpened his challenge still further and challenged Samuel Wilberforce in particular, as the self-appointed leader of the episcopal campaign against Colenso:

> Does he, a Fellow of the Royal and other Scientific Societies, believe unfeignedly in the literal historical truth of the account of the Creation, the Noachian Deluge, or the numbers of the Exodus? If the Bishop will say that he does 'unfeignedly believe' in all these matters as related in the Pentateuch, of course, I have nothing more to say as regards this part of my argument. But, if he does not, then how, I repeat, does his present conduct differ essentially from mine? *He* has some way of explaining these matters, which satisfies his own mind, as I have. And the only difference is this, that I think it to be

my duty, and shall make it my practice, to tell my people plainly, on such points, what I believe, and what I know to be true; and the Bishop of Oxford has not yet, as far as I am aware, thought it necessary to say what he really thinks upon any one of these subjects.

(Colenso, 1863b, p. xxvii)

Thus did Colenso respond to those who charged *him* with dishonesty for remaining a bishop whilst publishing liberal and critical theological views. He turned the moral argument back upon his accusers and charged them with dishonesty if they would not say plainly—as plainly as Colenso himself—what they really believed.[8] The challenge was not, however, taken up. Instead, the bishops sought to silence Colenso by forbidding him to preach in their dioceses; they asserted his wrongheadedness and naïvety, and then they ignored him. What they would not do was answer him, point for point, on his chosen ground. And all the while, popular jibes about the bishop converted to heresy by the Zulu and his own arithmetic served their purposes well—for if Colenso could be made to look ridiculous, there would be no need to answer him (Guy, 1983a, pp. 137 and 146).

In southern Africa, however, the tactics of Gray and other conservatively minded clergy were different. Gray was back in southern Africa by April 1863 and within a month was presented, by several clergy, with a formal charge against Colenso of 'false teaching'. The charge listed nine issues on which Colenso was alleged to be at odds with the Church's teaching, including the atonement, the sacraments, eternal punishment, the Bible and its inspiration, the extent of Christ's knowledge, and the status of the Prayer Book. Colenso was informed that he must answer these accusations before the South African bishops, led by Gray, in November 1863. Colenso believed the procedure to be without legality, gave notice that he would appeal against any adverse verdict and remained in England. Gray and his fellow bishops met, having discussed the issues with the prosecuting clergy before the trial. Colenso was duly found guilty of the charges against him and given four months to retract or be deposed.

In England, Colenso appealed against the decision through the courts and the matter went to the Judicial Committee of the Privy

---

[8] Colenso thereby made an important contribution to the mid-Victorian debate over plain-speaking and the 'ethics of belief', an issue already being hotly debated in the early 1860s in connection with the controversy over *Essays and Reviews*. For the broader debate on this theme, see *RVB*, II, 9.

Council. In April 1864, Gray travelled to Pietermaritzburg and from the pulpit of Colenso's own cathedral declared Colenso deposed and the bishopric vacant: Colenso, he said, had turned away from God, '... led captive by the Evil one' (Guy, 1983a, p. 149). In March 1865, the Judicial Committee found Gray's sentence null and void on the grounds that the terms of Gray's own appointment did not give him such authority. Colenso also successfully sued the Colonial Bishoprics Fund in order to secure his stipend, which had been suspended following Gray's actions. Whilst his stipend was suspended, and to pay for his legal expenses, supporters had subscribed to a fund on his behalf. Subscribers included scientists such as Lyell, Darwin, Huxley and Hooker; literary figures such as Dickens and Trollope; the lawyer Fitzjames Stephen (who had defended Rowland Williams in the *Essays and Reviews* case); and theologians such as A. P. Stanley the Dean of Westminster, Henry Milman the Dean of St Paul's, Frederick Temple, Rowland Williams and Benjamin Jowett of *Essays and Reviews* fame, and James Martineau, the leading Unitarian.

At the same time, however, many of his liberal supporters also began to fear that involvement in prolonged legal confrontations would obscure the original issues for which Colenso was fighting and lose him whatever sympathy he might have. Colenso himself was aware of the ambiguities of his position. He believed, however, that he could not now give up the position for which he had fought without seeming to concede too much to his opponents. It was also his view that his duty lay in seeking to defend the right to freedom of thought within the Church of England (Guy, 1983a, pp. 146–7). In August 1865, therefore, after the publication of the fifth part of *The Pentateuch and Book of Joshua Critically Examined* (Colenso, 1865c), the Colensos embarked once more for Natal.

Before doing so, however, Colenso presented two revealing papers to learned societies in London. The first, 'On the efforts of missionaries among savages', was presented in March 1865 to the Anthropological Society (Colenso, 1865a). The second, 'On missions to the Zulus in Natal and Zululand', was presented in May 1865 at the Marylebone Literary Institution (Colenso, 1865b). The two papers constituted a telling summary and restatement of the theological position and understanding of the missionary task which Colenso had developed over the preceding decade. The true task of the missionary, Colenso affirmed, was not merely to save a few individual souls, but '... to raise a whole race to the true dignity of man, as a child of God, a being endowed with intellectual, moral and spiritual faculties' (Colenso, 1865a, p. cclxvii). To this end the missionary must not present a version of Christianity which will cause moral revulsion or sheer incomprehension in the non-Christian hearer, which adds new fears and superstitions to existing ones, or denies the true Christian spirit by, for example, breaking up polygamous families. On the contrary, the missionary must build upon the 'common ground of our humanity'—an echo of his own sermon in Cambridge before first leaving for Natal in 1854—searching for seeds already planted in the heart of the 'heathen' by God. Missionary efforts must begin, therefore, not with complete systems of dogmatic theology but with the undogmatic teaching of the Lord's Prayer and the Sermon on the Mount. Nor must missionaries avoid the implications of modern science; they must themselves teach what modern science reveals about the age of the earth, and thus also explain the non-literal nature of much of the biblical text (Colenso, 1865a and b).

The two papers were not only significant for their bold and succinct restatement of Colenso's theological and missionary ideals, however. They also constituted an emphatic statement of Colenso's belief in the essential humanity and dignity of the Zulu—and by implication of all other 'heathen' and 'primitive' peoples, in Africa and elsewhere—and his utter rejection of the emerging social Darwinism which sought to assign such peoples to a fundamentally inferior and transient stage in the evolution of the human race.[9] In speaking in this way, Colenso—for all his paternalistic conviction that the British were providentially destined to bring Christianity and civilization to less advanced peoples—signalled a potential radicalism not only in religion, but in the ideology and politics of race as well. A decade later that potential was to be fulfilled.

IV   PROCLAIMING THE FAITH OF A 'HERETIC'

Colenso arrived back in Natal in November 1865. By the end of the month he was already embroiled in the opening phases of a struggle with Dean Green and other supporters of Bishop Gray that was to last for years. Green and his supporters sought to obstruct Colenso from carrying out his duties as Bishop of Natal. Scuffles occurred between Colenso's and Green's supporters. Rival services were held at different times. Bell ropes were removed, the harmonium was locked, and items such as the Bible, Prayer Book, Baptismal Register and communion plate were hidden from Colenso and his supporters. Repeatedly, over the next few years, Colenso

---

[9] It is clear that Colenso was replying directly to a paper by Winwood Reade, an explorer of markedly social evolutionist and racist views (Guy, 1983a, p. 75; Edgecombe, 1982, pp. xxxiv–vi). It has also been suggested that he was responding to the no less overtly racist views of John Crawfurd, a prominent member of the Ethnological Society of London. There does not appear to be direct evidence for this however (Hinchliff, 1986, pp. 105–9).

was obliged to go to law to secure access to such items and to secure his right to various church properties and endowments in Natal, including possession of St Peter's Cathedral. In January 1866, Gray formally excommunicated Colenso, and in 1869 consecrated a new bishop, W. K. Macrorie, to replace him. From then until Colenso's death in 1883 there were two bishops in Natal, although Macrorie had to be called bishop of Maritzburg—a place which, technically, did not exist, the name being an abbreviation of Pietermaritzburg (Guy, 1983a, pp. 154–9). There were also in due course two cathedrals, the new cathedral of St Saviour's eventually being consecrated in 1877.

Although, for some years, he retained a significant following among the laity of Natal—not least because many of the laity shared his opposition to Gray's highly autocratic exercise of his episcopal authority—Colenso's options were now severely restricted. Few of the clergy in his diocese remained loyal to him and lack of funds meant that he could not recruit sufficient numbers of qualified replacements. From 1865 onwards, Colenso never had more than six or seven clergy at most, whilst the 'orthodox' party enjoyed two or three times that number. Moreover, this desperate need for clergy and limited means led Colenso to make a number of ill-judged and unsuitable appointments (Hinchliff, 1964, pp. 188–9; Guy, 1983a, pp. 157–9). The bulk of the work of running the diocese thus fell upon Colenso himself. His mission work was now limited to further Zulu translations and an African school run at Bishopstowe by his daughters. The seemingly endless court cases, meanwhile, seemed to lend credence to the charge that Colenso was a perverse and obsessive controversialist. Even more painfully, however, his theological ideas and biblical scholarship were increasingly ignored. The episcopal tactic of at once ignoring Colenso's arguments and repeatedly asserting that he had been answered, together with his sheer distance from England, resulted in the commercial failure of his later works (Guy, 1983a, pp. 159–61).

In retrospect, the injustice of such treatment is clear. Even at the time there were some voices ready to acclaim his contribution to the study of the Old Testament. For example, the leading contemporary Dutch Old Testament scholar, Abraham Kuenen, paid tribute to Colenso's work and acknowledged his impact upon his own studies (Deist, 1984, pp. 110–12; Rogerson, 1984, p. 233).[10] And Benjamin Jowett, on hearing of Colenso's

---

[10] Kuenen's work had, in its turn, been an important influence on Colenso's early studies of the Pentateuch. The two men corresponded, met in both Holland and England, and enjoyed a mutual friendship and respect for each other's work, Colenso translating one of Kuenen's works into English. For the history of their friendship and influence upon one another, see Rogerson, 1993.

death, remarked that, he had '... made an epoch in criticism by his straight-forwardness. No one now talks of verbal inspiration ... the effects of his writings, though they are no longer read, is permanent' (Abbott and Campbell, 1897, Vol. 2, p. 64). It was a judgement echoed, albeit in different terms, by a modern historian of Old Testament criticism in the nineteenth century (Rogerson, 1984, p. 234; 1988, p. 124).[11] Arguably, however, it was not Colenso's contribution to Old Testament studies and biblical criticism which became the most neglected aspect of his legacy. Rather, it was his attempt to provide a positive, constructive and systematic statement of his liberal theological and religious ideas which suffered that fate.

Despite his opponents' repeated insistence that Colenso was a negative and destructive critic, it is abundantly clear, even in his most overtly critical works, that his underlying aim was constructive and positive. Thus, for example, in the conclusion to the second part of *The Pentateuch and Book of Joshua Critically Examined*, Colenso turned to the questions—also famously raised by Benjamin Jowett and Rowland Williams in their contributions to *Essays and Reviews*—'should the Bible be read like any other book?' and 'was the Bible God's Word?' He answered, plainly and robustly—and in terms that showed clearly his continuing debt to Coleridge—that the Bible was to be read with both the mind and the heart. In respect of the mind, it was, indeed, to be read as any other book, as the work of 'fellow-men, like ourselves', and thus inclusive of legendary elements, contradictions and unhistorical narratives. The Bible was not, therefore, in itself, 'God's Word'. But when read with the heart, humbly and devoutly, the Bible would surely be found to contain 'God's Word', for it remained 'a gracious gift of God' by means of which '... with a few simple words, the springs of life within our own hearts are touched, and the whole inner man is stirred' (Colenso, 1863a, pp. 382–4).

For Colenso, moreover, the recognition that the Bible contained 'God's Word' but was not in itself literally, word for word, 'the Word of God' was not only intellectually but also spiritually liberating. Not only did such recognition free one, intellectually, from having to try to believe in the historicity of ancient narratives and legends which patently conflicted with the discoveries of contemporary science and biblical criticism, but in

[11] For Colenso's place within the broader story of the history of biblical criticism in Victorian Britain, see *RVB*, II, 11. Similarly, for a positive assessment of the potential significance of Colenso's principles of biblical interpretation in the pastoral context of modern South Africa, see Draper and West, 1989, pp. 30–2.

addition it brought moral and spiritual relief from the apparent necessity of believing that certain manifestly and appallingly immoral teachings and incidents in the Old Testament were authentic expressions of the will of God. For example, as Colenso pointed out in the chapter on 'The War on Midian' in the first volume of *The Pentateuch and Book of Joshua Critically Examined*, once it was demonstrated that the narrative in Exodus was unreliable and inaccurate,

> ... how thankful we must be, that we are no longer obliged to believe, *as a matter of fact*, of vital consequence to our eternal hope ... that a force of 12,000 Israelites slew all the males of the Midianites, took captive all the females and children, seized all their cattle and flocks ... and all their goods, and burnt all their cities ... without the loss of one single man, and then by command of Moses, butchered in cold blood all the women and children.

> (Colenso, 1862, p. 143; see also Hinchliff, 1963, p. 97, and 1986, pp. 104–5)

Similarly, in examining the text of Exodus, chapter 21, verses 2–6 and 20–21, Colenso noted that a critical understanding of the biblical text meant that

> ... we shall be relieved in future from the necessity of holding, and teaching authoritatively from the pulpit, the revolting doctrine, that the practice of *slavery* may be supported by express Divine utterances, like that which permits the flogging by a master of his slave, man or woman, even unto death, provided that he or she 'continue a day or two, for he is his money'... or which orders that a Hebrew slave shall work only for six years, and then 'go out free for nothing', but 'if his master have given him a wife, and she have borne him sons or daughters, the wife and children shall be her master's, and he shall go out by himself' unless, indeed, he be willing to sell himself for their sakes into perpetual bondage.

> (Colenso, 1872, pp. 206–8 and 619)

Or again, it is important to note that, even as Colenso deployed his critical skills in a devastating assault on the literal reading of the story of Noah and the Flood, yet he also insisted that the story remained an inspired and religiously significant text. Thus it expressed the profound religious principles that God was the creator and preserver of all, that humanity was made in God's image, and that what God made was good (Colenso, 1863c, pp. 111–12; see also Rogerson, 1984, p. 227).

Above all, however, it was in a long sequence of sermons, preached in St Peter's Cathedral, Pietermaritzburg, after his return from England in late 1865 and throughout 1866, that Colenso sought to set out, systematically, the positive and constructive nature of his theology. Delivered to substantial congregations, there were ninety-seven sermons in all in the series and, in addition to printing them for circulation in South Africa, Colenso hoped also to publish them in England. In the latter project he was only partially successful. Of the four volumes of sermons assembled in Natal, only two, containing but fifty-one of the sermons, were ever published in England, the first in 1867 and the second in 1868. With Colenso now back in Natal the *Natal Sermons* aroused little interest among the English public, and with various lawsuits grinding on, Colenso's lawyers in England advised against the publication of the last two volumes. They remain, however, a telling demonstration of the underlying coherence of Colenso's theological position and a testimony to the depth of his own faith.

Many of the themes are familiar. The liberating effect of biblical criticism is repeatedly emphasized, as is the value of Scripture, provided that it is studied with honesty and rigour and provided that it is not regarded as the literal or infallible 'word of God'. Indeed, Colenso affirms, the more the Bible is studied, the more Divine, grand and wonderful it will seem (Colenso, 1867, sermons iv–v). The discoveries of modern science are similarly welcomed and Colenso repeatedly affirms that modern science need not pose any threat to true religious faith, but on the contrary might deepen Christian understanding. For example, the discoveries of science concerning the age of the earth, the vastness of the universe, or the teeming profusion of life at the microscopic level may all excite awe and amazement and prompt the contemporary Christian to echo the Psalmist's wonder that the creator of such vastness and complexity should also be intimately concerned with humanity (Colenso, Natal Sermons, Series 3, p. 235; quoted in Guy, 1983a, p. 173, and 1983b, p. 12). Also reiterated are Colenso's moral and theological objections to the doctrines of eternal punishment and substitutionary atonement, together with his universalistic and symbolic understanding of baptism and his interpretation of Holy Communion as at once the highest and holiest form of worship, yet by no means the only expression of the 'real presence' of Christ (Colenso, 1867, sermons ii, ix–x, xiii–iv and xix; 1868, sermons ix–x and xxvii; see also Darby, 1984 and 1989).

In the *Natal Sermons*, however, Colenso not only restated themes already familiar from his previous theological works, but also ranged over many other subjects. He protested, for example, against the effects of restrictive and dogmatic sabbatarianism (Colenso, 1867, sermons xiv–xviii). He challenged belief in both demonic possession and the Devil conceived as a distinct personality, suggesting in the latter case that one of the inherent dangers of such belief was the legitimation of hatred for that personality—a hatred which might then, all too easily, be transferred to those human beings who were thought by such believers to be the Devil's agents. Moreover, to challenge belief in the personal existence of a Devil was not, Colenso insisted, to underestimate or make light of either sin or evil, rather it was to free the Christian from superstition in order to confront the genuine struggle of good and evil within the heart of each individual (Colenso, 1867, sermon xxii; 1868, sermons i–ii). Similarly, Colenso considered the nature of prophecy, arguing that, rightly understood, a prophet was not a predictor of future events, but one who spoke forth God's message, renewing the power of general moral and spiritual insights and principles in the particular circumstances of the prophet's own day (Colenso, 1867, sermons xix–xx).

Perhaps most significantly, however, in the *Natal Sermons* Colenso began to apply his critical approach to the Old Testament to the New Testament as well, to the Gospels and to the figure of Jesus. He recognized that the life of Jesus as portrayed in the Gospels was but a 'slight sketch'; that there were few details of his life; and that the various New Testament documents were of varying types and degrees of authenticity. Similarly, he acknowledged that the resurrection narratives were full of difficulties, often at variance with each other, and contained some 'legendary additions'; and he argued that the doctrine of the second coming of Christ, though once understood literally, could no longer appropriately be held in this way (Colenso, 1867, sermons vi and xxi; 1868, sermons x, xi and xxvi). At the same time, however, he affirmed that the spirit of Jesus' life, the principle that ruled it, was clear, namely the surrender and conformity of his own will to that of God. In the life, teaching and death of Jesus, Colenso asserted, God's own character was revealed, in all its graciousness. Thus the substance of both the New Testament and the Old was shown to be not 'a system of religious worship' or 'a summary of many and various things to be believed', but '... a revelation of God, and of our relation to Him, as that of children to a loving Father' (Colenso, 1867, sermons ii and xxi; 1868, sermon xxvi). In one of the later Natal Sermons, never published in England, Colenso elaborated upon this 'sum and substance' and defined Jesus' essential teaching as '... the Fatherhood of God, the Brotherhood of Man, [and] the manifestation of the Divine in the Human through the Incarnation of the Living Word, through the Indwelling Presence of the Spirit, bearing witness with our spirits that we are all in very deed the sons of God' (Colenso, Natal Sermons, Series 3, pp. 189–90, quoted in Guy, 1983a, p. 170, and 1983b, p. 17).

Looking back upon the Natal Sermons in 1871, in the preface to the sixth part of *The Pentateuch and Book of Joshua Critically Examined*, Colenso echoed this summary of the essence of Jesus' teaching and added that in his sermons he had done his best to show that these 'central truths of Christianity' were unaffected by the results of scientific enquiry—'... or rather are confirmed by the witness which the Pentateuch, when stripped of its fictitious character, gives of the working of the one Divine Spirit in all ages' (Colenso, 1872, p. xv).

Although relatively little read at the time—and for the most part similarly neglected by historians—the Natal Sermons were an affirmation of Colenso's passionate belief in the spiritual and moral truths which, as he understood it, lay at the heart of Christianity. As such, the sermons also reveal the absurdity of the charge, frequently levelled at Colenso by his opponents, that his theological position was essentially destructive and negative, the result of doubt, scepticism and disbelief. It was a charge which haunted Colenso's reputation both during his life and after his death—and it was a charge which drew repeated protests from Frances Colenso. In 1866, in a letter to Lady Mary Lyell, she expressed her regret and frustration that her husband's lawyers in London were already advising against the publication of any of the Natal Sermons. He was, she complained,

> ... so abominably calumniated in the so-called Church papers, that I am sure many would be quite astonished if they could see what he really does preach and teach, how far removed from infidelity, how absolutely the opposite of atheism. It is hard to be looked on as a monster by so many good people, who if they could only hear you speak for yourself, would think so very differently of you. The bitterness of these orthodox people is something one could not have imagined beforehand.
>
> (Rees, 1958, p. 119)

Almost twenty years later, in January 1885, some eighteen months after her husband's death, Frances Colenso wrote another letter, this time to Katherine Lyell. Prompted by passages in a newly published volume of *Memoirs of F. D. Maurice*, she protested that

> I am annoyed to see in one of Mr Maurice's letters the old unreasonable charge against him [Colenso] as if he had given his

doubts to the world. He never ventilated *doubts*, he always believed in God, but it seems as if many of the clever men thought that impossible in one who maintained the inauthenticity of the histories of Abraham, Isaac and Jacob ... Do you not agree with me that there is all the difference between a man's publishing his doubts, which is a sign of weakness ... and laying conclusions before the minds of others which are sure to be repugnant to them, but which need to be sifted and viewed by many minds, that the truth may be brought out?

(*Ibid.*, p. 391)

Her husband had been amazed, Frances Colenso recalled in the same letter, by the ignorance he had found on all sides in England when he began publishing his studies of the Pentateuch, and also by the fact that

... instead of the victorious faith which enabled him to hold fast to the living God, and Father of Jesus and of all men, there was amongst them a kind of shrieking, shrinking dread of looking the facts in the face, as if they were afraid of finding out that there was no God, no Heavenly Father! Why should that follow to simple minds from the Old Testament being regarded as partly mythical!

(*Ibid.*, pp. 390–1)

Colenso himself had continued to affirm his own faith until the very end of his life, and in what was to be one of his last sermons in St Peter's Cathedral, Pietermaritzburg, he provided a succinct and fitting summation of his beliefs. The central truth of all religion, Colenso proclaimed,

... is the existence of an Unseen Power, transcending all our knowledge; and the central, essential truth of Christianity is this, that this Unseen Power, in its moral nature, is revealed in human life and action, in that of Jesus and of all true sons of God in every age—that in the human the Divine is manifested, full of grace and truth.

(Colenso, 1883, p. 11)

By then, however, the furore over Colenso's theological opinions had been overshadowed by another conflict. For in the last decade of his life Colenso's conviction that Christian faith must be concretely expressed in human life, together with his long concern for the Zulu and their relationship with white society, led him into new—and now political—controversy.

V CONCLUSION: A POLITICAL POSTSCRIPT

During the final decade of his life, Colenso became immersed in a second sequence of controversies. This time, however, the issues were political, not theological—although for Colenso himself the costly political stand that he now took was one which flowed, both naturally and necessarily, from his religious beliefs. Colenso, as we have seen, was at once a paternalistic Christian imperialist—a believer in the providential role of the British in bringing Christianity and civilization to less advanced peoples—and yet also a passionate advocate of the right of such peoples to respect and of their essential and God-given humanity and dignity. From the mid-1870s onwards, however, the relationship between these two aspects of his beliefs was to become increasingly strained as Colenso steadily discovered the distance between his own religious and imperial ideals and the realities of imperial politics and white attitudes to black Africans.

The process began in 1873 with the so-called 'rebellion' of a minor Zulu chief, Langalibalele, whose clan lived within the borders of Natal. The complex details of the affair cannot be explored in the present context.[12] What is significant, however, is that, from late 1873 onwards, Colenso became increasingly convinced that Langalibalele's alleged rebellion had not only been the subject of official contrivance and duplicity in its origins, but had then been suppressed with great brutality, overt racism and a plain lust for vengeance. When Langalibalele was subsequently tried and banished to Robben Island, Colenso protested not only about the procedural irregularities of the trial and the illegality of the sentence, but also about the way in which the entire process had been organized to justify white acts of oppression and to conceal a long history of duplicity in official dealings with the Zulu in Natal.

Colenso felt bound to act. He protested in the Natal press. He appealed on Langalibalele's behalf in the Natal courts. He compiled careful analyses of the contradictions in the various records and accounts relating to the issue. He enlisted the support of the Aborigines Protection Society in London—to whom his own London lawyer acted as Secretary. Finally, he travelled to England, for the last time, in 1874 to present the case directly to the Colonial Office. And throughout Colenso brought to the attention of the authorities and public the alternative version of events which his black African contacts supplied to him, and which the white colonists and officials had sought to suppress. Although he

---

[12] For a detailed account of the affair and its context, see Guy, 1983a, chs. 13–14.

returned to Natal in December 1874 with promises from the Colonial Secretary that Langalibalele would receive some alleviation of his sentence, Colenso was soon to discover that the efforts of local politicians and officials would render such assurances virtually worthless.

He also returned to scorn and hate from the white community in Natal. To theological heresy, he had now added racial heresy. Most of the white support that he had retained until this point now evaporated. His ecclesiastical opponents rejoiced to see him thus isolate himself yet further. The overwhelming majority of clergy and missionaries signed a statement affirming that the proceedings against Langalibalele were humane, just and necessary; describing Colenso's arguments as nonsense; and claiming that the government of Natal had merely acted as God's own instrument of judgement against Langalibalele. Those who opposed the Natal government on this issue, they asserted, opposed Almighty God. In the aftermath of the affair, meanwhile, Colenso came to learn more and more about the realities of white attitudes to black Africans. Increasing numbers of Africans came to him for advice and assistance—and in seeking to help them Colenso encountered more and more individual cases of injustice, abuse and brutality.

Colenso's enemies accused him of using the issue for his own ends and of seeking to regain the limelight, now that his theological ideas were no longer exciting controversy. In a letter to her brother, Frances Colenso observed that she supposed that those who thought in this way simply could not understand

> ... a man's sacrificing his own private friendships and public supporters on account of a question of wide general interest, of justice or humanity. The Enemy already suggests that he is trying again to make himself conspicuous!! I don't believe there are many in this world who can understand his single-mindedness. Whatever he has done, whether in criticisms of the Old Testament, or his protests against the action of the Government here against this poor chief, it has always been because, like Luther, *he could not do otherwise.*

(Rees, 1958, p. 283)

John Colenso confirmed the accuracy of Frances Colenso's linking of his respective stands upon matters of religious and political principle. Replying to a letter from a member of his congregation in 1874, Colenso thanked him for the kindness and frankness of his letter and then explained that:

I am very sure that you would not be the man to wish me to preach, Sunday after Sunday, what I do not practice—to tell my people to take up, when the occasion comes, heavy burdens of duty on behalf of their fellow-men, when I myself shrink from touching such work with my own hands, though here it has been laid in the providence of God at my very doors. Year after year since I returned to Natal from England I have been *saying this and that from the pulpit*, but my life has been on the whole a very quiet, calm, and happy one. I have not been called to do anything which required resolution and painful effort since in 1862 I published the First Part of my work on the Pentateuch; and I little expected when this year began that the middle would find me in this most distressing conflict, in which I know I am at variance with very many whom I respect, and whose good opinion I would not willingly throw away ... But there is no help for it. I should belie my whole past life, and be false to all my teaching, and should be ashamed in fact to face you all in the pulpit again, if I was not true to my own convictions in this matter. I believe that a fellow-man has been most unfairly tried, and he and his tribe unjustly and cruelly treated.

(Quoted in Cox, 1888, Vol. 2, pp. 373–4)

By 1875, therefore, Colenso was more isolated than ever. He was also increasingly disposed to distrust the aims and actions of colonial and imperial officials in Natal and southern Africa. By 1877, he was coming to suspect that those officials were conspiring to provoke the still independent Zulu kingdom to the north of Natal into war—thereby securing an excuse for annexation.[13] To this end, the Zulu king, Cetshwayo, was portrayed as a bloodthirsty tyrant who both oppressed his own people and posed a military threat to the settlers of Natal and of southern Africa in general. Colenso, again, had reason to doubt both charges, and equal reason to believe that British policy was both deceitful and unjust. Again, he contacted the Aborigines Protection Society, and again he studied the various official records and compared these with other sources, including Zulu ones. In January 1879, Colenso's suspicions were proved correct. After delivering an impossible ultimatum to the Zulu king, British and colonial troops entered Zululand. Confident of easy victory, they and the colony of Natal were shocked by a crushing Zulu victory at the battle of Isandhlwana in which an entire column of British and native troops was wiped out, leaving some 1,800 dead.

---

[13] Again, the present context prevents a full account of this: for details, see Guy, 1983a, chs. 15–20.

Along with an initial panic and a determination for revenge, the colony of Natal proclaimed 12 March 1879 a 'Day of Humiliation and Prayer, in consequence of the great Disaster at Isandhlwana'. The purpose of the day was to be 'to confess our sins and ask for victory'. 'On the former point, at all events,' observed Colenso to the Aborigines Protection Society, 'there is much to be said' (quoted in Guy, 1983a, p. 275). On the Day of Humiliation, Colenso preached in St Peter's Cathedral, Pietermaritzburg. In a sermon that has been described as 'one of the great sermons of the world' and an example of 'the true rhetoric of integrity' (Jarrett-Kerr, 1989, pp. 154–5), Colenso presented a devastating analysis of the origins of the war and a biting critique of official policy, and then called upon his congregation to abjure vengeance, to recognize Zulu grief as well as their own, and to be willing to make peace, even now, with the Zulu. Preaching from a favourite text from the Book of Micah—'What doth the Lord require of thee, but to do justly, and to love mercy, and to walk humbly with thy God?'—Colenso asked:

Wherein, in our invasion of Zululand, have we shown that we are men who 'love mercy'? Did we not lay upon the people heavily, from the very moment we crossed their border, the terrible scourge of war? Have we not killed already, it is said 5,000 human beings, and plundered 10,000 head of cattle? It is true that, in that dreadful disaster, on account of which we are this day humbling ourselves before God, we ourselves have lost many precious lives, and widows and orphans, parents, brothers, sisters, friends, are mourning bitterly their sad bereavements. But are there no griefs—no relatives that mourn their dead—in Zululand? Have we not heard how the wail has gone up in all parts of the country for those who have bravely died—no gallant soldier, no generous colonist, will deny this—have bravely and nobly died in repelling the invader and fighting for their King and fatherland? And shall we kill 10,000 more to avenge the losses of that dreadful day? Will that restore to us those we have lost? Will that endear their memories more to us? Will that please the spirits of any true men, true sons of God, among the dead? Above all, will that please God, who 'requires of us' that we 'do justly' and 'love mercy'? Will such vengeance be anything else but loathsome and abominable in His sight, a pandering to one of the basest passions of our nature, bringing us Christians below the level of the heathen with whom we fight?

(Quoted in Guy, 1983a, p. 278)

If they were to walk humbly with God, Colenso concluded, then they must put their trust in him, and not in the god of force. And if—as Colenso believed was likely—the Zulu king sued for peace, then they should not reject this overture but meet him part way.

Colenso's plea was ignored. The Zulu were bloodily defeated. Cetshwayo was banished and imprisoned in Cape Town, and the Zulu kingdom was partitioned under thirteen British-appointed 'chiefs'. Colenso and his family warned of the instability of the partition and worked for the restoration of Cetshwayo as a belated symbol of British recognition of the wrongs of the Zulu war. Colenso's family believed that the continued campaigning was damaging his health and shortening his life. The Natal press attacked him with increasing ferocity. The colonial government and officials sought to discredit him and smear his reputation with the Colonial Office in London. Colenso and his family continued to produce digests and summaries and analyses of official records, printing them on the press at Bishopstowe.

Eventually, in 1882, King Cetshwayo was finally allowed to visit England—a development for which the Colensos had long been campaigning. Cetshwayo was told that he could return to Zululand, but only to a kingdom reduced in size, the chiefs appointed by Britain retaining control of a substantial part of the former kingdom. In January 1883, Cetshwayo was formally restored, but amidst warnings from the Zulu that the partition imposed on Zululand would result in civil war. By March that war had begun—and the Natal press blamed it on Colenso, accusing him of 'meddling' in Zulu affairs and supporting the 'tyrant' Cetshwayo. On Wednesday 20 June 1883, John Colenso died, peacefully, at Bishopstowe, after a short illness which had begun the previous Saturday. Within a short time, in early 1884, Cetshwayo too was dead, in suspicious circumstances, after an attack upon his lands by other Zulu. The Zulu kingdom had been all but destroyed in the civil war and much of Zululand had been occupied by Boer farmers.

Colenso was buried in front of the altar of 'his' cathedral, St Peter's. The funeral was a moving affair. His coffin was carried from Bishopstowe to Pietermaritzburg on a gun carriage and in Pietermaritzburg shops were closed, shutters drawn and the streets lined with onlookers. St Peter's itself was packed. It was, according to the local press, an occasion unparalleled in the history of Natal. The service included Colenso's favourite hymns—'O God our help in ages past' and 'Through all the changing scenes of life'—and after the service more than 3,000 people filed past the altar and his final resting place (Cox, 1888, Vol. 2, p. 635; Guy, 1983a, pp. 344–5).

Among the Zulu, an affectionate remembrance of Colenso continued into the early twentieth century. But there soon began a long process in which the memory of his life and the causes he espoused became fragmented. Only rarely are the various strands of Colenso's life as missionary, Zulu scholar, biblical critic, theologian and preacher, and political campaigner brought together—and even less often are they understood to have formed a coherent whole, his various concerns and commitments having worked creatively upon each other as his life and career developed. More usually, he is remembered as a supporting player—but one who appears only briefly, if entertainingly, on the stage—in one or other of the ecclesiastical or political dramas in which he participated. Thus there is Colenso the missionary heretic and arithmetical biblical critic; there is Colenso the litigant, repeatedly calling the courts to his aid in his theological and ecclesiastical disputes; and there is Colenso the politician and campaigner for the Zulu—a figure who, it has appropriately been observed, can all too easily be mistaken for 'a twentieth-century liberal who somehow wandered into the wrong century' (Etherington, 1978, p. 40).

Because of this fragmentation—and because Colenso so often found himself on the losing side—it is easy to write him off as a failure. But there are grounds for another, more positive, assessment. Consistency is one such ground. We have seen that the various aspects of his life in fact formed a coherent whole, his Maurician theology leading him to a particular understanding of the missionary vocation; his missionary experience further shaping his theology; and his theology and missionary experience alike leading him to political commitment and engagement. And for some recent historians and theologians—concerned primarily with the history of Christianity in Africa rather than that of the Victorian Church of England—this is enough to have prompted a re-assessment of Colenso as one of the most remarkable Victorian bishops and missionaries, who understood the dilemmas of the encounter between European Christianity and traditional African culture, and who may even be described as a pioneer of the exploration of an authentically African understanding of Christianity (Hastings, 1994, p. 265; Isichei, 1995, p. 94; Mosothoane, 1991; Pato 1989, pp. 169–70). But there is another consistency to be found in Colenso also. A careful reading of his theological works, from the *Village Sermons*, through the commentary on Romans and the studies of the Pentateuch, to the *Natal Sermons*, reveals a steadily developing but remarkably coherent and internally consistent example of Broad Church theology, and one forged, moreover, not in the relative security of academic life but in the midst of the pastoral and evangelistic demands of parochial, episcopal and missionary ministry.

Perhaps most of all, however, we should reassess Colenso because of the consistency he sought to display not only in the preaching but also in the living of his faith. When back in England in 1874 to plead the case of Langalibalele, Colenso visited the Archbishop of Canterbury, A. C. Tait. Tait told him that his name was associated with infidelity and that he needed to clear himself of this charge. Colenso replied, Tait recorded in his diary, that he was engaged continually in preaching Christian truth but that he '... held indeed that it was the Christian life, rather than the formal assertion of Christian doctrine, that he was bound to preach' (Davidson and Benham, 1891, Vol. 2, p. 305). Twenty-five years later John Khumalo, a Zulu educated at Ekukhanyeni, recognized that same quality in Colenso's story:

> His deeds on behalf of the natives, his questionings, discussions, the briefs he held, were themselves of the nature of light; they tended to produce light; they tended to glow. The circumstances in which he laboured may pass and vanish from view, but his example is a beacon of light.
>
> (Quoted in Guy, 1983a, p. 352)

And in so thinking, Khumalo echoed the sentiments of no less a figure than King Cetshwayo. For on hearing the news of Colenso's death, Cetshwayo wrote asking '... that a stone may be bought in my name, which shall be set up over the grave of my Father, to show that we loved him in return for his so great love to us, and his efforts to deliver us out of our distress' (Guy, 1983a, p. 345). So it was that Colenso's tombstone carried the word 'Sobantu'—the name first given to him over a quarter of a century earlier by the Zulu. It was a fitting memorial. For Colenso—in his own blunt, uncompromising manner—had already engaged, in his own day and way, with both the relationship between Christianity and other religions and with the implications of Christian discipleship in the realms of social justice and racial oppression. It was to take most of the Christian churches the better part of another century before they even began seriously to confront such issues. And after more than another quarter of a century of such belated (re)engagement, the churches' struggle with these issues still remains nearer its beginning than its end. Perhaps, then, Colenso's life was not such a failure after all.

BIBLIOGRAPHY

E. Abbott and L. Campbell (1897) *Life and Letters of Benjamin Jowett*, Volume 2, London.

R. apRoberts (ed.) (1974) *Anthony Trollope: Clergymen of the Church of England*, Leicester, Leicester University Press.

J. B. Brain (1984) 'Toleration and persecution in colonial Natal' in W. J. Sheils (ed.) *Persecution and Toleration*, pp. 379–92, Oxford, Blackwell.

O. Chadwick (1972) *The Victorian Church*, Part 2, London, Adam & Charles Black.

J. W. Colenso (1853) *Village Sermons*, Cambridge, Macmillan.

J. W. Colenson (1854) *Church Missions among the Heathen in the Diocese of Natal*, reprinted in Edgecombe (1982), pp. 1–21.

J. W. Colenso (1855) *Ten Weeks in Natal: a journal of a first tour of visitation among the colonists and Zulu Kafirs of Natal*, Cambridge, Macmillan.

J. W. Colenso (1861a) *A Letter to His Grace the Archbishop of Canterbury, upon the question of the proper treatment of cases of polygamy, as found already existing in converts from heathenism.*

J. W. Colenso (1861b) *St Paul's Epistle to the Romans: newly translated and explained from a missionary point of view*, Cambridge, Macmillan.

J. W. Colenso (1862) *The Pentateuch and Book of Joshua Critically Examined*, Part 1, London, Longman.

J. W. Colenso (1863a) *The Pentateuch and Book of Joshua Critically Examined*, Part 2, London, Longman.

J. W. Colenso (1863b) *The Pentateuch and Book of Joshua Critically Examined*, Part 3, London, Longman.

J. W. Colenso (1863c) *The Pentateuch and Book of Joshua Critically Examined*, Part 4, London, Longman.

J. W. Colenso (1865a) 'On the efforts of missionaries among savages', *Journal of the Anthropological Society*, Vol. 3, pp. ccxlviii–cclxxxix.

J. W. Colenso (1865b) *On Missions to the Zulus in Natal and Zululand*, London, printed for private circulation (reprinted in Edgecombe, 1982).

J. W. Colenso (1865c) *The Pentateuch and Book of Joshua Critically Examined*, Part 5, London, Longman.

J. W. Colenso (1867) *Natal Sermons*, Series 1, London, Trübner.

J. W. Colenso (1868) *Natal Sermons*, Series 2, London, Trübner.

J. W. Colenso (1872) *The Pentateuch and Book of Joshua Critically Examined*, Part 6, London, Longman.

J. W. Colenso (1883) *Three Sermons Preached in the Cathedral Church of St Peter's Maritzburg*, Pietermaritzburg.

G. W. Cox (1888) *The Life of John William Colenso D.D. Bishop of Natal*, 2 vols., London, Ridgway.

I. Darby (1984) 'Bishop Colenso and eucharistic theology', *Journal of Theology for Southern Africa*, Vol. 46, pp. 20–8.

I. Darby (1989) 'Colenso and baptism', *Journal of Theology for Southern Africa*, Vol. 67, pp. 63–6.

R. Davidson and W. Benham (1891) *Life of Archibald Campbell Tait: Archbishop of Canterbury*, 2 vols., London, Macmillan.

F. E. Deist (1984) 'John William Colenso: biblical scholar' in J. A. Loader and J. H. Le Roux (eds.) *Old Testament Essays*, Vol. 2, pp. 98–132, Pretoria, Department of Old Testament, University of South Africa.

J. Draper and G. West (1989) 'Anglicans and scripture in South Africa' in England and Paterson (1989), pp. 30–52.

R. Edgecombe (1980) 'Bishop Colenso and the Zulu nation', *Journal of Natal and Zulu History*, Vol. 3, pp. 15–29.

R. Edgecombe (ed.) (1982) *Bringing Forth Light: Five Tracts on Bishop Colenso's Zulu Mission*, Pietermaritzburg, University of Natal Press and Durban, Killie Campbell Africana Library.

F. England and T. Paterson (1989) *Bounty in Bondage: Essays in Honour of Edward King, Dean of Cape Town*, Johannesburg, Raven Press.

N. Etherington (1978) *Preachers, Peasants and Politics in Southeast Africa 1835–1880: African Christian Communication in Natal, Pondoland, and Zululand*, Royal Historical Society, London.

S. Gilley (1994) 'The Church of England in the nineteenth century' in S. Gilley and W. J. Sheils (eds.) *A History of Religion in Britain: Practice and Belief from Pre-Roman Times to the Present*, pp. 291–305, Oxford, Blackwell.

C. Gray (1876) *The Life of Robert Gray*, 2 vols., London, Rivington.

*J. Guy (1983a) *The Heretic: A Study of the Life of John William Colenso 1814–1883*, Pietermaritzburg, University of Natal Press and Johannesburg, Raven Press.

J. Guy (1983b) 'The religious thinking of J. W. Colenso: the theology of a heretic', *Religion in Southern Africa*, Vol. 4, pp. 3–20.

J. Guy (1991) 'Learning from history: religion, politics, and the problem of contextualization—the case of J. W. Colenso' in C. F. Hallencreutz and M. Palmberg (eds.) *Religion and Politics in Southern Africa*, pp. 185–93, Uppsala, Scandinavian Institute of African Studies.

A. Hastings (1994) *The Church in Africa 1450–1950*, Oxford, Oxford University Press.

P. Hinchliff (1962) 'John William Colenso: a fresh appraisal', *Journal of Ecclesiastical History*, Vol. 13, pp. 203–16.

P. Hinchliff (1963) *The Anglican Church in South Africa*, London, Darton, Longman & Todd.

P. Hinchliff (1964) *John William Colenso: Bishop of Natal*, London, Nelson.

*P. Hinchliff (1986) 'Ethics, evolution and biblical criticism in the thought of Benjamin Jowett and John William Colenso', *Journal of Ecclesiastical History*, Vol. 37, pp. 91–110.

E. Isichei (1995) *A History of Christianity in Africa: From Antiquity to the Present*, London, Society for Promoting Christian Knowledge.

*M. Jarrett-Kerr (1989) 'Victorian certainty and Zulu doubt: a study in Christian missionary hermeneutics from Shaka to Colenso' in D. Jasper and T. R. Wright (eds.) *The Critical Spirit and the Will to Believe: Essays in Nineteenth-century Literature and Religion*, pp. 145–57, London, Macmillan.

E. Mosothoane (1991) 'John William Colenso: pioneer in the quest for an authentic African Christianity', *Scottish Journal of Theology*, Vol. 44, pp. 215–36.

L. Pato (1989) 'Becoming an African church' in England and Paterson (1989), pp. 159–76.

W. Rees (1958) *Colenso Letters from Natal*, Pietermaritzburg, Shuter & Shooter.

S. Ridge (1994) 'A sifting process: the truth, language and Bishop Colenso', *Journal of Theology for Southern Africa*, Vol. 88, pp. 21–33.

*J. Rogerson (1984) *Old Testament Criticism in the Nineteenth Century: England and Germany*, London, Society for Promoting Christian Knowledge.

J. Rogerson (1988) 'The Old Testament' in P. Avis (ed.) *The History of Christian Theology Volume 2: The Study and Use of the Bible*, pp. 1–150, Basingstoke, Marshall Pickering.

J. Rogerson (1993) 'British responses to Kuenen's Pentateuchal studies' in P. Dirksen and A. Van der Kooij (eds.) *Abraham Kuenen (1828–1891): His Major Contributions to the Study of the Old Testament*, pp. 91–104, Leiden, E. J. Brill.

CHAPTER 5

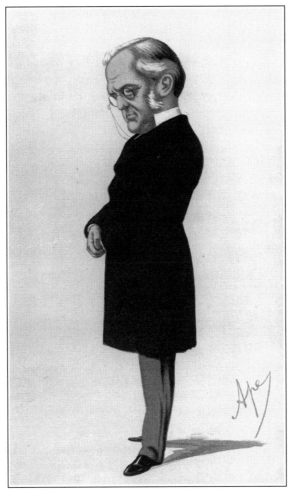

FRIEDRICH MAX MÜLLER

PROFESSOR FRIEDRICH MAX MÜLLER AND THE MISSIONARY CAUSE

I N 1860, when Professor Friedrich Max Müller squared up to face his rival, Professor Monier Williams (later Sir Monier Monier-Williams), the prize was the occupancy of the prestigious and handsomely remunerated Boden Professorship at the University of Oxford. Many of those involved on the sidelines during the contest between these scholars, however, believed that what was at stake was far more than simply the advancement of one or other of the two candidates. They held that the future success of Britain's missionary efforts in the subcontinent of India,[1] and even the future stability of British rule in this region might be directly affected by the calibre of the person appointed to the vacant professorial chair. Those judging the merits of the two candidates were only too well aware that, barely two years earlier, British territories in India had been convulsed by the 'Indian Mutiny', and that the Established Church in Britain had been similarly shaken by the publication of *Essays and Reviews* but months previously. This was not a time to make a mistake when choosing the right man to bolster both Britain's standing in the subcontinent and the momentum of the missionary cause.

This chapter will be devoted to an exploration of the career and ideas of one of the personalities at the centre of the fiercely contended competition for the Boden Chair in 1860, namely, Max Müller. (The reasons for his unsuccessful candidacy will be discussed in section IV.) As we will see in section I, Müller was dismissed by many of his peers as a controversial maverick, but was popularly held in the latter part of the nineteenth century to be Britain's foremost voice on anything touching upon the nation's relationship with India. Müller's opinions about Christian mission are of particular interest, and not just because of his national, and indeed international, reputation as an expert on India past and present. Müller's views reveal the moral, intellectual and religious difficulties that had to be faced at that time by individuals who continued to profess the Christian faith while actively working to promote a more tolerant and even-handed study of other religious traditions. In seeking to advance what they regarded as the 'civilizing' influence of Christianity, they also found themselves searching for ways in which to defend, albeit selectively, the worth of those other religious and cultural traditions to which they had devoted long years of study. We will begin by briefly setting Müller's scholarly career in context before devoting the remainder of the chapter to an examination of his attitudes to Christian mission in India.

---

[1] In the nineteenth century, 'India' included the countries now known as Pakistan, Bangladesh, Myanmar (formerly Burma) and Sri Lanka (formerly Ceylon).

I MÜLLER'S ACADEMIC CAREER

Max Müller has been ranked alongside great Victorians such as John Ruskin, Charles Kingsley and Matthew Arnold as one of the 'father-figures of the Victorian fireside' (Trompf, 1968, p. 200). Now that Müller's work is no longer generally known, such a claim made on behalf of an expatriate German scholar whose interests lay in the study of language, religion and mythology may seem extravagant. In late Victorian Britain, however, Müller occupied a central role in the intellectual life of the nation, particularly as a 'pundit' on matters pertaining to Britain's relationship with India. By the time of his death in 1900, Müller had emerged as 'one of the giants of the English intellectual world' (Kitagawa and Strong, 1985, p. 184). *The Times*, for example, noted in Müller's obituary that his lectures had become 'part of the staple of conversation at dinner tables' (Voigt, 1981, p. 2). Such was Müller's reputation that he has been portrayed not only as 'the father of comparative religion' (Sharpe, 1975, p. 35) but also as introducing to Britain, if not actually inventing, the scientific study of language (Dowling, 1982, p. 161). His writings, particularly on India, were internationally known and read by eminent contemporaries including the Russian novelist, Leo Tolstoy, and the American psychologist, William James. Müller's home in Oxford became almost a place of pilgrimage for visiting Indians. Keshub Chunder Sen, P. C. Mozoomdar and Swami Vivekananda, among the most prominent Hindu thinkers of their day,[2] all spent time at Müller's home.

Müller was born in 1823 in Dessau, which was then the capital of the ducal state of Anhalt-Dessau in eastern Germany, and his earliest days were spent in a home which was a centre of artistic life in Dessau. Müller's father was the romantic poet, Wilhelm Müller, who served as librarian at the ducal palace and as a teacher in the Gymnasium (grammar school) of Dessau. Tragically, Wilhelm Müller died when his son was only four years of age and, consequently, Müller and his mother, Adelheide von Basedow, were forced to live in more straightened circumstances. The von Basedow family had long been prominent in the affairs of the Duchy of Anhalt-Dessau and had supplied the small state with political and military officials. Adelheide von Basedow was well educated and moved in circles that included the poet Johann von Goethe and the composer Felix Mendelssohn. She was also deeply religious and the Lutheran religion played an important part in the life shared by Müller and his mother.

---

[2] See Chapter 6.

After the death of Wilhelm Müller, the Duke and the von Basedow family helped the struggling Adelheide to support herself and her children. The Duke continued to take an interest in the young Müller, whose precocious skill as a musician led to him being invited to play at the ducal palace long after the death of his father. The experience of poverty was one that was to stay with Müller as he looked for financial security in later life. He also had a strong sense that he had to live up to the memory of his father.

In 1836, Müller was sent to Leipzig to finish his school education and remained there to complete an undergraduate degree and then a doctorate on the philosophy of Spinoza at the University. Already fluent in Latin and Greek from his earlier schooling, Müller's linguistic studies at university expanded to include Hebrew and Arabic before he undertook the study of Sanskrit, the language preserved in the texts of ancient India. Urged on by childhood memories of seeing pictures of Benares, a city sacred to Hindus, in books at Dessau and by more recent reading about Hindu philosophy, Müller became a student under Professor Hermann Brockhaus, the holder of the first professorship in Sanskrit at the University of Leipzig. Knowledge of Sanskrit was relatively new to Europe and was largely sought by specialists interested in comparative philology and the history of languages, and by those who wished to penetrate the still mysterious worlds of Indian religion, philosophy and literature. By the second decade of the nineteenth century, linguistic links between Greek and Latin, the classical languages of Europe, and Sanskrit had been established, thus exciting scholars with the prospect of new discoveries to be made through comparative studies. Müller was drawn to the study of Sanskrit, both as a further tool in his linguistic studies and as a gateway to understanding Hindu philosophy: 'I began to feel that I must know something special, something that no other philosopher knew' (Müller, 1901, p. 142).

On graduating, Müller moved from Leipzig to Berlin to study under Franz Bopp, an eminent Sanskritist and comparative philologist, and the idealist philosopher Friedrich Schelling. It was at this time that Müller committed himself to what would become his lifelong interest in India, while, as in Dessau after the death of his father, living a meagre lifestyle haunted by financial insecurity. During his long years as a student, Müller was further shaped by the German romantic-idealist tradition to which he had been first exposed through the ethos of his family home. Its influence was never to leave him and was evident in his mature thinking, for example in his fascination with language and symbolism and in his quest to understand the processes of development at work in nature and history. Yet his reliance upon a historical approach made him critical of thinkers who were cavalier in their treatment of the historical facts of religious traditions. Thus, although Müller began his higher studies in the field of philosophy, he increasingly became impatient with what he viewed as a trend in German idealist philosophy, which encouraged generalizations about the development of 'religion' rather than addressing the histories of particular religions. His doubts made Müller critical of both Schelling and Hegelianism, which was then at the peak of its influence in German universities. Müller makes plain that the beginning of his Sanskrit studies under Brockhaus at Leipzig marked the end of his specialized study of philosophy (Müller, 1901, pp. 142f.).[3,4] The same misgivings about the lack of attention paid to historical detail later shaped his responses both to Charles Darwin and to the wide-ranging theories of British evolutionist anthropologists such as Herbert Spencer, E. B. Tylor and Andrew Lang. Müller was similarly critical of the so-called 'quest for the historical Jesus' undertaken by continental scholars, including his friend E. Renan, which Müller believed produced little more than the author's own image of Jesus (*ibid.*, p. 279). It would be history and philology that would provide the 'basic building blocks' of Müller's own theory of religion (Kitagawa and Strong, 1985, p. 191).

In 1845, Müller moved to Paris, where he studied under Eugène Burnouf, 'Europe's greatest pioneer orientalist' (*ibid.*, p. 182), who shared the religious eclecticism and dislike of what Müller called 'priestcraft' that, as we shall see, characterized Müller's own outlook (*ibid.*; Müller, 1902, Vol. I, p. 34). Through his involvement with scholars of the stature of Bopp and Burnouf, Müller was able to extend and exploit his own considerable abilities as a student of European classical languages and Sanskrit. It was Müller's association with Burnouf that was to guide him into the project with which his name would become indissolubly linked. This was the translation of the Rig-Veda, a work which took shape between the twelfth and eighth centuries BCE[5] and which is part of the extensive body of Hindu scriptures known as the Veda ('Knowledge'). The Veda, which was originally transmitted orally, is believed by Hindus to contain eternal truths made known by ancient seers. It has been preserved by Brahmins, members of the highest caste, specializing in ritual, and committed to textual form in the language of Sanskrit. The Rig-Veda contains the oldest portions of the Veda, in particular the verses that

[3] Müller's philosophical training and outlook is discussed at length in Kitagawa and Strong, 1985 and Trompf, 1978.

[4] The abbreviations f. and ff. indicate that the reference continues onto the page or pages following the one cited.

[5] Before the Common, or Christian, Era.

would have been recited by one of the chief officiants at the sacrificial rites. Müller's decision to devote himself to the study of the Rig-Veda was greatly influenced by Burnouf's advice that such a study would provide a key to understanding Indian religion and mythology as distinct from Indian philosophy (Müller, 1901, pp. 172f.). In keeping with his growing scepticism about the value of philosophers' pronouncements on the nature and development of religious traditions, Müller may also have reacted against the idealist philosopher Arthur Schopenhauer's dismissal of the then little-known early portions of the Veda as 'priestly rubbish' (Voigt, 1981, p. 3).

The quest for Sanskrit manuscripts took Müller to London, where he arrived in 1846 as a penniless and virtually unknown scholar. There he was taken under the wing of the Prussian ambassador and amateur scholar, Baron von Bunsen, who took an interest in Müller not only as a fellow German but also as a young scholar researching in areas close to Bunsen's own heart. Müller worked in London for two years and then found his resting place in Oxford, where he remained until his death in 1900. Müller's life as a scholar in England, therefore, coincided almost exactly with the second half of the nineteenth century. In one sense, Müller put down deep roots in Oxford. He became a member of Christ Church College and consequently of the University, and, having first held the post of deputy professor, was made Taylorian Professor of Modern European Languages in 1854. Other University appointments followed, but not positions that gave formal recognition to Müller's reputation as a Sanskritist. After a lengthy struggle to convince his future wife's family of the soundness of both his financial prospects and his Christian beliefs, Müller married Georgina Grenfell at Bray Church in Berkshire in 1859. He thus became connected by marriage to Charles Kingsley and J. A. Froude. Müller's family life was happy and three daughters and a son followed. As his life advanced, the earlier anxieties over financial insecurity were eased. However, Müller had to face yet again the agony of family bereavement when first his eldest daughter, Ada, died from meningitis just before her sixteenth birthday in 1876 and then Mary, his second daughter, died in 1886, having fallen ill during pregnancy. These fresh blows, falling on childhood memories of the death of his father, left Müller broken in spirit and acutely conscious of life as the mere waiting-room to death.

Over a long working life, Müller gathered numerous academic awards and many honours, and yet it has been suggested that, whether in terms of his own experience or from the more detached standpoint of the historian, 'Müller's career seems a failure from either point of view'

(Dowling, 1982, p. 160). Indeed, Müller's academic career at the University of Oxford, although distinguished, was not without its disappointments, of which the greatest was his failure to win the Boden Professorship in Sanskrit in 1860. According to his rival, Monier Williams, such was Müller's disappointment that after 1860 Müller regularly avoided or snubbed Monier Williams and his family on the streets of Oxford (Monier-Williams, unpublished autobiography, pp. 373ff.).

Müller was given a specially created professorship in comparative philology in 1868 but tendered his resignation in 1875, giving as his public reason that he wished to devote more time to his study of India and in particular to the study of the language of Sanskrit. Privately, however, Müller declared to his friends that he was tired of Oxford's university and ecclesiastical intrigues and confessed to a sense of remaining an outsider due to his German birth. Müller's friends and supporters, including Lord Salisbury, then Secretary of State for India, and Benjamin Jowett, the scholar and prominent Broad Churchman, campaigned for Müller to be given a post that would enable him to continue his Sanskrit studies and retain a connection with the University. Early in 1876, a deputy professor was appointed to relieve Müller of the routine duties associated with the chair in comparative philology and Müller pursued his researches in Oxford until his death in 1900.

As well as experiencing a lingering, bitter disappointment over the outcome of his candidacy for the Boden Chair, Müller found himself at the centre of a number of scholarly controversies about the reliability and value of his researches. The translation of the Rig-Veda is often presented as the culmination of Müller's scholarly endeavours as a Sanskritist. This translation was undertaken with the support of H. H. Wilson (the first Boden Professor of Sanskrit at the University of Oxford from 1832) and under the patronage initially of von Bunsen and then of the East India Company. Müller laboured on this project from 1849 until 1873, but the result was the translation of just over 1 per cent of the original Sanskrit text. W. D. Whitney, an eminent American Sanskritist at the University of Yale, savaged the published fruits of Müller's lengthy study of the Rig-Veda as mostly made up of 'padding' (quoted in Tull, 1991, pp. 28f.). Müller himself admitted that other demands on his time had slowed his progress, but much of Whitney's criticism was aimed at Müller's decision to rely heavily upon a much later Sanskrit commentary, which itself had to be translated. It was left to another German scholar, Theodor Aufrecht, to complete the first full translation of the Rig-Veda—without a commentary. From this point on, Müller's reputation among his peers as one of the world's leading Sanskritists remained the subject of debate.

As he worked on his translation of the Rig-Veda, Müller also gave time to writing a series of lectures on the Science of Language (1861–4). He wrote subsequently on the Science of Religion (1873), the Science of Thought (1888) and the Science of Mythology (1897). Apart from other substantial volumes on topics falling under these broad headings, Müller wrote and lectured prolifically on a wide range of subjects of literary, political and historical interest. From 1876, he also undertook to edit the series, The Sacred Books of the East, a mammoth undertaking comprising fifty volumes including several volumes of translations by Müller himself.

Müller's interests broadened beyond the confines of pure scholarship as he gave more time to exploring the origins and development of religion and mythology, a decision possibly shaped by his failure to win the Boden Chair (MacDonnell, 1967–8 edn (a), p. 1025). In his writings, both on language and on the development of religion and mythology, was to be found the unwavering assumption that human beings were rational: 'As far as we can trace back the footsteps of man' (quoted in Sharpe, 1975, p. 41). Müller's construction of a theory to illustrate the truth of this claim, in the guise of the science of language, again drew the withering fire of Whitney, who at one point referred to Müller as 'one of the greatest humbugs of the century' (quoted in Dowling, 1982, p. 160). On the other hand, it has been observed that Müller's insistence upon the nobility and rationality of the human being was deeply reassuring in an age troubled by Darwinism and that this was one reason for the popularity of Müller's ideas with Victorian audiences (*ibid.*, p. 161).

Müller's forays into the comparative study of religion and mythology similarly led to fierce controversy. His reliance upon texts at the expense of other forms of evidence and his conviction that human beings were rational from the earliest days of the human race resulted in a collision of opinions with the emergent schools of anthropology and folklore, then heavily influenced by Darwinism. Again, Müller found himself beset by a persistent and hardly less virulent critic in the person of the folklorist, Andrew Lang.[6] To many later academics, the criticisms levelled against Müller by the likes of Whitney and Lang appear to be well founded and the honours heaped on Müller out of proportion to his lasting contribution to scholarship. But few would question that Müller probably did more than any other scholar of his day to open up the minds of the

[6] A full evaluation of Müller's contribution to these various areas of late Victorian scholarship goes beyond the scope of the present discussion of his attitudes to Christian mission. For fuller discussion of Müller's work as a comparative philologist and Sanskritist, see Dowling, 1982 and Tull, 1991; on Müller's theories about the origins of religion and the development of mythology, see Sharpe, 1975 and Kitagawa and Strong, 1985; on Müller as the founder of the 'science of religion', see Wiebe, 1995.

educated public to the varied forms that religion may take and thus to the importance of the new discipline of the comparative study of religions (see, for example, Chadwick, 1970, p. 36).

Although the value of Müller's work, both as a translator and as a theorist, was vigorously questioned by other scholars even during his lifetime, his reputation in the eyes of the reading public was clearly enhanced by the fact that his work was not confined by boundaries prescribed by strict adherence to the methods of objective, historical science. Müller has aptly been described as an 'eirenic enthusiast' (from the Greek *eirenicon*, meaning 'a proposal making for peace'), namely, one for whom 'the attempt to understand religion was an attempt to understand man, and an attempt, too, to persuade men to understand one another' (Sharpe, 1975, p. 44). The comparative study of religion, therefore, was for Müller more than a pure, historical science; it was a practical activity, which was concerned to bring together those of differing religious persuasions (*ibid.*, p. 252). Müller's work was held in high regard by Queen Victoria and the royal household as a result of links forged with Albert, the Prince Consort, to whom Müller had been introduced by von Bunsen. In 1896, at the Queen's initiative, Müller was made a Privy Counsellor, although this was for his scholarly work and not for his services to the Indian Empire as Queen Victoria had originally proposed. As a consequence of such recognition, Müller felt fully justified in referring in the closing pages of his autobiography to having spent 'nearly a whole life in the service of my adopted country', namely Britain (Müller, 1901, p. 304).

II PUBLIC DEBATES ON MISSIONARY ACTIVITY IN INDIA

One aspect of Müller's 'life in the service of my adopted country' was his willingness to participate in the national debates of late Victorian Britain. A topical question, which generated considerable controversy, concerned the legitimacy and scope of Christian missionary activity, particularly within Britain's expanding Empire, which included subjects of different religious faiths. The place of missionary work in India had provided the focus for especially heated controversy in Britain at the beginning of the nineteenth century, partly as a result of growing public dissatisfaction with the administration of British territories in India. In fact, by the time Müller arrived in Oxford in the middle of the century, a considerable modification had taken place in British policy relating to missionary work in India.

Before 1813, the East India Company, which regulated British territories in India, had employed a licensing system to control the entry of missionaries, not least because the Company favoured a policy of non-interference in local customs. Gaining such licences, however, in general had not proved to be a problem and even missionaries without licences had been tolerated in practice. This acceptance was not extended so readily to missionaries of the Evangelical wing. Officials of the East India Company distrusted dissenting Evangelical missionaries, suspecting them of harbouring radical political views. As a consequence, Evangelical missionary societies had not applied for licenses prior to 1813 (Stanley, 1990, pp. 98f.). All the while, India, in the eyes of many Evangelicals and others, appeared to be rife with 'idolaters' and calling out for rapid and effective evangelization.

Growing dissatisfaction with limitations imposed on missionary activity, coupled with accusations that the East India Company was actively supporting Hindu practice through its policy of non-interference, led to increased pressure on the British government and the East India Company for a change of policy. The Evangelical Revival in England played no small part in bringing this about and in motivating missionaries and administrators to spread the Christian gospel in British India. Charles Grant, a director of the East India Company and a member of the Evangelical Clapham Sect, was a powerful voice in support of change, whilst Charles Simeon, Vicar of Holy Trinity, Cambridge, inspired a number of undergraduates at Cambridge to offer themselves for missionary service. Policies that were held to have limited the effectiveness of missionary activity were reversed in 1813 and an Anglican bishop was appointed to Calcutta in 1814. In 1833, Calcutta was accorded the status of a metropolitan see and bishops were appointed to Madras and Bombay. The appointment of Lord William Bentinck (a Benthamite) to the Governor-Generalship of the East India Company in Calcutta in 1828 saw an increasing shift towards active interference in local customs, including religion, as Evangelical missionaries joined forces with utilitarian officials of the East India Company in condemnation of popular Hindu practices.

In 1857–8, British assumptions about the duration and stability of British rule in India were challenged by the uprising referred to variously by British commentators of the time as the 'Indian Mutiny' and by later Indian historians as the First War of Indian Independence.[7] In the reorganization of the administration of British possessions in India that

---

[7] See Chapter 3, pp. 122–4.

followed, territories formerly held by the East India Company were incorporated within the British Empire in 1858. The aftermath of the 'Mutiny' made the British government cautious about adopting policies that might be seen as interference and thus be liable to provoke renewed unrest among the Indian population. However, the transition from administration under the East India Company to direct imperial rule was effected by the 'great Evangelical administrators and soldiers' who were among 'the best friends of the missionaries' (Neill, 1964, p. 269). By that time, the furtherance of Christian mission had become inextricably bound up with attempts to define Britain's role in India and indeed to justify Britain's presence in India. The marked growth in the number of Protestant missionaries working in India between 1789 and 1860 was merely the prelude to the 'phenomenal growth' that took place in the latter half of the century (Williams, 1994, p. 389). This expansion of missionary activity, however, was not accomplished without considerable debate about both the principles upon which it should be based and the practical methods by which it should be pursued—a debate to which Evangelicals, Anglo-Catholics and Broad Church followers all contributed.

The uncompromising rejection of other religions as routes to damnation and as sources of moral depravity, and the profound horror of 'idolatry', which typified the attitudes of many Evangelicals, were challenged in the theological questionings of members of the Broad Church. F. D. Maurice, for example, in his Boyle Lectures of 1845, made a plea that Christians, when dealing with other religions, 'deal fairly with facts which Christian apologists have often perverted' (Maurice, 1877, p. x). He acknowledged that Christianity could learn from other religions, all of which express something of God's relationship to humanity; in spite of their differences, there is in the religions 'a witness of unity' (*ibid.*, p.127). In 1853, Maurice was removed from his post at King's College, London, for expressing his doubts about the morality of eternal punishment. In the process of questioning this teaching of the Athanasian Creed, Maurice also indirectly undermined one of the main justifications for missionary work: namely, to save those who would otherwise be damned.[8]

If Britain's interests in India had a considerable bearing upon the debate about Christian mission, they had no less an impact upon the ways in which India and its ancient language of Sanskrit were studied in Britain during the nineteenth century. Increasingly vociferous demands for a

---

[8] *RVB*, II, 10, p. 224; *RVB*, III, 1.2.3, pp. 19ff.

more concerted attempt to spread the gospel throughout the length and breadth of India shaped expectations of the purposes that the study of India and its languages might fulfil. The study of Sanskrit in Britain was already under way before Müller's arrival in Britain in 1846. From its beginnings, it had been closely linked to Britain's extensive interests in India, managed as these were until 1858 by the East India Company. Sanskrit was taught to officials of the East India Company both at Haileybury College in England and at the College of Fort William in Calcutta, which were financed by the East India Company. Its study served to produce translations of ancient texts which, it was believed, would help those directly involved in the administration of the affairs of the East India Company by throwing light on India's customs and social institutions. Some of those brought to the study of Sanskrit in this way, however, found that it opened the door to Indian literature, religion and philosophy, and so came to devote their lives to the translation of Sanskrit classics out of a love of the language and the sentiments that they found expressed in its great works. Many of these early British students of Sanskrit, including H. H. Wilson (the first Boden Professor of Sanskrit at the University of Oxford), knew India well, having lived and worked there in some cases for decades.

Müller took up the study of Sanskrit having followed a path that was significantly different from that commonly trod by his British counter-parts. Müller, as we have seen, embraced the study of Sanskrit as part of a new continental tradition of comparative philology, sometimes referred to as 'the science of language'. Germany did not share Britain's commercial and political interests in India and so German scholars coming to the study of Sanskrit through the route of comparative philology felt less compulsion to take an interest in contemporary India. Few German scholars had first-hand experience of India, and this was the case with Müller, who never visited India. On coming to Britain, therefore, Müller had to establish himself in the eyes of British Sanskritists, who tended to be suspicious of the dense theorizing of continental, and particularly German, philologists. British Sanskritists were more inclined to view India's remote past through eyes that had surveyed India's present, and to draw upon later Indian commentators rather than rely solely upon the linguistic evidence contained within ancient texts. It has been suggested that Müller's reliance on a later commentary in his translation of the Rig-Veda, which so incensed his arch-critic, Whitney, might have been influenced by Wilson, on whose support Müller then depended (Tull, 1991, p. 37). If this was indeed the case, it would not have been out of keeping with Müller's need to find a place within Britain's Sanskrit 'establishment' and especially with the holder of a chair in Sanskrit that Müller himself might have hoped in time to occupy. In fact, Müller's hope of securing this well-paid position appears to have figured in the delicate and lengthy negotiations that took place prior to his marriage (Chaudhuri, 1974, p. 114).

As a scholar working in Britain, Müller repeatedly turned his mind to the question of what contribution, if any, the study of Sanskrit and India's cultural traditions could make to resolving current problems being faced by British officials and policy makers in nineteenth-century India (see, for example, Müller, 1893). Could a knowledge of Sanskrit and the Sanskrit tradition be of practical use to administrators and missionaries? Facing such questions took on a greater urgency after 1835 when the British administration in India adopted the policy of promoting English as the medium of education. The arguments leading to this decision had included intemperate and negative judgements on the value of the legacy of the Sanskrit tradition, which Sanskrit scholars working in Britain were understandably anxious to refute. In addition to being a Sanskritist, Müller was also an early pioneer in the comparative study of religion at the University of Oxford at a time when that University continued to be dominated by the interests of the Anglican Church. With his particular interest in the religious traditions of India, it is hardly surprising that Müller felt called upon to speak about the whole enterprise of Christian mission in India and its relationship to the comparative study of religion. His thoughts about these questions were voiced most clearly during his candidacy for the Boden Chair in 1860 and in his later writings and lectures, which expressed his hopes for future religious reform in India.

In exploring Müller's attitudes to Christian mission in India, we shall find that his position underwent substantial changes, from speaking crudely about assisting in overthrowing Hindu 'idolatry', in 1860, to searching out 'common ground' on which to stand with Hindus, in the latter years of his life. His judgements on the value of the Hindu religious tradition, relative to Christianity, were frequently shaded by a degree of ambivalence. This may at first glance appear surprising in one who, at least initially, actively advocated Christian missionary endeavour in Britain's most prized possession. Müller's background as a Lutheran German and his identification with the Broad Church party perhaps made it inevitable that his contribution to the public debate about Christian missions would be treated with suspicion by those opposed to the political and religious positions that they felt Müller represented.

III   MÜLLER'S RELIGIOUS POSITION

Reflecting in his autobiography, Müller wrote: 'I know that many of my friends on both sides looked upon me as a latitudinarian, but my conviction has always been that we could not be broad enough' (Müller, 1901, p. 291). He offered this remark partly to explain his friendship in Oxford with clerics as different as Edward Pusey and Arthur Stanley. In speaking specifically of the animosity that Pusey displayed to the ideas of Maurice, Müller commented: 'To me everything that was said of God seemed imperfect, and never to apply to God Himself but only to the idea which the human mind had formed of Him.' Müller felt that the Hindu, 'in spite of the idolatrous epithets which he used' no less aimed, like himself, at the true God (*ibid.*, pp. 291f.). This may at first sight appear to suggest the acceptance of an extremely 'broad' theological position by the standards of his day, but it was a faith that Müller himself spoke of as being based upon 'simple' and 'childish' elements. To locate the origins of Müller's search for a 'broad' outlook, we have to go back to his child-hood.

On the surface, Müller's profession of Christian conviction appears to have been constant and unambiguous. In his autobiography, he declared 'My practical religion was what I had learnt from my mother; that remained unshaken in all storms, and in its extreme simplicity and childishness answered all the purposes for which religion is meant' (*ibid.*, p. 294). It remained his 'safe harbour' (*ibid.*, p. 295). Even in later life Müller repeatedly spoke of the will of God as the basis of his belief that 'everything is ordered, and ordered for our true interests' (Müller, 1902, Vol. I, p. 238). But he also remembered the cold and boredom attendant upon enforced attendance at church (Müller, 1901, p. 59). There are, of course, evident dangers in trying to reconstruct the religious outlook of the child from an account written from the vantage point of old age, but in this case it is Müller's religious outlook during the latter part of his life with which we are concerned. This hint of a growing impatience with institutionalized Christianity, the seeds of which may have been planted in childhood, prefigures a distinction that Müller frequently invoked between the Christianity of Christ and the Christianity of the Church and theology. Arguably, it anticipates the 'broadness' for which he was to search in later life.

Müller also recalled that in his youth the same building was often used for Protestant and Roman Catholic services, yet, by the time he came to write his autobiography, this practice had come to be 'stygmatized as indifference, and by other ugly names'. He declared that 'this so-called indifferentism should be classed among the highest Christian virtues, and as the fullest realization of the spirit of Christ' (*ibid.*, p. 63). Müller's mature attitude to the outward forms of Christian worship was amplified in a recollected discussion with Keshub Chunder Sen, a leading light in the reformist-inclined Brahmo (Brahma) Samaj, a Hindu theistic movement. In this discussion, Müller urged that 'service of God should be service of men', an emphasis on personal morality that chimed well with the stated views of members of the Broad Church persuasion such as Jowett (*ibid.*, pp. 59f., cf. p. 280).

Once resident in Oxford, Müller was soon absorbed into a circle whose members, like himself, were not averse to distinguishing between the religion of Christ and the religion of the Church and theology. His early friendship with von Bunsen and J. A. Froude led to friendships with, among others, Stanley, Jowett, Arnold and Kingsley. In the eyes of the University community in Oxford, Müller soon appeared to have been fully assimilated into the Broad Church or Liberal Anglican party. This was hardly surprising given the keen interest shown by Liberal Anglicans in the fruits of German critical scholarship. Moreover, Luther was held in high regard by members of Müller's circle who, suspicious of the High Church tendency in Oxford, regarded the German Reformation as a decisive moment in the history of Christianity. Shocked to find Luther, who had been 'represented to us as a perfect saint', spoken of in other Oxford circles 'like any other mortal, nay, as a heretic', Müller found that he had much in common with the Liberal Anglicans (*ibid.*, p. 63). In 1851, in Oxford and isolated from fellow Lutherans, Müller joined the Anglican communion. In the same year he was given an honorary MA, enabling him to become a member of Christ Church College and of the University. His change of allegiance, however, should be viewed within the context of his statements about denominational divisions. Later in life, he explained his attachment to the Church of England in terms of the freedom and 'immunity from priestcraft' that it offered (Müller, 1902, Vol. II, p. 413).

Such was the preoccupation of Müller's new friends in Oxford with the fierce debates provoked by German critical scholarship that he commented that they were 'indifferent or unprepared' when it came to facing the religious questions that still troubled him. Yet, in the main, Müller spoke of his own religious struggles as being behind him by that time. From his earliest schooling in Germany, Müller had been exposed to 'chiefly historical and moral' religious teaching (Müller, 1901, p. 62):

Thus we grew up from our earliest youth, being taught to look ... on Christ and His disciples as historical characters, on the Old and New Testaments as real historical books. Though we did not understand as yet the deeper meaning of Christ and of His words, we had at least nothing to unlearn in later times.

(*Ibid.*, p. 63)

At university, there followed schooling in 'the purely historical and scientific treatment of religion' which, Müller maintained, 'never interfered with my early ideas of right and wrong, never disturbed my life with God and in God' (*ibid.*, p. 294). His studies in Berlin left Müller convinced 'that the Old and New Testaments were historical books, and to be treated according to the same critical principles as any other ancient book, particularly the sacred books of the East' (*ibid.*, p. 277). Speaking of his theological outlook on first arriving in Oxford, Müller declared that 'Anything like revelation, in the old sense of the word ... was to me a standpoint long left behind' (*ibid.*). He 'claimed for each man the liberty of believing in his own Christ' (*ibid.*, p. 279). Having come to the 'simple conclusion that revelation can never be objective, but must always be subjective', he tried to show Kingsley and others 'how entirely self-made some of their difficulties were' (*ibid.*, p. 64).

At Oxford, Müller also discovered individuals who, although publicly known for their orthodoxy, would privately confess their lack of Christian belief to Müller with a 'Voltairian levity' on the assumption that, as a German scholar, he would share it (*ibid.*, pp. 295f.). Müller's simple faith did not merely surprise the sceptics in Oxford. One contemporary at Oxford, Canon Frederic W. Farrar, confessed to having been impressed by Müller's sincere religious conviction, given the widespread perception in Oxford of Müller, as one of those who were 'though Christians in life, most indefinite in their religious views, and probably suspected of excessive broadness' (Müller, 1902, Vol. I, p. 168).[9] This perception was sufficiently widespread for it to reach the ears of the family of Georgina Grenfell, whom Müller was determined to marry. Müller refuted the accusation in letters to her aunt (Chaudhuri, 1974, pp. 162f.).

Müller's 'broadness', in fact, although shaped by German critical scholarship, did not lead him anywhere close to a radical rejection of the Christian gospel. Writing to Gladstone in later life, Müller confessed his unease at the cumulative effect of the questions raised by writers such as David Strauss, Darwin and Spencer (letter of 1872 in Müller, 1902, Vol. I, p. 442). Instinctively, however, Müller felt a lack of sympathy for the

---

[9] On Farrar, see *RVB*, III, 7.3, p. 425.

rigidities imposed by the various forms of Christian denominationalism. It was this, coupled with his Lutheran upbringing, that led to his identification with the Broad Church, whose style of theological liberalism was mild compared to the radicalism of Strauss (Trompf, 1978, p. 38). Questions about ecclesiastical vestments, genuflection and the use of incense then troubling the University community in Oxford left Müller cold; these were mere 'paraphernalia' and not the 'service of God' (Müller, 1901, p. 280). It was in this spirit that he would eventually reach out to religions other than Christianity and in particular to Hinduism.

Müller was sufficiently aware of the highly charged atmosphere in Oxford to confine his discussion of theologically sensitive matters to members of 'the Stanley party' and so to avoid becoming embroiled in the theological controversies that gripped the University in the middle and latter parts of the nineteenth century (*ibid.*; see also Müller, 1902, Vol. I, pp. 185ff.). When it came to his judgements on religious traditions other than Christianity, he was warned by intimate friends that his public statements were likely to be misunderstood (Müller, 1901, pp. 277ff.).

IV THE BODEN PROFESSORSHIP: A QUESTION OF NATIONAL INTEREST

Müller's public contribution to the debate about missions fuelled a controversy that simmered and periodically boiled over throughout the last forty years of his life. A natural starting-point for a consideration of his attitudes to missionary activity is the controversy that surrounded his candidacy for the Boden Professorship in Sanskrit at the University of Oxford, then a centre of Anglican influence and profoundly affected by the controversies between the different factions within the Anglican Church. Following the death of Wilson, the first holder of the Boden Chair, in May 1860, a successor to the Chair had to be elected by members of the Convocation of the University of Oxford, an assembly made up of MAs of the University. This assembly included non-resident graduates of the University, many of whom were country clergy, and not just the dons. Although four candidates originally entered their names for the contest for the Boden Chair in 1860, only two went forward to the election, namely, those of Müller and Monier Williams. The competition within the University was fierce, with both candidates having their supporters. The outcome of such votes in Convocation could be determined by the success of different parties in inducing MAs living at some distance from the University to return to Oxford in order to cast their votes. Personal manifestos were issued, circulars sent out, promises of support extracted from members of Convocation and letters written to newspapers. The progress of the contest was followed by *The Times* and other national and provincial newspapers, and by scholars as far away as India, some of whom had lent their support to one or other of the candidates. The matter was resolved in December 1860, when the election showed Monier Williams to be the winner by 833 votes to 610.

Monier Williams, Müller's successful rival, was born in India in 1819 but educated in England. As the son of an army officer and the daughter of an official of the East India Company, a career in the East India Company beckoned. Monier Williams was educated at the East India Company's Haileybury College, having initially entered Balliol College, Oxford. His move to Haileybury was brought about by the offer of an appointment in the East India Company and his career as a student at Haileybury was distinguished. A death in the family led to a change of plans and, instead of returning to India in the service of the East India Company, he returned to Oxford, this time to University College, where he studied Sanskrit under the Boden Professor, Wilson, and was awarded a Boden Sanskrit scholarship. He was then appointed Professor of Sanskrit at Haileybury until 1858 when the College was closed with the winding-up of the East India Company. By the time of his appointment to the Boden Professorship in 1860, Monier Williams had published both Sanskrit and Hindustani dictionaries and grammars and translations of Sanskrit texts, particularly dramas. Like Müller, he had also, since 1855, acted as an examiner in Sanskrit of students sitting the entrance examination for the Indian Civil Service.

When Monier Williams offered himself for the Boden Chair, his supporters equalled those of Müller but, it has been said, were not so distinguished (Chaudhuri, 1974, p. 222). It is probably more accurate to say that Müller gathered testimonials more widely from scholars of international repute. Somewhat surprisingly, this list included Whitney! Monier Williams's list of supporters, however, included many influential figures in the University, including heads of colleges, and individuals connected to India through service in the East India Company or in the mission field. Even so, we are still left with the question of why Monier Williams triumphed over Müller, whose international reputation at that time was the greater. The answer to this is to be found within the debate about missionary work in India that enveloped the contest for the Boden Professorship.

It could be argued that, in the minds of the Oxford electorate, Monier Williams's links with the former East India Company and the then prestigious Indian Civil Service rated more highly than the lists of foreign academics who had rallied to Müller's flag. Also, Monier Williams was known both as a teacher and as an examiner of Sanskrit whereas Müller's reputation was that of a translator, writer and lecturer. Outside the University, Monier Williams had taught both at Haileybury and at Cheltenham College and could call upon local constituencies outside Oxford for support. Monier Williams was also an 'Oxford man' and had been a Boden Scholar.

However, when Müller had to reconcile himself to the fact that he had failed to win the prestigious and well-paid Boden Professorship, his bitterness over the outcome of his candidacy was fuelled by his conviction that he had been treated at Oxford as a foreigner. Müller also believed that his own brand of Christian faith was regarded as sufficiently 'broad' as to be suspect and so used against him by those who opposed his advancement within the University. He was convinced that he had lost the election because his opponents used his nationality and religious leanings particularly to sway the mass of voters no longer resident at the University. Müller's supporters and other observers certainly believed that he had been disadvantaged by his German descent at a time of anti-German feeling in Britain (see, for example, MacDonnell, 1967–8 edn (a), p. 1024).

For many of Müller's opponents, however, the issue of Müller's nationality was inseparable from what they held to be the substance of his religious beliefs (Müller, 1902, Vol. I, pp. 244f.). His very descent was deemed to imply acceptance of a liberal theological outlook. Thus, Müller was portrayed as less 'orthodox' in his Christian belief than Monier Williams and as infected by an association with the Broad Church faction that had published *Essays and Reviews* barely ten months prior to Müller's unsuccessful candidacy. Müller's connection with the Broad Church wing was strengthened through the support that he received on arrival in England from von Bunsen, whose own researches were incorporated into Rowland Williams's provocative contribution to *Essays and Reviews*.

In his unpublished autobiography, Monier Williams acknowledged that he was 'favoured by circumstances' during the contest and that he was widely regarded as conservative in both politics and religion, whilst Müller was seen as a liberal and as a representative of German theology. He also maintained that these differences were made much of by the contestants' respective supporters when 'volleys were discharged in earnest' in September 1860 (Monier-Williams, unpublished autobiography, pp. 346f.). However, the wider ramifications of the contest appear most clearly in the coverage given to it by newspapers and in the circulars put out by the candidates' supporters. *The Record*, the leading Anglican Evangelical newspaper, in announcing the death of Wilson, commented in its issue of 18 May 1860 on both Müller and Monier Williams. Müller is presented as youthful and known to readers of *The Times* on account of his reviews which 'have made him and his researches in Comparative Philology familiar to all persons interested in literature, while they have destroyed confidence in his religious opinions' (Monier-Williams, misc. papers). Monier Williams, on the other hand, is presented as the chosen successor of Wilson and as 'a man of sincere piety, and one who is likely, by the blessing of God on his labours, to promote the ultimate object which the founder of the Professorship had in view' (*ibid.*).

Whilst *The Times* was steadfast in its support for Müller, in other newspapers Monier Williams's piety, practical scholarship and Englishness were given prominence. The *Homeward Mail* of 22 May 1860 posed this question for the Oxford electors: 'Will you have a stranger in the University, a stranger and a foreigner, or will you choose one of your own body, whose qualifications, moreover, are at least the equal of other candidates?' (*ibid.*). The *Cheltenham Chronicle* of 6 November 1860 proclaimed: 'Our every sympathy, as Englishmen and Churchmen, is with our distinguished townsman [Monier Williams]' and questioned whether the 'interests of Christianity' would be as safe in the hands of Müller (*ibid.*). Writing in the *Morning Post* of 27 November 1860, 'Detur Anglicano' denied that Monier Williams's supporters had made an issue of Max Müller's religious belief, but pleaded that members of the University 'recognise the merits of their own countryman, and to keep the great prizes of the English universities for English students' (*ibid.*). Articles from Indian publications pleading the cause of Monier Williams, the Englishman, were reproduced in *The Record* on 28 November 1860 (*ibid.*). The implications of this line of argument were made explicit in the *Morning Herald* which, just prior to the election, declared on 5 December 1860 that the outcome of the contest was 'a question of national interest'. Its outcome would directly effect the efficient training of civil servants and missionaries and so ultimately 'the progress of Christianity in India and the maintenance of British authority in that empire' (*ibid.*). Imagine the sneers in Calcutta, the *Morning Herald* added, should the outcome suggest that Britain, with its Indian Empire, has to look to Germany to fill its premier university appointment in Sanskrit! Voting for the Boden Chair was increasingly taking on the appearance of being a test of patriotism.

Two circulars published by supporters of Monier Williams added another dimension to the arguments in the press that the appointment of an Englishman to the Boden Professorship would be in the national interest. The two circulars entitled *Boden Sanskrit Professorship* were issued

on 30 November and 1 December under the signatures respectively of
'M.A.' and 'D.D.' Both appealed powerfully to what they presented as the
known wishes of the majority of Englishman living in India, namely, to
elect Monier Williams. They believed that these expatriates who had no
vote were the ones who knew India and its needs best and thus should be
heeded. For

> The Professorship is not for Oxford alone.
> It is not for 'the Continent and America'.
> It is for India.
> It is for Christianity. (signed 'M.A.')
>
> (*Ibid.*)

Amidst the flurry of exchanges between their supporters, Müller and
Monier Williams set out their own positions in more formal submissions
to members of the University Convocation.[10] Whilst Müller's nationality
and religious belief clearly weighed heavily in the minds of some, as we
shall see the two candidates for the Boden Professorship held significantly
different views about the way in which Sanskrit study and Indological
research could best help the missionary. Given the nature of the post for
which both Müller and Monier Williams were competing, these
differences exercised a considerable influence upon the ways in which
the two candidates presented their cases.

It has been observed that the Convocation of the University of Oxford
had generally disregarded the intentions of benefactors in the working of
the University as a whole. Yet, in respect of the election to the Boden
Chair in Sanskrit in 1860, Müller's opponents gave primacy to the
intention of its founder, Joseph Boden. This was that the promotion of a
knowledge of Sanskrit would enable 'his [Boden's] countrymen to
proceed in the conversion of the Natives of India to the Christian
Religion' (Chaudhuri, 1974, pp. 221ff.). Thus, as Monier Williams
insisted, while distancing himself from the tactics of some of his
supporters, the personal religious beliefs of the contestants for the
Boden Professorship were of relevance in securing a holder who would
discharge the conditions attached to the Professorship by its founder
(Monier-Williams, unpublished autobiography, p. 347). In fact, as Monier
Williams recalled, questions had been raised about the religious
convictions of the two main contenders during the first election to the
Boden Professorship in 1832. In this earlier election, doubts had been

---

[10] See 'Monier Williams's and Max Müller's submissions to the members of Convocation of
the University of Oxford, 1860', Part II, pp. 332–5.

expressed about the degree of support that Wilson would provide for the missionary cause.

In his submission to members of the University Convocation, dated 16 May 1860, Müller offered himself as a candidate for the Boden Professorship and drew attention to his translation of the Rig-Veda and his collaboration with Wilson. He argued that 'The Veda is ... to the Hindus what the Koran is to the Mohammedans' and that lack of knowledge of the Veda had 'hitherto proved a serious bar to Missionary exertions'. Müller argued that, in translating the Rig-Veda, he had already spent the greater part of his life in promoting the object of the Boden Professorship. He promised testimonials from missionaries in India who would confirm the importance of his work in assisting them 'to overthrow the ancient systems of idolatry still prevalent in that country, and to establish the truths of Christianity among the believers of the Veda' (Müller, The Papers etc.). Not unreasonably, Müller also confessed his wish to hold a professorial chair that would allow him to devote all his time to the study of Sanskrit.

Monier Williams's submission pointed to his personal connections with India, his distinguished record at Haileybury and his publications, but in particular to the debt he already owed as a former Boden Sanskrit Scholar to the founder of the Professorship. He closed by affirming that, if elected, 'my utmost energies shall be devoted to the one object which its Founder had in view;—namely, "*The promotion of a more general and critical knowledge of the Sanskrit Language, as a means of enabling Englishmen to proceed in the conversion of the natives of India to the Christian religion*"' (Monier-Williams, misc. papers).

In view of the way in which the contest was being presented more widely in the press, Müller arguably disclosed too much of his hand in a later and fuller communication sent to members of Convocation. In this statement dated 30 August 1860, Müller combined a refutation of some of the personal attacks made against him with a fuller outline of his plans, if elected. He pointed out, in the face of questions raised about his religious beliefs, that the University had had 'ample opportunity of judging of the sincerity of my profession as a Christian, a Protestant, and a Member of the Church of England' (*ibid.*). He made plain that, if elected, in addition to offering instruction in Sanskrit, he would use the Boden Chair to promote Sanskrit scholarship and comparative philology. He would also offer classes on the history and literature of India, particularly with the needs of future entrants to the Indian Civil Service in mind. Merely to offer instruction in Sanskrit 'would be but a mean return for the liberality of the founder of the Chair of Sanskrit at Oxford' (*ibid.*). The strategy he proposed, Müller suggested, would build upon the legacy of Wilson and would establish a school of Sanskrit Scholarship and Comparative Philology at Oxford, which in turn would 'supply efficient Missionaries for the propagation of the Gospel in India, useful members of the Indian Civil Service, and distinguished Boden Scholars' (*ibid.*).

To Monier Williams, Müller's plans for the Boden Professorship represented a dilution in the energy that could be devoted to fulfilling the primary condition attached to the Chair, namely, assisting in the conversion of Hindu India. Müller's scheme also smacked of continental preoccupations with the 'science of language'. In his own lengthy statement to members of Convocation, issued on 12 October 1860, Monier Williams resolutely pointed to what he held to be the intentions of the founder of the Chair: not to promote European comparative philology but to aid 'by means of Sanskrit, the diffusion of Christianity in India' (*ibid.*). It was necessary for Convocation, therefore, to determine which of the applicants would be the most likely to apply a knowledge of Sanskrit to the greatest effect in aiding the evangelization of India.

In Monier Williams's opinion, it was not simply that Max Müller had plans for the future of the Boden Chair that were not in keeping with its founder's intentions, but that Müller's record as a scholar to date suggested that he might not be the best suited to pursue the stated aim of the founder, even if he adopted this single-mindedly. Monier Williams contrasted Müller's 'continental' approach to the study of Sanskrit with his own approach which was 'suited to English ideas'. He declared that for practical Englishmen, unlike the 'philosophical' continentals, the study of Sanskrit was not an end in itself but was a means to an end, and Monier Williams pointed to his compilation of grammars and dictionaries shaped to the English mind. In contrast, he argued, too much of Müller's scholarship had been devoted to ancient and abstruse Sanskrit texts relating to the earliest parts of the Vedic tradition, which no longer had a direct and daily relevance in the religious lives of contemporary Hindus. Consequently, the study of these texts could reveal little of any relevance to the missionary who needed to understand the nature of contemporary, popular Hindu belief and practice. For example, many of the deities referred to in the Rig-Veda were no longer central to the practice of living Hinduism. To devote so much time and energy as Müller had done to the translation of the Rig-Veda, according to Monier Williams, was merely to focus on the first in a voluminous series of texts which collectively comprise the Veda. Moreover, in his statement to members of Convocation of 12 October, Monier Williams made the very telling observation that to treat the Veda as the 'Scripture' of Hinduism in the way in which the Bible is the Scripture of Christianity, or the Qur'an (Koran) is the Scripture of Islam, would be to misunderstand both the nature of the Veda and its use by Hindus (Monier-Williams, misc. papers).

For his part, Monier Williams emphasized his familiarity with the major categories and periods of Sanskrit literature but laid special claim to a close acquaintance with what he called 'classical' or, speaking comparatively, 'modern' Sanskrit literature. In this category, Monier Williams found the 'storehouse of their [Hindus] household legends, their social institutions, customs, laws, and jurisprudence' and not ancient liturgical materials written in an obsolete form of Sanskrit or philosophical treatises so abstruse as to be understood by only a handful of learned Hindus (*ibid.*). The relevance of these 'classical' texts to the work of the missionary was plain to Monier Williams: 'It is in these works that the Hindu mind, as it now presents itself, is reflected. These are the real Sanskrit scriptures, which every missionary must study if he wishes to understand the natives of India, and to be understood by them' (*ibid.*).

Not only did Monier Williams challenge the extent of Müller's commitment to the stated purpose of the Boden Professorship and the relevance to the missionary of what Müller saw as his life's work, but he also observed that Müller had devoted to the translation of the Rig-Veda 'an expenditure of time, labour, money, and erudition, far greater than was ever bestowed on any edition of the Holy Bible' (*ibid.*). Harping on the stated purpose of the Professorship, Monier Williams suggested that the founder of the Professorship had never envisaged that simply teaching Sanskrit at Oxford would in itself increase the numbers of missionaries offering themselves for service in India. The purpose of the Chair was to encourage a more critical understanding of the language and thus a way into 'the Indian mind' and into the spoken languages of contemporary India, which have their roots in Sanskrit. Armed with such an understanding, Christian missionaries would be better able to debate with Hindus and to render Christian Scripture into the living languages of contemporary India.[11] This was the way in which the holder of the Chair would aid the missionary and 'not by perpetuating and diffusing the

---

[11] Monier Williams outlined this line of argument more fully in his inaugural lecture after he was appointed to the Boden Professorship (see Monier Williams, 1861). This lecture did not repeat his judgement on the relative usefulness to the missionary of the different categories of Sanskrit literature which he had deployed against Müller. It did, however, repeat Monier Williams's earlier insistence that the learning of Sanskrit had to be tailored to the 'practical spirit' of the English. This lecture confines itself entirely to an outline of the features of the Hindu religious tradition, the place of Sanskrit within this and thus the relevance of a knowledge of this language to the missionary. At no point does Monier Williams offer a theology of mission.

obsolescent Vedic scriptures, but by "disseminating a knowledge of the sacred scriptures" of our own religion' (*ibid.*).

Monier Williams's criticism of the relevance of Müller's work to the missionary sufficiently provoked Müller to reply through the columns of *The Times* on 29 October 1860. This, in turn, stung Monier Williams to reproach Müller for using the newspapers to conduct his campaign and to issue a further circular to members of the University Convocation in which Monier Williams protested that Müller had misrepresented his arguments. These exchanges added little that was new to the debate, but do illustrate the increasingly heated tone of the exchanges between the two contestants and their followers. For example, one of Müller's supporters asserted that Monier Williams had yet to prove that he could translate a Sanskrit text that existed only in manuscript form rather than read the Sanskrit of texts that had already been translated. This tactic rather backfired on the writer, Robinson Ellis. Once the contest was over, Ellis, who was himself a Boden Sanskrit Scholar, had to present himself for instruction to the new Boden Professor whom he had but recently judged unable to read a Sanskrit manuscript!

Leaving to one side the acrimony generated during the contest, in challenging the relevance of Müller's work and hinting that it did more to perpetuate the ancient sacred texts of Hinduism than to assist in the translation and dissemination of Christian Scripture, Monier Williams had touched on a wider set of questions, which both missionaries and administrators in India had had to face. The debate centred upon the value that the British administrator and the Christian missionary should place on India's indigenous and classical traditions. Should the British administrator merely govern India in accordance with the established conventions of Indian society, or were the British in India *to change* Indian society, to 'civilize' India? If change was to be the order of the day, could this change be effected by drawing selectively upon India's past and present traditions and her social instituitions to manipulate the future? Or did this legacy have first to be destroyed in order to re-shape India according to a European design in which Christianity would provide a cornerstone for India's future? Was the purpose of the missionary, therefore, to eradicate the religious traditions already in place before the coming of European Christianity to India?

We have already seen that, supported by the different, but in this instance convergent, interests of utilitarian officials and Evangelical Christians, the cause of bringing about more sweeping religious and social change in India had gathered momentum by the 1830s. The *laissez-faire* policies of the East India Company had come under sustained criticism, missionary activity was made easier and the policy to promote English as the medium of learning in India was adopted. Monier Williams's criticisms of Müller's work thus seemed to place Müller in the same camp as other romantic antiquarians who, through their absorption in India's past, were not concerned to change her present and future. Unspoken in the text of Monier Williams's argument is the charge laid by others against these 'romantic antiquarians' that they had, in effect, given a new lease of life to India's religious and philosophical texts by making them more accessible, not just to European students, but more significantly to educated Hindus who knew little of Vedic Sanskrit but who read English with ease and proficiency.

The difference in the approaches of Müller and Monier Williams to Sanskrit learning was to some extent but a reflection of the difference in style between continental Sanskrit scholarship and British Sanskrit scholarship, which was noted earlier in this chapter. Monier Williams drew attention to this difference when he argued that the practical English would have little patience with Müller's continental scholarship and preoccupation with the Rig-Veda. Although followers of Müller also appealed to conversations with Wilson in which it was reported that Wilson acknowledged Müller's pre-eminence (letter from W. S. Vaux in Müller, The Papers etc.), supporters of Monier Williams were able to produce a letter in which Wilson spoke unequivocally of his hope that Monier Williams would succeed him (reprinted in the *Morning Herald*, 24 May 1860).

What the contest for the Boden Professorship in 1860 showed beyond question was the extent to which, in the minds of many within the University of Oxford and beyond, the effectiveness of the conduct of the Christian mission in India was indissolubly linked to the permanence and stability of British rule in India. It should not be forgotten that the Boden contest took place barely two years after the 'Indian Mutiny' of 1857–8. In the minds of many supporters of the missionary cause in India, the horror of the uprising was nothing less than a divine judgement upon a style of British administration in India that to date had been inconsistent, if not actually ambivalent, in its support of the missionary cause. The future of British rule in India, they believed, would depend, not upon the success of policies designed not to antagonize the indigenous population, but upon doing the will of God and bringing the population of India to the acceptance of the Christian gospel. Measured against this consideration, with its religious, political and economic ramifications, the appointment of a German Sanskritist of international renown, but with a reputation for unsound religious opinions, seemed to many to represent an unnecessary risk when the alternative was an English Sanskritist of distinction known for his conservatism and piety. Farrar, who was on Müller's committee, expressed surprise after the election that Müller had collected as many votes as he had (Müller, 1902, Vol. I, p. 245).

V TOWARDS A STRATEGY FOR THE 'PRACTICAL MISSIONARY'

During the contest for the Boden Professorship, both Müller and his advocates attempted to demonstrate his past achievements in supporting Christian mission in India. Indeed Pusey, the staunchly conservative Tractarian and ardent opponent of *Essays and Reviews*, came forward, together with the Bishop of Calcutta, strongly in favour of Müller, who, they claimed, had done more than any other scholar to make the Sanskrit Scriptures of the Hindu religious tradition accessible to the Christian missionary (*ibid.*, pp. 236ff.). Pusey's support is interesting, because he had little sympathy for Müller's 'broad' attitudes and therefore it is reasonable to view his contribution as a judgement on the academic calibre of the candidate who, he believed, would be most able to further the missionary cause. Another supporter, Reverend C. Matheson, urged Müller to remind the Oxford electorate that he had previously acted as a judge in determining the winner of the Mr John Muir Prize for the best refutation of the Hindu religious system (Müller, The Papers etc.).

It has been suggested that, during the Boden contest, Müller did exaggerate the practical importance that his edition of the Rig-Veda would have for missionaries when he argued that direct access to this tradition would enable them to counter Hindu claims that there was nothing in Christianity that had not been anticipated in the Veda (Tull, 1991, p. 53, fn. 33). On the other hand, Müller's supporters were able to include among his testimonials a list of missionary societies that had approached the East India Company for copies of Müller's edition of the Rig-Veda. These included the Church Missionary Society, the Society for the Propagation of the Gospel, the Free Church of Scotland Missionary Society, and American and German missions. Two missionaries who had supported Müller during the Boden contest, R. Rost of St Augustine's Missionary College, Canterbury, and C. Graul, late Director of the Leipzig Mission, shared Müller's view that access to the Rig-Veda provided a key to 'the Indian mind' and enabled missionaries to debate with 'the heathen' (Müller, The Papers etc.). In fact, Müller's claims for the practical applications of the fruits of his scholarship for Christian missionaries were repeatedly stated in his extensive writings both prior to the competition for the Boden Chair and long afterwards, when he would no longer have had a personal interest in being seen to aid the missionary endeavour. As we shall see, the nature of the strategy that he advocated for the evangelization of India changed in step with his personal response to the religious developments within India and with his own changing religious belief.

In 1853 and 1854, for example, Müller devoted considerable time to helping von Bunsen produce a Uniform Alphabet to assist missionaries in committing languages to writing for the first time, although the conference of academics and missionaries called to ratify the adoption of this alphabet ended before an agreement was reached. In 1876, in the prospectus for the series, The Sacred Books of the East, Müller wrote of the value of such a series to the missionary 'to whom an accurate knowledge of them [sacred books] is as indispensable as a knowledge of the enemy's country is to a general' (Müller, 1902, Vol. II, p. 10). Some years later, in 1887, at a missionary meeting in St John's College, Oxford, Müller reaffirmed that one of his objects in editing The Sacred Books of the East series was 'to assist missionaries' and he asked his audience to consider how they would respond to a missionary who attempted to convert them without any knowledge of the Christian Bible (*ibid.*, p. 481).

In addition to regarding his work as a translator as supportive of missionary activity, Müller publicly advocated that Christian missionary activity should be extended as a matter of urgency to those of other faiths. In 1858, Charles Hardwick, Christian Advocate of the University of Cambridge, published a work entitled *Christ and Other Masters*, which ranged widely over the world's religious traditions and offered comments by the author on the 'merits' and 'defects' of each system judged from a Christian standpoint. In reviewing this work, Müller took issue with Hardwick's statement that the latter's work was not intended for Christian missionaries on the grounds that there were 'difficulties nearer home' which were more pressing than 'to conciliate the more thoughtful minds of heathendom in favor of the Christian faith' (Müller, 1985 edn, p. 51). Müller argued that such a restriction in the scope of Christian missionary work could only be acceptable to one who had not met the sincere 'pagan' face to face. Like John Colenso, the missionary bishop of Natal who had been greatly influenced by Maurice's rejection of the doctrine of eternal damnation, Müller declared that no 'sensible missionary' would tell those who had honestly lived by a religious code other than Christianity that they were destined for eternal damnation due to an accident of birth which had denied them knowledge of the Christian gospel.[12]

Müller also observed that Hardwick treated ancient religious teachers of the stature of Lao-tzu and Buddha 'too much in the spirit of a policeman who tells a poor blind beggar that he is only shamming blindness' (*ibid.*, p. 53). Müller was no less troubled by the way in which Hardwick appeared to find resemblances between the tenets of Lao-tzu and the 'modern heathens', the philosophers Auguste Comte and Spinoza, and accused Hardwick of using the history of religion as 'a masked battery against modern infidelity' (*ibid.*, p. 55). The harshness of Hardwick's language when dealing with Chinese and Hindu beliefs, according to Müller, stemmed from the fact that, when Hardwick was writing about these systems of belief, he did so partly in order to attack those contemporary philosophers whom he regarded as 'modern heathens'. In a manner reminiscent of Maurice, Müller suggested that, given Hardwick's lack of sympathy with his subject-matter, 'the cold judgement of the historian would have been better than the excited pleading of a partisan', and argued that the defence of Christianity did not require 'that we should insist on the utter falseness of all other forms of belief' (*ibid.*, pp. 52–3).

The 'practical missionary', according to Müller, was one who 'put a charitable interpretation on many doctrines of ancient heathenism', and Müller argued that, unless a similar generosity was extended to 'modern heathenism', Christian charity and sense of justice would be lost in 'wrangling for victory'. Moreover, he insisted that Christianity does not require Christians to criticize the 'Divine policy which has governed the whole world from the very beginning', and he appealed to earlier Christians like St Augustine, who had the confidence to admit the existence of traces of truth in the religions and philosophies of other people: 'Surely it is not necessary, in order to prove that our religion is the only true religion, that we should insist on the utter falseness of all other forms of belief' (*ibid.*).

The concept that Müller commonly employed when attempting to explain how the different religions could point to a common and underlying truth was *Logos*. Translated from the Greek as 'word' or 'reason', the concept of *Logos* had its place in Neo-Platonism and in Christian theology—most notably in the preface to St John's Gospel, which Müller appears to have regarded as encapsulating the Christian revelation (Müller, 1894b, p. 895). Put simply, for Müller *Logos*

---

[12] See Chapter 4, p. 145.

represented the highest truth to which all religions pointed. In offering this interpretation of the meaning of *Logos*, however, Müller was not merely reaching back to the Church Fathers but was also incorporating modifications of the philosophies of those who had introduced him to Sanskrit studies while he was a student in Germany and France.

Studying in Paris under Eugène Burnouf, Müller was exposed to the belief that the Neo-Platonic concept of *Logos* lay at the heart of Christianity and that Christianity as a consequence owed more to Greek philosophy than to Judaism. Burnouf traced this philosophic inheritance back to a group of people who came to be labelled 'Aryans' or 'Indo-Europeans' by nineteenth-century students of philology and mythology. These people were believed to have migrated from the Caucasus during the second millennium BCE and to have settled in regions as far apart as western Europe and northern India. The language, religion and mythology of these early peoples, it was argued, provided the source of later Sanskrit, Greek and other related traditions.

The racial bias encouraged by Burnouf's understanding of the Aryan past was embraced by Müller because it lent additional cohesion to the philosophy of religion that Müller was building up. This theory had its roots in Müller's simple belief in divine providence, but expanded as he was exposed to the influence of his German and French teachers and the ideas of religious liberals like von Bunsen. It was fine-tuned in the light of his own historical and linguistic studies of ancient Indo-European people, and in particular of the textual tradition contained within the Rig-Veda. This, Müller believed, provided the earliest surviving insights into the nature and development of the Indo-European tradition. Thus, Müller came to embrace a view of religious history that identified a thread running from the early portions of the Vedic texts of ancient India through Hellenistic Christian philosophy to Immanuel Kant's *Critique of Pure Reason* (1781). His historical and linguistic studies therefore confirmed Müller in the belief that God's Providence was to be discerned in the religious history of the world as a whole and was not confined in a narrow fashion to the Judaeo-Christian revelation. The religious history of humanity, Müller believed, demonstrated a reaching out for the infinite, a 'natural religion' that shone through most clearly in the earliest forms of religion before these were sullied by later accretions (Müller, 1985 edn, pp. xiiff.). It was, in essence, a theory of degeneration that was at odds with the evolutionary spirit of both Hegel's philosophy of history and Darwinist understandings of the development of human institutions including religion. When dressed up in the language of comparative philology, as we saw earlier, it brought down on Müller's head the scorn of critics such as Whitney and Lang. This theory also enabled Müller to distinguish between what he regarded as the 'higher' (that is, the earliest and purest) and the 'lower' forms of religion (that is, the later accretions), thus accounting for the mixture of generous and severe judgements on the worth of the Hindu tradition that peppers his writing.

Müller also echoed the contention of Schelling, the philosopher who had been one of his teachers in Berlin, that Christianity was and has been in all religions. For example, Müller quoted the words of St Augustine with evident approval: 'What is now called the Christian religion, has existed among the ancients, and was not absent from the beginning of the human race' (*ibid.*, p. xi). Other Church Fathers, such as Justin Martyr and Clement of Alexandria, were also called upon by Müller to support this claim (*ibid.*, pp. xxviiiff.). Consequently, Müller could urge his readers to expect that 'Every religion, even the most imperfect and degraded, has something that ought to be sacred to us, for there is in all religions a secret yearning after the true, though unknown God' (*ibid.*, p. xxx).

Although Müller's understanding of the course of religious history may have struck his Victorian readers as novel, his interpretation of a providence at work would have at least the appearance of familiarity to anyone acquainted with Christian theology. For example, early Christian apologists, including Justin Martyr, had adopted from Stoic usage the concept of *Logos spermatikos* ('seminal' *Logos*) to explain what united human beings to God and gave them knowledge of God before the coming of Jesus Christ. It was this capacity that enabled those born before Christ, including Hellenistic philosophers, to have glimpses of the truth and so anticipate elements of Christian teaching. Put to the service of Victorian mission, this strand of early Christian theology was given a new dimension in what has come to be known as 'fulfilment theology', which proclaimed that Christianity was both the fulfilment and the goal of all other religions and that, as such, it was the religion for the modern age.

'Fulfilment theology' has been most closely associated with the work of the Protestant missionary J. N. Farquhar (1861–1929), although points of similarity may be found in the writings of Maurice and Rowland Williams.[13] Farquhar argued that India was ready to fall to Christianity because 'Only in the riches of Christianity ... can Hindus find the universal principles needed for a new intellectual, moral, and social life' (Farquhar, 1912, p. 202). In his view, only Christianity could answer what he believed was the unfulfilled desire of the Hindu population for an incarnate saviour. Similarly, for Farquhar, only exposure to Christianity

---

[13] The attitudes of F. D. Maurice and Rowland Williams to non-Christian religions are outlined in *RVB*, II, 13, pp. 289ff.

would provide the dynamism that he believed India needed to develop materially. In the writings of Monier Williams, we also find the assertions that Hinduism is 'everywhere tottering and ready to fall' and that Christianity is 'exactly suited to the needs of the masses of the people of India' (Monier Williams, 1878 pp. 184ff.). Writing in 1868, Müller too gave voice to this sense that the time was right for India to fall to Christianity: 'the ancient religion of India is doomed—and if Christianity does not step in, whose fault will it be?' (Müller, 1902, Vol. I, p. 358).[14]

The differences between Müller's position and that of others who regarded Christianity as the answer to the unspoken prayers of Hindus are to be seen in his forthright criticism of destructive missionary strategies, in his particular understanding of the history of religions, which placed a value on the pristine purity of India's ancient Vedic heritage, and in his vision of the changes that Christianity had itself to undergo. His proclamation in a letter to the Duke of Argyll of 1869 that 'the ancient religion of India is doomed', was preceded by his assertion that 'The Christianity of our nineteenth century will hardly be the Christianity of India' (Müller, 1902, Vol. I, p. 358).

Müller's support for missionary activity, although of a sort already outlined in his criticism of Hardwick's *Christ and Other Masters*, was spelled out in a letter of November 1873 to Sir Henry Acland, Regius Professor of Medicine at Oxford. The letter described a meeting on the subject of mission, which was held in Oxford barely a month before Müller delivered his controversial Westminster Lecture on missions. Müller referred in this letter to a united view among Christians in Britain who, no matter how they disagreed over matters of doctrine, would prefer to see a convert made to any Christian denomination than left outside the fold of Christianity: ' we want him [*sic*] to love—to love God and to love his neighbour for God's sake' (Müller, 1902, Vol. II, p. 491). Having commended the value of missionary work at home, Müller expressed his judgement on the worth of missionary work abroad in stronger language in this private letter than he had in his review of Hardwick's book, declaring that 'I consider it blasphemous to call them ['the great religions of the world'] the work of the Devil, when they are the work of God' (*ibid.*).

Müller's contention that all 'the great religions' are the work of God would appear to raise a question about what he saw as the purpose of Christian missionary work. This is a point that Müller addressed in the following manner:

[14] See also *RVB*, III, 8.3.1, p. 505.

I do not wish to see the old religions destroyed. I want to see them reformed, reanimated, resuscitated by contact with Christianity. There is much rubbish in the present form of Brahmanism [Hinduism], but so there is in the present form of Christianity. Let us try to get rid of the whitewash and the plaster—the work of men, whether Popes, Bishops, or Philosophers—and try to discover the original plan and purpose, whether in Christianity or Hinduism.

(*Ibid.*)

In so doing, Müller believed, 'we shall arrive at the deep and only safe and solid foundation of religious belief, and a truly religious life ... in all the religions of mankind. I could not call myself a Christian if I were to believe otherwise' (*ibid.*). Müller ended the letter to Acland in a memorable manner: 'All religions are mere stammerings, our own as much as that of the Brahmans [Hindus of the highest caste]—they all have to be translated, and, I have no doubt, they all will be translated, whatever their shortcomings may be' (*ibid.*).

It is apparent, therefore, that by the early 1870s Müller's support for Christian mission rested upon a number of convictions, which were shaped by his involvement not just in the translation of Sanskrit texts but in his more general comparative studies of religion. In the Preface to a collection of essays published in 1869, Müller declared that the comparison of Christianity and other religions was useful because comparison carried out on a sound 'scientific' basis 'will for the first time assign to Christianity its right place among the religions of the world ... it will restore to the whole history of the world, in its unconscious progress towards Christianity, its true and sacred character' (Müller, 1985 edn, p. xx). In the light of this assertion, it is hardly surprising that Müller could make the claim that the comparative study of religions would be of the 'greatest assistance' to the Christian missionary. Yet a closer reading of Müller's argument reveals that it was not his intention to reduce the role of comparative religion to that of a handmaiden in a celebratory procession of Christian triumphalism. Although he argued that the comparative study of religions would be advantageous to missionaries and to 'other defenders of the faith', as would knowledge of the world's sacred texts, such advantages should not be 'the chief object of these researches', which should be of a scientific character, independent and aiming at the truth, even when unpalatable to Christians (*ibid.*, p. xxvi).

Müller looked to comparative religion to combat the tendency on the part of missionaries to regard religions other than Christianity as 'barbarous' and to encourage them to 'look out more anxiously for any common ground, any spark of the true light that may still be revived, any altar that may be dedicated afresh to the true God' (*ibid.*, p. xxi). Whilst the 'true God' is the God revealed in the Christian religion, the line of Müller's argument makes it plain that the voice of this 'true God' has been and still can be heard, if not with full clarity, in other religious traditions. In a 'Lecture on the Vedas', delivered in Leeds in 1865, Müller brought together two important strands in his understanding of the religious history of the world when he declared that 'there is hardly one religion which does not contain some ... important truth' and that 'religions in their most ancient form ... are generally free from many of the blemishes that attach to them in later times' (*ibid.*, p. 48).

Moreover, Müller pointed out that only a person of little faith would wish to exempt his or her own faith from 'the same critical tests to which the historian subjects all other religions'. Müller asserted that 'we can decline no comparisons, nor claim any immunities for Christianity, as little as the missionary can, when wrestling with the subtle Brahman, or the fanatical Mussulman, or the plain speaking Zulu' (*ibid.*, p. xx). Müller's language reveals much about the spirit of his age, but at the same time suggests that, in his view, the Christian missionary cannot merely assume the superiority of Christianity and must be prepared to demonstrate it in the arena of the history of religions. In a later paper sent to the World's Parliament of Religions held in Chicago in 1893, it becomes abundantly clear that Müller, as a result of his studies, had come to hope for 'not simply a reform, but a complete revival of religion, more particularly of the Christian Religion' (Barrow, 1893, Vol. II, p. 935).

The benefits that Müller believed the encounter with Christianity would bring to the Hindu religion are detailed in a letter of 1868 to the Duke of Argyll, shortly after the latter's appointment as Secretary of State for India. In this letter, Müller called for a second conquest of India through education, and spoke of western education leading to an invigoration of India that would be expressed in a 'new national literature ... impregnated with western ideas, yet retaining its native spirit and character' (Müller, 1902, Vol. I, p. 357). In a second letter to Argyll in the following year, Müller spoke specifically of the benefits to India that would follow from a recovery of the 'simple' form of religion found in the Veda, although Müller spoke frankly of what he deemed to be the moral and metaphysical deficiencies of this early Hindu tradition (*ibid.*, p. 362).

When Müller came to deliver his widely reported lecture 'On Missions' at Westminster Abbey in December 1873, his ideas gave offence both to some Hindus and to some Christians. In this lecture, delivered at the invitation of the Dean of Westminster—none other than Müller's Broad Church friend, Stanley—many of the themes in Müller's earlier works reappear. However, in this context they are part of a discussion of what Müller envisaged would be the 'decisive battle' to be fought between 'the three missionary religions, Buddhism, Mohammedanism, and Christianity'. Müller defended the costs of foreign missions in terms of the value of each 'living seed' and distinguished between three types of missionary strategy: (i) the *parental*, (ii) the *controversial* and (iii) sustained *contact* between religions, which abstains from direct attempts at conversion.[15] For Müller, only the latter strategy can be successful in the long term. Unlike the *parental* strategy, which Müller located in the missionary's encounter with the simplest and least technologically developed societies, the *contact* strategy places the truths of Christianity before the convert but, unlike the *controversial* strategy, not in such a way as to destroy the fibres and roots of the religious faith that has been challenged.

Applying to India his analysis of types of missionary activity, Müller pointed to what he regarded as the 'purifying' influence that Islam and Hinduism had exercised over each other, once Muslims ceased in the attempt to convert Hindus to Islam. Müller argued that an even more lofty influence would be exerted upon the minds of Hindus through the mere presence of Christianity in India and saw the fruits of this appearing in the Brahmo Samaj under the leadership of men such as Rammohun Roy, Keshub Chunder Sen and Debendranath Tagore. Müller observed that this vital development within the wider Hindu tradition, which he described in general terms as 'dying or dead' (thus offending Hindus who read reports of the lecture), had found little favour in the eyes of missionaries who were committed to 'transplanting' English Christianity to India and who feared that this new movement might hold individuals within the Hindu fold who might otherwise have embraced Christianity. This was certainly the view taken by Farquhar, who tended to see new Hindu movements like the Brahmo Samaj as examples of either reforming tendencies wholly dependent upon the stimulus provided by contact with Christianity or nothing more than reactions against the challenge of Christianity. To regard these groups as authentic expressions of Hinduism, even if stimulated by the contact with European and Christian ideas, would clearly undermine the missionary assertion that Hinduism had nothing left to offer its followers and that their spiritual needs could only be met by embracing Christianity.

[15] *RVB*, III, 8.3.2, pp. 506ff.

Müller, however, in his lecture 'On Missions', commended the 'Indian puritans' of the Brahmo Samaj to his audience, observing that 'If missionaries admit to their fold converts who can hardly understand the equivocal abstractions of our Creeds and formulas, is it necessary to exclude those who understand them but too well to submit the wings of their free spirit to such galling chains?'. In line with his memories of the religion of his childhood and his understanding of a providence at work in the history of the world's religions, Müller returned again to his judgement upon credal formulas—'the stammerings of children'—and located the 'fundamentals of our religion' not in creeds or beliefs but in '*our love of God, and in our love of man, founded on our love of God*'. Creeds, ceremony, solemnity and doctrine are to be set aside in favour of trust, work, genial honesty and love. For, as Müller reminded his audience, it was not possible 'to have one creed to preach abroad, another to preach at home', and he urged missionaries to remember that 'the Christian faith at home is no longer what it was'.[16] Commenting on Müller's ready setting aside of creeds, Sir Alfred Lyall, who was appointed Home Secretary in India in 1873, noted: 'Missionaries will even yet hardly agree that the essentials of their religion are not in the creeds, but in love; because they are sent forth to propound scriptures which say clearly that what we believe or disbelieve is literally a *burning question*' (quoted in Chaudhuri, 1974, pp. 336f.).

VI THE SEARCH FOR 'A COMMON GROUND'

From 1873, Müller's writings became increasingly dominated by his interests in Hindu philosophy and in theoretical questions concerning the origins of religions and their subsequent development and relationships. It has been suggested that this change in Müller's interests and methods may have reflected his desire to find a way of answering the challenge to Christian faith in the works of Darwin and Strauss, as hinted in his letter of 1872 to Gladstone, which has been cited above (Voigt, 1981, pp. 14ff.). Müller's preoccupation with the contest for the Boden Chair, and with building a life for his family, may explain the apparent delay before he turned his mind to a challenge laid down during the previous two decades. However, Müller's eclecticism and dislike of denominational divides were established characteristics in his earlier writings and provided the impetus for the quest for the 'common ground' between religions, which became more pronounced in his later writings.

---

[16] *RVB*, III, 8.3.2, p. 510.

When, in the last decade of his life, Müller declared that 'the points on which the great religions differ are far less numerous, and certainly far less important, than are the points on which they all agree', he picked up a theme already touched on in his earlier writings (quoted in Sharpe, 1977, p. 17).

Müller's extensive studies of India's Sanskrit literature had convinced him of the existence of a lost Vedic 'golden age' and, in keeping with his wider theories about the histories of religions, led him to view the subsequent history of the Hindu tradition as one of degeneration. On the basis of this judgement, Müller reflected on the means to bring about the revitalization of Hindu society and cherished certain expectations in the areas of religious, educational and social reform.

Having modified his earlier conviction that the reforms that he believed necessary could only be realized through the replacement of Hinduism by Christianity, Müller came instead to place his reliance upon Vedic studies as a way of encouraging Hindus 'to recast their religious life in the light of what he was placing before them as its highest expression' (Chaudhuri, 1974, p. 321). Müller, however, lived to see both India's past history and the Veda being treated by various Hindu groups for their own ends in a way that he felt was essentially uncritical (*ibid.*, pp. 358ff.). Although he had helped to make ancient texts like the Rig-Veda more accessible, it became apparent to Müller that he could not control how those texts would then be used by others, especially those in the grip of heady nationalist feelings. Thus, by the end of his life Müller looked increasingly towards Hindu leaders like Keshub Chunder Sen, P. C. Mozoomdar and Swami Vivekananda, who appeared to be working towards the reformist goals that he shared. He responded warmly, although not uncritically, to what he saw as the monotheistic quality of their teachings and their energetic efforts to promote religious and social change. In their avowed intention of purifying popular religion, Müller recognized what he perceived to be the spirit of 'the old Indian philosophy, properly called Vedânta' (Müller, 1975 edn, p. 70).

At a personal level, following the example of Schopenhauer, Müller turned for inspiration during the last decade of his life to the classical Vedanta system of Hindu philosophy, of which he said 'I know of no better preparation for it [death] than the Vedanta philosophy' (Müller, 1894a, p. 8). This affirmation on Müller's part was noted by the Hindu thinker, Swami Vivekananda, who spoke in 1895 of Müller 'swallowing the whole of it [Vedanta]—reincarnation and all' and as having 'taken in Vedanta, bones and all' (Swami Vivekananda, 1990, pp. 337 and 342). The timing of Müller's commendation of Vedanta philosophy also shows the extent to which his personal attitudes towards this aspect of Hinduism had changed in just over a decade. In his translation of the Upanishads, that part of the Veda from which Vedantic philosophy has been largely developed, Müller made a very different reference to Schopenhauer's evaluation of Vedanta philosophy. Writing in 1879, Müller noted Schopenhauer's conviction that Christianity would not take root in India and that Indian wisdom, in fact, would penetrate and change European thought. Müller declared 'the great philosopher [Schopenhauer] seems to me to have allowed himself to be carried away too far by his enthusiasm for the less known. He is blind for the dark sides of the Upanishads, and he wilfully shuts his eyes against the bright rays of eternal truth in the Gospels' (Müller, 1900, p. lxiv). Just as Müller's views about Vedanta and its roots in the Upanishads had dramatically changed by the last six years of his life, so too had his opinions about Christian mission in India.

Although he never lost his abhorrence of Hindu forms of popular worship, Müller's links with the leaders of 'modern' Hindu movements, including the Brahmo Samaj, strengthened in step with his growing appreciation of the 'common ground' on which they all stood. Müller's contacts with Hindu contemporaries whom he held to be exponents of 'living Vedanta' thus provided more than merely the basis for a prescription for the new India. It also prompted the following personal reflection on the sense of the presence of God to be found in India: a common ground on 'which Hindus and non-Hindus may join hands and hearts in worshipping the same Supreme Spirit—who is not far from every one of us, for in Him we live and move and have our being' (Müller, 1975 edn, p. x).

It was in this spirit that Müller wrote in 1899 to P. C. Mozoomdar, as a leader of the Brahmo Samaj, to entreat him to declare himself a Christian, to accept the Christ of the gospels. Müller added 'There is no necessity whatever of your being formally received into the membership of one or the other sect of the Christian Church' (Müller, 1902, Vol. II, p. 412). Sects, bishops and other accretions were, he felt, of no importance. Of his own allegiance, Müller wrote 'I am, myself, a devoted member of the English Church, because I think its members enjoy greater freedom and more immunity from priestcraft than those of any other Church' (*ibid.*, p. 413). Once again, Müller found himself at the centre of criticism: from Mozoomdar, who rejected Müller's enticement to abandon the Hindu tradition, and from Christians, like the Principal of Pusey House, Oxford, who believed that Müller had sacrificed the doctrines of the Church in making such an offer to Mozoomdar.

By the last decade of his life, Müller's deeply engrained dislike of formal religion had been further strengthened by the eclecticism that led him to look for the 'common ground' on which he believed, as a committed Christian, he could stand with those of other faiths. It is evident, however, that by this time Müller's distrust of denominationalism had brought him to require a 'profession' of Christianity from others who stood with him on this 'common ground' that was very different from the conversion sought by the Christian missionary. Indeed, in the case of India, Müller had come increasingly to look to the Brahmo Samaj as the means by which to reform and reinvigorate the religion of the people. It is at this point that we may recognize both the distinctive nature of Müller's contribution to the late Victorian debate about Christian mission and indeed the difference between Müller's religious beliefs and expectations and those held by others popularly identified with the Broad Church. As Müller himself wrote: 'my conviction has always been that we could not be broad enough' (Müller, 1901, p. 291). It was a difference that saw him embattled in religious controversy, even in the last year of his life, when he declared: 'Woe to him, who is not a heretic, who does not choose for himself!' (Müller, 1902, Vol. II, p. 421).

VII CONCLUSION

In an assessment of Müller's career, a contemporary Indologist likened Müller to the scientists John Tyndall and T. H. Huxley. All three of these famous Victorian thinkers were held by the world at large to be 'the oracles of their respective fields of knowledge' but were not held in similar regard by their scholarly peers. Of the three, only Müller lived beyond the period of 'the full glory of popular applause' and thus saw his fame wane in his own lifetime (Hopkins, 1966, p. 396).

Those assessing Müller's achievements nearly a century after his death face a difficult task because later scholarship has provided no basis upon which to reject the broad thrust of the criticism levelled against Müller's work during his own lifetime. Whilst the value of some of Müller's translations is still acknowledged, few scholars today, if any, would choose to identify themselves with Müller's theories concerning the development of religion and mythology. His role in promoting the embryonic 'science of religion', or comparative study of religion, has to be balanced against the excessive emphasis that he placed upon the study of texts. Like so many other scholars of his day, the study of texts took the place of direct experience of the culture of which he wrote. Müller was no less a child of his age in his willingness to pass often hostile and negative judgements upon the religious traditions he described.

Yet Müller continues to be remembered with respect in India as a European who devoted much of his life to making India known to Europeans and India's past better known to Indians of his generation. His less charitable judgements on India's traditions and the shortcomings in his reconstructions of India's past are felt, on balance, to have been outweighed by his unremitting efforts to promote a wider understanding among less than sympathetic audiences of India's past and its present and future needs. His name is still to be found on Indian street signs and research institutes long after the monuments to others associated with Britain's imperial rule have been removed or re-named.

Müller's contribution to the debate surrounding the promotion of Christian mission was characterized by a degree of tolerance, which was far more generous than that shown by many of his contemporaries, but was rooted in the very methods and assumptions that had led critics to question the value of his scholarship more widely. Müller's confident expectation that popular forms of Hinduism would wither away and be replaced by the style of Hinduism promoted by the likes of Keshub Chunder Sen, P. C. Mozoomdar and Swami Vivekananda has yet to be fulfilled. It has been said that only one without direct experience of India could have entertained such a belief.[17]

Müller's conviction that Christianity would itself be changed by the encounter with other religions and that its role was to reform rather than eradicate these other faiths remained out of line with the generally shared hope of those of his contemporaries who worked in mission fields. At the first World Missionary Conference held at Edinburgh in 1910, a decade after Müller's death, delegates remained united in their belief that, where Christianity was planted, other religions would disappear; for them, Christianity alone offered certainty of salvation (Neill, 1964, p. 454).

During the twentieth century, however, there have been considerable changes in Christian attitudes towards both other faiths and the purpose of missionary activity. The confidence of the Edinburgh Conference has been tempered by more liberal theological attitudes, which have balked at accepting the kind of exclusive claims made on behalf of Christianity that united the delegates at the Edinburgh Conference. Missionary work has also been re-cast as a life of service through which the spirit of Christianity is made known to non-Christians rather than being seen as an activity in which success is measured simply through its number of conversions. The

[17] On Müller's study of modern Hindu movements, see Beckerlegge, 1995.

causes of such changes were many and complex and there is little evidence that Müller's particular contribution to the Victorian debate about Christian mission played any great part in directly bringing about these changes.

Nevertheless, it may be justifiably said that Müller's assertion that all religions are the 'work of God' and his advocacy of a missionary strategy of 'contact' rather than 'controversy' were anticipations of the later developments in the conduct of Christian mission. His pioneering role as a translator of Indian religious texts, as his candidacy for the Boden Chair illustrated, was valued by many involved in mission who would thus have been exposed in varying degrees to his views about the history of religions and the future of Christian mission. Müller's scholarly endeavours, for all their limitations, brought the comparative study of religion to the attention of a broader reading public and his research opened doors through which others would pass, including those who felt impelled to question Müller's own findings. His frequently expressed dislike of religious parochialism and his rejection of missionary activity intended to eradicate religions other than Christianity provoked controversy and hostility during his own lifetime, but has left a legacy that may prove more enduring than his scholarly theories, which were so soon to be set aside.

BIBLIOGRAPHY

J. H. Barrow (ed.) (1893) *The World's Parliament of Religions*, 2 vols., Chicago, Parliament Publishing.

G. Beckerlegge (1995) 'Sri Ramakrishna Paramahamsa—F. Max Müller's "A Real Mahatman"': a study in nineteenth century Indology', *International Journal of Comparative Religion and Philosophy*, Vol. 1, pp. 16–26.

O. Chadwick (1970) *The Victorian Church*, Part II, London, Adam & Charles Black.

*N. C. Chaudhuri (1974) *Scholar Extraordinary—The Life of Professor the Rt. Hon. Friedrich Max Müller PC*, London, Chatto & Windus.

L. Dowling (1982) 'Victorian Oxford and the science of religion', *Publications of the Modern Language Association of America*, Vol. 97, pp. 160–78.

J. N. Farquhar (1906) *Gita and Gospel*, London, Christian Literature Society.

J. N. Farquhar (1912) *A Primer of Hinduism*, 2nd edn, Oxford, Oxford University Press.

E. W. Hopkins (1966) 'Max Müller' in T. A. Sebeok (ed.) *Portraits of Linguists*, Volume 1, Bloomington and London, Indiana University Press (first published 1900).

*J. Kitagawa and J. S. Strong (1985) 'Friedrich Max Müller and the comparative study of religion' in N. Smart, J. Clayton, S. Katz and P. Sherry (eds.) *Nineteenth-century Religious Thought in the West*, Volume 3, Cambridge, Cambridge University Press.

A. A. MacDonnell (1967–8 edn (a)) 'Max Müller, Friedrich', *National Dictionary of Biography*, Oxford, Oxford University Press (first published 1917).

A. A. MacDonnell (1967–8 edn (b)) 'Monier-Williams, Sir Monier', *National Dictionary of Biography*, Oxford, Oxford University Press (first published 1917).

F. D. Maurice (1877) *The Religions of the World*, 5th edn, London, Macmillan.

M. Monier-Williams, Miscellaneous papers, press cuttings and articles covering the life and work of Sir M. Monier-Williams and especially the foundation and early history of the Indian Institute, Oxford (on microfilm in the Indian Institute Library, University of Oxford).

M. Monier-Williams, Unpublished autobiography (in manuscript in the Indian Institute Library, University of Oxford).

Monier Williams (1861) *The Study of Sanskrit in Relation to Missionary Work in India*: *An Inaugural Lecture*, delivered before the University of Oxford on 19 April 1861, London and Edinburgh, Williams & Norgate.

Monier Williams (1878) *Hinduism*, London, Society for Promoting Christian Knowledge.

F. Max Müller, The Papers of Friedrich Max Müller (1823–1900). Testimonials and letters relating to the election of the Boden Professorship of Sanskrit at Oxford, 1860–1 (98 leaves: MS.Eng.c.2807, Bodleian Library, University of Oxford).

F. Max Müller (1985 edn) *Chips from a German Workshop: Volume I Essays on the Science of Religion*, California, Scholars Press (first published 1869).

F. Max Müller (1976 edn) *Lectures on the Origin and Growth of Religion*, New York, AMS (first published 1882).

F. Max Müller (1883) *India: What Can It Teach Us?*, London, Longmans, Green.

F. Max Müller (1894a) *Three Lectures on the Vedanta Philosophy*, London, Longmans, Green.

F. Max Müller (1894b) 'Why I am not an agnostic', *The Nineteenth Century*, Vol. 36, pp. 890–5.

F. Max Müller (1975 edn) *Râmakrishna: His Life and Sayings*, New York, Charles Scribner's, New York, AMS (first published 1899).

F. Max Müller (1900) *The Upanishads*, Part 1 (The Sacred Books of the East series, Volume 1), Oxford, Clarendon Press.

F. Max Müller (1901) *My Autobiography—A Fragment*, London, Longmans, Green.

G. A. Müller (ed.) (1902) *The Life and Letters of the Right Honourable Friedrich Max Müller Edited by his Wife*, 2 vols., New York, London and Bombay, Longmans, Green.

S. Neil (1964) *Christian Missions*, Harmondsworth, Penguin Books.

E. J. Sharpe (1975) *Comparative Religion—A History*, London, Duckworth.

E. J. Sharpe (1977) *Faith Meets Faith: Some Christian Attitudes to Hinduism in the Nineteenth and Twentieth Centuries*, London, Student Christian Movement.

B.Stanley (1990) *The Bible and the Flag: Protestant Missions and British Imperialism in the Nineteenth and Twentieth Centuries*, Leicester, Apollos.

*G. W. Trompf (1968) 'Friedrich Max Müller: some preliminary chips from his German workshop', *Journal of Religious History*, Vol. 5, pp. 200–17.

G. W. Trompf (1978) *Friedrich Max Mueller as a Theorist of Comparative Religion*, Bombay, Shakuntala.

H. W. Tull (1991) 'F. Max Müller and A. B. Keith: "twaddle", the "stupid" myth, and the disease of Indology', *Numen*, Vol. 38, pp. 27–58.

D. Wiebe (1995) 'Religion and the scientific impulse in the nineteenth century: Friedrick Max Müller and the birth of the science of religion', *International Journal of Comparative Religion and Philosophy*, Vol. 1, pp. 76–97.

C. P. Williams (1994) 'British religion and the wider world: mission and Empire, 1800–1940' in S. Gilley and W. J. Sheils (eds.) *A History of Religion in Britain: Practice and Belief from Pre-Roman Times to the Present*, pp. 381–405, Oxford, Blackwell.

Swami Vivekananda (1990) *The Complete Works of Swami Vivekananda*, Volume 8, Calcutta, Advaita Ashrama.

*J. H. Voigt (1981) *Max Müller—The Man and His Ideas*, Calcutta, Firma KLM.

T. E. Yates (1978) *Venn and the Victorian Bishops Abroad*, London, Society for Promoting Christian Knowledge.

CHAPTER 6

MR QUILLIAM IN A PRAYING POSTURE AS BRITISH CHIEF OF THE
ISLAMIC FAITH

ABDULLAH QUILLIAM

FOLLOWERS OF 'MOHAMMED, KALEE AND DADA NANUK': THE PRESENCE OF ISLAM AND SOUTH ASIAN RELIGIONS IN VICTORIAN BRITAIN

I N 1888, a shy Hindu student set out for Britain from western India. His mother was concerned that he would be seduced by the freedom of being in a foreign land. His uncle, the head of the family, also hesitated, for in his opinion crossing the seas to England would constitute an irreligious act. The young man did not simply have to contend with the reservations of his immediate family. As a Hindu he had been born into caste, a social group defined broadly by marriage, occupation and custom. Maintaining the status of one's caste, relative to those of other castes which comprised Hindu society, depended greatly upon observing the customs of the caste and the ritual obligations imposed upon its members by Hindu tradition. In fact, it had been traditionally assumed that it would be impossible to observe these requirements beyond the confines of Hindu India; anyone travelling across the 'black sea' thus would lose their caste status. This was certainly the view that the young man's caste took. He remained resolved, however, to make the journey. He placated his mother and uncle by taking a vow not to touch wine, women and meat and took an early passage from Bombay. He arrived in London with four introductions to expatriate Indians. The young man was Mohandas Karamchand Gandhi, later known as Mahatma Gandhi and held by many to be 'the father of modern India'.

Although Gandhi's later life was truly exceptional, his experiences on coming to London in the late nineteenth century were not untypical of those shared by other Hindus of his class in Britain at that time. At their most general level, these experiences would have been recognized by many travellers of other faiths coming to London from abroad. Like them, Gandhi had no community to go to. Without a community of the same faith to support it, there could be no place of worship. It was left to these individuals to contrive a lifestyle that would enable them to retain what they wished of their religious practice. Barely three-quarters of a century later, the religious face of Britain had been transformed. As a result of migration during the 1950s and 1960s, many large towns and most cities had sizeable communities of Hindus and many other faiths besides.

The religious diversity that Victorians knew, however, was almost exclusively the 'internal pluralism' within institutionalized British Christianity. During the nineteenth century, a gradual acknowledgement of the full citizenship of Roman Catholics, Nonconformists, Jews and secularists was achieved through various legal reforms enacted by Parliament. But, whilst part of the impetus leading to this reappraisal of the relationship between the state and its established religion, Anglicanism, came from the challenge of secular attitudes to the institutional dominance of Christianity, much of the pressure was exerted by claims for recognition by other Christian denominations and, indeed, from within the Anglican tradition, as its various factions sought a basis for coexistence. Although the Church of England of the late Victorian period has been described as 'an internally pluralistic established church in a religiously pluralist state',[1] the movement towards a religiously pluralist state during the Victorian period was not a direct consequence of a reappraisal of the relationship between Christianity and other religions found within British society.

To speak of 'other religions' suggests a hidden reference point from which to determine the 'other'. The experience of the vast majority of Victorians would have given them little or no reason to question the appropriateness of assuming that Christianity was that hidden reference point. In fact, many Victorians would doubtless have been puzzled by references to 'other religions' within the context of British society apart from the presence of Judaism.[2] It was known, of course, that individuals of different faiths were to be found in Britain, but many of these, like Gandhi, were birds of passage—students or visitors.

The purpose of this chapter is to uncover the ways in which certain 'other religions' began to establish a presence in late Victorian Britain. Although the character of Britain's post World War II religious pluralism owes much to a colonial past and period of decolonization, we shall see that Britain's imperial role in the latter part of the nineteenth century stimulated movement between Britain and its Empire.[3] British interests in India and the Middle East forged links with regions dominated by different religions. Whilst this encouraged an interest in these religions by British scholars,[4] these links also induced and on occasion compelled members of these faiths to travel to Britain. The position of these religions in Victorian Britain was very different from that which developed after World War II. Yet, uncovering this earlier presence is part of the same story and offers a new perspective on the 'British' nature of faiths that even today are all too often sadly labelled as 'alien'.

This chapter will deal largely with Hinduism and Islam but will also make reference to Buddhists, Parsis and Sikhs. These traditions established different presences within Victorian society and, after World War II, became the focal points of communities of substantial numbers of

[1] *RVB*, I, 1, p. 62.

[2] See *RVB*, I, 7.

[3] For an account of the growth of post-war religious pluralism in Britain, see Parsons, 1993.

[4] See *RVB*, II, 13.

Britons. The limitation in the scope of this study has proved necessary because of the need to include an account of the features of the traditions in question, the regions from which these traditions were carried to Britain, and Britain's links with these regions during the Victorian period. An inevitable consequence will be the neglect of other examples of equal interest and significance. African and Chinese religious beliefs, for example, also had their place within Victorian society.

Like many traditions, the religions that will be discussed in this chapter characteristically promote individual and communal religious behaviour and certainly do not locate the whole of the religious life or even its most important parts in collective activity. Nevertheless, in examining the place of these religions in late nineteenth-century Britain, we will focus particularly on the creation of specifically religious organizations as significant indicators of the extent and nature of the presence of these religions within British society.

I THE PRESENCE OF DIFFERENT RELIGIONS AND THE GROWTH OF BRITAIN'S BLACK AND ASIAN POPULATION

Long before communities marked by different religions became commonplace in Britain, there were individuals from various parts of Africa and Asia living and working in this country. P. Fryer (1984), for example, traces a continuous but largely unrecognized black presence in Britain since the Roman occupation, throughout the Middle Ages and down to the nineteenth century. The very presence of black people of different ethnic backgrounds suggests that religions other than Christianity regulated the lives of some individuals in Britain even during these early periods. Muslims were certainly known as traders in medieval Britain, although there is no firm evidence to suggest the existence of a settled Muslim community at that time (Badawi, 1981, p. 7).

The growth of slavery from the sixteenth century increased the number of black people in Britain. By the end of the seventeenth century, black people were to be found scattered all over England, with concentrations in London and the slaving ports of Liverpool and Bristol (Fryer, 1984, p. 32). Yet, not all black people in England were slaves. In the 1780s, for example, there were at least fifty African school-children living in Liverpool and nearby villages, sent there by wealthy parents from the Gold Coast (*ibid.*, p. 60). Less fortunate were destitute blacks who lived by begging on the streets of London. This floating population included ex-servicemen and lascars. It was the plight of the lascars that attracted public attention.

In the eighteenth century a 'lascar' was defined as a native of the territories administered by the East India Company, who sailed the East India Company's ships. These Indian sailors came mainly from Bengal, Gujarat and Punjab, suggesting that many of the lascars would have been Muslims whilst others would have been Hindus and Sikhs.

The shortage of manpower caused by the outbreak of the French Wars at the end of the eighteenth century brought lascars in greater numbers to Britain, although both the government and the East India Company took stringent measures to ensure that lascars could not settle here (Sherwood, 1991, pp. 230f.[5]). Nevertheless, a number of lascars who had been illegally discharged, had jumped ship or had been unable to find a passage eastwards, joined other destitutes on the streets of London. One Evangelical, campaigning in 1842 for better conditions for lascars, estimated that 3,000 lascars visited the port of London alone every year (Salter, 1873, p. 3). During the winter of 1856–7, lascars died on the streets of London due to cold and hunger (Fryer, 1984, p. 262). In response to this, the Church Missionary Society opened a Strangers' Home for Asiatics, Africans and South Sea Islanders in 1857. The public interest shown in the conditions of lascars during the late eighteenth and nineteenth centuries resulted in more careful record-keeping relating to their numbers and needs and thus clues about the nature of the religious traditions that they brought to Britain. Early signs of this interest resulted in popular reports of religious festivals and rituals, such as burial, carried out by lascars (see, for example, Anon., 1805; Anon., 1823).

One source that offers a detailed account of the lives of lascars in Britain and their religious affiliations is that written by Joseph Salter, who was appointed as a missionary to Asiatics in Britain as part of the initiative that led to the founding of the Strangers' Home. Those who supported these projects believed that it made little sense to send missionaries to India when Indian seamen could travel regularly to Britain, and even become temporary residents, without ever hearing the Christian gospel. Salter's account, for all its genuine concern for the wretched treatment of lascars, is highly polemical in its references to their religious beliefs. When treated with care, however, his *Sketches of Sixteen Years' Work Among Orientals* (1873) is an important source of information, because he travelled extensively through England, Scotland and Wales in his attempt to 'search out and make inquiries into the case of every Asiatic, African and Polynesian found or met with wandering about or begging' (Salter, 1873, p. 12). He received instruction

---

[5] The abbreviations f. and ff. indicate that the reference continues onto the page or pages following the one cited.

in Hindustani and visited lascars in their lodging-houses, in hospitals and in prison.

From Salter's references to 'worshippers of Mohammed, Kalee and Juggernaut' and to followers of 'Dada Nanuk', it is evident that there were indeed Muslims, Hindus and Sikhs among those to whom he took the gospel (*ibid.*, pp. 25 and 104). The personal names of those in his record often indicate their allegiance to one of these faiths. Like many Victorians, Salter spoke of Muslims as 'worshippers of Mohammed' which would be blasphemous to Muslims who revere the Prophet Muhammad but worship only Allah (God). The term 'Mohammedan', used by Salter, was no less common and born of the same misunderstanding. Salter's reference to 'Dada Nanuk' (Guru Nanak) as the 'prophet' of the Sikhs was in one sense more accurate, as *guru* in its broadest sense means 'spiritual teacher'. It fails to disclose the particular place that Guru Nanak occupied as the first in a line of ten historical gurus revered by the majority of Sikhs. In common with others of his day, Salter represented the variety of Hinduism with stereotyped references to the goddess Kali ('Kalee'), who was portrayed in the writings of many Victorians as the embodiment of everything that they found alien and repulsive in Hindu culture. The great temple procession in honour of the deity Jagannatha ('Juggernaut'), which takes place annually in the east Indian city of Puri, was viewed with equal horror. Victorian literature had already begun to shape an image of the great wooden vehicles upon which the temple images are carried as symbols of brutality and extravagance and indicative of the moral condition of those who followed such a religion.[6] However, we do learn more from Salter than just about his own understanding of these faiths.

Salter's work as a missionary was not confined to lascars and homeless Asians. Salter refers to members of India's élite classes who supported the Strangers' Home. One of these was Maharaja Duleep Singh, a Christian convert from Sikhism who had contributed towards the costs of the Home, whilst others were Muslim rulers.[7] Meer Jaffier Ali, the Nawab of Surat, took up residence in Paddington with a small retinue, and Salter's

[6] For fuller reviews of Victorian stereotyped images of Hinduism and Islam, see Kiernan, 1969 and Parry, 1971. Images of Islam as a political threat will be discussed later in this chapter when we consider the Liverpool Muslim Institute.

[7] In the interests of consistency, names of individuals referred to by Salter are being given in the form found in his account rather than according to more recent systems of transliteration. 'Maharaja' (from Hindi) is a title ascribed traditionally to certain Indian kings and princes, whereas 'raja', although also given more generally to kings and princes, has been extended to lesser dignitaries such as landlords. The title 'Nawab' (from Urdu) means a governor or nobleman. 'Meer' (Mir) is similarly a title traditionally given to a leader or ruler, as in 'Amir' or 'Emir'.

contacts with this Muslim ruler's household aided his study of Hindustani. Salter noted that the Nawab, although hospitable, would not take European food. Salter also described the Nawab's doorman performing the Muslim ritual of evening prayer in the kitchen amidst the bustle of the household.[8]

The Nawab's party, however, was small compared to that of the Queen of Oude and her 130 retainers. Coming to plead for the restoration of her son to the throne of Oude, which had recently been annexed by the British, the Queen's cause was overtaken by the uprising of 1857 in India (the 'Indian Mutiny') and she left England before Salter had the opportunity to fulfil his missionary vocation. Nevertheless, Salter's contact with members of the Muslim Queen's entourage led him to observe 'The Ramadhan, or Mohammedan fast, was strictly observed by these natives of India', possibly implying that the month of obligatory fasting for Muslims had been observed during the Queen's stay in London (Salter, 1873, p. 62, cf. pp. 240ff.).

Apart from his brushes with Indian nobility, it was Salter's work with lascars and less fortunate travellers from Africa and Asia that took up most of his time. His account illustrates the range of different linguistic and ethnic groups then found in Britain, and also the extent to which individuals from these groups would travel through the country and way beyond the docklands areas, for example to the Isle of Man (see, for example, *ibid.*, p. 221). Salter was thus well qualified to make the judgement that, although the West was regarded as defiling to Hindus and others, those who made the journey were often admired by their countrymen (*ibid.*, p. 92). He glimpsed into lives nurtured by different faiths in India and other countries and saw the persistence of beliefs and practices absorbed from birth. Salter knew enough to realize the horror experienced by Muslim seamen when forced to eat pork on ship (*ibid.*, p. 151) and occasionally appeared to acknowledge the devotion to their faiths displayed by individuals in the uncongenial and hostile setting of Britain (*ibid.*, p. 228).

Not all of Britain's Indian population during the middle and latter parts of the nineteenth century fell into the category of the least advantaged. Improved forms of travel encouraged more of those with means to make extended visits to Britain from parts of Africa and India. Princes from independent Indian states were regular visitors to Britain from 1870. Indian academics, doctors, barristers, entrepreneurs and entertainers all found employment in Britain, where many made their

---

[8] See 'J. Salter on the Asiatic in England', Part II, pp. 336–7.

permanent homes.[9] Some academics, for example, found employment in coaching students for the examination for entry into the prestigious Indian Civil Service. In the 1870s, Maharaja Duleep Singh (the benefactor of the Strangers' Home for Asiatics) considered offering himself as a prospective Member of Parliament (Alexander and Anand, 1980, pp. 117f.). If nothing else, this suggests something about the way Duleep Singh viewed his standing in British society at that time. By 1892, Dadabhai Naoroji, an Indian Parsi, had been elected to Parliament by the voters of Finsbury Central.

At a more modest level, the majority of Indian seamen pursued their trade independently of philanthropic assistance and congregated in lodgings and houses in the docklands, some marrying local women. Embryonic communities of seamen and ex-seamen distinguished by ethnicity thus began to develop in the docklands of port cities such as Cardiff and Liverpool. In addition to Indian seamen, these included Arabs from Aden and the Yemen, Chinese and Malays. While waiting for ships, these seamen took up a wide range of shore-based occupations including providing services like shops and lodging-houses for each other, and, as Salter observed, travelling widely as entertainers. Servants and ayahs (nannies) brought to Britain by returning officials of the East India Company or by visiting Indian rulers found service or other employment at a time when the employment of Indian servants was regarded as fashionable in some sectors of society.

Queen Victoria has been described as having had a 'soft spot' for visiting Indian maharajas and rajas and took a considerable interest in the fortunes of expatriate members of the Indian nobility, like Maharaja Duleep Singh and Princess Gouramma, who took up residence in Britain (Visram, 1986, p. 174). She also employed Indian servants, most notably Abdul Karim, a Muslim and former clerk from Agra who joined her service at Balmoral in 1887 soon after the Golden Jubilee celebrations. He later became known as the Queen's 'munshi' (teacher) after Victoria employed him to give her instruction in the religions and culture of India and in rudimentary Hindustani so that she might greet Indian rulers. Further attempts by the Queen to advance the career of Abdul Karim were fiercely resisted by members of her court (*ibid.*, pp. 32f.).

[9] For a broad account of the lives of Indians in Britain during this period, see Visram, 1986. In this context, it is interesting to note that the characters in Wilkie Collins's *The Moonstone* (1868) expressed no surprise at finding *Indian* jugglers at their door.

An increasing number of students from Africa and India travelled to England after 1871,[10] compared to the handful who had studied in Britain prior to this, once the religious qualifications for entry to the universities at Oxford and Cambridge had been removed. Some, like Gandhi, came to gain qualifications in medicine or law and others to sit the entrance examination to the Indian Civil Service. Entry into professional occupations in India at that time depended almost exclusively upon successful completion of courses of study in Britain. Many Indian students were from wealthy families and others were sponsored by missionaries and philanthropists. In London and in the university cities, Indian students could join societies concerned with Indian affairs, such as that formed in Edinburgh in 1883, or organizations like the National Indian Association, founded in 1870 to promote good relations between Indians and Britons.

With few exceptions, the categories of Indians we have identified were made up of individuals, or small clusters of individuals, rather than communities. These were largely professional people and individuals whose work, and not infrequently British racism, required that they adopt transitory lifestyles or whose period of residence in Britain was relatively short. The exceptions were the princely retinues and the lodgings of sailors in which different experiences of community life were evident.

The socio-economic differences that divided co-religionists coming to Britain during the latter half of the nineteenth century significantly shaped the presence of all the religions with which we are concerned. In particular, these differences affected the ways in which, and ultimately the extent to which, these individuals were able, if they so chose, to maintain the practice of their faith in an alien and often hostile environment. For example, dietary problems had to be resolved both by seamen and visiting nobility. Carrying out prescribed rituals of prayer and worship required facilities, no matter how rudimentary. Such problems, of course, were not peculiar to Asians in Victorian Britain and have been commonly faced by migrants who constitute religious minorities. These problems, however, are clearly felt more acutely in proportion to the degree of isolation and powerlessness of the individual. The religious needs of the wealthy individuals, whether dietary, ritual or spiritual, could often be met from within the resources of their retinues. But these resources were not generally available except to those granted entry to these élite circles. The Nawab of Surat who refused to take European food had it in his power to

---

[10] Visram (1986, pp. 178f.) states that the first Indian students, four in number, arrived in England in 1845 and that this number increased to 160 studying in Britain in 1885. By 1910, this number had risen to 700.

make other arrangements in a way in which a lascar offered pork on a ship did not.

Thus, although Hinduism, Islam and Sikhism directed the lives of many in late nineteenth-century Britain, these individuals were so divided by class and by their vastly different reasons for being in Britain that their long-term interests did not initially draw them together with a view to forming overtly religious organizations. The movement towards the establishment of religious organizations and institutions in Britain was gradual. For example, some of the Arab Muslim communities in the docklands, made up mainly of Yemenis and Adenese, began to support *zawiyas*—centres for prayer, religious instruction and accommodation for Muslim travellers. The first of these was established by Yemenis in Cardiff by the end of the nineteenth century (Ally, 1981, pp. 26ff.). In large measure, however, the movement towards more complex and stable arrangements for communal religious practice did not take place until after World War II with the emergence of multi-generational, permanent communities with sufficient human and economic resources to undertake and sustain such projects. The experience of the Parsi community was the outstanding exception to this generalization and was due in part to the greater concentration of its members within a narrower socio-economic banding.

II   THE OLDEST OF THE ASIAN COMMUNITIES IN THE UNITED KINGDOM

It has been claimed that a member of the Parsi faith was the first known Indian to visit England, arriving in 1742. The Parsi community has been described as 'the oldest of the Asian communities in the United Kingdom' and it created 'the first Asian religious association founded in Britain' (Hinnells, 1996, pp. 1 and 107).

The name 'Parsi' (or 'Persian') has been given to Indian followers of the ancient Iranian prophet Zoroaster (Zarathustra), whom many scholars now date to *c.*1200 BCE. The Zoroastrian religion is centred upon belief in one wholly good God (Ahura Mazda), who is opposed by the evil spirit Angra Mainyu. Believing in the ultimate victory of good over evil, Zoroastrians have a duty to contribute to the defeat of evil and to take responsibility for both the spiritual and material aspects of existence. Zoroastrians are required not merely to observe a high moral code. As the material world is regarded as God's creation, they are also required to observe codes of purity that avoid polluting the earth, fire or water. This concern is particularly evident in the disposal of the dead. Traditionally, this was done in 'Towers of Silence' where bodies were exposed for consumption by wild animals.

Parsis are the descendants of Iranian Zoroastrians who migrated from Iran to India in the tenth century CE rather than live under Muslim rule following the Arab conquest of Iran. Settling largely in the region around Bombay, Parsis became, in effect, another caste within Hindu society, but never adopted the Hindu practice of defining their identity by following certain occupations to the exclusion of others. Although traditionally prominent in the manufacture of textiles, Parsis were quick to take up educational and occupational opportunities offered under British rule. They rapidly rose to prominence in business and in the professions and played a vital role in the expansion of Bombay as a commercial centre. Coming to Britain in increasing numbers in the latter half of the nineteenth century for reasons of study and trade, some Parsi business-men and professionals subsequently brought their families to settle permanently. Small numbers of Parsis were to be found in centres of commerce and learning across the country, but the largest numbers were concentrated in London. Of these, Dadabhai Naoroji was not the only Parsi to achieve political prominence in late Victorian Britain. Sir Muncherji Bhownagree was the Member of Parliament for Bethnal Green between 1895 and 1906.

By 1861, the Parsi community in London was sufficiently large and wealthy to found the Religious Society of Zoroastrians and in 1862 to acquire a burial area in the cemetery at Brookwood near Woking.[11] A 'chapel' for prayer and the performance of purification rituals was opened at the cemetery in 1901. Among other things, the Society helped destitute Zoroastrians and sought to establish a 'House of Prayer'. In so doing, members of the Society faced charges from their co-religionists in India that a Zoroastrian temple could not be built in a social context where it would prove impossible to observe strictly regulations relating to purity. In fact, the Parsis in London had not planned to establish a Zoroastrian temple, but merely a place for meeting and prayer. However, this concern foreshadowed later controversies within the Parsi commu-nity, and within the other religions discussed in this chapter, over the

---

[11] The Parsi Burial Ground at Woking was visited in 1890 by Behramji M. Malabari, a Parsi visitor to Britain. In his account of his visit to the cemetery, Malabari mused 'No vultures here' (a reference to the traditional Parsi method of exposing the dead for consumption by wild animals in 'Towers of Silence') and spoke of the anguish of those families whose relatives were now buried in a distant land. Malabari also recorded wandering through 'the spots assigned to other nationalities for the rites of sepulture' in the same cemetery (Malabari, 1895, pp. 228f.). For a definitive account of early Parsi activity in Britain, see Hinnells, 1996. See also Visram, 1986.

extent to which a community away from its homeland could properly practise its religion, that is, adapt traditional notions of religious purity in the light of local circumstances and legal provisions (Hinnells, 1996, p. 137).

III   MAHARAJA DULEEP SINGH—A SIKH IN VICTORIAN BRITAIN

In contrast to the Parsis, the Sikh religion did not establish an organized presence in Britain until 1908 when the first Sikh society, the Khalsa Jatha British Isles, was formed. In 1911, the Khalsa Jatha opened the first Sikh *gurdwara* (temple) in Britain with funding from Maharaja Bhupinder Singh of Patiala. Those who supported the *gurdwara* were the small number of more affluent and educated Sikhs who had come to London for professional, educational or commercial reasons. Before that time, the most well-known Sikh personality living in Britain was beyond question Maharaja Duleep Singh, but this ruler had come to Britain as a convert to Christianity. The son of Maharaja Ranjit Singh, the last ruler of an independent Sikh kingdom, Duleep Singh left India after the British annexation of the Punjab in 1849. He became a Christian in 1853 and moved to England in 1854, where he received an annuity and a knighthood in exchange for signing away the right to his kingdom and surrendering the Koh-i-noor diamond. A favourite of Queen Victoria, Duleep Singh took up the lifestyle of a country gentleman at Elvedon Estate. He emerged as something of a public figure, thinking about standing for Parliament and acting as benefactor of the Strangers' Home for Asiatics. After a long-festering dispute about the level of his annuity, Duleep Singh came increasingly to be cast as a person of extravagance. His lifestyle provoked an inquiry into his debts in 1880. After this, his attitudes towards the British changed and he attempted to return to the Punjab in 1886. On making a public claim for the restoration of his right to rule Punjab, he was stopped at Aden where he renounced Christianity and reverted to Sikhism. He died in Paris in 1893 but was buried at Elvedon. The re-adoption of Sikhism by Duleep Singh in 1886 had a symbolic significance for some Sikhs in India but, in the absence of a Sikh community in Britain, made no impact upon religious life in Britain.[12] In fact, it seems probable that many Britons in Duleep Singh's circle saw little difference between Hinduism and Sikhism and that they would have been

---

[12] In more recent years, some Sikhs have chosen to visit Elvedon because of its associations with Britain's first prominent Sikh.

far more conscious of his renunciation of Christianity than of the implications of his re-adoption of Sikhism.[13]

In broad terms, therefore, the movement of Sikhism into Britain during the nineteenth century followed much the same pattern as that of Hinduism and Islam, carried as it was by scatterings of individuals at different ends of the socio-economic spectrum. In addition to the small number of Sikhs from professional backgrounds, Sikh royal visitors with their retinues also came to Britain for stays of different lengths, for example to attend the Jubilee celebrations of Queen Victoria in 1887 and 1897. Sikhs were also to be found among the lascars and the servant classes. This small, floating population was enlarged by Sikh pedlars who began to appear in Britain in the early twentieth century and who became more familiar after World War I. That Hinduism and Islam, unlike Sikhism, were able to generate active organizations in Britain during the last quarter of the nineteenth century was, as we shall shortly see, largely due to the quite different ways in which both these traditions succeeded in eliciting the support of Britons not born into these faiths.

IV HINDUISM IN VICTORIAN BRITAIN

Until the nineteenth century, the practice of the religion known in the West as 'Hinduism' had been confined to those born into Hindu society and thus into caste. The term 'Hinduism' was, in fact, a western invention and not a translation of a concept indigenous to India. Confronted by the rich diversity of Indian religious practice, Europeans coined the term 'Hinduism' to refer to the religion and culture of the majority of India's population who were not followers of Islam. The term thus had a geographical reference point but did not signify explicitly the vast diversity of religious beliefs and practices that it concealed. Amidst this diversity, many observers were struck by the intimate relationship between what they referred to as 'Hinduism' and the social system of caste. Indeed, the religious development of Hindus was perceived to be closely dependent upon discharging responsibilities that were only able to be undertaken by those born into a specific caste. As we noted in the earlier reference to the experience of Gandhi, this intimate connection between the more narrowly religious aspects of the Hindu tradition and membership of a Hindu social system based upon caste had produced scepticism

---

[13] For a fuller account of the life of Duleep Singh, see Alexander and Anand, 1980.

about whether it was possible in any sense to live an authentically Hindu lifestyle beyond the shores of India.

Yet, even a glance at the history of south and south-east Asia during the last two millennia reveals that Hindus did travel beyond the confines of India, and that Hinduism was spread as a result of the migrations of Hindus, rather than by conversions, beyond the shores of the subcontinent of India. Earlier migrations were broadly replicated in the nineteenth and twentieth centuries by Hindus who sought work and education in east Africa or Britain and then settled in these places with their families. Once a substantial community had been created, and one typically comprising multi-generational families requiring the performance of life-cycle rituals, then Brahmins (members of the highest caste, specializing in ritual) could be brought from India and temples created. For other Hindus, living beyond the shores of India was never more than a temporary expedient even when involving lengthy periods of absence. They maintained their family homes in India and returned to India to fulfil necessary religious obligations. On return, some would have been expected to undergo rituals of purification to restore their status as caste members. Transplanting Hinduism, as we can see, has traditionally been hedged around by a certain amount of difficulty.

Thus, when Madhao Singh, the Hindu Maharaja of Jaipur, attended the coronation of Edward VII in 1902, he found it necessary to make careful preparations. His ship was ritually cleansed and stocked with vegetarian food and cows to provide milk. Earth from India and water from the sacred river, Ganges, were placed aboard the ship so that the Maharaja could purify his new environment (Burghart, 1987, pp. 1f.). In effect, Madhao Singh took 'Mother India' with him on his journey to London. Gandhi, on the other hand, who was born into a lower stratum of Hindu society and came to London for very different reasons, adopted a different strategy. For Gandhi, this would mean remaining true to the vows he had made before leaving India and, in the process, making common cause with English vegetarians. He also chose to cover his Hindu background to some extent by adopting the manners and dress of an English gentleman.

Whereas the Maharaja of Jaipur attempted to create, so to speak, a 'portable India' while in Britain, the accommodation that Gandhi attempted to reach with the daily realities of Victorian life had an unforeseen and profound effect on his understanding of his own faith. Towards the end of his second year in London, he was introduced to Sir Edwin Arnold's *Song Celestial* (1885), a rendering in verse of the *Bhagavad Gita*, a Hindu religious text originally composed in Sanskrit. In later life,

Gandhi was to say of this text 'When I fancied I was taking my last breath, the Gita was my solace' (Gandhi, 1971, p. 181). However, as Gandhi acknowledged, when he was introduced to Arnold's rendering of the text he 'felt ashamed, as I had read the divine poem neither in Sanskrit nor Gujarati' (Gandhi, 1982, p. 76). This was to be his first reading of the text that would later shape so much of his personal interpretation of his Hindu heritage. In addition, Gandhi also acknowledged that a friend in London had persuaded him to read Thomas Carlyle's *Heroes and Hero Worship* (1841) in which Gandhi 'learnt of the Prophet's [Muhammad] greatness and bravery and austere living' (*ibid.*, p. 78). Much of Gandhi's life on his eventual return to India was given over to the cause of promoting better relations between Hindus and Muslims.

The fact that Gandhi was introduced to the *Bhagavad Gita* in London and by two brothers whom he identified as members of the Theosophical Society adds an important element to our understanding of the nature of the presence of Hinduism in late Victorian Britain. The Theosophical Society had been founded in New York in 1875. Initially, it owed much to the personality of Helena Petrovna Blavatsky (1831–91), whose interests lay in occultism, spiritualism and the esoteric knowledge that she believed was preserved in religious traditions from the ancient world down to her own day. From its beginnings, the Theosophical Society looked towards the East for wisdom, as Blavatsky claimed that truths had been revealed to her by Tibetan spiritual masters or mahatmas (literally, 'great souls'). A British wing of the Theosophical Society was formed in 1878 and drew for membership upon individuals already interested in spiritualism and psychic research.

The early history of the Theosophical Society was clouded by controversy centred upon disputes about the veracity and general character of Blavatsky and her immediate associates. It has been suggested that increasingly hostile public attitudes in the United States of America may have influenced Blavatsky's decision to transfer her operations to India. Whatever the reason, this move brought the Theosophical Society into closer contact with Indian thought. In 1882, the headquarters of the Theosophical Society was established in Madras. The Theosophical Society, with its universalist outlook and acknowledgement of the power of Indian spiritual wisdom, was well received, both in Madras and more widely in India during a period of intensifying nationalist sentiment. Branches of the Theosophical Society sprang up throughout India and the Society was vocal in its defence of the abiding value of Hindu and Buddhist religious thought. Even so, scandal continued to dog the Theosophical Society in India during the 1880s with fresh accusations of the fraudulent manufacturing of psychic phenomena. Yet, this did not deter a most remarkable woman from joining the movement in London. This woman was Annie Besant.

Annie Besant (1847–1933) was of Irish descent and by the age of twenty-five had experienced a loss of Christian faith which resulted in the break-up of her marriage to an Anglican clergyman. Not quite a professing atheist, she joined the National Secular Society in 1874 and so began a close association with Charles Bradlaugh. The causes she supported included contraception, women's rights, republicanism and trade unionism. Having been asked to review Blavatsky's *Secret Doctrine* in 1889, she declared that 'The light had been seen, and in that flash of illumination I knew that the search was over and the very Truth was found' (Dinnage, 1986, p. 67). She became the most important figure in the Theosophical Society after the death of Blavatsky in 1891. By 1893, Besant had moved to India and, due at least in part to her influence, the occultism and spiritualism of Blavatsky were gradually overlaid by interests shaped by the interaction with Hinduism. In 1898, she was instrumental in establishing the Benares Central Hindu College, which in time provided a foundation for the Benares Hindu University. Besant became President of the Theosophical Society in 1907 and such was her subsequent level of involvement with Indian affairs that in 1917 she was elected President of the Congress Party during the struggle for independence from British rule.[14]

The Theosophical Society in the United States and Europe was no less active in disseminating knowledge of Indian religious and philosophical thought than its Indian counterpart. As the Society moved away from the 'secret doctrines' of Blavatsky, it presented Hindu and Buddhist thought increasingly on its own terms through the publication of translations of classical religious and philosophical texts. Members of the western branches of the organization were also keen to make common cause with Indians whom they met. Thus, Gandhi's association with members of the Theosophical Society in London and, in a sense, his receiving instruction in his own religion from them was, if not predictable, then certainly not surprising, given the known interests of Theosophists and the understandable social needs of isolated expatriate Hindus. Although he never joined the Theosophical Society, Gandhi declared in an interview given in 1946 that Theosophy 'is Hinduism at its best' (Fischer, 1951, p. 469).

In examining the presence of Hinduism in late nineteenth-century Britain, we come, therefore, to the question of whether the Theosophical

[14] For a fuller account of Besant, see Dinnage, 1986 and Taylor, 1992. References also occur in earlier volumes of *Religion in Victorian Britain*.

Society was itself one manifestation of this presence. Theosophists certainly incorporated aspects of the Hindu religious world-view into their own personal philosophies and in so doing entered into a relationship with Hinduism that was significantly different from that of the merely interested student. The *Bhagavad Gita*, which Gandhi read at the bidding of Theosophists, had first been translated into English in 1785 (Sharpe, 1985). Translations of many other Hindu texts were completed in the following century. Studying a text of an Indian religion, no matter how unusual that might have been at the time, was not, however, the same thing as absorbing it existentially and living by it.[15] It is for this reason that Buddhism has not been discussed in detail within this chapter. Buddhist scriptures were translated by Victorian scholars, and some translators and scholars, such as T. W. Rhys Davids (1843–1922) and Edwin Arnold (1832–1904), testified personally to the appeal of Buddhist thought and morality. The earliest British organization of practising Buddhists, however, was not created until 1907.[16]

Yet, in spite of their personal assimilation of Hindu religious teaching, Theosophists were not drawn into the cultic patterns of Hindu popular devotion. Nor could they find a place within the Hindu caste system, membership of which had traditionally been the prerequisite for being a Hindu. In this respect, any notion of 'converting' to Hinduism was problematic in a way in which adopting a Buddhist way of life was not. Buddhism historically has not been confined by ethnic and social boundaries. Thus, leaving aside the complex and technical question of whether Theosophists voiced versions of Hindu belief that would have been regarded as authentic by Hindus, we have to determine whether by the latter part of the nineteenth century the Hindu tradition offered any niche for those not born of Hindu parents and so into caste. We can go some way towards answering this question by examining the effects of visits made to Britain by Swami Vivekananda, a prominent Hindu religious teacher, during the closing years of the nineteenth century.

[15] Chapter 5 on Max Müller traces the process whereby one prominent Victorian Indologist came to a personal acceptance of certain aspects of Hindu philosophy while remaining hostile to popular expressions of Hindu religiosity.

[16] The Buddhist Society of Great Britain and Ireland was created in 1907. A second important but later impetus to the growth of British Buddhism was the foundation of the British Mahabodhi Society in 1925. The founder of the Mahabodhi Society, originally established in Calcutta in 1881, was Anagarika Dharmapala, a Sri Lankan and a close associate of Blavatsky, who has been described as a 'Buddhist Theosophist' (Oliver, 1979, p. 51). Theosophists thus played an important role in the propagation of both Hindu and Buddhist ideas in late nineteenth- and early twentieth-century Britain. See Oliver, 1979, for a fuller account of the growth of Buddhism in Britain.

Swami Vivekananda (1863–1902) was not the first Hindu to visit Britain. He was preceded by two equally well-known Hindu leaders, Raja Rammohun Roy (1772–1833) and Keshub Chunder Sen (1838–84), who visited Britain in 1830 and 1870, respectively. In fact, it has been said that two Brahmins from Bombay had made the journey to England about forty years before Rammohun Roy's visit but, lacking personal prominence, their journeys went unmarked (Collet, 1962, p. 303, n. 1).

Rammohun Roy, Keshub Chunder Sen and Swami Vivekananda were representatives of styles of Hinduism that have been collectively labelled 'reformed Hinduism', 'Renaissance Hinduism' or simply 'modern Hinduism'. As these titles imply, the individuals and the movements that they represented were all committed to changing the nature of the Hindu tradition in line with what they perceived to be the needs of their age. What is less certain is the degree of fundamental change that they sought and the sources of the impetus for this change. It is beyond dispute that these movements had their roots in the nineteenth-century Hindu encounter with European, including Christian, thought. What is contested is the extent to which these movements retained continuity with traditional Hinduism, as opposed to absorbing so much western and specifically Christian influence as to constitute a break with earlier Hindu tradition. Much of the scholarly debate about the status of these movements has centred not just upon their treatment of received Hindu belief and practice but also upon the prominence that they gave to organized philanthropic activity and, in certain cases, upon the extent to which they offered their style of Hinduism to those not born Hindus.

The reasons that brought Rammohun Roy and Keshub Chunder Sen to Britain were very different from those that motivated Swami Vivekananda. Both Rammohun Roy and Keshub Chunder Sen were leading lights in the Brahmo Samaj, a Hindu theistic society created by Rammohun Roy in Calcutta, which devoted considerable efforts to the reform of popular Hindu religious practices. Although the movement fractured after the death of Rammohun Roy, and Keshub Chunder Sen formed a new society in 1866 called the Brahmo Samaj of India, both leaders held many ideas in common. Their practical humanitarianism, sympathy for Christian ethical teaching and universalist outlook commended them to Unitarians in India and thus to Unitarians in Britain and the United States.

When Rammohun Roy travelled to Britain in late 1830, he took a Brahmin cook and two cows with him, in order, according to one well-informed missionary source, 'that he might keep caste on sea and in England' (Farquhar, 1967, p. 36). He came to study Christianity in the

West and western institutions more generally, to contribute to the discussions taking place in Britain preparatory to the renewal of the charter of the East India Company in 1833, and to strengthen his links with Unitarians and other sympathetic parties. His chief preoccupation at the time was judged by his biographer to have been 'political rather than social or ceremonial' (Collett, 1962, p. 331). He died in Bristol in 1833. Keshub Chunder Sen also came to Britain fortified by a sense of sharing in a common cause with British Unitarians and with letters of introduction to the government. He declared that he had come to Britain 'to study Christianity in its living and spiritual forms ... and to study the spirit of Christian philanthropy' (Mozoomdar, 1887, p. 217). The cause of promoting theism and universal fellowship dominated his concerns.[17] After an audience with Queen Victoria, Keshub Chunder Sen returned to India in September of 1870.

Unlike Rammohun Roy and Keshub Chunder Sen, Swami Vivekananda did not come to Britain largely to see more of Christianity in the West, nor was he absorbed to the same extent into the Unitarian network. When Vivekananda returned to India, English and Irish 'converts' to Hinduism went with him, while other supporters continued the work he had begun in London.

Vivekananda made two visits to Britain, the first in 1895 during an extended stay in the United States. Vivekananda had travelled to the United States in 1893 in order to offer himself as an independent representative of Hinduism at the World's Parliament of Religions, which was held in Chicago in 1893. He came primarily to find support to create an organization that would alleviate the material condition of the Indian masses and so, ultimately, lift his people out of the spiritual trough into which, he believed, they had fallen. While in the United States, however, Vivekananda increasingly took on the role of an apologist for Hinduism and in so doing began to gather American disciples who were drawn to his presentation of Hindu religious philosophy. He began to speak increasingly of a mutually beneficial exchange between East and West from which India would improve materially and western countries like Britain spiritually. It has been pointed out that the movement of yoga into the West has been part of a cross-cultural process accelerated by the founding of the Theosophical Society in 1875 and Vivekananda's journey to the West in 1893 (De Michelis, 1995, p. 243). Vivekananda's repeated reference to an exchange of material and spiritual insights between West and East further contributed to this process. Having met Theosophists in

[17] For a record of the topics on which Keshub Chunder Sen spoke while in Britain, see Sen, 1980.

India and again at Chicago in 1893, Vivekananda travelled to Britain in September 1895. He accepted invitations from two of his new disciples, Henrietta Muller and E. T. Sturdy, both of whom had had close links with the Theosophical Society, the latter having lived in India. During the next month, Vivekananda gave public lectures and offered classes on Hindu thought, particularly on the philosophical tradition known as Vedanta.[18] Sturdy furnished most of the introductions but Vivekananda also spoke at the Ethical Society run by Moncure Conway, a former Unitarian who had been one of those who had played host to Keshub Chunder Sen.

In the next year, Vivekananda paid a second visit to Britain from the United States, this time staying from April until December 1896, broken by a two-month excursion to the continent. Vivekananda had arranged for a brother monk to join him from India and the seeds of an organization were being planted. Significantly, at this time the attention of Vivekananda and his brother monk was centred upon the spiritual needs of those not born into the Hindu tradition but who were negotiating ways in which to become part of it. J. J. Goodwin, an Englishman who had met Vivekananda in the United States, devoted the remainder of his life to serving Vivekananda as a secretary and personal attendant. By 1896, Goodwin is described as having undertaken 'the vow of a Brahmachari', a *brahmachari* being a student of Vedic knowledge and bound to celibacy (*The Life of Swami Vivekananda*, 1979, Vol. 2, p. 96). More strikingly, before leaving the United States for Britain, Vivekananda had initiated two of his American disciples into *sannyasa,* the state of renunciation that technically could only be entered by a member of the highest caste in Hindu society who had passed through the preceding stages of being a *brahmachari* and a householder. Thus, we see that the boundaries of Hinduism had been redrawn by Vivekananda in a novel way so as to grant admission to individuals not born into Hindu society.

Vivekananda's second stay in Britain passed rapidly in a whirl of speaking arrangements—classes, Sunday lectures, lectures to associations and talks at private functions. His links with the Theosophical Society and Unitarianism continued, and it is clear that he drew many of his listeners from the ranks of those with liberal religious views and universalist inclinations. Overwhelmingly, Vivekananda addressed a white British

---

[18] Vedanta (literally, 'end of the Veda') refers to one of the traditional schools of Hindu religious philosophy, which claimed to encapsulate the essence of Vedic teaching. As presented by Vivekananda, Vedanta took on the form of a universal religion, a common core to be found in all religions but most fully expressed within the Hindu tradition. Vivekananda's tailoring of Vedanta to the needs of western audiences has led some scholars to suggest that what Vivekananda offered his listeners was a form of 'neo-Vedanta', which differed significantly from earlier Hindu expositions.

audience, although in July 1896 he did preside over a special meeting of Indian students, called under the auspices of the London Hindu Association, which was also attended by many Europeans. He attended another function for Indian students at Cambridge later in the year. Vivekananda spoke on many topics relating to India, and the composition of his audiences changed accordingly, but a small core of devoted disciples began to define itself as in the United States. To Goodwin, Henrietta Muller and Sturdy were added Margaret Noble, who later took the name Sister Nivedita, and Captain and Mrs Sevier. When Vivekananda returned to India, Goodwin and the Seviers accompanied him, shortly to be followed by Noble. Whilst these disciples fashioned new lives in India under Vivekananda's spiritual direction, other western disciples, like Henrietta Muller, made extended visits to India.

Of all Vivekananda's western disciples, Noble (1867–1911) built a reputation in India, and more particularly Bengal, that has lasted to the present day. Of Scottish ancestry, Noble was born and raised in Ireland in a Nonconformist family, but one with sympathies for the cause of Irish nationalism. Trained as a teacher in a Congregationalist college, she took up teaching posts in England and Wales and was influenced by the pioneering work of Pestalozzi and Froebel. Her involvement in the development of novel teaching methods led eventually to London where she was invited to assist in the creation of a new school. Gaining a reputation as an educator, Noble joined the Sesame Club and it was here that she first heard Vivekananda.[19] She accepted him as her guru and later received the name of Sister Nivedita ('The Dedicated'). Her life of dedication to Vivekananda and her adopted home, India, was expressed through her efforts as an educator, philanthropist and her passionate attachment to the cause of Indian nationalism.

On his return to India in 1897, much of Vivekananda's energy was committed to creating the Ramakrishna Math and Mission. This movement, which took the name of Vivekananda's own spiritual mentor, Ramakrishna, brought together a monastic wing (the Math) and a lay organization devoted to service to humanity (the Mission). Vivekananda's title of 'Swami' indicates that he was a member of the Math and thus bound by the ascetic and celibate lifestyle of a monastic. The Ramakrishna Math and Mission is an active force in India today, but the innovations for which Vivekananda was largely responsible have provoked the same sort of debate about the extent of its continuity with earlier Hindu tradition as that centred upon the status of 'Renaissance

[19] See 'Sister Nivedita on "How and why I adopted the Hindu religion"', Part II, pp. 337–8.

Hinduism' more generally. One of Vivekananda's innovations, as we have seen, was initiating western disciples into aspects of Hindu religious life previously open only to those born into Hindu society.

The religious duties performed by Hindus take place largely within the home, sometimes supervised by a Brahmin. Attendance at temples is not compulsory for Hindus and yet it is a regular practice for many. The presence of Hinduism in late Victorian Britain did not conform to this model. Beyond the lives of individual Hindus either resident or staying in Britain, Hindu religious ideas and elements of Hindu religious practice, such as meditation, were disseminated through organizations that largely addressed the needs and interests of those born outside Hinduism. The 'presence' of Hinduism within Theosophy helped to stimulate a more popular interest in Indian religious traditions that has survived. Theosophy has been an important feeder into what are now known as 'New Age' movements, many of which have been influenced by some level of acquaintance with Hindu thought.

Many of the Vedanta societies that Vivekananda began in the West, such as that started in New York in 1894, have continued down to the present day and remain under the direction of the Ramakrishna Math and Mission. In spite of the scholarly debate about the status of 'modern' or 'reformed Hinduism', it is probably fair to say that few Hindus have denied the place of the Remakrishna Math and Mission within Hinduism. The vast majority of its centres today are to be found in India, but, as the Ramakrishna Math and Mission has expanded during the last century, so it has attracted more western 'converts', who look back with gratitude to the seeds sown by Vivekananda in New York and London in the 1890s. Although Vivekananda did not inaugurate a formally constituted society in London, clusters of his followers created informal Vedanta organizations from time to time. Writing in 1897, Sister Nivedita described Vivekananda's London followers meeting 'over afternoon tea, or evening coffee' (Nivedita, 1972, p. 394). A more organized group was active in 1907 but on a self-supporting basis. An official branch of the Ramakrishna Math and Mission has flourished in Britain since 1948 supported by white devotees and by families of Indian descent.

Finally, the fact that several of Vivekananda's closest British disciples followed him to India implies something of a judgement upon the constraints experienced by some at that time. The acceptance of Vivekananda's version of Hindu religious philosophy offered a less rigid, less dogmatic and, Vivekananda claimed, more 'spiritual' religion than institutionalized Christianity. However, for followers like Noble, moving to India also constituted a statement about the limitations imposed upon the lives of women in British society and about British imperialism in much the same way as did Besant's adoption of Theosophy and a new life in India.

V THE LIVERPOOL MOSQUE AND THE MUSLIM INSTITUTE

If the Hindu tradition has found its distinctive social expression through the maintenance of the caste system, in Islam it has been the notion of a 'house of believers' united against the unbelievers that has provided both an ideal and a social reality that has crossed ethnic and national boundaries. The Islamic calendar begins from the year when the Prophet Muhammad organized an *ummah* (from the Arabic, 'community' or 'people') at the city of Medina, which has served as the prototype for all later Muslim communities. A Muslim is simply one who submits to or accepts the will of Allah (God) and whose life is consequently an expression of Islam or submission to Allah. Acknowledging much of the same prophetic tradition as that shared by Jews and Christians, Muslims believe that it fell to Muhammad to be God's final prophetic messenger. Muhammad acted as the medium through which the divine revelation later written down in the Qur'an was given, a revelation that supersedes and completes earlier prophetic revelations.

The core of Muslim belief may be summarized succinctly as an uncompromising insistence upon the oneness and transcendence of God, who will call every human to account on the day of judgement, and the proclamation of the role of the Prophet Muhammad. There is a similarly concise set of basic obligations, popularly known as the 'Five Pillars of Islam', comprising the profession of faith, prayer, fasting, charity and pilgrimage. The lifestyle of the individual, however, has been enveloped in Muslim countries within the way of life of the whole community based upon the practice of Islam, which traditionally has recognized no distinction between the sacred and the secular and thus between religion and politics. The life of the community has been regulated by *shari'ah* or the 'sacred law' of Islam, which has been derived from the Qur'an and in differing degrees, according to which interpretative school has been regionally influential, from the precedents set by Muhammad and his companions and from the judgement of the Muslim community.

Until the expansion of European colonialism, Islam had largely been practised in countries in which it constituted the dominant religion and in which religious, political, economic and indeed military interests were thus integrated within an Islamic framework. In Britain, its practice would have been almost exclusively confined to foreign visitors and workers of the type identified earlier in this chapter. One intriguing exception to this generalization is suggested by references in diocesan records to English sailors 'returning from captivity' who had 'outwardly conformed to Mohammedanism'. A correspondence between the Bishop of Exeter and the Archbishop of Canterbury in 1637 deals with the creation of a church service through which a 'Renegade or Apostate from the Christian Religion to Turkism' may be brought back into the Christian communion.[20] It should not be assumed, however, that these English sailors were coerced into adopting Islam. Although popular images have often portrayed Islam as spread by the 'fire and the sword', history shows that trade and the process of acculturation resulting from close contact have been far more significant factors than conquest. As we will see shortly, the members of the first British Muslim organization embraced Islam through choice—in spite of the negative images of Islam that have long been a part of popular British culture.

The nineteenth century saw a 'renewal of thought about Islam' in Britain and Europe more generally because of the expansion of Europe into regions where Islam had been historically dominant (Hourani, 1991, p. 15). Evidence of this may be seen, for example, in the number of articles on subjects relating to Islam in popular nineteenth-century British reviews.[21] Some writers, like Thomas Carlyle and Edmund Gibbon before him, were attracted to the achievements of the Prophet Muhammad as a leader, and Christians of different complexions wrestled with the relationship between Islam and Christianity, but it was the political threat posed by Islam that preoccupied many Victorians. Although some were prepared to follow Carlyle in recognizing the sincerity of the Prophet, such a concession did not necessarily lead to sympathy with 'existing Mahometanism' (Almond, 1989, p. 4). The *British Quarterly Review* for 1872, for example, acknowledged Muhammad as one of the greatest reformers but referred to Islam, once it had spread beyond Arabia, as 'the greatest of curses to mankind' (quoted in Almond, 1989, p. 82).

In Victorian Britain, Islam was widely identified as the religious faith held by nations and groups that were regarded as hostile to Britain's political and economic interests. During the course of the nineteenth century, Britain found itself in conflict with Afghanistan (1839 and

---

[20] I am grateful to Dr Mary Wolffe for information concerning this correspondence between Joseph Hall, the Bishop of Exeter and Archbishop Laud, which she discovered in Chanter 57, Pattern Book 1 (24 May 1628–20 September 1732) held at Devon Record Office (Exeter).

[21] For specific examples, see A. A. H., 1878, Davey, 1896 and Salome, 1896. For more comprehensive treatments of Victorian attitude to Islam, see Almond, 1989, Hourani, 1991 and Bennett, 1992.

1878–80) and Persia (1856–7). It was involved in containing the rise of the Mahdi in the Sudan and General Gordon's name passed into the national mythology as the heroic defender of Khartoum in 1885. In India, regarded by many as the most important part of the British Empire, Britain had taken over much of the territory that had formerly been part of the Mughal Empire, and British rule in India subsequently was characterized by a mistrust of the Muslim population and its ruling class as the erstwhile rulers of India. The attempt made by the British after the 'Indian Mutiny' to treat the Muslim élite as a special interest group, and so to entice collaboration with British rule, was merely part of a broader 'divide and rule' strategy designed to forestall political collaboration between Hindus and Muslims. It did not mark a new degree of trust in India's Muslim population (Beckerlegge, 1991, pp. 204–7).

Like the other European powers of the nineteenth century, Britain was keenly interested in the fate of the crumbling Ottoman Empire, which held on tenuously to the control of vast territories and the vital waterways of the Dardanelles, the Bosporus and the Suez Canal, which had been opened in 1869. The titles of the Ottoman emperor included that of 'caliph' (from the Arabic *khalifah*: literally, 'successor' or 'viceroy'), this being the name given to first ruler of the Islamic community who was elected to this role after the death of the Prophet Muhammad. The caliphate had been based in various locations throughout Islamic history. The Ottoman rulers in Istanbul claimed that the title had been ceded to Selim I in CE 1517 when he conquered Cairo, where previously the Abbasid dynasty had held the title.

When the expansion of the interests of the European powers threatened the fragile stability of the Ottoman Empire in the nineteenth century, Abdul Hamid II, then Sultan of Turkey and ruler of the Ottoman Empire, began to utilize the traditional title of caliph to encourage Muslims to support his regime in its struggle against the weight of European colonial ambitions: an early expression of what has come to be known as 'Pan-Islamism'. The British, pointing to the uncertainties surrounding the circumstances in which the Ottoman rulers had acquired the title of caliph, countered Abdul Hamid's appeal to the authority invested in the position of caliph by questioning the legitimacy of his use of the title (see, for example, Davey, 1896, p. 2). During the 1890s, Britain's relations with the Ottoman Empire were further strained over the treatment of Armenians under Turkish rule. A minority even in their own homeland, the Armenians suffered the more so because of their allegiance to Christianity, as had other Christians under Ottoman rule, including Bulgarians in 1876. The reported ill-treatment of

Christian minorities under Ottoman rule provoked intense anger in Britain and strong public condemnation by many including the Liberal leader William Gladstone.

Britain's relations with its Muslim subjects in India and with the Ottoman Empire in the last quarter of the nineteenth century breathed new life into stereotyped images of Islam, which had been handed down in popular culture since the Middle Ages. Islam appeared as a force brutally opposed to the practice of Christianity, its rulers the very embodiments of the corruption long held to be the hallmark of the 'oriental despot', and its followers models of duplicity. None other than Gladstone had described the mind of Abdul Hamid, the Ottoman ruler, as 'a bottomless pit of fraud and falsehood' (quoted in Anderson, 1966, p. 224). The perceived relationship between Islam and despotism encouraged Victorians to view Turkey and its political system as representative of all the characteristics that they regarded as the worst features of Islamic societies, and to see the Turks as 'paradigmatic Muslims' (Almond, 1989, p. 84). It is all the more remarkable, therefore, that, in this atmosphere of antipathy and distrust, a thriving Muslim organization was created in Liverpool in the 1890s, largely due to the efforts of a local solicitor, a convert to Islam.

William Henry Quilliam was born in 1856 of Manx decent.[22] His ancestor, John Quilliam, steered *HMS Victory* at the Battle of Trafalgar and was a pall-bearer at Nelson's funeral. William Quilliam was born and bred in Liverpool. Educated in Liverpool, Wrexham and the Isle of Man, Quilliam retained property on the island and was active in the Liverpool Manx Society and other local organizations. From the age of eighteen, he studied to become a solicitor, working as a journalist to support himself. He qualified in 1878 and subsequently became well known as a prominent advocate in the north of England.

Of Quilliam's religious beliefs prior to his conversion to Islam, little is known. His mother, who followed him into Islam, had formerly been active as a Methodist, so from this certain inferences may reasonably be drawn about the ethos in which Quilliam was raised (Ally, 1981, p. 49). It is said that Quilliam's conversion to Islam followed extensive travels in Morocco, which he visited for a period of three months in 1882, having been advised to travel on medical grounds due to overwork. Here he would have encountered the style of Islam associated with that region of

---

[22] Quilliam's biographical details are summarized from 'Men who are talked about', *Porcupine*, 21 November 1895, p. 10; a longer version of basically the same account reproduced under the same title in *Islamic World*, Vol. 4, No. 43, November 1896, pp. 212–15; 'Sheik Abdullah Quilliam', *Porcupine*, 7 April 1900, p. 8; 'A man of many parts—Mr. W. H. Quilliam and his varied life', *Liverpool Freeman*, 8 July 1905, p. 11.

North Africa known as the Magreb, including the distinctively North African style of mosque architecture. This visit led him to study Arabic and in 1887 publicly to renounce Christianity and embrace Islam, taking the name Abdullah Quilliam. The news of this conversion came to the ears of the rulers of several Muslim countries. Their interest in this Islamic shoot sprouting in the uncongenial climate of Liverpool at the close of the nineteenth century led to honours being given to Quilliam, financial support for his attempt to propagate Islam in the north of England, and invitations to spend more time in Islamic countries, some of which then had highly sensitive political relations with Britain.

In 1890, Quilliam was invited with his son to visit Abdul Hamid, the Sultan of Turkey and Caliph of the Faithful in Istanbul. Although Quilliam refused the personal honours that the Sultan pressed upon him, Quilliam's son was given several honorary titles. In 1893, Quilliam returned to Morocco, where he was honoured by the Islamic University of Fez and recognized as an *àlim*, one qualified to offer Islamic legal opinions. His position as Britain's most prominent Muslim was ratified in the following year when both the Sultan of Turkey and the Amir of Afghanistan conferred upon him the title of 'Sheikh-ul-Islam of the British Isles', or leader of British Muslims. Gifts and honours from other Muslim countries followed, as did requests to carry out commissions on behalf of the Sultan of Turkey, which took Quilliam again to Africa. Quilliam's eldest son served for a time as aide-de-camp to the Ottoman ruler. When Prince Nasrullah Khan, the Shahzada (the son of the Shah or ruler) of Afghanistan, visited Liverpool in 1895, it fell to Quilliam to ensure that a civic banquet in honour of the visitor observed Muslim etiquette. The generous gift that was then made to Quilliam was put to the use of improving the facilities for Muslims in Liverpool. In 1899, the Shah of Persia appointed Quilliam to the post of Persian Consul in Liverpool.

The Liverpool Mosque and Muslim Institute that were established under Quilliam's dynamic leadership continued as long as Quilliam remained in Liverpool. The phases of the development of the Institute followed closely Quilliam's own rise to prominence in the eyes of the Muslim world. The minutes of the Annual General Meeting of the Institute held in June 1896 refer to this meeting as the tenth of its kind, thus suggesting that the Institute was created in 1887 (*Islamic World*, July 1896, p. 65). This was the year of Quilliam's formal conversion to Islam. From the year of his conversion, it seems that Quilliam had begun to preach Islam and that the public lecture had been the main vehicle for this mission (*Islamic World*, August 1896, p. 99). By 1890, Quilliam had also published two pamphlets, 'The faith of Islam' and 'Fanatics and fanaticism', the first of which was translated into thirteen languages.[23] It has been suggested that it was as a result of the dissemination of these pamphlets that 'Abdullah Quilliam became a household name among the nobility of the Muslim world' (Ally, 1981, p. 50). Certainly, by this year, a small Muslim community was taking shape in Liverpool. This was substantially made up of converts to Islam rather than those born into the faith, whether seamen or transitory members of the Muslim professional and social élites. The minutes of the Annual General Meeting of 1896 state that the members of the Institute used to worship in Mount Vernon Street, Liverpool, in 1887, a location not far from the area now occupied by the University.

The mature Muslim Institute, however, was associated with a site that it occupied from 1891 in Brougham Terrace in West Derby Road, which was more towards the outskirts of Liverpool. The premises were further enlarged in 1895. Both these phases in the improvements made to the Institute followed the receipt of gifts presented to Quilliam by Muslim rulers. By the middle of the 1890s the Liverpool Muslim Institute had reached the final phase of its development. Its activities, and those of Quilliam, attracted increasing public notice, not all of which was sympathetic. Speakers at the Institute took pleasure in noting the warnings uttered by Christians, including the Archbishop of Canterbury, about the danger posed by the power of Islam (see, for example, *Islamic World*, July 1896, pp. 84f.).

Although the Liverpool Muslim Institute was relatively short-lived, it proved to be an extremely active organization. Once relocated to Brougham Terrace, the complex expanded through a series of terraced houses to comprise a mosque, an oriental library and lecture hall for adult education, a boys' day and boarding school, a girls' day school, a literary and debating society, a printing works and accommodation for guests (Figure 1). By 1896, Quilliam had opened the 'Medina Home for Children', his response to the increase in illegitimate births in the city (Figure 2). With Quilliam as its Sheikh, or leader, the Muslim Institute also had its appointed *imam* (leader of prayer) the Moulvie Barakat-Ullah and two *muezzins* (those who call to prayer).[24] The printing works at the Institute produced two regular publications, the weekly *Crescent* and the monthly *Islamic World*. From surviving issues of the latter can be glimpsed something of the life and concerns of this early British Muslim community.

---

[23] A series of articles entitled 'Fanatics and fanaticism' was published in the *Islamic World*, beginning in Vol. 5, No. 57, March/April 1898.

[24] The Moulvie Mahomet Barakatullah (Barakat-Ullah) was a contributor to the *Westminster Review*, see 'Islam and Soofeeism', *Westminster Review*, December 1895, pp. 674–8.

Figure 1   The inside cover of the *Islamic World* regularly advertised the range of activities
taking place at the Liverpool Muslim Institute

MEDINA HOME FOR CHILDREN

(Established 1896),

12, Brougham Terrace, West Derby Road, Liverpool.

This Institution has been established after having given the following facts a careful consideration :—

Unfortunately seduction is a frequent occurrence in our midst, and the result is that a large number of girls in fairly respectable positions in life give birth to illegitimate children. Over 200 cases came before the Liverpool Police Courts last year, in which girls sought to obtain orders of affiliation against the putative fathers of children to which they had given birth, and at least ten times as many cases were probably settled privately and never came before the courts at all.

Quite *two thousand* illegitimate children are born each year in the City of Liverpool and neighbourhood—the second city of the British Empire, the centre of Christendom ! What becomes of these children ? In many instances they are put out to nurse, or a small sum of money paid for them to be adopted. Cases are continually leaking out showing that baby-farming is still being conducted on a large scale in this country. Very often the parents of these children would be only too glad to pay a reasonable sum for their maintenance, provided that a suitable place was established for their reception where the children would receive proper attention and care.

The advantages of such a Home are manifold :—

1.—It will be a check upon infanticide.

2.—It will ensure the children being well cared for and trained under good surroundings.

3.—It will give the mothers of the children an opportunity to retrieve their character, and once more return to the path of virtue and respectability.

With reference to this last matter it is unfortunately the case in England that while society forgives the man any transgressions of this nature, it remembers for ever a woman's slip. The way for a woman to return to virtue is made difficult, while the way for a man to commit indiscretions of this character is facilitated. Those who so cruelly hound down the weaker sex for the slightest deviation from the strictest morality appear to have entirely forgotten the teaching of Christ upon the subject. When an unfortunate erring woman was brought before him, he wrote on the sand—" Let him who is without sin among you cast the first stone," and one by one her accusers, conscience-stricken, stole away, until none but Jesus of Nazareth and the woman were left, and then he turned to her and kindly said—" Neither do I condemn you. Go in peace and sin no more."

Critics may think such an institution as this will make it easy for wrongdoers to get rid of the fruits of their folly. Such is not the intention of the promoters, and proper precautions will be taken to prevent as far as possible such being the case. Enquiries will be made into each case before the child is admitted into the Home, and a second child will not be taken from the same mother.

We earnestly hope you will co-operate with us in this work of charity. We are anxious "to do some *little* good," and try if we cannot succeed in making *one* life even more bright—more good. That

Figure 2   Appeals for support for the Medina Home for Children appeared regularly in the *Islamic World* and included a robust justification for the founding of a Muslim orphanage in Liverpool

An account of a Sunday meeting at the Institute in 1891 provided by a Liverpool periodical referred to a 'confusion of tongues' and the presence of speakers of Gujarati, Urdu, Arabic, Turkish and French, in addition to English (*Liverpool Review,* 29 August 1891, p. 13). By 1896, the list of those associated with the Muslim Institute included patrons and honorary vice-presidents drawn from throughout the Islamic world and local, active members whose names indicate that they were converts to Islam, for example Professor H. Nasrullah Warren, T. Omar Byrne and several members of Quilliam's own family. One of the local members is identified as a resident of Accrington, quite a distance from Liverpool. Quilliam's report to the 1896 Annual General Meeting referred to twenty-one new members joining the Institute during the past year, of whom fourteen were converts from Christianity and seven Muslims from birth. However, he also noted that a 'large percentage', twenty-three members, of the Institute had died since 1887. The reason for this, he observed, was that 'Those who become Muslims from conviction are almost in all cases persons of mature age.' Nevertheless, the Institute also included younger people, some married and others soon to be so, and so he anticipated 'a succession of pupils, born, trained, and for ever living in the true faith' (*Islamic World,* July 1896, pp. 66f.).

T. Omar Byrne (the Honorary Secretary of the Institute), in his report to the Annual General Meeting of 1896, referred to the efforts of Quilliam resulting in over 150 persons embracing the faith of Islam (*Islamic World,* August 1896, p. 99). It cannot be assumed that this number corresponded to the actual membership of the Institute, but it is reasonable to assume that the total membership of the Institute would not have exceeded this figure. This figure would be consistent with Quilliam's observation that the death of twenty-three members since 1887 constituted a 'large percentage' of the Institute's total membership during the preceding decade. A report in the May 1896 issue of the Liverpool journal *Sunday at Home* referred to the mosque having 'upwards of one hundred members, besides children' (Anon., 1896, p. 442). Although the Institute's numbers were never large, they were remarkable for that time and that place, bolstered as they were by a steady trickle of converts from Christianity.[25] Unfortunately, the available sources do not

[25] A report of a Muslim funeral, in the *Liverpool Review* of 18 April 1891, shows that the Muslim community was carrying out such life-cycle rituals by this time. Intriguingly, the report begins by noting that the funeral 'was the first of the kind that had taken place in this city for over thirty-five years' (p. 7). As one of the mourners attempted to place a floral cross on the coffin, it is reasonable to infer that the deceased was a convert from Christianity. The reference to an earlier Muslim funeral, which predated the formation of the Liverpool Muslim Institute, indicated a familiarity with or remembrance of Muslim practice that had its source in an earlier acquaintance with Islam in Liverpool.

allow us to estimate with confidence the respective numbers of converts to Islam and of Muslims from birth within the membership of the Institute over the span of its existence. According to Quilliam, the Institute was 'mainly composed of Englishmen' (*Islamic World*, July 1896, p. 84). It may well be that the increase in membership that Quilliam reported for 1896, which he broke down into one-third who were Muslims from birth and two-thirds who were converts, reflected more generally the balance of membership within the Institute.

At the heart of the Institute was the mosque or place of prayer ('mosque' is the Anglicization of the Arabic *masjid*: literally, 'a place of prostration'). Devout Muslims are required to offer set prayers five times daily, except in special circumstances. These prayers may be performed individually by a person who has carried out ablutions according to rules of Muslim hygiene and should be carried out facing Mecca. Men in particular are expected to gather for communal prayer at midday on Fridays, and facilitating this prayer is one important function fulfilled by a mosque. In practice, many Muslims also choose to perform their daily prayers in their local mosque, choosing one of their number to lead the prayer, to be the *imam*. The mosque is also the place where the Qur'an (Koran), the sacred book of Islam, is read and expounded by those knowledgeable in the faith. Consequently, mosques have served as centres of Islamic education where young boys in particular have been instructed in Arabic and the Qur'an. The mosque is thus more than a place of prayer for a Muslim community, but it fulfils no sacramental functions and is not regulated by a priestly hierarchy, since there is none in Islam.

Mosques throughout the Muslim world share certain common features, although they differ in appearance according to local architectural styles and, to some extent, in their conduct, depending upon the particulars of the school of Islamic law influential in the surrounding region. In a purpose-built mosque, the direction of Mecca is marked by a *mihrab*, a niche in the middle of the wall facing Mecca. To the side of the *mihrab*, there is a point from which worshippers can be addressed during the communal midday prayer on Fridays. The extent to which worshippers pray under cover, as distinct from simply being within an enclosed courtyard, varies considerably according to country. A mosque should be devoid of any representation of the human form and under no circumstances would a pictorial representation of the divine be tolerated. As a consequence, Islamic art has relied heavily upon geometric design and the use of decorative calligraphy employed in the copying of passages from the Qur'an. Music is not permitted in mosques, where reciting the Qur'an has become an art form itself. The need to call the community to prayer has resulted in the incorporation of minarets in the design of many mosques, from which the *muezzin* can summon the faithful to prayer. The inclusion of a dome, although often associated in the popular imagination with the image of a mosque, is not a universal feature of mosque architecture.

Quilliam recalled the earliest members of the Liverpool Muslim Institute 'worshipping' when they met at Mount Vernon Street in 1887. He did not give an account of the specifics of the practice at Mount Vernon Street, but, if this involved the performance of the prescribed daily prayers according to strict Muslim practice, this implies that part of the accommodation at Mount Vernon Street must have been arranged in the style of a mosque to conform to Muslim convention. This would have involved, among other things, establishing the direction of Mecca in order to orientate prayer in that direction. Worshippers would have been required to remove their shoes before entering the place of prayer and to have followed prescribed forms of ablution.[26]

The public practice of Islam provoked hostility. Calling to prayer from the balcony in Brougham Terrace led to demonstrations by local residents and to the *muezzin* being stoned (*Islamic World,* July 1896, p. 73). As early as November 1891, voices were raised in protest against the practice of Islam in Liverpool and against the 'public advertisement of him [Muhammad]' (*Liverpool Review,* 28 November 1891, p. 14). Fireworks and missiles were thrown at the mosque. The *Liverpool Review* took the side of the protesters and, reminding its readers of the antipathy to Islam that had been part of the Christian heritage in Europe since the time of the Crusades, judged the public 'advertisement' of Muslim practice in Liverpool to be 'most incongruous, unusual, silly and unwelcome' (*ibid.*). It did not state explicitly that the call to prayer had been a source of inconvenience to local residents because of its timing or volume, rather it served as a reminder of the 'Eastern humbug' which was 'detested' by 'Western folk' (*ibid.*).[27]

Following gifts to Quilliam by Muslim rulers, the Liverpool Muslim Institute devoted resources to ensure 'the establishment of Islam on a permanent footing in this country' and this included plans for expanding existing facilities and a larger, purpose-built mosque (*Islamic World,* July 1896, p. 67).

---

[26] A simple description of worship at the mosque as seen through the eyes of a non-Muslim reporter formed part of an article entitled 'Sunday in Liverpool' in the journal *Sunday at Home* in May 1896. See Anon., 1896 and 'Sunday in Liverpool: with the Moslems', Part II, pp. 347–9.

[27] See 'Moslemism in Liverpool: Quilliam, father and son', Part II, pp. 345–7.

Quilliam's first extended experience of Islam had been in North Africa and this may be the reason why the enlarged mosque of the Liverpool Muslim Institute was influenced by the Saracenic style found in the cloistered mosques of Egypt and more generally in North Africa. In this model, an open courtyard was surrounded on four sides by cloisters or colonnades, thus combining shade for regular, extended users with a larger, open area for more occasional use by larger numbers of people. The mosque was separated from the noise and dirt of the street by a plain wall decorated only by a crenellated parapet. Located in Brougham Terrace, the Liverpool Mosque could not rival the glories of the Ibn Tulun Mosque of Cairo but it did borrow certain motifs from this mosque. The design of the *mihrab* in the Liverpool Mosque was modelled on that at Ibn Tulun and the arches over the entrance to the lecture hall, constructed at the Institute in 1895–6, were of 'Mooresque style, with Saracenic ornamentation, after the famed Tulun Mosque in Cairo' (*Islamic World*, 1896, p. 366) (see Figures 3 and 4). From a description of the alterations made to the interior of the Institute in 1895 (after the gift from the Shahzada of Afghanistan), we learn that latrines were constructed in the playground used by children attending the school at the Institute, and that 'in draining same quite an engineering feat has been accomplished in excavating a tunnel twenty-feet long to the main sewer in the centre of the street at a depth of twelve feet' (*ibid.*, p. 367).

The longer-term plans of the Institute were ambitious. Securing additional houses in Brougham Terrace was seen as a way to create the space in which to build a 'Mosque and courtyard of considerable extent'. The new mosque would have a *mihrab* crowned with a cupola and would be in true Saracenic style in respect of its arches, capitals, minaret and flat roof. The courtyard of the new mosque, or 'British Muslim Cathedral', would contain in due time the tomb of Sheikh W. H. Abdullah Quilliam, the first Sheikh-ul-Islam of the British Isles: 'The sacred structure when erected will be worthy of its being the Moslem Cathedral of the British Isles, to whose holy shrine votaries from the Far East can then make their pilgrimage' (*ibid.*). This was not to be, for reasons that will shortly become apparent.

The use of the term 'cathedral' to refer to a centre of Muslim worship is worthy of comment. It suggests that a parallel was being drawn between a cathedral—literally, the seat of a Christian bishop—and a proposed Muslim 'cathedral' that would be the 'seat' of the Sheikh-ul-Islam of the British Isles. This might be viewed simply as an example of acculturation as an Islamic institution donned the more familiar garb of a British

INTERIOR VIEW OF LECTURE HALL, LIVERPOOL MUSLIM
INSTITUTE.

INTERIOR ELEVATION OF LECTURE HALL, LIVERPOOL MUSLIM
INSTITUTE.

Figure 3 The interior of the lecture hall at the Liverpool Muslim Institute, revealing the influence of Saracenic decoration

Christian institution. Yet, it also reveals something of the needs of a minority religious community and, in this respect, may be compared with the role given to the Great Synagogue in London by the Ashkenazi Jewish community. By 1764, when Jewish communities had begun to spread beyond London, a controversy arose over the appointment of a rabbi to serve the Jewish community in Portsmouth. One consequence of this dispute was the decision to recognize the rabbi of the Great Synagogue, the largest of the Ashkenazi synagogues in London, as the Chief Rabbi of Great Britain. Consequently, Jewish charitable and educational activities were clustered around this synagogue. This decision had the effect of encouraging an efficient use of resources and provided a way of adjudicating disputes. In the light of the considerable distance between Britain's Muslim community and the traditional centres of learning in the Islamic world, the designation of a centre of authority within the British Isles was no less understandable.

The next British mosque, built in Woking in 1889, was constructed according to Indian design and resulted from Indian patronage (see Figure 5).[28] The *Illustrated London News* reported that the proximity of Woking to Windsor enabled Abdul Karim, 'Her Majesty's munshi', and 'several of her Mohammedan servants at Windsor' to attend this mosque on more than one occasion and, in particular, to celebrate one of the two major festivals in the Muslim calendar (Anon., 1889, p. 591). This account of Victoria's servants' attendance at the Woking Mosque indirectly reveals something of the Queen's own attitude to religious pluralism. The report also hailed as a 'sign of the times' the way in which 'enlightened Christians unite with pious Mohammedans on what is the common ground in their respective faiths' (Anon., 1889, p. 591). In passing,

Figure 4   The design of the *mihrab* at the Liverpool Mosque based on the *mihrab* at the Ibn Tulun Mosque at Cairo

[28] An account of the founding of the Woking Mosque and its relationship to the 'Oriental Institute', opened in 1884 as a hostel for Indian students by Dr G. W. Leitner, a Hungarian orientalist and humanitarian, is given in Anon., 1889. See also Ally, 1981, pp. 64–7.

THE MOSQUE AT THE ORIENTAL INSTITUTE, MAYBURY, WOKING.

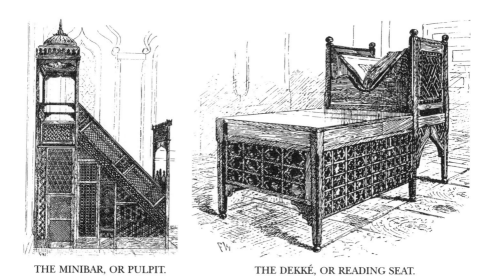

THE MINIBAR, OR PULPIT.   THE DEKKÉ, OR READING SEAT.

Figure 5   The exterior of the Woking Mosque and its internal features, in contrast to the Liverpool Mosque, show the influence of north Indian styles of mosque architecture and decorative design

it is plain that both Sunni and Shi'ite Muslims attended this mosque and that the mosque was used for some activities in 1889 before its final completion and formal opening.[29]

That British Islam should embrace two such very different models within the first decade of its organized presence in Britain is not surprising. The early Muslim converts were largely brought to Islam through residing in Muslim countries rather than simply reading about it. It was natural that they would consequently attempt to transplant the particular expression of Islam with which they were familiar, a tendency reinforced when they received financial support from Muslims in the country where they had imbibed the faith. This diversity of style also reflected the diversity within the Islamic world more widely, whilst still embodying the universals of Islam to be found in the confession of faith, the obligatory duties of the believer and the function and ethos of the mosque.

In addition to catering to the religious needs of its existing members, the Liverpool Muslim Institute continued in its attempt to bring Islam to the notice of the wider public. It did this primarily through its lecture programmes and publications. The phrase 'lecture programme', in fact, covered two rather different types of activity. Like many other nineteenth-century organizations, the Liverpool Muslim Institute ran an extensive programme of public lectures on a wide range of subjects, many of which were related to topics of popular scientific interest. By 1896, the Institute had a small laboratory for use by its students adjacent to the ablution room in the basement beneath the lecture hall. Clearly, one purpose served by its general lecture programme was to encourage adults to enter the Institute. Since 1887, however, Quilliam had also organized open meetings of a more narrowly religious nature in which lectures on Islam were given. Once the Institute was created, these meetings took place on Sundays.

From references to the Sunday meetings made during the Annual General Meeting of 1896, it is plain that secondhand reports of the nature and purpose of these meetings had stirred a controversy among Muslims abroad, in a manner not dissimilar to the concern voiced by Indian Parsis about the proposed creation of a Zoroastrian 'House of Prayer' in London. These distant Muslims formed the impression that the public meetings were 'Muslim services' of a style and nature contrary to Islam, which were being conducted in the mosque with musical accompaniment from an organ. The refutation of the accusations levelled against the

[29] Sunni Muslims (the majority) and Shi'ite Muslims are divided over the question of authority within Islamic tradition.

Sunday meetings throws considerable light on the way in which Quilliam and his closest followers attempted to bring Islam to Liverpool. Over a period of nine years, a style of meeting developed that was designed 'to bring people gradually into faith', by tailoring the proceedings in a manner that would be familiar to those used to Christian worship. Instead of 'chants in praise of the trinity, the blood-atonement for sins, and other foolishness', the meetings offered an initial recitation of the opening *surah*, or section, of the Qur'an, various other readings from the Qur'an, the singing of Christian hymns adapted for Muslims by Quilliam and a brief lecture on an aspect of Islamic history or thought. The hymns, standards like 'Abide with me', which would have been well known to Victorians, had been compiled by Quilliam 'eliminating objectionable verses from them and making their whole tone Unitarian and Islamic' (*Islamic World*, August 1896, p. 100). Thus, once having removed the 'objectionable' first line ('Hold thou thy cross before my closing eyes'), the last verse of 'Abide with me' became

> Abide with me when close these mortal eyes!
> Shine through the gloom, and point me to the skies!
> Heaven's morning breaks, and earth's vain shadows flee;
> In life, in death, Allah abide with me![30]

Byrne, the Honorary Secretary of the Institute, who provided the account of the Sunday meetings, was emphatic about the effect of these meetings and stated that it was 'doubtful if our beloved leader could have made a dozen converts' without these meetings (*Islamic World*, August 1896, p. 99). He observed 'In England Islam is in its infancy, and it is therefore necessary for us not only to provide for the religious exercises of our brethren in the faith, but also to conduct an active *propaganda* of our principles' (*Islamic World*, August 1896, pp. 98f.). Nevertheless, conscious of the misgivings to which reports of the Sunday meetings had given rise in the minds of other Muslims, Byrne went on to insist that these meetings were entirely separate from prayer that took place in the mosque and was shared only by Muslims. The Sunday meetings were open to all—Muslims and non-Muslims alike—but it had never been incumbent upon Muslims to attend them. The meetings were held in the lecture hall, never in the mosque, and had never been regarded as a substitute for the prescribed prayers of Islam. Of the conduct of prayers in the mosque, Byrne declared '*Jumma* and every other *Nimaz* in Liverpool is made exactly in the same manner as it is in every Mosque of the Hanifee school of Muslims

---

[30] See the other examples of Muslim hymns from the *Islamic World* given in Part II, pp. 344–5.

throughout the world' (*Islamic World*, August 1896, p. 98). The 'Hanifee school' is a reference to one of the surviving Muslim legal schools specializing in the interpretation of *shari'ah*, the corpus of law and precedent derived primarily from the Qur'an. The Hanafi school, as we might expect from Quilliam's associations, was the school dominant in both the Ottoman Empire and in Afghanistan. In this way, the Liverpool Muslim community placed itself squarely within the 'house of Islam' when it declared that its conduct of *jumma* (Friday communal prayer) and *nimaz* (or *namaz* from the Persian for 'prayer') was in accord with strict precedents.[31]

The contents of the *Islamic World* were not confined narrowly to topics relating to the propagation of Islam and many of the items found in this journal could have had a place in other popular periodicals of the time. Accounts of recent scientific discoveries were to be found alongside papers on mythology and Manx folklore and history together with many articles of historical and geographical interest. Many of these contributions, in fact, had been reproduced from other journals. The underlying Islamic concerns of the *Islamic World* were manifested in references to the work of the Muslim Institute, articles explaining Muslim belief and practices (some translated from Turkish sources by Quilliam) and extended articles on the place of Islam within the contemporary world. It was largely in discussions of the latter sort that polemical references were made to Christianity, frequently when pleading for fair treatment of Muslims in Britain and more generally, or when criticizing the tactics employed by Christian missionaries among Muslims (see, for example, *Islamic World*, July 1896, pp. 71f.).

One problem that loomed large in the minds of the Liverpool Muslim community was the so-called 'Eastern Question' relating to Europe's interests in the Balkans and the relationship between the European powers and the declining Ottoman Empire. Indeed, it was suggested at the outset of this account of the growth of the Liverpool Muslim Institute that Britain's diplomatic relationship with Ottoman Turkey was a delicate one and that there was popular dislike of the Sultan in Britain at that time. Yet, we have seen that the prime mover in the organization of the Liverpool Muslim Institute, Quilliam, maintained close contacts with Ottoman Turkey, received honours and support from the Sultan, and, like other members of his family, undertook missions in the service of the Sultan. It is hardly surprising, therefore, that the question of Britain's

---

[31] Given the lack of detail about the style of worship conducted at Mount Vernon Street, it is possible that the existing facilities there limited communal worship to the style associated with the Sunday meetings.

relationship with Turkey and its ruler was addressed at length and with passion in the *Islamic World*. By considering Quilliam's role as an apologist on behalf of the Muslim faith and as a defender of the authority of the Ottoman ruler as the 'Caliph of the Faithful', it will be possible to suggest reasons that might account for Quilliam's sudden departure from Liverpool and the almost immediate decline and disappearance of the Muslim Institute.

The experiences of the Liverpool Muslims in the late nineteenth century bear comparison with those of Victorian Catholics. The profession of the faith of Islam was taken by those hostile to it as indicative of a divided political loyalty. In short, a Muslim living according to the imperatives of Muslim law was seen to be answerable to authorities beyond and other than the British monarch and the British state. In the latter half of the nineteenth century, the practice of Catholicism was similarly regarded by many of its critics as suggestive of a dual allegiance to a foreign power, and also as conducive to the acceptance of arbitrary power that ran contrary, it was believed, to the civil and religious liberty that flourished in the ethos of Protestantism.[32] In the late nineteenth century, it was the Muslim Institute's links with the Ottoman Turks and Quilliam's defence of the caliphate that incited public outcry. The two major issues on which Quilliam chose to speak were the legitimacy of the Ottoman caliphate, at a time when it was being reviled in Britain because of its treatment of Armenian Christians, and the conduct of the military campaign against the followers of the Mahdi in the Sudan.

The killing of Armenians in the Ottoman Empire provoked heated public debate in Britain in 1896. Writers in the *Islamic World* responded vigorously to accusations levelled against the caliph in particular and Muslims in general for perpetrating atrocities against Christians. In the face of public outcry against 'Muslim atrocities', Quilliam produced a lengthy article under the heading of 'Christian atrocities' which was published in parts in late 1896 and early 1897. In it, having catalogued 'Christian atrocities' in the Philippines and South Africa, Quilliam called upon Gladstone publicly to condemn these atrocities, asking whether Gladstone had an ear only for Armenians (*Islamic World*, November 1896, pp. 193–6). This tone was in keeping with other articles in the *Islamic World*, which tended to make their most bitter and polemical references to Christianity when defending the claims of Islam and the rights of Muslims. However, it was the public attack on the legitimacy of the Ottoman caliphate to which the *Islamic World* replied most systematically.

---

[32] *RVB*, I, 4, p. 150.

In March 1896, Ghazanfar Ali Khan responded at length to an article by H. A. Salomé in the widely read journal *Nineteenth Century*, in which Salomé had argued that the maintenance of the Ottoman Empire with its centre at Istanbul, and thus the caliphate, was not synonymous with the preservation of Islam. Salomé argued that the Ottomans were not universally accepted as the leaders of the Muslim world by other Muslims, and that the Ottoman ruler was not the legitimate holder of the office of caliph because, according to tradition, the caliph should be an Arab of the same clan as the Prophet Muhammad, the Quraish (Salomé, 1896, p. 174). In response, Ghazanfar Ali Khan insisted that retaining Istanbul was a matter of pride to Muslims the world over and, citing scholarly Muslim opinion, refuted the argument that membership of the Quraish clan was a condition for holding the office of caliph. He pointed out that each Ottoman ruler in turn had been ratified as caliph through an election, that the Ottomans had fulfilled the duties of the caliph through their protection of the cities of Mecca and Medina (places of pilgrimage for Muslims), and that the claims of rival contenders had never gathered more than parochial support. As for reported atrocities, the Armenians had brought down upon their own heads the wrath of the Turks due to their involvement in conspiracies, acts of violence and rebellion that would not have been tolerated by European governments. Britain's current policy towards the Ottoman caliphate was likely, said Ghazanfar Ali Khan, to lead to disaffection among the sizeable population of Muslims in British India and to drive Turkey into an alliance with Russia, thus effectively cutting Britain off from India (*Islamic World*, March 1896, pp. 327–34).

Quilliam's defence of the caliphate was similarly built upon arguments based upon religious conviction that appealed to British interests (*Islamic World*, April 1896, pp. 353–9). Quilliam declared himself to be 'a loyal British subject by birth, and a sincere Muslim from conviction' (*ibid.*, p. 358). Thus, he too warned Britain of the strategic losses that might result from driving Turkey into the arms of an alliance with Russia. For Quilliam, moreover, the Turks should be Britain's natural allies: 'They are a God-fearing, sober, brave, unselfish people, who can be the best of friends, and unless interfered with as regards their religion, the enemy of no man' (*ibid.*, p. 356). Although not denying atrocities carried out in Turkey and some failings in the administration of the Ottoman Empire, Quilliam blamed much of this upon individuals whose actions were not directed by the caliph. He, Quilliam felt, was 'one of the most remarkable men of his age' but not always well advised (*ibid.*). Quilliam argued that the Ottoman Empire was frequently judged against a double standard, which allowed Christian countries to avoid censure:

'The Christian may steal a horse with impunity, but a Muslim must be hung if he only peeps at the quatruped from over a hedge. Such is Christian charity and British fair-mindedness in the year of grace 1896' (*ibid.*).

If Quilliam's defence of Ottoman Turkey seemed out of line with British national feeling at the time, his public judgement on British conduct in the Sudan appeared to many to be little other than treasonous. In 1881, Muhammad Ahmad declared himself to be the Mahdi (literally, the 'Rightly Guided One'), an expected leader who would revivify Islam. This expectation, shared by some Islamic traditions, had had a tendency to promote political instability, and Muhammad Ahmad was not the first to claim to be the long-expected leader. The revolutionary war centred upon the charismatic figure of Muhammad Ahmad led to widespread turbulence in the Egyptian Sudan, and was fed by resentment against the Ottoman and Egyptian rulers of the Sudan and the increasing intrusion of European influence and interests. The British had occupied Egypt in 1882 in order to protect British interests in the Suez Canal as the most direct route to India, and were thus involved in the direction of the campaign to recapture the territory taken by the Mahdi and his followers. This, however, necessitated the use of Egyptian troops in the fight against the Sudanese, Muslims being asked to fight Muslims. In 1896, a decade after the death of the much revered General Gordon at Khartoum, Quilliam, as Sheikh-ul-Islam of the British Isles and a recognized *àlim* or Islamic jurist, issued a declaration that was clearly designed to have the status of a *fatwa*, a formal judgement by one qualified to pronounce on Islamic law. In this judgement, he stated: 'I warn every True Believer that, if he give the slightest assistance in this projected expedition against the Muslims of the Soudan ... his name will be unworthy to be continued on the roll of the faithful' (*Islamic World*, July 1896, pp. 76f.).[33]

It is difficult to measure the repercussions of Quilliam's *fatwa*. He reported that the judgement was widely debated abroad in Muslim publications and that it was reported in some English papers. It was widely condemned, according to Quilliam, in the Indian press, which, he noted, was then controlled by Europeans and Christians. His *fatwa* was a further illustration of how Quilliam, a nineteenth-century British Muslim, tried to hold in balance his religious conviction and his loyalty to Britain. Yet, it must not be forgotten that both Quilliam and the Institute continued to thrive for several years after the publication of the *fatwa*. There is probably more than a grain of truth in Quilliam's paraphrase of

[33] See Quilliam's address to the 1896 Annual General Meeting of the Muslim Institute: 'Abdullah Quilliam, "Minutes of AGM"', Part II, pp. 339–43.

the attacks made upon him in some Indian newspapers, namely that 'Only my insignificance saved me from being prosecuted for High Treason' (*Islamic World*, July 1896, p. 77). Ultimately, however, it seems probable that Quilliam's close links with Turkey made residence in Britain increasingly difficult, leaving aside the hostility displayed towards Muslims in Liverpool at that time.

Quilliam left Liverpool in 1908 in somewhat mysterious circumstances relating to legal proceedings that were then subjudice, and it was popularly supposed that he had taken up permanent residence 'in the East' (*Porcupine*, 31 October 1908, p. 1). It has been suggested that he went to live in Turkey as Britain moved closer to war with Germany and Turkey, but that he later returned to Britain under the name of Professor Marcel Leon (Khan-Cheema, 1979, p. 17). It may be significant that a prominent member of the Liverpool Muslim community was Henri Mustapha Leon, M.D., who published under that name in the same issues of the *Islamic World* as Quilliam in 1898. Once Quilliam had gone, the Liverpool Mosque and Muslim Institute rapidly declined and closed, and there appears to have been no reason for this other than the removal of the personality who had sustained the community from its beginnings in 1887.

The Liverpool Mosque of the 1890s was the first place in Britain to be designated a 'mosque', but the honour of being the oldest living mosque goes to the mosque built in Woking in 1889, which has survived down to the present day. For this reason, some writers prefer to speak of the Woking Mosque as Britain's 'oldest' mosque. Some commentators at the time of its founding referred to it in error as 'England's first mosque' (for example, Anon., 1889). Several of the most active members of the Liverpool Muslim Institute joined the Muslim organization at Woking after the decline of the Liverpool Mosque, including Professor H. Mustapha Leon (Ally, 1981, p. 72). One historian of the Liverpool Muslim community has argued that Quilliam, under the name of Marcel Leon, also worked for the Woking Mosque. He notes that, when Marcel Leon died in April 1932 and was buried after prayers at the Woking Mosque, the names of both Leon and Quilliam were used (Khan-Cheema, 1979, p. 17).[34] Whatever the

[34] The mature development of the Woking Mosque and the Muslim Mission took place after 1912. The Woking Mosque, although built in 1889, almost immediately fell into disuse until revived in 1912. For a brief history of the Woking Mosque and Woking Muslim Mission, see Ally, 1981, pp. 64ff. and Siddiq, 1934. The early years of the twentieth century also saw the first British converts to the Baha'i faith—a nineteenth-century movement that had its origins in the Iranian Shi'ite tradition of Islam but then developed into an independent religion. Given what has been said in this chapter about the role of Theosophy in mediating Indian religious thought to Britain, it is interesting to note that the first British converts to Baha'ism were largely drawn from 'the cultic milieu' of the period and in many cases retained their links with 'cult movements such as Theosophy' (MacEoin, 1984, p. 282).

individual fate of Abdullah Quilliam, Sheikh-ul-Islam of the British Isles, the influence of the Muslim community that he created in Liverpool fed into the more lasting activities at Woking.

VI   CONCLUSION

Unlike Roman Catholicism and Judaism, the two most prominent minority religious communities outside the boundaries of Protestantism, the religious traditions considered in this chapter, with the exception of Zoroastrianism, did not strengthen their presence in late Victorian Britain due to a change in the ethnic composition of Britain's permanent population. In fact, as we have seen, Victorian expressions of Islam and of aspects of Hinduism depended largely upon the commitment and efforts of individuals not born into these faiths. Nevertheless, like more long-standing religious minorities, Parsis and those adventurous individuals who dared to identify themselves as Muslims or followers of Hindu Vedanta philosophy were able to benefit from Victorian reforms that ensured that those of minority religious persuasions or none were no longer excluded from public life.

In spite of the greater latitude afforded to religious, and, in particular, non-Christian, minorities by Victorian legal reforms, it remained true that individuals espousing religious traditions whose centre of authority lay abroad were popularly regarded with deep suspicion, especially when the foreign country was hostile to Britain. Although this chapter has shown how such suspicion often took the form of a general expression of religious prejudice, we have also seen that individuals who converted to Islam or identified themselves with Hinduism were inclined to hold views that were forthrightly critical of British imperialism. For William Quilliam and Margaret Noble, the encounter with 'other religions' enabled them to express their dissatis-faction with Victorian Christianity and encouraged them, as Abdullah Quilliam and Sister Nivedita, to adopt political sympathies that were no less challenging at that time than their newly found religious identities.

Members of religious minorities, however, did not merely have to face the suspicion of their fellow citizens. On occasion, they also risked the censure of their co-religionists abroad who were sceptical about the authenticity of attempts to create new patterns of faith and practice in Britain. Later generations of the same but enlarged religious minorities would strive to construct their religious lives in Britain after World War II amidst comparable expressions of hostility and indifference at local and national level. At the same time they too would be watched from a distance by co-religionists in other countries anxious lest accommodations reached with British society compromise their understanding of the purity and authenticity of their faith.

BIBLIOGRAPHY

A. H. A. (A. H. Atteridge) (1878) 'Islam' (reprinted from the *Dublin Review*), London, Burns & Oates.

M. Alexander and S. Anand (1980) *Queen Victoria's Maharaja: Duleep Singh 1838–93*, London, Weidenfeld & Nicolson.

M. M. Ally (1981) *History of Muslims in Britain 1850–1980*, MA dissertation, University of Birmingham.

P. Almond (1989) *Heretic and Hero—Muhammad and the Victorians*, Wiesbaden, Otto Harrassowitz.

M. S. Anderson (1966) *The Eastern Question 1774–1923*, London, Macmillan.

Anonymous (1805) 'Country news—domestic occurrences', *Gentleman's Magazine*, May, p. 479.

Anonymous (1823) 'Domestic occurrences', *Gentleman's Magazine*, January, p. 80.

Anonymous (1889) 'The first mosque in Britain', *Illustrated London News*, 9 November, pp. 590f.

Anonymous (1896) 'Sunday in Liverpool: with the Moslems', *Sunday at Home*, Part 19, May, pp. 441–7.

M. A. Badawi (1981) *Islam in Britain*, London, Ta Ha.

G. Beckerlegge (1991) '"Strong" cultures and distinctive religions: the influence of imperialism upon British communities of South Asian origin', *New Community*, Vol. 17, No. 2, pp. 201–10.

C. Bennett (1992) *Victorian Images of Islam*, London, Grey Seal.

R. Burghart (ed.) (1987) *Hinduism in Great Britain*, London, Tavistock.

S. D. Collet (1962) *The Life and Letters of Raja Rammohun Roy*, ed. D. K. Biswas and P. C. Ganguli, 3rd edn, Calcutta, Sadharan Brahmo Samaj (first published 1900).

R. Davey (1896) 'The Sultan and his priests', *Fortnightly Review*, No. 349 (New Series), 1 January, pp. 1–17.

E. De Michelis (1995) 'Contemporary Hatha Yoga in the UK', *Journal of Contemporary Religion*, Vol. 10, No. 3, pp. 242–56.

R. Dinnage (1986) *Annie Besant*, Harmondsworth, Penguin.

J. N. Farquhar (1967) *Modern Religious Movements in India*, Dehli, Mushiram Manoharlal (first published 1914).

L. Fischer (1951) *The Life of Mahatma Gandhi*, London, Jonathan Cape.

P. Fryer (1984) *Staying Power: The History of Black People in Britain*, London and Sydney, Pluto Press.

M. K. Gandhi (1971) *Selected Writings of Mahatma Gandhi*, ed. R. Duncan, London, Fontana/Collins.

M. K. Gandhi (1982) *An Autobiography or The Story of My Experiments with Truth*, Harmondsworth, Penguin.

J. R. Hinnells (1996) *Zoroastrians in Britain*, Oxford, Clarendon Press.

A. Hourani (1991) *Islam in European Thought*, Cambridge, Cambridge University Press.

M. A. Khan-Cheema (1979) *Islam and the Muslims in Liverpool*, MA dissertation, University of Liverpool.

V. G. Kiernan (1969) *The Lords of Human Kind: European Attitudes towards the Outside World in the Imperial Age*, London, Weidenfeld & Nicolson.

The Life of Swami Vivekananda by His Eastern and Western Disciples (1979), Volume 2, Calcutta, Advaita Ashrama.

D. MacEoin (1984) 'Baha'ism' in J. Hinnells (ed.) *A Handbook of Living Religions*, pp. 475–98, Harmondsworth, Penguin.

B. M. Malabari (1895) *The Indian Eye on English Life or Rambles of a Pilgrim Reformer*, 3rd edn, Bombay, Apollo Printing Works.

P. C. Mozoomdar (1887) *The Life and Teachings of Keshub Chunder Sen*, Calcutta, J. W. Thomas, Baptist Mission Press.

I. P. Oliver (1979) *Buddhism in Britain*, London, Rider.

Sister Nivedita (1972) *The Complete Works of Sister Nivedita*, Volume 2, Calcutta, Advaita Ashrama.

B. Parry (1971) *Delusions and Discoveries: Studies on India in the British Imagination 1880–1930*, Berkeley and Los Angeles, University of California Press.

G. Parsons (ed.) (1993) *The Growth of Religious Diversity: Britain from 1945*, London, Routledge/The Open University.

H. A. Salomé (1896) 'Is the Sultan of Turkey the true khaliph of Islam?', *Nineteenth Century*, January, pp. 173–80.

J. S. Salter (1873) *The Asiatic in England: Sketches of Sixteen Years' Work Among Orientals*, London, Seeley, Jackson & Halliday.

K. C. Sen (1980) *Keshub Chunder Sen in England—Diaries, Sermons, Addresses and Epistles*, Calcutta, A Writers Workshop Greybird Book, 4th Navavidhan Centenary edn (1st English edn 1871).

E. J. Sharpe (1985) *The Universal Gita*, London, Duckworth.

M. Sherwood (1991) 'Race, nationality and employment among Lascar seamen, 1660–1945', *New Community*, Vol. 17, No. 2, pp. 229–44.

S. M. Siddiq (1934) 'Islam in England', *Islamic Review*, Vol. 22, Nos. 1–2, pp. 14–25.

A. Taylor (1992) *Annie Besant: A Biography*, Oxford, Oxford University Press.

R. Visram (1986) *Ayahs, Lascars and Princes: The Story of Indians in Britain 1700–1947*, London, Pluto.

Liverpool Periodicals

  The Islamic World

  The Liverpool Freeman

  The Liverpool Review

  The Porcupine

  Sunday at Home

PART II

1 MEN, WOMEN AND THE QUESTION OF GENDER

(A) BENJAMIN PARSONS ON ADAM AND EVE, AND THE EDUCATION OF WOMEN, 1842

Benjamin Parsons (1797–1855) was a Congregational minister whose views on women form a marked contrast to those of his co-religionist John Angell James. His book The Mental and Moral Dignity of Woman *was intended to refute notions of female intellectual inferiority. Two chapters were devoted to the story of Adam and Eve, which Parsons understood literally, deducing from it that no good purpose would have been served if God had created woman as an 'imbecile'.*

There are millions who imagine that woman was created for hardly any higher purpose than to cook the food, wash the linen, look after the domestic affairs, and gratify the wants and wishes of the other sex. Such is their meaning of the words "*help meet,*" and therefore, in thousands of cases, women are educated to be little more than a superior description of domestic animals. But what a perfect contrast to these grovelling sentiments is the scriptural account of the origin and design of the creation of woman. She was created equal in dignity to man, and intended to be his intellectual and moral associate. Adam was no sensualist; his reason and conscience duly controlled and regulated all his propensities. To him the self-denial of such appetites as were common to him with brutes afforded far more exquisite pleasure than any sensual gratifications would have yielded. Adam lived on the fruits of Paradise, and therefore needed no female attendant to cook his meals. In that state of primæval innocency there was no wardrobe to be looked after. The laundress and the laundry were offices not in use then. The cold, drizzling, bucking-day never ruffled the temper of Eve, nor drove Adam from home. Woman, therefore, was not needed in Paradise for any of those grovelling and selfish purposes, which many a philosopher, and many a professed Christian, too, in our day, supposes to be the chief end of her existence; and for which alone, perhaps, ninety-nine out of every hundred marry. An intellectual, a moral, and spiritual companion, was the being which the first man required as his associate; and it is chiefly to these godlike qualities that the Creator referred, when he said, "I will make him an help meet for him." And never will society make any rapid advances in knowledge and religion, until the true dignity of woman is recognized. We must think of woman as Adam did, yea, as God himself did, before she will be raised to the proper rank and sphere assigned her by the Creator. I have often thought, that the ideas of woman contained in "Paradise Lost," fall very far short of what ought to have been conceived by the writer. Probably the Adam of that poem, was rather Milton himself than the husband of Eve. One is almost ready to conclude that, however democratic the poet was as a politician, yet, as a husband, he was rather aristocratical. Some of his most elaborate descriptions of the intercourse of Adam and Eve, exhibit but a low estimate of the mental powers of the other sex. This opinion seems to have influenced him in the education of his daughters, whom he doomed to read Latin, Greek, and Hebrew, without understanding the meaning of a word in either of those languages, assigning as a reason "That one tongue was enough for a woman." In "Paradise Lost," Eve often refers to her inferiority, and previous to the fall is made as obsequious as the poet wished his refractory wife to have been. But as we have reason to believe that Adam was a much better husband than even our great poet, so Eve, associated with such a partner, had no need to gratify her lord with any of those flattering compliments which the poet puts into the mouth of our mother. It is not improbable that even Milton's wife, if she had been yoked to a companion like Adam, who had set a proper value upon the mental and moral powers of woman, would never have run away, and left the chagrined poet to write his essay on divorce. [...]

Females, in a particular manner, ought to have an objective education; for in a majority of cases their lot is cast amidst the most interesting realities of life. The servant, the nurse, the mother, the sister, the daughter, and the mistress of a family, fill stations of usefulness which angels might envy, and often have to combat with difficulties, and perform duties, which demand all the subsidies of truth. But how ill prepared for any of these relations must that individual be whose mind has been fed with nothing but fiction, or who has never been shown the practical use of a very considerable portion of her learning. Of thousands of girls it might be said that their memories are either stored with useless notions, or with such opinions as they know not how to employ for their own advantage or the good of others. To imbue all the faculties of the soul with real knowledge, and to instruct the pupil how all this knowledge may be used for its own benefit and the profit of society is the perfection of education. But neither abstractions nor fictions can be thus applied. The soul is a reality, society is a reality, and the wants of the soul and of society are real, and must be fed with substantial food. You might as well expect to satisfy the hunger of a child with pictures or shadows, as to hope to mature the mind by amusing it with abstractions or fictions. The body, fed on plain substantial food, gradually and proportionally arrives at maturity, so the mental faculties, early introduced to the realities of truth and constantly nourished with this solid aliment, must arrive at perfection. [...]

Women have so much good sense, that were the objects of real knowledge set before them in all their native attractions, they would soon forsake the worlds of fiction for the universe of fact. And were it generally understood that they were become our fellow-students in all the departments of truth, literature would soon be brought to perfection. Literary chivalry would then be an object of ambition, and science, history, and religion would be invested with all the charms of truth, for the purpose of interesting the attention and obtaining the approbation of the other sex. What mystic, who desired to gain the patronage of women, would dare attenuate truth into an abstraction, or conceal his meaning under an ambiguous or metaphysical style? Science would be represented in all her native beauty; history, as the record of life in its myriads of forms, would be vital and thrilling; language, as the vehicle of thought and passion, would be invested with all the feeling and intellectuality which essentially belongs to such an interpreter of the soul; and theology and religion, as the philosophy of God, of man, and eternity, would stand forth in all the glory and sublimity of their original character. The bane of knowledge has been that learned men have written for learned men, scientific men for men of science, and theologians for theologians alone. The initiated few have been addressed, and the ignorant many forgotten. In not a few instances abstruseness has been rendered more abstruse, and "confusion has been confounded." How few philosophers have ever dreamt of writing philosophical treatises for women. If this lucky thought had only entered their heads, from what mazes they would have extricated their crabbed productions, and what benefactors they would have been to the world. Girls might then, from the cradle, have been tutored in real knowledge, and thus would have been qualified to be in after years the intellectual companions of the other sex, and the scientific guides of their own offspring.

(From Benjamin Parsons, *The Mental and Moral Dignity of Woman*, London, John Snow, 1842, pp. 19–20, 307–9)

(B)   SARAH MARTIN ON PRISON VISITING, 1844

The philanthropic activities of the Evangelical Anglican Sarah Martin, known as 'the Yarmouth Prison Visitor' (1791–1843), might have been forgotten had not the Religious Tract Society published an autobiographical memoir, Brief Sketch of the Life of the Late Sarah Martin of Great Yarmouth, *together with some of the addresses that she delivered to the prisoners.*

In August 1819, I heard of a woman being sent to the gaol for having cruelly beaten her child, and having learned her name, went to the gaol, and asked permission to see her, which, on a second application, was allowed. When I told the woman, who was surprised at the sight of a stranger, the motive of my visit, her guilt, her need of God's mercy, etc., she burst into tears, and thanked me, whilst I read to her the twenty-third chapter of St. Luke. For the first few months, I only made a short visit to read the Scriptures to the prisoners, but desiring more time to instruct them in reading and writing, I soon thought it right to give up a day in a week from dress-making, by which I earned my living, to serve the prisoners. This regularly given, with many an additional one, was never felt as a pecuniary loss, but was ever followed with abundant satisfaction, for the blessing of God was upon me.

At this time there was no Divine worship in the gaol on the Lord's day, nor any respect paid to it, at which I was particularly struck, when in going one Sunday to see a female convict, before her departure for transportation, I found her making a bonnet. I had long desired and recommended the prisoners to form a Sunday service, by one reading to the rest. It was at length adopted; but aware of the instability of a practice in itself good, without any corresponding principle of preservation, and thinking that my presence might exert a beneficial tendency, I joined their Sunday morning worship as a regular hearer. On discovering that their afternoon service had been resigned, I proposed attending on that part of the day also, and it was resumed. After several changes of readers, the office devolved on me. That happy privilege thus graciously opened to me, and embraced from necessity, and in much fear, was acceptable to the prisoners, for God made it so; and also an unspeakable advantage and comfort to myself. I continued the two services on Sundays, until 1831, when, as my strength seemed failing for both, it pleased God that a good minister, who then came to reside in our parish, should undertake the afternoon service, which was a timely relief to me. [...]

The manner in which instruction has been carried forward amongst the prisoners, was as follows:—Any who could not read I encouraged to learn, whilst others in my absence assisted them. They were taught to write also, whilst such as could write already, copied extracts from books lent to them. Prisoners, who were able to read, committed verses from the Holy Scriptures to memory every day, according to their ability or inclination. I, as an example, also committed a few verses to memory to repeat to them every day, and the effect was remarkable; always silencing excuse, when the pride of some prisoners would have prevented their doing it. Many said at first, "it would be of no use," and my reply was, "It is of use to me, and why should it not be so to you? you have not tried it, but I have." Tracts and children's books, and larger books, four or five in number, of which they were very fond, were exchanged in every room daily, whilst any who could read more, were supplied with larger books, all of which were principally procured from the Religious Tract Society.

Surely the power of God might here be distinctly seen, where a number of persons, differing in temper, although conceited, prejudiced, and ignorant, yet obeyed what was recommended with the docility of children; and if I left home for a day or two, yet all learned the same, and most of them more, in my absence, with the view of giving me pleasure on my return. From the commencement of my labours to 1832, I read printed sermons on Sundays; and from that time to 1837, wrote my own observations; but after the appointment of the present governor, when a new system arose, and no attention on my part was required for the preservation of order, I was enabled, by the help of God, to address the prisoners without writing beforehand, simply from the Holy Scriptures.

(From *Brief Sketch of the Life of the Late Sarah Martin of Great Yarmouth*, London, Religious Tract Society, 1844, pp. 10–11, 25–7)

(C) FANNY TAYLOR ON CATHERINE MCAULEY AND THE ORDER OF OUR LADY OF MERCY, 1862

The Order of Our Lady of Mercy was by far the largest Roman Catholic women's order in Victorian Britain and Ireland. It was responsible for a vast amount of work among the poor. In an appendix to her book Religious Orders or Sketches of Some of the Orders and Congregations of Women, *Fanny Taylor noted that it had ninety-six convents, and the number increased further during the century. In the late 1860s, Taylor herself became the foundress of a Congregation, the Poor Servants of the Mother of God.*

It was thought advisable that Miss McAuley and two of her companions should make their noviciate in an enclosed order, in order to learn the practice of the convent life, which was to form so important a part of their

Institute. In December, 1829, they entered the Convent of the Presentation, and after spending a year in the noviciate, made their vows, adding to the three vows of religion a fourth, of devoting their lives to the service of the sick and poor. During the time of their absence learned ecclesiastics were engaged in compiling the Rules and Constitutions of the new Order. The Rule was to be that of St. Augustine, modified by the Constitutions as the scope of the new Order required. The "peculiar characteristic of this Congregation," says the Rule, "is a most serious application to the instruction of poor girls, visitation of the sick, and protection of distressed women of good character."

The duties of the Sisters of Mercy are most minutely defined by their holy Rule. They are taught by it how to act in their schools, how to instruct the children, how to visit the sick, and how to guide and instruct those who are inmates of the "House of Mercy." The Sisters are also taught to observe strictly the vow of Poverty, remembering His example who " in His own person consecrated this virtue, and bequeathed it as a most valuable patrimony to His followers." They are told also to obey "rather through love than by servile fear;" and "they shall never murmur, but with humility and spiritual joy carry the sweet yoke of Jesus Christ." They are also instructed how to say their Office with "attention and devotion," and how to practise mental prayer; to "seek in it their comfort and refreshment from the labours and fatigues of the Institute." They are to have "the tenderest and most affectionate devotion towards the Adorable Sacrament." Also, most "tender devotion to the Passion of our Lord and Saviour Jesus Christ; they shall therefore offer the labours and fatigues of their state, the mortifications they undergo, and all their pains of mind and body, in union with the sufferings of their Crucified Spouse;" "in all their fears, afflictions, and temptations, they shall seek comfort and consolation at the foot of the altar." "They shall be devout to the Sacred Heart of Jesus" They are bid to remember that their congregation is under the especial protection of the Mother of God, and that they look on her "as their Mother, and the great Model they are obliged to imitate;" they shall have "unlimited confidence in her, have recourse to her in all their difficulties or spiritual wants," and on the Feast of our Lady of Mercy they make a solemn act of consecration to her love and service. The interior spirit of the Order is most beautiful, and is founded on a deep humility and perfect charity; they are told to strive after the perfection of their ordinary actions, and to attain great recollection. No one could observe the Rule of this Order without making sure and rapid progress in the ways of sanctity. It is governed, as we have said, by the Bishop, or a priest delegated by him, and the Bishop or his substitute shall make the visitation of the convent once a year. The Mother Superior must be thirty years of age, and must have been professed for five years (except in the case of a new foundation). She is elected by the votes of the Sisters; she can only govern three years, but may be re-elected for three more. [...]

Such was the Order Miss McAuley was called upon to found; such the design she was to carry out.

And well did she fulfil her task. The Order spread rapidly. Bishop after Bishop requested the religious to come into their dioceses. To all these foundations Mother McAuley went herself. She spared no fatigue, and cared for no inconvenience. She taught the Sisters more by example than by words; she won the hearts of all who came near her by her winning manners, and by the sweet humility which characterised her. As foundress, she was obliged by the Bishop, against her own wishes, to be Superioress for life, yet she was not ashamed to kneel at the feet of those whom she thought she had inadvertently offended and beg their pardon. She was always calm and serene, trusting only in God; she would say, "All the hopes and fears of a religious ought to be centred in God." She had a great horror of singularity and high-flown expressions, and her favourite aspiration was, "Mortify in me, dear Jesus, all that displeases Thee, and make me according to Thy own heart's desire."

(Extracts from Anon. (Fanny Taylor) *Religious Orders or Sketches of Some of the Orders and Congregations of Women*, London, Burns & Lambert, 1862, pp. 305–7, 310)

(D)   FRANCES POWER COBBE ON WIVES, 1862

Frances Power Cobbe (1822–1904) was a Freethinker from an Irish Evangelical background and a vociferous writer on many subjects as well as a philanthropist. Her observations about wives in an essay on 'Celibacy v. marriage' were prompted by an article (which she refers to as 'the article under debate') about the difficulties married men encountered in 'keeping up appearances', because of the financial drain of maintaining a wife.

The author of the article under debate admits with astonishing candour, that the *woman's* interest and happiness are necessarily sacrificed by the proper fulfilment of the man's destiny. He quotes Kingsley's aphorism with approbation—

Man must work and woman must weep.

Truly this conclusion, whereby no inconsiderable portion of the human race is consigned to the highly unprofitable occupation of "weeping," might have excited some doubts of the accuracy of the foregoing ratiocinations. It is not easy, we should suppose, for women generally to accept this matter of "weeping" as the proper end of their creation! At all events, if they occasionally indulge henceforth in the solace of tears, we cannot believe they will shed them for the loss of the connubial felicity to be enjoyed with those "workers," who so readily appoint them such a place in the order of the world.

Leaving aside, however, this piece of "muscular sociology," let us seriously inquire whether the true destiny of woman, if rightly understood, would not serve to make right this puzzle of life, and show that *if the wife were what the wife should be*, the husband would not need to grow more mercenary and more worldly to supply her wants, but would rather find her pure and religious influence raise him to higher modes of thinking, and a nobler and more devoted life, than either man or woman can attain alone.

The *actual* fact must, alas! be admitted. The cares of a family have a tendency to make a man interested; and what is much worse, the wife too frequently uses her influence the wrong way, and prompts her husband even to more worldly and prudential considerations than he would be inclined spontaneously to entertain.

Woman's natural refinement leads her to give too high a value to outward polish, and, consequently, to tend always to seek social intercourse above her own natural circle. It is nearly always the *wives* of shopkeepers, merchants, professional men, and the smaller gentry, who are found pushing their families into the grade a step higher, and urging the often-recalcitrant husband to the needful toadyism and expenditure. Woman is Conservative, or rather feudal, by instinct, if she be not by some accident vehemently prejudiced the other way; and her unacknowledged but very real political influence is constantly exercised to check aspirations after progress of the rational kind

Of Freedom slowly broadening down
From precedent to precedent.

Worse than all, the education she now receives, makes her a bigot in religion. To *her*, the sources of wider and broader thought on the greatest of all subjects, are usually closed from childhood. The result is, that a timid and narrow creed constantly fetters the natural religious instincts of her heart, and she can exercise in no degree the influence over her husband's soul which her genuine piety might otherwise effect. If he venture to speak to her of the limits of his belief, she gives him reproach instead of sympathy; if he tell her he doubts the conclusions of her favourite preacher, she bursts into tears! Men have kept women from all share in the religious progress of the age, and the deplorable result is, that women are notoriously the drags on that progress. Instead of feeling like their Teuton forefathers, that their wives were "in nearer intercourse with the divinity than men," the Englishmen of to-day feel that their wives are the last persons with whom they can seek sympathy on religious matters. Half with tenderness for their good hears, half with contempt for their weak minds, they leave them to the faith of the nursery, and seek for congenial intercourse only among men, hardheaded and honest, perhaps, in the fullest degree, yet without a woman's native spring of trust and reverence.

All these things tend to make wives fail in performing their proper part of inspiring feelings of devotion to noble causes. And further, a woman's ignorance of real life leads her to attach to outward show a value which it actually bears only in the opinion of other women as foolish as herself, and by no means in the eyes of anything which deserves to be called society at large. The *real* world—"the world of women and men,"

Alive with sorrow and sin,
Alive with pain and with passion,

does *not* concern itself so very earnestly with the number of the domestics and the antiquity of the millinery of its friends, as these ladies fondly imagine.

(From Frances Power Cobbe, 'Celibacy v. marriage' in *Essays on the Pursuits of Women Reprinted from Fraser's and Macmillan's Magazines,* London, Emily Faithfull, 1863, pp. 42–5)

(E)   JOHN RUSKIN ON WOMEN'S EDUCATION, 1865

John Ruskin (1819–1900) is chiefly remembered as an art critic, although he wrote on a variety of other subjects. Like so many prominent Victorians, Ruskin was the product of an Evangelical home. His book Sesame and Lilies *began as two lectures. The extract below is from the second lecture, 'Lilies—of queens' gardens', which seeks to explore how far women are 'called to a true queenly power'.*

Thus, then, you have first to mould her physical frame, and then, as the strength she gains will permit you, to fill and temper her mind with all knowledge and thoughts which tend to confirm its natural instincts of justice, and refine its natural tact of love.

All such knowledge should be given her as may enable her to understand, and even to aid, the work of men: and yet it should be given, not as knowledge—not as if it were, or could be, for her an object to know; but only to feel, and to judge. It is of no moment, as a matter of pride or perfectness in herself, whether she knows many languages or one; but it is of the utmost, that she should be able to show kindness to a stranger, and to understand the sweetness of a stranger's tongue. It is of no moment to her own worth or dignity that she should be acquainted with this science or that; but it is of the highest that she should be trained in habits of accurate thought; that she should understand the meaning, the inevitableness, and the loveliness of natural laws; and follow at least some one path of scientific attainment, as far as to the threshold of the bitter Valley of Humiliation, into which only the wisest and bravest of men can descend, owning themselves for ever children, gathering pebbles on a boundless shore. It is of little consequence how many positions of cities she knows, or how many dates of events, or names of celebrated persons—it is not the object of education to turn the woman into a dictionary; but it is deeply necessary that she should be taught to enter with her whole personality into the history she reads; to picture the passages of it vitally in her own bright imagination; to apprehend, with her fine instincts, the pathetic circumstances and dramatic relations, which the historian too often only eclipses by his reasoning, and disconnects by his arrangement: it is for her to trace the hidden equities of divine reward, and catch sight, through the darkness, of the fateful threads of woven fire that connect error with retribution. But, chiefly of all, she is to be taught to extend the limits of her sympathy with respect to that history which is being for ever determined as the moments pass in which she draws her peaceful breath; and to the contemporary calamity, which, were it but rightly mourned by her, would recur no more hereafter. She is to exercise herself in imagining what would be the effects upon her mind and conduct, if she were daily brought into the presence of the suffering which is not the less real because shut from her sight. She is to be taught somewhat to understand the nothingness of the proportion which that little world in which she lives and loves, bears to the world in which God lives and loves;—and solemnly she is to be taught to strive that her thoughts of piety may not be feeble in proportion to the number they embrace, nor her prayer more languid than it is for the momentary relief from pain of her husband or her child, when it is uttered for the multitudes of those who have none to love them,—and is "for all who are desolate and oppressed."

Thus far, I think, I have had your concurrence; perhaps you will not be with me in what I believe is most needful for me to say. There *is* one dangerous science for women—one which they must indeed beware how they profanely touch—that of theology. Strange, and miserably strange, that while they are modest enough to doubt their powers, and pause at the threshold of sciences where every step is demonstrable and sure, they will plunge headlong, and without one thought of incompetency, into that science in which the greatest men have trembled, and the wisest erred. Strange, that they will complacently and pridefully bind up whatever vice or folly there is in them, whatever arrogance, petulance, or blind incomprehensiveness, into one bitter bundle of consecrated myrrh. Strange, in creatures born to be Love visible, that where they can know least, they will condemn first, and think to recommend themselves to their Master, by crawling up the steps of His judgment-throne, to divide it with Him. Strangest of all, that they should think they were led by the Spirit of the Comforter into habits of mind which have become in them the unmixed elements of home discomfort; and that they dare to turn the Household Gods of Christianity into ugly idols of their own;—spiritual dolls, for them to dress according to their caprice; and from which their husbands must turn away in grieved contempt, lest they should be shrieked at for breaking them.

I believe, then, with this exception, that a girl's education should be nearly, in its course and material of study, the same as a boy's; but quite differently directed. A woman, in any rank of life, ought to know whatever her husband is likely to know, but to know it in a different way. His command of it should be foundational and progressive; hers, general and accomplished for daily and helpful use. Not but that it would often be wiser in men to learn things in a womanly sort of way, for present use, and to seek for the discipline and training of their mental powers in such branches of study as will be afterwards fittest for social service; but, speaking broadly, a man ought to know any language or science he learns, thoroughly—while a woman ought to know the same language, or science, only so far as may enable her to sympathise in her husband's pleasures, and in those of his best friends.

(From John Ruskin, *Sesame and Lilies*, London, George Allen, 4th edn, 1880, pp. 96–100)

(F)   THOMAS HUGHES ON THE TESTS OF MANLINESS, 1879

Thomas Hughes (1822–96) was a Broad Church Anglican who is probably best remembered as the author of Tom Brown's Schooldays. *With Charles Kingsley, he became a leading proponent of 'Christian manliness'. His book* The Manliness of Christ *grew out of what Hughes had taught in a bible class at the Working Men's College. The extract below outlines the ethos of Christian manliness, and reveals something of the tensions inherent within that creed.*

One other precaution we must take at the outset of our inquiry, and that is, to settle for ourselves, without diverging into useless metaphysics—what we mean by "manliness, manfulness, courage." My friends of "the Christian Guild" seemed to assume that these words all have the same meaning, and denote the same qualities. Now, is this so? I think not, if we take the common use of the words. "Manliness and manfulness" are synonymous, but they embrace more than we ordinarily mean by the word "courage;" for instance, tenderness, and thoughtfulness for others. They include that courage, which lies at the root of all manliness, but is, in fact, only its lowest or rudest form. Indeed, we must admit that it is not exclusively a human quality at all, but one which we share with other animals, and which some of them—for instance, the bulldog and weasel—exhibit with a certainty and a thoroughness which is very rare amongst mankind.

In what, then, does courage, in this ordinary sense of the word, consist? First, in persistency, or the determination to have one's own way, coupled with contempt for safety and ease, and readiness to risk pain or death in getting one's own way. This is, let us readily admit, a valuable, even a noble quality, but an animal quality rather than a human or manly one, and obviously not that quality of which the promoters of the Christian Guild were in search. [...]

Athleticism is a good thing if kept in its place, but it has come to be very much over-praised and over-valued amongst us, as I think these proposals of the Christian Guild for the attainment of their most admirable and needful aim, tend to show clearly enough, if proof were needed. We may say, then, I think, without doubt, that its promoters were not on the right scent, or likely to get what they were in search of by the methods they proposed to use. For after getting their Society of Athletes it might quite possibly turn out to be composed of persons deficient in real manliness.

While, however, keeping this conclusion well in mind, we need not at all depreciate athleticism, which has in it much that is useful to society, and is indeed admirable enough in its own way. But as the next step in our inquiry, let us bear well in mind that athleticism is not what we mean here. True manliness is as likely to be found in a weak as in a strong body. Other things being equal, we may perhaps admit (though I should hesitate to do so), that a man with a highly trained and developed body will be more courageous than a weak man. But we must take this caution with us, that a great athlete may be a brute or a coward, while a truly manly man can be neither. [...]

And in this life-long fight, to be waged by every one of us single-handed against a host of foes, the last requisite for a good fight, the last proof and test of our courage and manfulness, must be loyalty to truth—the most rare and difficult of all human qualities. For such loyalty, as it grows in perfection, asks ever more and more of us, and sets before us a standard of manliness always rising higher and higher.

And this is the great lesson which we shall learn from Christ's life the more earnestly and faithfully we study it. "For this end was I born, and for this cause came I into the world, to bear witness to the truth." To bear this witness against avowed and open enemies is comparatively easy. But to bear it against those we love, against those whose judgment and opinions we respect, in defence or furtherance of that which approves itself as true to our own inmost conscience, this is the last and abiding test of courage and of manliness. How natural, nay, how inevitable it is that we should fall into the habit of appreciating and judging things mainly by the standards in common use amongst those we respect and love. But these very standards are apt to break down with us when we are brought face to face with some question which takes us ever so little out of ourselves and our usual moods. At such times we are driven to admit in our hearts that we, and those we respect and love, have been looking at and judging things, not truthfully, and therefore not courageously and manfully, but conventionally. And then comes one of the most searching of all trials of courage and manliness, when a man or woman is called to stand by what approves itself to their consciences as true, and to protest for it through evil report and good report, against all discouragement and opposition from those they love or respect. The sense of antagonism instead of rest, of distrust and alienation instead of approval and sympathy, which such times bring, is a test which tries the very heart and reins, and it is one which meets us at all ages, and in all conditions of life. Emerson's hero is the man who, "taking both reputation and life in his hand, will with perfect urbanity dare the gibbet and the mob, by the absolute truth of his speech and rectitude of his behaviour." And, even in our peaceful and prosperous England, absolute truth of speech and rectitude of behaviour will not fail to bring their fiery trials, if also in the end their exceeding great rewards.

(From Thomas Hughes, *The Manliness of Christ,* London, Macmillan, 1879, pp. 20–2, 24–6, 34–7)

2 HYMNS AND CHURCH MUSIC

(A) SAMUEL SEBASTIAN WESLEY ON CATHEDRAL MUSIC, 1849

Samuel Sebastian Wesley (1810–76) wrote this impassioned plea in the year of his move from Leeds Parish Church to Winchester Cathedral. It indicates the perspective of the leading professional church musician of his generation, and sets out an agenda for reform, achieved partly by Wesley himself but more fully realized in the decades after his death.

A Bill relating to Church affairs will, it is said, shortly be brought under the consideration of Parliament, by which it is, among other things, proposed to reduce the Cathedral Choirs to the "least possible state of efficiency."

Now, the Cathedral Choirs have long been in a state very far *below* one of *the least* "efficiency."

It may appear too sweeping an assertion to declare that *no* Cathedral in this country possesses, at this day, a musical force competent to embody and give effect to the evident intentions of the Church with regard to music; but such is the state of things, nevertheless.

The impressions of either the occasional visitor or the regular attendant at Cathedrals, if analyzed, would afford nothing like well-defined criticism of the service, as a *musical* performance, which it really is; novelty in the one case, or the utter hopelessness of reform, or entire ignorance, in the other, serving either to palliate, or to exclude from all open complaint, that mass of inferiority and error which has long rendered our Church music a source of grief and shame to well disposed and well instructed persons.

To arrive at a right understanding of the matter, it is obviously requisite to consider what Cathedral service is intended to be, and what it has hitherto been. On this basis alone can be formed any adequate idea of its just claims on the religious world at the present moment, as to what *it should be.*

The subject is so vast, laying open such an immense field for inquiry and research, that a merely *musical* writer must find himself perplexed in his attempts to treat it with anything like due consideration and effect; but it is the opinion of *musicians* which is so greatly needed at this moment. A professional statement from them seems indispensable. In the following pages it is hoped the reader will find, although in but a scattered form, the necessary details to enable him to arrive at something like correct views, and to see that before you can accomplish even any moderately correct and impressive performance of the Choral Service of the Church, it is absolutely necessary that there should be, first, *competent performers,* (*or Ministers;*) secondly, *the guidance of an able conductor,* (*or Precentor;*) and thirdly, *that the musical compositions performed should be the emanations of genius, or of the highest order of talent.* Such is the Church system. How that system has been departed from will presently appear.

To begin with the arrangement of Church music; it is antiphonal. It must, from the nature of its composition, be sung by TWO CHOIRS.

The least number of men which can constitute a Cathedral Choir capable of performing the service is twelve; because each Choir must have *three* for the solo or verse parts, and an extra *three* (one to a part) to form the chorus; six on a side, that is: now so far from this, the least amount of necessary strength, being what is found in anything like constant attendance at our Cathedrals generally, there is *not one* where such is the case: not one which has the requisite number of singers in daily attendance. [...]

The Choral Service of the Church claims admiration from the musician upon the score of the exquisite *keeping* preserved throughout. Its solemn and beautiful inflexions of tone—its glorious contrasts and analogies—its monotone—its responses and anthem; all should be governed by one feeling. And so it once *was,* thanks to the wisdom of ages. But it is not so now; disorder reigns throughout. From the errors in style of the chant, service, or anthem, all is disjointed and "in bad keeping." There is, perhaps, not one unexceptionable performance of the service at the present day. It would, no doubt, be difficult to impart to the richer portions of the service all the high quality of modern art, and yet preserve the necessary regard to the features in detail. To accomplish this is the task of the modern Church musician. Still, viewing the Choral Service generally, and in comparison with any of the endless varieties of the Parochial, how superior is the former;—the prostration of all individuality in its ministering servant!—the withering familiarity in this respect of the latter!

The mixture of the Choral and Parochial modes, now so common, is inconsistent with a just appreciation of the Choral Service; and may not the propriety of making the congregation take prominent part in the ceremonial of religion be questionable, considering that it was not permitted for so many centuries in England, and that persons who take part in and perform a public ceremony, can never be so thoroughly imbued with its spirit as those who preserve a silent attention? It was a very early law in the Church, that none but those qualified by previous study and preparation should be allowed to sing in the service; confusion being the inevitable result of a different course. The beautiful Choral Service of the Church, like other sublime things, would necessarily render the auditor speechless, and produce a tone of feeling far different from that which results in utterance. Paley, in his sermon on the text: "Lest that, by any means, when I have preached to others, I myself should be a castaway," describes the danger even to the Clergy themselves which attends the frequent and formal "intermixture with religious offices;" and it is surely one of the most beautiful attributes of Choral Service that the worshipper is not compelled at any time to utter anything to interrupt the prostration of mind which would ever attend a perfect performance of that service in our beautiful Cathedrals. [...]

THE PLAN

which the writer would suggest for remedying the evils of which he so deplores the existence, is as follows:–

The number of lay Choir-men in daily attendance should never be less than *twelve*, this being the *least* number by which the choral service can be properly performed.

To ensure the constant attendance of *twelve* it would be necessary to retain at least three *additional* voices (one of each kind) to meet the frequent deficiencies arising from illness or other unavoidable causes. The stipend of the former might be £85 per annum; of the latter £52.

These lay singers should be required to give the degree of attention to *rehearsals* and every other musical duty exacted of all such persons at ordinary performances of music, and, like others, they should be subject to an early removal in cases of wilful inattention.

Should it not be deemed desirable for them to occupy themselves in trade, or other pursuits, (and that it is *not* desirable cannot be a question, their Cathedral duty, if properly followed, being the work of a life,) the salaries should be higher, and not less than from £100 to £150 per annum.[1]

The election to the office of lay Choir men should rest with the organists or musical conductors of three Cathedrals, namely the one in which the vacancy occurs, and the two nearest to it, the Dean and Chapter of the former exercising their judgment as to the religious fitness of the candidate. In fixing, as is here proposed, the number of the lay singers at the *minimum* number, twelve, it may be added, that in any Cathedral town where the musical services of the Cathedral were conducted in a meritorious manner, they would undoubtedly enjoy great popularity, and enlist the voluntary aid of many competent persons. An addition of *six* such might probably be relied on; and this, although inadequate—the requirements of such large buildings as our Cathedrals being considered—would be a great advance upon present things.[2]

A MUSICAL COLLEGE, in connection with one of the Cathedrals, and under the government of its Dean and Chapter, seems indispensably necessary for the tuition of lay singers; and, what is more important, for the complete education of the higher order of musical officer employed as the Organist, Composer, or Director of the Choir. Lay singers for Cathedrals are not easily procured; and the above arrangement would greatly facilitate the object of providing every Cathedral with the required number for its Choir, and for imparting a thorough and complete musical education to the musical professors employed by the Church. A School of this kind might not be self-supporting, possibly; every Cathedral, therefore, should be required to contribute something to its maintenance.

THE CATHEDRAL ORGANIST should, in every instance, be a professor of the highest ability,—a master in the most elevated departments of composition,—and efficient in the conducting and superintendance of a Choral body.

(From S. S. Wesley, *A Few Words on Cathedral Music*, 1849, pp. 5–7, 33–4, 56–8)

---

[1] The constant vibration of the lay clerk between his shop and his Cathedral, as at present, is productive of serious results; rendering him, but too often, a tradesman amongst singers, and a singer amongst tradesmen. The serving two masters in disastrous, as inquiry into the position of these parties at the present time would show.

[2] At Leeds Parish Church, where the Choral Service is performed, and supported by voluntary contributions, several gentlemen attend on this footing, and with regularity and good effect.

(B)   FREDERICK W. FABER ON CATHOLIC HYMNS, 1849

Frederick W. Faber here sets out the rationale for a Roman Catholic hymnbook, acknowledging the impact of Evangelical precursors, and explaining the devotional function of hymns.

The following Hymns do not, as will be seen, form anything like a perfect collection, but are given as a specimen of a much larger and more complete work. The Author has had a double end in view in the composition of them; first, to furnish some simple and original hymns for singing; secondly, to provide English Catholics with a hymn-book for reading, in the simplest and least involved metres: and both these objects have not unfrequently required considerable sacrifice in a literary point of view. [...]

The few [hymns] in the Garden of the Soul were all that were at hand, and of course they were not numerous enough to furnish the requisite variety. As to translations, they do not express Saxon thoughts and feelings, and consequently the poor do not seem to take to them. The domestic wants of the Oratory, too, kept alive the feeling that something of the sort was needed; though at the same time the Author's ignorance of music appeared in some measure to disqualify him for the work of supplying the defect. Eleven, however, of the hymns were written, most of them, for particular tunes and on particular occasions, and became very popular with a country congregation. They were afterwards printed for the schools at St. Wilfrid's, and the very numerous applications to the printer for them seemed to show that, in spite of very glaring literary defects, such as careless grammar and slipshod metre, people were anxious to have Catholic hymns of any sort. The MS. of the present volume was submitted to a musical friend, who replied that certain verses of all or nearly all the hymns would do for singing: and this encouragement has led to the publication of the volume.

This, however, as the length and character of many of the hymns will show, was not the only object of the volume. There is scarcely anything which takes so strong a hold upon people as religion in metre, hymns or poems on doctrinal subjects. Every one, who has had experience among the English poor, knows the influence of Wesley's Hymns and the Olney Collection. Less than moderate literary excellence, a very tame versification, indeed often the simple recurrence of a rhyme is sufficient: the spell seems to lie in that. Catholics even are not unfrequently found poring with a devout and unsuspecting delight over the verses of the

Olney Hymns, which the Author himself can remember acting like a spell upon him for years, strong enough to be for long a counter influence to very grave convictions, and even now to come back from time to time unbidden into the mind. The Welsh Hymn-book is in two goodly volumes, and helps to keep alive the well-known Welsh fanaticism. The German Hymn-book, with its captivating double rhymes, outdoes Luther's Bible, as a support of the now decaying cause of Protestantism there. The Cantiques of the French Missions and the Laudi Spirituali of Italy are reckoned among the necessary weapons of the successful missionary; and it would seem that the Oratory, with its "perpetual domestic mission," first led the way in this matter; and St. Alphonso, the pupil of St. Philip's Neapolitan children, and himself once under a vow to join them, used to sing his own hymns in the pulpit before the sermon. It seemed then in every way desirable that Catholics should have a hymn-book *for reading*, which should contain the mysteries of the faith in easy verse, or different states of heart and conscience depicted, with the same unadorned simplicity, for example, as the "O for a closer walk with God" of the Olney Hymns; and that the metres should be of the simplest and least intricate sort, so as not to stand in the way of the understanding or enjoyment of the poor, which has always been found to be the case with anything like elaborate metre, however simple the diction and touching the thoughts might be. The means of influence which one school of Protestantism has in Wesley's, Newton's and Cowper's hymns, and another in the more refined and engaging works of Oxford writers, and foreign Catholics in the Cantiques and Laudi, are unfortunately entirely wanting to us in our labours among the hymn-loving English.

The kind reader is requested then to consider these Hymns as a sample, upon which the Author wishes to invite criticism, with a view to future composition, if sufficient leisure should ever be allowed him for such labour; and they may perhaps be permitted, provisionally at least, to stand in the gap, which they are certainly not fitted permanently to fill, in our popular Catholic literature.

F.W. FABER
PRIEST OF THE ORATORY OF ST. PHILIP NERI.
The Oratory, London.
Feast of the Sacred Heart of Jesus.
1849.

(From F. W. Faber, *Jesus and Mary: or Catholic Hymns, for Singing and Reading*, London, Richardson, 1849, pp. v–x)

(C)   THE MUSIC OF THE MOODY–SANKEY MEETINGS

The author of this appraisal was John Spencer Curwen (1847–1916), a Nonconformist musician and publisher, and the son of John Curwen, who had been a leading promoter of the tonic sol-fa system. It well illustrates the ambivalence of cultivated Congregationalism towards the revivalists.

There has been plenty of debate over these American gospel song-tunes. Are they legitimate church music, and if not, is it wise to employ a musical idiom in the prayer-meeting and mission service which cannot be tolerated in the church? The taste formed on Bach, on the simpler counterpoint of our stately old English hymn-tunes, or on the warmly-coloured modern tunes of Dykes and Barnby, find these American pieces hopelessly insipid, not to say vulgar. Their structure is, indeed, extremely slight. The old hymn-tune, with fundamental harmony at each beat, moves with the stride and strength of a giant, while the attenuated effect of these American tunes is largely due to their changing the harmony but once in the bar. The frequent employment of march rhythm is also distasteful to the ear which has fed itself upon good models. Again, the plan of these tunes is bad enough to start with, but still worse when they multiply by the hundred, so that it settles into a mannerism. Not much fluency or power of caricature are needed to manufacture them by the dozen at the pianoforte extempore.

Yet, after the musician has vented his spleen upon this degenerate psalmody, an important fact remains. Music in worship is a means, not an end, and we are bound to consider how far these tunes serve their end in mission work, which, after all, has not musical training for its object, so much as the kindling of the divine spark in the hearts of the worshippers. Without doubt these songs touch the common throng; they match the words to which they are sung, and carry them. The American Gospel hymn is nothing if it is not emotional [...]

Mr. Sankey and his singing have in several ways distinctly advanced our church music. To him more than to any living person must be attributed the ripening of opinion in favour of organs in Scotland. He did not argue the lawfulness of instrumental accompaniments in divine worship, but he superseded argument by making people *feel* that organs were consistent with devotion and helpful to it. [...]

Mr. Sankey was not the first "Gospel singer", but he has, more than any other, inspired imitators. Singing such as his is now a common part of the services by which all the churches are endeavouring to reach the masses. He is not a trained vocalist. A singing-master would find faults in every measure that he sings. His style is more recitative than singing; he sacrifices time unnecessarily to impulse and feeling. The effect is often jerky, intermittent, disconnected. It is not speaking with a sustained voice. But his earnestness is so apparent that it covers a multitude of faults; indeed, his transparent naturalness and his fervour so fix our attention upon what he is singing that we do not think of the faults. If Mr. Sankey were a finished singer, it is possible that he would touch his audience less. He is utterly lost in his theme, and thinks no more of how he looks or how his voice sounds while he is singing than does Mr. Moody while he is preaching. Every word throbs with feeling, and in yearning, pleading phrases the large tender heart of the man is especially conspicuous. "Gospel singers" who wish to follow in Mr. Sankey's footsteps may go elsewhere to learn vocalisation, but from Mr. Sankey, if from no higher source, they must learn to forget themselves and sing straight from the heart.

(From J. S. Curwen, *Studies in Worship Music* (Second Series), London, J. Curwen, 1885, pp. 39–40, 42–3)

(D)   PREFACE TO *THE CHURCH HYMNARY*, 1898

This Preface to the authoritative end-of-century Scottish Presbyterian hymnbook gives some indication of the motivation of the compilers and the challenges that faced them. The hymns that follow were all included in the first edition of The Church Hymnary *and are thus indicative of the taste of the period. The writers and dates are as follows:*

No. 24 'My God, how wonderful Thou art' F. W. Faber, 1849
No. 25 'Praise to the Holiest in the height' J. H. Newman, from *The Dream of Gerontius*, 1865
No. 172 'I heard the voice of Jesus say' H. Bonar, 1846
No. 257 'True-hearted' F. R. Havergal, 1878
No. 308 'Hark! hark, my soul!' F. W. Faber, 1849. The two stanzas in parentheses appeared in the original version but not in *The Church Hymnary.*
No. 339 'For all the saints' W. W. How, 1864
No. 365 'Abide with me' Words by H. F. Lyte, 1820 or 1847 (see above, p. 66); tune by W. H. Monk, 1861. The tune is reproduced both in standard stave notation and in tonic sol-fa, to illustrate the use of the latter.

This collection of hymns, authorized for use in public worship by the Church of Scotland, the Free Church of Scotland, the United Presbyterian Church, and the Presbyterian Church in Ireland, has been prepared by a Committee appointed in equal numbers by those Churches. It is catholic, as including hymns by authors belonging to almost every branch of the Church from the second century to the present day, and comprehensive, as intended for the use of various Churches and congregations.

Particular attention has been devoted to verifying the text of the hymns; and, as far as possible, the words of the author have been preserved. Variations from the original or authorized text will be found recorded in the Notes appended to the large-type edition of the words.

The music for the hymns has been selected by another Committee similarly appointed. The duties of Musical Editor were entrusted to Sir John Stainer, to whom grateful acknowledgement is due for the cordial and painstaking interest he has shown in the work. At the request of the Committee he has procured for THE CHURCH HYMNARY a number of new tunes by composers of known ability, and has himself written and arranged several expressly for it. While seeking from all available sources the music best adapted to each hymn, the Committee felt it necessary in some instances, especially in the section for the young, to adhere to tunes recommended only by long association with the hymns to which they are set. In the case of a few tunes also, they judged it advisable to retain the form which, though a departure from the original, is that in general use. The transcription of the music into the Tonic Sol-fa notation has been made by Dr. W. G. McNaught, to whom thanks are due for the care and attention he has bestowed on the work.

Both Committees entrusted with the preparation of THE CHURCH HYMNARY have to return sincere thanks for the courtesy of authors and proprietors of copyright, to whom they applied for permission to use their hymns and tunes. They trust that they will be pardoned any unintentional infringement of copyright, as well as the omission of special acknowledgement where they have been unable to trace the authors or proprietors of words or of music.

THE CHURCH HYMNARY is issued with the fervent prayer that its use in the praises of the sanctuary may be to the glory of God and the edification of His people.

April, 1898.

(From *The Church Hymnary*, Edinburgh, Henry Froude, 1898, pp. v–vi)

My God, how wonderful Thou art,
Thy majesty how bright!
How beautiful Thy mercy-seat,
In depths of burning light!

How dread are Thine eternal years,
O everlasting Lord,
By prostrate spirits day and night
Incessantly adored!

O how I fear Thee, living God,
With deepest, tenderest fears,
And worship Thee with trembling hope
And penitential tears!

Yet I may love Thee too, O Lord,
Almighty as Thou art,
For Thou hast stooped to ask of me
The love of my poor heart.

No earthly father loves like Thee;
No mother, e'er so mild,
Bears and forbears as Thou hast done
With me, Thy sinful child.

Father of Jesus, love's reward,
What rapture will it be
Prostrate before Thy throne to lie,
And ever gaze on Thee!

Praise to the Holiest in the height,
And in the depth be praise,
In all His words most wonderful,
Most sure in all His ways.

O loving wisdom of our God!
When all was sin and shame,
A second Adam to the fight
And to the rescue came.

O wisest love! that flesh and blood,
Which did in Adam fail,
Should strive afresh against the foe,
Should strive and should prevail;

And that a higher gift than grace
Should flesh and blood refine,
God's presence, and His very self
And essence all-Divine.

O generous love! that He who smote
In Man, for man, the foe
The double agony in Man,
For man, should undergo,

And in the garden secretly,
And on the cross on high,
Should teach His brethren, and inspire
To suffer and to die.

Praise to the Holiest in the height,
And in the depth be praise,
In all His words most wonderful,
Most sure in all His ways.

I heard the voice of Jesus say,
'Come unto Me and rest;
Lay down, thou weary one, lay down
Thy head upon My breast':
I came to Jesus as I was,
Weary, and worn, and sad;
I found in Him a resting-place,
And He has made me glad.

I heard the voice of Jesus say,
'Behold, I freely give
The living water; thirsty one,
Stoop down and drink, and live':

I came to Jesus, and I drank
Of that life-giving stream;
My thirst was quenched, my soul revived,
And now I live in Him.

I heard the voice of Jesus say,
'I am this dark world's Light;
Look unto Me, thy morn shall rise,
And all thy day be bright':
I looked to Jesus, and I found
In Him my Star, my Sun;
And in that light of life I'll walk
Till travelling days are done.

True hearted, whole-hearted, faithful, and loyal,
King of our lives, by Thy grace we will be!
Under Thy standard exalted and royal,
Strong in Thy strength, we will battle for Thee.

Peal out the watchword, and silence it never,
Song of our spirits rejoicing and free:
'True-hearted, whole-hearted, now and for ever,
King of our lives, by Thy grace we will be!'

True-hearted, whole-hearted! fullest allegiance
Yielding henceforth to our glorious King,
Valiant endeavour and loving obedience
Freely and joyously now would we bring.

True-hearted! Saviour, Thou knowest our story;
Weak are the hearts that we lay at Thy feet,
Sinful and treacherous; yet, for Thy glory,
Heal them, and cleanse them from sin and deceit.

Whole hearted! Saviour, beloved and glorious,
Take Thy great power and reign Thou alone
Over our wills and affections victorious,
Freely surrendered, and wholly Thine own.

Hark! hark, my soul! angelic songs are swelling
O'er earth's green fields and ocean's wave-beat shore:
How sweet the truth those blessed strains are telling
Of that new life when sin shall be no more.
Angels of Jesus, angels of light,
Singing to welcome the pilgrims of the night!

[Darker than night life's shadows fall around us,
And like benighted men, we miss our mark;
God hides himself, and grace hath scarcely found us,
Ere death finds out his victims in the dark.]

Onward we go, for still we hear them singing,
'Come, weary souls, for Jesus bids you come';
And through the dark, its echoes sweetly ringing,
The music of the gospel leads us home.

Far, far away, like bells at evening pealing,
The voice of Jesus sounds o'er land and sea,
And laden souls, by thousands meekly stealing,
Kind Shepherd, turn their weary steps to Thee.

Rest comes at length; though life be long and dreary,
The day must dawn, and darksome night be past;
Faith's journey ends in welcomes to the weary,
And heaven, the heart's true home, will come at last.

[Cheer up, my soul! faith's moonbeams softly glisten
Upon the breast of life most troubled sea;
And it will cheer thy drooping heart to listen
To those brave songs which angels mean for thee!]

Angels, sing on, your faithful watches keeping;
Sing us sweet fragments of the songs above,
Till morning's joy shall end the night of weeping,
And life's long shadows break in cloudless love.

For all the saints who from their labours rest,
Who Thee by faith before the world confessed,
Thy name, O Jesus, be for ever blest.
Hallelujah!

Thou wast their Rock, their Fortress, and their Might;
Thou, Lord, their Captain in the well-fought fight;
Thou, in the darkness drear, their one true Light.
Hallelujah!

O may Thy soldiers, faithful, true, and bold,
Fight as the saints who nobly fought of old,
And win, with them, the victor's crown of gold.
Hallelujah!

O blest communion, fellowship Divine!
We feebly struggle, they in glory shine;
Yet all are one in Thee, for all are Thine.
Hallelujah!

And when the strife is fierce, the warfare long,
Steals on the ear the distant triumph song,
And hearts are brave again, and arms are strong.
Hallelujah!

The golden evening brightens in the west;
Soon, soon to faithful warriors cometh rest;
Sweet is the calm of Paradise the blest.
Hallelujah!

But, lo! there breaks a yet more glorious day:
The saints triumphant rise in bright array;
The King of Glory passes on His way.
Hallelujah!

From earth's wide bounds, from ocean's furthest coast,
Through gates of pearl streams in the countless host,
Singing to Father, Son, and Holy Ghost,
Hallelujah!

Abide with me: fast falls the eventide;
The darkness deepens; Lord, with me abide:
When other helpers fail, and comforts flee,
Help of the helpless, O abide with me.

Swift to its close ebbs out life's little day;
Earth's joys grow dim, its glories pass away;
Change and decay in all around I see:
O Thou who changest not, abide with me.

Not a brief glance I beg, a passing word;
But, as Thou dwell'st with Thy disciples, Lord,
Familiar, condescending, patient, free,
Come, not to sojourn, but abide with me.

Come not in terrors, as the King of kings,
But kind and good, with healing in Thy wings
Tears for all woes, a heart for every plea;
Come, Friend of sinners, thus abide with me.

Thou on my head in early youth didst smile;
And, though rebellious and perverse meanwhile,
Thou hast not left me, oft as I left Thee:
On to the close, O Lord, abide with me.

I need Thy presence every passing hour;
What but Thy grace can foil the tempter's power?
Who like Thyself my guide and stay can be?
Through cloud and sunshine, O abide with me.

I fear no foe, with Thee at hand to bless;
Ills have no weight, and tears no bitterness:
Where is death's sting? where, grave, thy victory?
I triumph still if Thou abide with me.

Hold Thou Thy cross before my closing eyes,
Shine through the gloom, and point me to the skies;
Heaven's morning breaks, and earth's vain shadows flee:
In life and death, O Lord, abide with me.

EVENTIDE.   W. H. Monk.
DOH = Eb.

m :—	m :r	d :—	s :—	l :s	s :f	m :—	— :—
d :—	t₁ :t₁	d :—	d :—	d :t₁	d :r	d :—	— :—
s :—	s :f	m :—	d :—	d :s	s :s	s :—	— :—
d :—	s₁ :s₁	l₁ :—	m₁ :—	f₁ :s₁	l₁ :t₁	d :—	— :—

m :—	f :s	l :—	s :—	f :r	m :fe	s :—	— :—
d :—	d :d	d :—	d :—	d :r	d :d	t₁ :—	— :—
s :—	f :m	f :—	m :—	l :s	s :d	r :—	— :—
d :t₁	l₁ :s₁	f₁ :—	d :—	r :t₁	d :l₁	s₁ :—	— :—

m :—	m :r	d :—	s :—	s :f	f :m	r :—	— :—
d :—	t₁ :t₁	d :—	d :—	d :d	de :de	r :—	— :—
m :f	s :f	m :—	d¹ :t	l :l	l :s	f :—	— :—
d :—	s₁ :s₁	l₁ :—	m₁ :—	f₁ :—.s₁	l₁ :l₁	r :—	— :—

r :—	m :f	m :r	d :f	m :—	r :—	d :—	— :—	d	d
t₁ :—	d :t₁	d :t₁	d :r	d :—	t₁ :—	d :—	— :—	l₁	s₁
s :—	s :s	s :f	m :l	s :—	— :f	m :—	— :—	f	m
f :—	m :r	d :s₁	l₁ :f₁	s₁ :—	s₁ :—	d :—	— :—	f₁	d

3 FOREIGN MISSIONS AND MISSIONARIES IN VICTORIAN BRITAIN

(A) JOHN CLARK MARSHMAN ON THE CAUSES OF THE 'INDIAN MUTINY', 1859

This Preface from John Clark Marshman's book The Life and Times of Carey, Marshman, and Ward *gives a contemporary reaction to the 'Indian Mutiny' of 1858.*

In the course of this work it has been requisite to impugn the assertion made by the opponents of missions to India in 1793 and 1808, that any attempt to convert the Hindoos would result in insurrection and massacre. Those morbid apprehensions, the offspring of prejudice and timidity, have been treated with the contempt they appeared to merit: but while the work has been passing through the press an unparalleled tragedy has been exhibited in India; a hundred thousand sepoys have appeared in open revolt, and endeavoured to subvert our dominion and to extirpate our race; and this insurrection is stated by them to have been provoked by our attempts to tamper with their caste and religion. The fearful events of the last eighteen months would thus appear to substantiate those gloomy prognostications, and to countenance the doctrine that any attempt to interfere with the religious prejudices of the natives must be attended with imminent peril, and that if we would maintain our empire in the east, we must leave them for ever under the dominion of their superstitions. It is necessary, therefore, that the question of the mutiny and its motives should be dispassionately investigated. It is important to the interests of the conquerors that the real cause of this tragic event should be clearly ascertained, that we may be enabled to guard against the recurrence of it; it is equally important to the welfare of the natives that it should not be attributed to the wrong cause, that the prospects of their improvement may not be injured. The former investigation may be left to the politician; the latter belongs more especially to the philanthropist.

That the mutiny was not in any measure occasioned by the labours of the missionaries there is the most conclusive evidence. During the revolt diverse manifestos were promulgated by the insurrectionary chiefs, with the view of inflaming the minds of the people, by an exposition of the grievances to which they were subject under the dominion of the *Feringees*. But in this catalogue of grievances, some of which were merely plausible and others purely imaginary, there was not the most remote allusion to the exertions of the missionaries, and it is manifest that if their labours had been regarded as a popular grievance, which could be turned to account, they would not have been overlooked. But in addition to this negative evidence there is the positive testimony of large and influential bodies of natives who have, of their own accord, come forward and asserted that the endeavours of the missionaries were in no respect connected with the revolt; that their blameless life, their disinterested and benevolent exertions, and their sympathy with the feelings and the griefs of the people, had secured them the respect and admiration even of those whose creed they were endeavouring to subvert. An opinion has been disseminated in England that the government in India has of late years changed its policy, and given encouragement to the missionary cause; and this is said to have created a feeling of alarm among the natives and disposed them to rebellion. But so far from giving any support to the missionaries, government has omitted no opportunity of disavowing all connection with them. In one of the last proclamations, issued a short time before the mutiny, the natives were informed that the missionaries were only labouring in their vocation, and that government had nothing whatever to do with them. The language of that proclamation was calculated to bring them into contempt with the native community, and they had some reason to complain of such unprovoked contumely. About the same time an Act was passed prohibiting the publication of obscene books and pictures in India, but a clause was inserted, especially exempting from the operation of the Act every "representation, sculptured, engraved, or painted on or in any temple, or on any car used for the conveyance of idols." With what colour of truth can it then be affirmed, that there has been any change in the policy of government, either as it regards discouraging missionary efforts, or deferring to the popular idolatry?

But it may be affirmed with perfect confidence, that even if the missionaries had received the most open and direct support from the state, and if government had laboured to propagate Christianity by a system of rewards and penalties, there would have been little reason to dread a mutiny, or even an insurrection. Although a contrary opinion be prevalent in England, it has been adopted without investigation, and is contrary to all historical teaching in India. This assertion may at first appear paradoxical, but it is based on truth, and it is fully substantiated by the opinion of the late Sir William Macnaghten, the envoy at Cabul, one of the ablest public men of his day, who, moreover, was never charged with any undue partiality for missionary labours. He was required to give his opinion on the question whether suttees could be abolished consistently with the safety of our dominion. Admitting the sacrifice of suttee to be a religious act of the highest possible merit according to the notions of the Hindoos, "where," he inquires, "is danger to be apprehended from the abolition of it? Look to the genius of the people and their past history; under their Moosulman rulers they tamely endured all sorts of insults to their religion and violation of their prejudices. We have no record of any general or organised disaffection. We read that their temples were polluted and destroyed and that many of them were compelled to become converts to the creed of their oppressors. Neither tyranny nor endurance could well go further than this." Yet the Mahomedans never lost a province or a town in consequence of this bigoted and oppressive course. Nor is there any reason to suppose that if we had pursued the same policy—which we have justly and equitably abstained from doing—the result would have been of a different character. [...]

The magnitude of the unexpected calamity of 1857 has naturally disturbed the minds of men at home, and led to the advocacy of measures of very doubtful policy. In the first moments of a panic the most violent counsels are generally considered the most expedient. Hence we have the extreme section of the religious world attributing the mutiny to the too great respect which has been shown to the idolatrous prejudices of the natives, and recommending the destruction of caste, the prohibition of all superstitious practices, and the propagation of Christianity by the influence of government.

On the other hand we have the president and secretary of the late Board of Control, tracing the mutiny, in the despatch sent to India on the 29th of March last, to the too little regard which has of late been paid to the religious prejudices of the people, and more especially to the rapid impulse given to "educational schemes," and advocating measures which would lead to the interruption of all progress, if not to the extinction of education. India, however, is not to be governed by the favourite partialities or prejudices of either of these parties; we must discover some middle course, equally removed from the extreme views of both, if we would combine the consolidation of the empire, with the elevation of its inhabitants.

It is equally contrary to all sound policy and to the interests of Christian truth, that Christianity should be propagated in India by the direct instrumentality, or the indirect aid, of Government. From every attempt to evangelise the country, it is the bounden duty of Government most conscientiously and most scrupulously to abstain. The spread of the Gospel is the exclusive province of the missionary, and he must not appear as the delegate of the state. Dr. Carey's remark when the subject was once introduced, should ever be held in remembrance. "Whatever government may do, let it not touch my work; it can only succeed in making men hypocrites: I wish to make them Christians." At the same time it would be unworthy of a great, powerful, and enlightened government to shrink, as the government of India has hitherto done, from avowing its Christian character. It is to be lamented that the public authorities in India have been too much disposed to keep their religion in the back-ground, as if they were ashamed or afraid to acknowledge it in the presence of the heathen. This timid policy has not prevented the torrent of an exterminating mutiny, and this of itself furnishes a strong argument for the adoption of a more dignified course. It is a fallacy to suppose that we shall lose the confidence of the natives by the manly avowal of our creed. The Hindoos and Mahomedans are men of such intense religious feeling that they cannot be expected to entertain any respect for those who do not manifest the same strength of attachment to their own religion.

They cannot believe in the existence of religious indifference in a government, and our profession of perfect neutrality has only tended to bring our motives under suspicion, and to complicate our relations with them. The soundest policy is to adopt a just and fearless course; to tell our native subjects that the government of the Crown is a Christian government, and regulated by Christian principles, that, although it believes Christianity to be the only true religion, and desires to see it prevail throughout India, yet, in obedience to its principles, it will employ neither force nor fraud to convert its subjects, but will continue to allow them the fullest liberty of conscience, and to permit every man to profess and practise his own religion without any interference. [...]

The Proclamation issued by the Queen on assuming the government of India, prohibits the interference of the public officers with the belief of the people. The prohibition has reference necessarily to their official character, and the principle embodied in it is judicious and sound. For the last fifty years it has been the rule in India that the functionaries of Government should abstain from using their official influence for the diffusion of Christianity among the natives, and the Proclamation simply incorporates the ancient rule with the new government. At the same time the public servants have always been considered at liberty, in their private and individual capacity, to aid the promotion of Christian truth. The line of distinction was first defined under the government of Lord Minto, and it has been distinctly recognised under every succeeding administration. It was in the year 1808 that the Serampore missionaries had resolved to solicit subscriptions for the translating and printing of the Scriptures in the languages of India, and Dr. Marshman waited on Lord Minto to request his support. He asked time to consider the proposal, and consult his colleagues. At the next interview he said that if he could possibly step out of himself, and separate his public from his private character, he would at once head the list, but it was considered unadvisable for the head of the Government to appear in such an undertaking.

JOHN C. MARSHMAN.

KENSINGTON PALACE GARDENS,
Jan. 25th, 1859.

(From J. C. Marshman, *The Life and Times of Carey, Marshman, and Ward embracing the History of the Serampore Mission*, Volume I, London, Longman, Brown, Green, Longmans, & Roberts, 1859, pp. v–viii, x–xv)

(B)   SERMON BY SAMUEL WILBERFORCE, 'THE CONDITIONS OF MISSIONARY SUCCESS', 1850

This sermon by Samuel Wilberforce (1805–73) was preached in St Paul's Cathedral on 19 June 1850, at the 149th Anniversary Meeting of the Society for the Propagation of the Gospel in Foreign Parts.

ACTS xix. 20.

So mightily grew the word of God and prevailed.

[In] 1701, the united efforts of a few good men obtained the Charter, and began the labours of the Society for the Propagation of the Gospel in Foreign Parts; and, from that day to this, the Church of England has never ceased to bear abroad a witness for our Lord. But cold, dark, faithless times were yet before her. Year by year, indeed, throughout the following century, she raised her voice as we are this day doing; and planted or nurtured in some far land the Faith of Christ; and through God's goodness, even those seeds which lay so long as dead, did yet at last take root and grow; and from their scanty and imperfect scattering, His great grace has drawn up at length the full and joyous harvest of our daughter Church in America. But it was long before any such results were produced. It was a season when the Church's inward vitality languished beneath the dullness of a creeping lethargy, and her work for God was feeble and unfruitful. At length a time came when, by various instruments, God revived His work amongst us, and the Christian heart of England beat again; and at once, with this stirring of the inner life, began the work of Evangelization. To speak of no other Mission, the labours and successes of Schwartz and his associates seemed to promise the immediate conversion of a large part of Southern India.

Yet, after a season, all this promise withered. The good work hardly survived the natural lives of its founders; and, in obedience to a deep and universal law of the Spiritual Kingdom, none have been found so hardened against Christian teaching, as those who lapsed from it to heathendom.

And in what are we to find the cause of such a failure? Surely, I think, in this, my brethren, that, whilst the first success was the fruit of God's blessing on that reviving inner life which had put forth the efforts, they lacked those other conditions, both of perfected organization, and of gifts diligently used, which we at first noted as the sure correlatives of primitive success. For these were signally absent—not only were those Missions not formed on the Apostolic model of sending forth one chief pastor with his attendant Priests and Deacons, to re-produce the Church in her perfectness; but the chiefest agents in the work had never received from Apostolic hands that sure commission, without which the Church of England allows none to minister as Christ's witness even in her smallest parish. Thus, the work rested on the energy of individual agents, and not on the inherent reproductive power of Christ's spiritual appointment; and no wonder that it withered with the passing life of those who had begun it. And then, further, here was no calling forth of the Church's gifts. Instead of her choicest sons being stirred up to do the Lord's bidding, not one English clergyman was found to go; but aliens from our nation and our Church could alone be procured to endure the glorious trials and hardships of that blessed enterprise. Verily, though our good Lord had touched our eyes, we as yet but 'saw men as trees walking,' still of His mercy He left us not, but again He touched us, and the vision cleared. First at His call there went forth some of the best and worthiest of our Church's sons. Their prayers, sacrifices, and examples were not lost upon others. The spirit spread—and now, with the deepest sense of our unworthiness, we may yet dare to say, that of late the two hitherto unfulfilled conditions have in some measure been supplied. Twenty-three Bishops of the Anglican succession, with their distant Dioceses, now sit in the Apostles' seats, and lead the army of the faithful. For the first time, we have been permitted to send forth throughout the earth rightly constituted missions of the Church of Christ. And contemporaneously with this, there has also been a new calling forth of the Church's various gifts of grace. Hearts have been touched, and the wealth of England has been given as it never had before been offered; nor is this all, or even the chiefest matter. She has given to the work of her own sons, yea, her best and goodliest. To India and its isles, to Persia and the frozen Labrador, to Australasia and the coral reefs of the New Zealand islands, have her chosen messengers[3] gone forth, lured from all which makes an English home so precious, by the exceeding sweetness of His voice who called Abraham from Ur of the Chaldees, and drew Saul of Tarsus from his Jewish home to his long course of labours, sufferings, bonds, and martyrdom. And further, we may humbly dare to say that with us too, even beyond our hopes, the Word of God has grown and multiplied. To name now no other places, in New Zealand, in Southern India, in America, how rich and goodly is the brightening prospect! Surely, we need only faith, labour, patience, and perseverance, to see mighty works of God's converting grace, such as have scarcely been seen since the days when 'all they which dwelt in Asia heard the word of the Lord Jesus.'[4]

What then shall we do, in this our day of gracious influences, to help on this work? Suffer me, my brethren, to suggest for your consideration a few hints, as to the greater perfecting of our work in those particulars which, as we have seen, have always been conditions of success:—

And, *First*,—Let us seek to bring the outward framework of our Missionary labours into a more exact agreement with that of the Church of Christ. There is much which yet needs to be done herein, both at home and abroad. At home we have need to make it felt, that this work cannot be left merely to the zeal of those who undertake it as a task, however laudable; but that its hearty carrying on is a true correlative of our baptismal blessings;—so that every separate parish, because it is a parish with its church, and altar, and ministry, and grace; and every separate Christian, because he is a regenerate member of Christ's body, must be partakers, by prayers, and interest, and offerings, and labours, in its charge and care.[5] Abroad, we need greatly to increase the number of our

---

[3] With humble thankfulness let us record amongst others the names of Henry Martyn, Samuel Marsden, Reginald Heber, George Augustus Selwyn, and Robert Gray

[4] Acts, xix. 10.

[5] Actual experience makes me certain, that a zeal for this work may be stirred up in every parish, if due pains are taken to keep the people informed on the real history of our missions. Mere general exhortations are not what I mean. But, if the people are assembled quarterly in the school-room; if the geographical position, and actual moral, social, and religious state of those amongst whom we labour, and the details of that labour, are set plainly before them, they will always be deeply interested. The most common error is to seek to include too much at each meeting; and thus all the lines are made faint, and a wearisome sameness of statement is unavoidable. A small field of missionary labour thoroughly explained is what is needed.

bishoprics; to train up everywhere a native ministry;[6] to permit and facilitate by every means the efforts which our Church is making so to adapt itself to its special needs in those distant lands, as to gather in, by God's blessing, the largest harvest of souls.

And then, *Secondly,* we need exceedingly to call out for this great work the gifts which are inherent in her. These abound, and, alas! how few of them are really used. To take the lowest first: When and where was there ever a Church which, in the wealth of its children, and in their connexion with every part of the heathen world, had such latent powers of service? Let us look forth around us, brethren, on every side, from this House of God[7] in which we are now worshipping, and what do we see? Surely wealth, greatness, riches, luxury and commerce, such as never before poured their golden streams upon the merchant princes of the earth. And what are all these but the gifts which we should faithfully use if we would work the work of God.

Again, what is our Colonial Empire but another of such gifts? How, like some curious net-work, does it encircle the earth; how has it everywhere laid hold of harbours and navigable rivers, and fertile lands; how has it occupied all the vantage posts of the earth, both east and west, and north and south! What works of God might not be worked through it! How might we hereby lay so deep and wide the foundations of His earthly kingdom, that if the day should ever come when England's greatness shall be a tale of past generations, still she might survive amongst the nations, in the Christian realms which, in her day of strength, she founded with her seed, and nurtured in her truth! [...]

Nor is this all. It is one special attribute of Christ's church, that it has an ever-new power of self-adaptation to the wants and difficulties of men. Now, have we manifested duly in our missionary work this especial sign and action of our spiritual life? Are not, on the contrary, our efforts often grievously crippled by a sort of stiff and unbending transference to new scenes and other circumstances of that which has grown up at home, and is well suited for the nourishing at home our spiritual life? Are not many of our colonial bishoprics so large as to maintain rather a nominal than a real episcopate? Is it possible for the Bishop of Calcutta to do his proper work there, and to be at the same time a really presiding bishop over Delhi and its provinces? Again: ought we not to make provision, when God gives any wide district to the labours of one of our missionaries, that he should enter on its episcopal oversight, and so be enabled to maintain

---

[6] Every colonial diocese ought to have, under the immediate direction of its bishop, a diocesan college for training clergymen.

[7] St. Paul's Cathedral.

his own plans, extend their operation, and secure labourers under himself, like-minded with himself, for the perfecting the work he has been enabled, by God's blessing, so prosperously to begin? [...]

And then, lastly, as the root of all, let us seek to quicken our internal life. Here, brethren, is the last and greatest need of all. All true labour for God, in individual Christians and in churches, is the coming forth of an inner life; and in quickening that life at its source, is that outward labour best and most truly perfected.

By holding fast at home Christ's truth in greater purity; by growth in love; by devotion deepened and increased; by more frequent and earnest communions; by a wider, more enduring, more steadfast unity; by being more filled with the Spirit; by being transfigured into Christ's likeness; by sitting always beneath His cross; by bearing His burden; by learning to do common things in a higher spirit of self-sacrifice, and grateful love to Him;—by these beyond all other ways shall we become able as a Church to cast abroad a brighter light of truth, and to gather in more largely the fulness of the heathen to our Saviour's fold.

(From S. Wilberforce, *Sermons Preached and Published on Several Occasions*, London, 1854, pp. 155–9, 161–3)

(C)   ALEXANDER DUFF ON THE PROGRESS OF MISSION, 1832

These two letters from the Scottish missionary Alexander Duff (1806–78) to the Reverend Professor Ferrie of Kilconquhar give Duff's estimate of the early results of mission and also reflect something of mission politics in Scotland.

CALCUTTA, 9*th January,* 1832.

Here there is little change: much work of preparation silently carried on, little of the practical work of conversion from dumb idols to serve the living God. We cannot over-estimate the worth of an immortal soul, and should one be found cleaving to the Saviour steadfastly and immovably we cannot rejoice too much or ascribe too much glory to God. But methinks that, considering the millions still unreclaimed, our joy should be tempered and our glorying moderated, lest the one should be found to be mere self-gratulation and the other a vain boastfulness. How I fear that much, far too much, has been made of partial success in the work of conversion, and that many good people at home are under serious delusion as to its extent. Everything around me proves the necessity of more earnest prayer and redoubled exertion. I see nothing to satisfy me that any decisive victory has been won on the grand scale of national emancipation. The few converts that have been made can never be the seed of the Church: they resemble rather those somewhat unseasonable, somewhat short-lived germs which start up under the influence of a few peculiarly genial days in winter—an indication of the seminal power of mother earth, and a token of what may be expected in spring. Let us not then confine our views to the few shrivelled sprouts of a mild winter;—for these let us be thankful, as they tend to revive our hopes and reanimate our sinking spirits. But let us reach forward with restless longing and unceasing effort to the full glow and life and verdure of spring, when the whole earth shall be loosened from its cold torpor and the heavens pour down refreshing floods. It is not easy in Calcutta to congregate a decent audience to listen to Bengalee preaching. The people are naturally apathetic, and here there is superadded such pervading avarice, such money-making selfishness, that it is difficult to secure any degree of attention, or even to excite any alarm for the safety of their own religion. Thousands there are, in fact, who cannot be said to have any religion at all. Preaching generally becomes either a conversation, or a discussion in which the most arrant frivolities in argument are reiterated with an obstinacy that wastes precious time, and wholly impedes the free deliverance of truths that might quicken the conscience and save the soul alive. More, generally speaking, can be done by way of direct preaching in Bengalee in the neighbourhood than in the town of Calcutta, though I think that missionaries have often too readily given way to the accumulation of acknowledged difficulties to be encountered in town. To desert it is like abandoning one of the enemy's strongest holds and allowing him to occupy it undisturbed.

My labours in Bengalee preaching have hitherto been necessarily very limited. But there is a sphere now partially occupied, formerly almost unattempted: there is the instituting of English schools under a decidedly Christian management, and insisting on the inculcation of Christian truths. The field may become one of the richest in bearing luxuriant fruits. We only want the necessary funds and qualified agents. The success that has attended the large school first established has infused a kind of new stimulus into the minds of those most interested in the Christian education of the natives, and in that alone much real good has been achieved. The work is excessively laborious and not a little expensive, but time will show its vast importance. I trust that you are acquainted with the various proposals already forwarded to the Assembly's committee. I crave your special attention to the last, as being perhaps one of the most momentous that has ever been forwarded from a heathen land, referring chiefly to a union of all denominations in the support of a Central Institution for the more advanced literary and religious education of promising native youth; and to be under the exclusive control of the Assembly's committee. I refer you again to the printed proposals sent home, and expect your powerful advocacy of the measure.

Thousands can now talk English tolerably well. Amongst these I labour a good deal, as this class, being of the better sort, has generally been neglected. For the last two or three months I have been delivering a course of lectures on the evidences of natural and revealed religion, to about fifty of the more advanced young men who have been educated at the Hindoo College, as well as of the class of East Indians who have received a competent education. On the whole the effect is pleasing. Much discussion takes place at times, but in the end objections have hitherto been withdrawn.

Our church still droops. Were an acceptable preacher to officiate regularly it might yet be in some degree recovered from its degradation. I preach occasionally, and perceive clearly that many are willing to attend, and under a different state of things would, but refuse at present on the presentation of a plea which they hold to be sufficient. Consequently many have joined other communions permanently, many temporarily, and many live without the stated administration of ordinances. In this way that which once was a united community is now severed into fragments; and that aid which would once have been and now might be afforded can no longer be expected. Oh let us have a pious and talented successor to Dr. Brown, and much may yet be done. Another of the same stamp when the present incumbent retires, and a vast deal may be done towards restoring our Zion. Such appointments would immensely profit the Assembly's Mission. Mr. Mackay, if he enjoy good health, will do well. But he does not appear to be strong, nor capable of undergoing much bodily fatigue, nor exertion in speech, all of which is so essential to the active discharge of a missionary's duties. I wish the committee would bear in mind that a constitutional vigour of body is just as requisite as a vigorous activity of mind, and piety and learning. Indeed it is not studying men that we want, but hard-working men who have been and still are students.

Feb., 1834.—Awakened by the pleasing success which has attended our humble efforts in Calcutta, some zealous friends at home, as I hear, are beginning to think that a new station might be opened. Now, let me say at once that nothing would prove more disastrous. Of all stations in India Calcutta is by far the most important. Its population is a vast motley assemblage or congregation of persons from all parts of Eastern Asia. Of course the natives of Bengal greatly predominate, and next to these, immigrants from all the provinces of Gangetic India. A revolution of opinion here would be felt more or less throughout the Eastern world, and particularly among the millions that are the victims of idolatrous delusion and Brahmanical tyranny. It is of no ordinary importance, therefore, to make Calcutta the grand central station for conducting missionary operations on an extended scale. But we require a score more labourers, and if we had two score Calcutta alone and its neighbourhood would afford abundant scope for their best efforts for at least several years to come. It has hitherto been a radical error in the organization of missions, to scatter the pioneers and so dilute and fritter away their strength, instead of concentrating their efforts on some well-chosen field. I sincerely trust that this is an error which the committee of Assembly will endeavour to avoid, and that all their aim will be for years directed towards the strengthening of the Calcutta station.

I perceive it was stated in the last Assembly by Mr. Thomson, of Perth, that the Assembly's Institution should always remain a *mere school*. No remark has astounded me more for many a year—the utter ignorance which it betrays of the wants of this people and the most probable means of supplying these with success! If it is to continue a mere school, then I say that all the time, money and labour hitherto expended on it have been thrown away for nought. Instead of being an apparatus which God might bless as the means of leading heathens to the way of salvation through Christ, it would be much more likely to become a machine for transforming superstitious idolaters into rogues and infidels. It has been entirely overlooked that in this country there is a gigantic system of error to be rejected ere a system of truth can be embraced; and the few years which a boy can spend at a *mere* school can barely suffice to open his mind to the absurdity and irrationality of the religion of his ancestors, a religion that closely intertwines itself with every feeling and faculty of the soul, with every habit and every action of life. But supposing that in a mere school you could succeed in overthrowing Hindooism and in inculcating much of the knowledge of Christianity, still if the boy be not confirmed in any belief, and you turn him adrift amid a multitude of heathens the most licentious and depraved under the sun, what must be the consequence? I can only say from experience, that his latter end must be in all respects worse than the first.

Our only encouragement is the hope of being able to induce a certain proportion of those who enter as boys to remain with us till they reach the age of puberty, and consequently, attain that maturity of judgment which may render knowledge, through God's blessing, operative and impressions lasting. And were there no reasonable hope of securing this end, I would without hesitation say, 'the sooner you abandon the school, the better.' I, for one, could not lend myself as an instrument in wasting the funds of the benevolent in Scotland in teaching young men a mere smattering of knowledge, to enable them to become more mischievous pests to society than they would have been in a state of absolute heathenism. On the other hand, if out of every ten that enter the school even one were to advance to the higher branches of secular and Christian education; were he to become in head and in heart a disciple of the Lord Jesus; and were a number with minds thus disciplined, enlarged, and sanctified, to go forth from the Institution, what a leaven would be infused through the dense mass of the votaries of Hindooism! And what a rich and ample reward for all one's labours, what a glorious return for all the money expended! I look to you, my dear sir, as one whose superior discernment can penetrate this subject, and expose the erroneous views of such zealous but, in this instance, mistaken men as Mr. Thomson of Perth.

The school continues greatly to flourish. You may form some notion of what has been done, when I state that the highest class read and understand any English book with the greatest ease; write and speak English with tolerable fluency; have finished a course of geography and ancient history; have studied the greater part of the New Testament and portions of the Old; have mastered the evidence from prophecy and miracles; have, in addition, gone through the common rules of algebra, three books of Euclid, plane trigonometry and logarithms. And I venture to say that, on all these subjects, the youths that compose the first class would stand no unequal comparison with youths of the same standing in any seminary in Scotland. Other labours progress apace. My Tuesday evening lectures on the evidences and doctrines of Christianity are still continued. God has been pleased to bless them for the conversion of a few, and the obstinacy of many minds has been shaken. On Sunday evening I preach also in English to considerable numbers in a small native chapel. There is certainly much to encourage, while there is much also to damp one's zeal. Believe me, the people at home have far too exalted an idea of what has been done in India. Still, much has been done; and that draws out the hope of soon doing still more. Let us not rest till the whole of India be the Lord's.

(From G. Smith, *The Life of Alexander Duff, D.D., L.L.D*, Volume I, London, Hodder & Stoughton, 1879, pp. 171–6)

4   *BISHOP COLENSO OF NATAL*

(A)   JOHN WILLIAM COLENSO ON THE EFFORTS OF MISSIONARIES AMONG SAVAGES, 1865

In a paper read to the Anthropological Society of London in March 1865, Bishop Colenso not only replied to an attack upon missionary work by a previous speaker at the Society, but also provided a summary of key themes in his theology and understanding of missionary work, as these had developed over the previous decade.

We have all heard, I suppose, of the old Bulgarian chief, who, when told that his father and mother, and all the ancestors of his tribe, were burning in hell-fire, declared that he would rather go and burn with them, than live in such a gloomy heaven, with so inhuman and unjust a being as this God—a very Moloch—whom the missionary spoke of. I have heard substantially the same uttered from the mouth of a Zulu. And I do not hesitate to say that, on this particular point, the ideas of that Teuton and that Zulu were far more orthodox—or more truly Christian—than those of such a missionary, trained, though he may have been, in schools of Christian theology. It was Christian to feel there can be no happiness for me in heaven, if my friends and fellow men, for no fault of their own, are to be eternally shut out: it was Christian to think, "Better that we should all be consumed together, and the Great Spirit live alone in his glory, than believe such things of the good and blessed God, and ascribe to him such frightful partiality." [...]

There are not a few well-meaning missionaries, who will complain, no doubt, that my own publications on the Pentateuch have reached even the ears of their converts, and unsettled their minds, and made their work more difficult. I, on the other hand, complain that there are many, who with the best intentions have yet poisoned the native mind with their teachings of the kind just described—have made it difficult for the real "glad tidings," the message of their Father's Love, to reach them—have, in fact, unconsciously blasphemed (as I have said) the holy name of God, by these representations, so that the heathen can receive only a distorted view of His character, and are repelled from coming to the knowledge of the truth. Forgetting, or ignoring, or more frequently never having realised at all, the fact, that there is one Almighty Father of all mankind, who is the "Faithful Creator," the "Saviour of all men,"—who is present by His Spirit in the hearts of these Zulus as surely as He is present in our own,—from whom they have received that measure of light which they even now possess, and for which alone He holds them responsible,— Missionaries of narrow views seek not unfrequently to make that very light itself to be darkness, and try to teach their converts to renounce altogether the religious notions in which they have been reared, instead of meeting them, as it were, by the way, upon the common ground of our humanity, which a Divine Life has quickened, and showing how far what they have hitherto believed is really true, how far in their ignorance they have mingled falsehood with truth. They come to them, in short, as if they were beings from another world, commissioned by Divine authority to override or overrule all their questionings, and doubts, and prejudices, as being utterly groundless and worthless; telling them that in their heathen state there is nothing good in them, that they are utterly fallen and corrupt, all their thoughts evil, and all their practices abomination in God's sight. [...]

For among the Zulus, as among other nations, God has not left Himself without witness, in those thoughts which are stirred mysteriously within the depths of their inner being, as well as in the blessings poured upon them from without, "the rain from heaven and fruitful seasons, filling their hearts with food and gladness." I know that there are those who say that degraded tribes of human beings exist, which have no spark of religious life whatever. It may be so: I cannot contradict the assertions of those, who declare from their own personal knowledge that so it is—of missionaries or of travellers, who profess to have closely investigated the question, and who have expressed deliberately this conviction. [...]

But I confess that I very much doubt the accuracy of the statement. I doubt if the travellers or the missionaries, who have made such assertions, have ever mastered so thoroughly the native tongue, or mixed so long and intimately with the native mind, as to be competent to pronounce such a judgment. I doubt if they have been able—or willing if able—to sit down, hour by hour, in closest friendly intercourse with natives of all classes, and in the spirit of earnest, patient, research, with a full command of the native language, have sought to enter, as it were, within the heart, and search for the secret characters of light, which may be written by God's own finger there. [...]

Again, the Zulus distinctly recognise the existence of the double-heart, or, in the language of St. Paul, the constant strife of the flesh and spirit. They speak of the *ugovana*, which urges them to hate, kill, steal, commit adultery, and the *unembeza*, which bids them leave all this.

Further, they believe evidently in another life, since they make their prayers to their dead ancestors, the spirits of their tribe.

Thus we have seeds of religious truth, already planted by the Divine Hand in the minds of these natives; and our business is surely to cherish and prune the plants that have grown from those seeds,—if need be, to cut them down almost to the ground,—but not coarsely and violently to root them up altogether.

Great evil, also, is caused, as I conceive, by those who insist, in their teaching of the heathen, upon the absolute infallibility of the Scriptures a doctrine which happily is not held or taught by our National Church. [...]

I need not say that, with the daily increase of scientific knowledge among all classes, and with the facts that the first principles, at all events, of Geology and Astronomy, are taught in many of our schools, the maintenance of this dogma at home will soon become impossible for any persons of ordinary education. [...]

Are we, then, to perpetuate the same wrong in our schools set up among the heathen, the wrong I mean—rather the *sin*—of either deliberately keeping back from them such knowledge of His works as the Great God has already granted to *us*, that we may be stewards of His own good gifts for others, or else of distorting the plain results of Science, in order to prevent the discovery of their clashing with the statements of the Bible or the Prayer-Book? It would be a miserable, short-sighted, policy to do so; for the natives would soon learn from others what we did not choose to teach them ourselves. [...]

Once more, I believe that the course which the great body of missionaries have taken on the question of polygamy is a very serious impediment to the progress of our work. Here again, without any authority from the Church of which they are ministers, there are many of the missionary clergy, and even Bishops, of the Church of England, who have laid down the law, that every convert admitted into the Christian Church shall put away all his wives but one, if he had more than one, before baptism. It would be reasonable if they said, "You need not be baptised at all; you may be good men without being formally received into the Church, as there have been good men of old who were never baptised, and who had more wives than one, yet lived faithful lives. It is written in the Bible of the polygamist Abraham, from the mouth of Jehovah himself, "I know him that he will command his children and his household after him, and they shall keep the way of Jehovah to do justice and judgment;" and you, with your many wives, must try to do the same. As a Christian, you cannot take more; but you must not be false to those you have already taken, and to the obligations you have already contracted lawfully, according to your own native customs. You must not, in the selfish hope of saving your own soul, commit an act of wrong to any of your wives and children." [...]

For me, however, I feel it to be a matter of bounden duty, not a matter of choice, to communicate to our heathen converts those facts of Modern Science of which we ourselves are assured, so far as their simple minds are able to receive them; and this includes, I need hardly say, the geological conclusions as to the vast age of the world, the great antiquity of man, the impossibility of a universal deluge. The knowledge which I possess of these would make it sinful in me to teach any heathen brother to believe in the historical truths of the scriptural accounts of the Creation and the Flood,—as other scientific reasons make it equally impossible to teach them the scriptural story of the Fall, and other parts of the Bible narrative, as historical facts.

(From J. W. Colenso, 'On the efforts of missionaries among savages', *Journal of the Anthropological Society of London*, Vol. 3, 1865, pp. ccliv, cclxxi–iv and cclxxvii)

(B) JOHN WILLIAM COLENSO ON MISSIONS TO THE ZULUS IN NATAL AND ZULULAND, 1865

In a paper presented to the Marylebone Literary Institution in May 1865, Bishop Colenso included a further resounding statement of his conviction that the witness of God was to be found in all cultures and all peoples and concluded his paper with an equally resounding affirmation of the need for, and the positive implications of, a critical understanding of the Bible.

And I thank God that I *am* commissioned by the Queen of England, in the name of our National Church, to be "a preacher and a teacher" to these heathens, as well as to others, of God's eternal truth and love. And if I am asked, "Have we any ground of hope on which to pursue our labours?" I point at once to such instances as these of true, human affections—the love of a husband and a father, a love stronger than death,—and I say that wherever in Zululand or in England, in the hut of the savage or in the dens of vice and misery at home, there burns yet unquenched one spark of true human love, *there* still is the sign of life, *there* still is ground for steadily pursuing the "work of faith, and labour of love, and patience of hope," on behalf of our fellow-man, "in the sight of God our Father."

It is not, then, as we have seen, his outward form, his colour, or his hair, which makes the unspeakable difference between man and man—that one creature should be the child of God, a being of immortal hopes and fears, and another be only a beast, with more or less of craft and ferocity. Wherever we meet with the power of speech, with reason and conscience, with tender human affections, we must confess that the owner of such gifts is "a man and a brother,"—that he has a claim upon us as a member of the great human family;—for in his heart is beating, even now, however faintly, the Life which, we are told, is "the Light of men," and "lighteth every man that cometh into the world." [...]

How is it possible to teach the Zulus to cast off their superstitious belief in witchcraft, if they are required to believe that all the stories of sorcery and demonology which they find in the Bible—the witch of Endor, the appearance of Satan in the court of heaven—are infallibly and divinely true—that God's own voice pronounced on Sinai. "Thou shalt not suffer a witch to live?" I, for one, cannot do this. The time is come, through the revelations of modern science, when, thanks be to God, the traditionary belief in the divine infallibility of Scripture can, with a clear conscience, be abandoned—can, in fact, be no longer maintained.

(From J. W. Colenso, 'Missions to the Zulus in Natal and Zululand', reprinted from *Social Science Review*, 1865, pp. 15 and 23–4)

(C) LETTER TO JOHN WILLIAM COLENSO FROM ROBERT GRAY, BISHOP OF CAPETOWN, DECEMBER 1865

In late December 1865, Bishop Gray wrote to Bishop Colenso making a final appeal to him to retract his views and submit to the authority of the Church. Gray chose not to address Colenso personally, and the letter arrived without any name or formal greeting at its head. The letter included the following remarks.

As the time draws near in which I feel that I must take the most painful step I have ever taken in my life, my heart yearns over you; and I make this last, I fear ineffectual, attempt, to lead you to adopt one or other of the two only courses which can spare us both the pain and distress of a formal severance. My own feeling, since you entered upon the course which you have of late followed—and, I think, at first, your own also—has been, that having consciously departed from the faith of the Church of England, the true line for you, as a religious-minded man, was openly to admit this, and retire from a post which not only implied that you held that faith, but required you to see that others under you taught it. I think you must be conscious that you do not believe what the Church teaches. If you really held what it holds, you would, I am persuaded, have been shocked, and deeply pained, at what has been said of your supposed views, and at your having given any real grounds for the imputations cast upon you; and you would at once have eagerly pointed out that you had been misunderstood—misrepresented—and have declared what your real convictions were, and given to the world a full confession of your faith. You have not done this, and it leaves the impression on my mind, that you know and feel that, on the very gravest subjects and doctrines, you differ from the Church. If so, surely you ought, as a true man, to say so, and save us all the pain, anxiety, and many troubles, which your not saying so is entailing. Unless you are very much changed from what you were when we had free, confidential, and loving intercourse with each other, you will not be content to hold on to your position and endowments upon the miserable plea that the measure of the legal is the measure of the moral obligation.

But if your own judgement leads you to think that you have not departed from the truths which you have undertaken to teach, ought not the general voice of the Church on this matter to convince you?

(From G. W. Cox, *The Life of John William Colenso D.D.*, Volume 1, London, Ridgeway, 1888, pp. 375–6)

(D)   JOHN WILLIAM COLENSO'S REPLY TO ROBERT GRAY, BISHOP OF CAPETOWN, JANUARY 1866

On the opening day of 1866, Bishop Colenso replied to Bishop Gray's final letter asking him to retract to avoid excommunication. The letter was a long one, replying in detail to various matters raised by Gray, and included the following observations.

Your letter reached me on Christmas Day, just after I had come in from publishing to a crowded mass of native Christians and heathens the 'glad tidings of great joy,' and from commemorating with some of them at the Holy Table the dying love of our Lord. Though not properly addressed to myself—for it begins without even a common formula of courtesy—I read it at once and considered it; and I need not say how painfully its contents contrasted with the tenor of the Christmas song, 'Peace on earth, good will to man,'—and how soon it recalled to me the truth of our Lord's own words, 'Think not that I am come to send peace on earth. I come not to send peace but a sword.'

It must be so, then. I give you credit for doing what you believe to be your duty before God and man. I claim, in the name of Christian charity, that you shall think the same of me; that differing wholly, as we do, from one another—doing each what we think to be right—pointing out what appear to be the grave defects in each other's conduct—taking action, if need be, against each other, as we seem driven to do—we shall yet refrain, as far as possible, from judging one another with harsh and angry judgement, remembering that to one common Master we must each of us stand or fall. [...]

I cannot doubt that, as a *man,* you must feel pain, as you say, while about to take a step which, if it had the result which you anticipate—of severing me from the whole English Church and 'all the Churches of our communion throughout the world,'—would affect so seriously me and mine, after many years of hard labour in the Church at home, and in the missionary work of this diocese. That pain, I think, must be deepened by the consciousness that you have judged and condemned me *unheard.* [...]

But the *man,* alas! has too frequently, in the history of the Church, been sunk in the *theologian*; and such language as yours might be used—has been used repeatedly—by some pitiless inquisitor, while dooming a victim to the stake, and claiming for himself, and for his 'Church,' Divine authority, and the most absolute infallibility. [...]

Further, I do maintain the soundness of the principle—though you speak of it as a 'miserable plea'—that for the clergy of an Established Church, which notoriously tolerates such extreme views as are expressed within it by well-known opposite schools of theologians, whose laws are made and inforced, or, as the progress of the age in knowledge and charity may seem to require it, having first become practically relaxed by disuse, are from time to time (as in the recent case of clerical Subscription) rescinded and remodelled *by the State*—for the ministers of such a Church the measure of their legal is the only measure of their moral obligations, which others from without have a right to apply; while doubtless each clergyman, in the sanctuary of his own soul, will judge for himself how far his continuance in the active discharge of his ministerial office is consistent with his own sense of truth, and a due regard to those great objects for which, in the eyes of enlightened men, a National Church exists. [...]

You ask, 'Ought not the voice of the Church in this matter to convince you?' 'Ought you not to hear the Church?' I answer, most assuredly not, when I know by what processes that voice has been elicited; when I know that everything has been done, in England as well as here, to raise a storm of prejudice against me, without any fair attempt having been made to examine and answer my arguments; that not only the flocks, but even the clergy, have been frightened into expressing condemnation of my works without having made any personal acquaintance with them; that these Synods have simply endorsed your proceedings, well knowing that I have never been heard in my own defence, and not caring to know what my defence would be; when I see from their expressions that even his Grace the Archbishop of Canterbury, the Bishop of Oxford, and others of my brethren who have condemned me, have read my works very partially—nay, that Archdeacon Denison himself, when moving, in the Convocation of the Province of Canterbury, for a Committee to sit upon my works, did not hesitate to say, 'I have no doubt, at all events I hope, that there are many here who have not read the First Part of this work; and I am sure there are many who have not read the Second.'

No! I have no confidence in any of these judgements, and feel in no way bound to defer to the 'voice of the Church' expressed under such circumstances, even if it had been more unanimous than it really is. [...]

You put before me two alternatives, as the 'two only courses' which are open to me, by adopting one or other of which I may 'spare us both the pain and distress of a formal severance'; though I confess I do not see how the 'severance' can be more complete and 'formal' than it is now, when you have publicly denounced me in my own Cathedral as an 'infidel' and 'heretic,' 'led captive by the Evil one.'

The first of these alternatives is to resign my office, and 'withdraw of my own accord to lay communion'; though it is difficult to see how one who, according to your views, is so notorious an 'infidel' and 'heretic' can be allowed to exist even in 'lay communion' with your Church, without some 'recantation'on his part, of which you say nothing. I need hardly say, after all I have said already here and elsewhere, that I am *not* 'prepared for this.' On the contrary, I feel that it would be a dereliction of duty for me to do so—a cowardly forsaking of a post in which God's Providence and the will of my Sovereign have placed me; in which, however little such strife is congenial to my own feelings, I am called to maintain the sacred cause of religious liberty against the incroachments of the priestly system; in which I have been adjured to remain by not a few of the clergy and laity of the Church of England, men of devout mind, of deep thought, and far-reaching insight.

(From G. W. Cox, *The Life of John William Colenso D.D.*, Volume 1, London, Ridgeway, 1888, pp. 378–9, 385–6 and 387)

(E)   SERMON BY JOHN WILLIAM COLENSO, 'LOVE ABOUNDING IN KNOWLEDGE AND JUDGEMENT', 1865

This extract and the three following ones are all taken from sermons preached by Colenso in his cathedral at Pietermaritzburg after his return to Natal from England in late 1865. Each was subsequently published in either Series 1 or 2 of Colenso's Natal Sermons. This sermon was preached in St Peter's Cathedral, Pietermaritzburg on 12 November 1865.

When I say that 'the Bible contains God's Word,' I do not mean, as some have supposed, that we may pick and choose among the contents of the Bible—that we can separate those books or portions of the Bible, which *are* God's Word, from those books or portions, which are *not*. I mean that throughout the Bible the Word of God will be heard, by the listening ear and the obedient heart, reproving, exhorting, instructing, comforting; but I say that this Word is 'the spirit and the life,' which breathes in the written words, not the mere 'flesh' or letter of the words themselves. [...]

But, if God has given us so freely the knowledge of Himself in the Holy Scriptures, which His Providence has 'caused to be written for our learning,' He has also given us in this our day most wonderful illumination by the light of the different Sciences, which all come to us from Him, who is 'the Father of Lights, the Giver of every good and perfect gift.' So sudden has been the growth of this light, that, even in the childhood of many of us, the very names of many of those Sciences were hardly known. [...]

If the light of Modern Science comes from God—and surely we believe it does—it must be as great a *sin* to despise or to disregard it, as to despise and disregard the Bible. And perhaps this very light of our own days, when the Bible is in every hand, may be given us in God's gracious Providence for this reason among others, that we may not make an *idol* of it,—that we may not read it with unreasoning acquiescence in every line and letter of the book, or rather that series of books, written by different men in different ages, bound up in one, which we call the Bible, but may read it with an intelligent faith, with the understanding as well as the heart.

Thus we need not be disquieted though the progress of Modern Criticism should take from us much in the Scriptures, which perhaps without sufficient reason we had hitherto regarded as infallibly certain and true,—should show that the Scripture-writers were left to themselves, as men, in respect of all matters which God has meant to exercise our human industry, to be the objects of diligent, painstaking research. [...]

We must consider for what end the Bible is given to us, namely, to bring our spirits near to God; and we must seek, therefore, the proofs of the inspiration of its writers, not in matters of Science or History, but in those words of Eternal Life, which come to us with a power that is not of this world, and find us out in our inner being, with messages from God to the soul. [...]

I repeat, then, the views of God's character and doings, which we derive from the Bible, must be corrected and modified by those which we derive from other sources, by which He is pleased to reveal himself to

Man. It is Our Father's Will that so it should be—that our love towards Him should abound yet more and more, in the clearer, fuller, knowledge of Himself, which the study of His Works supplies to us, no less surely than the study of His Word. We cannot be truly glorifying God, if we do not make use, according to our powers and opportunities, of each of these means of growing in this knowledge.

(From J. W. Colenso, *Natal Sermons*, First Series, London, Trubner, 1867, pp. 8–10)

(F)   SERMON BY JOHN WILLIAM COLENSO, 'THE CHRISTIAN MINISTRY', 1865

This sermon was preached in St Peter's Cathedral, Pietermaritzburg on 31 December 1865.

It is God's will that we shall not have *certainty* in this world—that we shall 'walk by faith and not by sight'—that we shall 'stand by faith'—by grasping with the hand of the soul the Hand Unseen of our Father in Heaven. In this way, His Wisdom knows, we shall best be trained for our work here and for our Home hereafter. If all were made plain and clear before us,—if all were proved to demonstration beforehand,—if the senses and the understanding were thoroughly satisfied that nothing could be otherwise than as we expect or as we can calculate,—there would then be no ground for faith, for that truly human faculty which looks confidently for the final triumph of Truth and Goodness, which looks to God, the Good, the True, through all the clouds of sense, sees Him *behind* the cloud, through all the shocks of time and fate grasps His sustaining Hand. This, I say, is a truly human faculty, which as reasonable beings we all possess, each in our own measure. We have only to retire each into himself to feel that, what we see and hear and touch, and what we can infer from all which these senses tell us, is not our whole existence, is not our very selves. [...]

[...] the fear, which is (in the words of our great living poet) 'our ghastliest doubt,' is lest there should be no One in the upper sphere to receive us when we aspire towards Him,—lest we should be left in our self-degradation, to sink, and sink, unchastened, unrestrained.

Yet this fear—this 'ghastly doubt'—the adherents of the old traditionary system do not hesitate to foment, by saying, 'Unless you receive all our dicta, however revolting to reason, however contradicted by the revelations of Modern Science, you must sink into absolute Atheism, you will be left 'without hope, without God, in the world.' If 'without

God,' then 'without hope' indeed! But we have not so learned the lessons of the Gospel from the lips of Jesus Christ Himself. We 'stand by faith': but let our faith stand, not propped by the frail supports of man's devising, by the dogmas of an Infallible Book or an Infallible Church, but firmly based with its foundations deep in the Rock of God's Eternal Truth and Love. Let us trust Him who has revealed Himself to us—not in the Scriptures only, and to the hearts of our fellow-men in other ages, but in our own hearts also, as our Father and Friend, as our Faithful Creator, the object of our faith, the end of our hope, the goal of our desires,—whose children we are, whose glorious perfections are faintly shadowed forth in human excellencies,—whose Living Word, that has spoken to us 'at sundry times and in divers manners,' by the lips of prophets and apostles of old, and by the voice of Jesus Christ our Lord, is speaking to us still—commanding, reproving, exhorting, comforting,—is present even with the heathen world, as the Light of their eyes, the Life of their souls, whenever they choose the good, and reject the evil, 'walking by faith and not by sight,'—but will be heard in our hearts continually, if we will only listen, saying, 'This is the way: walk ye in it.'

(From J. W. Colenso, *Natal Sermons*, First Series, London, Trubner, 1867, pp. 120–2)

(G)   SERMON BY JOHN WILLIAM COLENSO, 'THE TEMPTATIONS OF A CHRISTIAN', 1866

This sermon was preached in St Peter's Cathedral, Pietermaritzburg on 18 February 1866. It relates to the biblical story of the temptation of Christ.

Far better will it be,—far less injurious to our moral sense, to our sense of truthfulness and honesty,—far more conducive to a spirit of devout reverence for what is excellent, to a firm belief in what is really God's Word, in the Bible,—that we should say at once that this narrative cannot be a narrative of actual fact: it is one of those numerous mythical or legendary additions to the true story of the life of our Lord, which the devout imaginations of his followers have developed in later days, while pondering in pious thought upon his work when on earth. When Jesus was about to enter on that work, in the full consciousness of His Divine Call to be the Messiah of his people, and to tell out plainly the Father's Love to the children of men, they seem to have thought that he must have been exposed to such temptations as these,—he must in the Divine Strength have overcome them. The forty days' fasting—the personal appearance of the Tempter—his words, his acts, and the answers by which his assaults were repelled,—these are but the colouring—the outward drapery, in which the substantial underlying fact was clothed, in accordance with the prevalent ideas of the time. The real fact, which lies at the basis of the narrative, is the fact of human experience, that all those who are called in the Providence of God to higher work, and gifted with greater powers, than others of their brethren, are exposed to special trials of their faithfulness, such as these which are here described,—such as these substantially, however differing in outward form. [...]

How is it, then, that we are able at once to appeal to Christ's Example, as the perfect model of what human beings ought to be, or ought to do, under all circumstances? It is because we appeal to the *spirit* of his life,—to the *principle* which ruled it,—to that conformity to the perfect Will of God, that desire to please his heavenly Father, that surrender of his own will to God's Will, which he manifested on all occasions. And, taught as we are ourselves by the Divine Word,—enlightened by the Light which is the Life of men,—we are able in our own minds to fill up that which is wanting, for our actual guidance amidst the duties of life,—to say to ourselves, in different situations, 'In this way Christ would act or would have acted.' We are able to set before us an ideal Christ, a perfect image of the Divine Man. That image of perfect beauty and holiness—of the perfect Man,—which we thus by Divine grace behold each in our own mind,—is not set before us at full length in the Gospels; nor could it possibly be: no record of his life could have supplied minutely all the details needed for this purpose,—for setting a mere *copy*, which we are closely to follow in all our different relations of life,—even if our Lord had actually entered into human relationships more fully than he has done.

(From J. W. Colenso, *Natal Sermons*, First Series, London, Trubner, 1867, pp. 313–16)

(H) SERMON BY JOHN WILLIAM COLENSO, 'SPIRITUAL RESURRECTION', 1866

This sermon was preached in St Peter's Cathedral, Pietermaritzburg on Easter Day, 1 April 1866.

I observed this morning that no one can read carefully the accounts of the Resurrection of Christ, as contained in the four Gospels, comparing them one with another, without finding that on many points they are at variance with each other, and present some very serious difficulties. That some portions, indeed, of these accounts are mere legendary additions,- which have sprung up in the common talk of Christians, who lived long after the time of the events described, can scarcely be doubted. [...]

But the one central truth in which we rejoice, the light which especially brightens and gladdens the hearts of Christian men on Easter-Day, is to know that though 'Jehovah's Servant,' the 'Messenger of the New Covenant,' the Son of Man, who brought us our Father's words of Eternal Life, was 'wounded' and 'bruised' even unto death, yet death 'had no dominion over him'; by the power of the Living Word that dwelt in him, by the glory of the Father, he overcame death, and, having died unto sin once, now liveth unto God eternally. And his triumph over death is a pledge of our own: nay, says the apostle, we are even now 'risen with Christ,' we are even now with him 'alive unto God,' and have thus the foretaste of eternal life. [...]

The hope of immortality, of a future life, is indeed unspeakably brightened by the consciousness that we are living even now a life above sense, 'in heavenly places,'—that we have even now, as St John says, 'fellowship with God,'—by the consciousness, in other words, that 'to know God *is* Life Eternal.' And the very imperfection of that fellowship in this world points to another world for its fulfilment, where, as St Paul says, we shall see face to face, instead of as now through a glass darkly, where we shall know, not as now in part, but even as we are known.

(From J. W. Colenso, *Natal Sermons*, Second Series, London, Trubner, 1868, pp. 122)

(I) LETTER FROM JOHN WILLIAM COLENSO TO A. P. STANLEY, DEAN OF WESTMINSTER, 17 DECEMBER 1874

While Bishop Colenso was in England in 1874 to present his version of the Langalibalele affair to the Colonial Office in person, several bishops, including the Bishop of London, reissued inhibitions preventing him from preaching in churches in their dioceses. A. P. Stanley, however, in a characteristic protest against this policy, invited Colenso to preach in Westminster Abbey—which lay outside the jurisdiction and authority of the Bishop of London. Colenso, as this extract shows, declined the invitation. In doing so he also provided a summary of both the paternalism and the idealism in his understanding of imperialism, a clear indication of the relationship between these and his religious beliefs, and evidence that—whatever his opponents might say—he was not motivated by a simple thirst for controversy.

I have come to the conclusion that I had better decline to comply with your kind request. I need hardly say that under other circumstances I should have gladly carried out your wishes. I might, perhaps, have tried to say a few words to comfort the hearts of some who, at this great crisis of religious thought in England, are looking anxiously to their spiritual advisers for help in their uncertainty. I might also have tried to impress upon my fellow-countrymen the duty which we owe, as English Christians, towards the inferior races under our charge; to say that surely the rule of a nation like ours over so many weaker communities means something more than the amount of property, of material wealth, she can squeeze out of the subject peoples; that if England extends her sway over the earth to inforce justice, to practise mercy, to show care and pity for the weak and helpless, to redress the wrongs of the downtrodden and oppressed, and to raise her dependents in the scale of humanity, there is then a reason for the existence of her vast colonial empire; that it is only such acts as these which will show that our religion is a reality and not a mere name; and that the passionate love of justice which God has planted in the bosom of his children is a sign that our Father thinks and feels as we do. But there are others who will teach these things when I am gone. I did not come home to assert my own personal position in the Church of England, if that were doubtful which has been recognised by his Grace the Primate of All England, and, above all, by the Crown; and I have no wish whatever to occupy the few remaining days of my stay in England with any such contention as might seem to be implied by my preaching at Westminster after the recent action of the Bishop of London, though, of course, I am aware that you are not under his jurisdiction. I therefore think it best not to avail myself of the invitation which you have given me to preach in the venerable Abbey so dear to the memories of Englishmen; and I shall return to my diocese rejoicing that I have been permitted to bear to England the cry of the oppressed, and thankful that by English hearts that cry has been heard and answered.

(From G. W. Cox, *The Life of John William Colenso D.D.*, Volume 2, London, Ridgway, 1888, pp. 394–5)

5 PROFESSOR FRIEDRICH MAX MÜLLER

(A) FRIEDRICH MAX MÜLLER ON THE STUDY OF RELIGIONS, 1869

This extract is taken from the Preface to a collection of essays by F. Max Müller, which had been published separately during the previous fifteen years but were bound together in one volume in 1869 under the title Chips from a German Workshop: Volume 1 Essays on the Science of Religion. *As the Preface makes clear, the volume enabled Müller to bring together his ideas concerning both the history of languages and the history of religions and was designed to promote a more general and sympathetic study of ancient religions.*

To the missionary, more particularly, a comparative study of the religious of mankind will be, I believe, of the greatest assistance. Missionaries are apt to look upon all other religions as something totally distinct from their own, as formerly they used to describe the languages of barbarous nations as something more like the twittering of birds than the articulate speech of men. The Science of Language has taught us that there is order and wisdom in all languages, and even the most degraded jargons contain the ruins of former greatness and beauty. The Science of Religion, I hope, will produce a similar change in our views of barbarous forms of faith and worship; and missionaries, instead of looking only for points of difference, will look out more anxiously for any common ground, any spark of the true light that may still be revived, any altar that may be dedicated afresh to the true God.[8]

And even to us at home, a wider view of the religious life of the world may teach many a useful lesson. Immense as is the difference between our own and all other religions of the world—and few can know that difference who have not honestly examined the foundations of their own

---

[8] Joguth Chundra Gangooly, a native convert, says: "I know from personal experience that the Hindu Scriptures have a great deal of truth. ... If you go to India, and examine the common sayings of the people, you will be surprised to see what a splendid religion the Hindu religion must be. Even the most ignorant women have proverbs that are full of the purest religion. Now I am not going to India to injure their feelings by saying, 'Your Scripture is all nonsense, is good for nothing; anything outside the Old and New Testament is a humbug.' No; I tell you I will appeal to the Hindu philosophers, and moralists, and poets, at the same time bringing to them my light, and reasoning with them in the spirit of Christ. That will be my work."–"A Brief Account of Joguth Chundra Gangooly, a Brahmin and a Covert to Christianity." *Christian Reformer*, August, 1860.

as well as of other religions—the position which believers and unbelievers occupy with regard to their various forms of faith is very much the same all over the world. The difficulties which trouble us, have troubled the hearts and minds of men as far back as we can trace the beginnings of religious life. The great problems touching the relation of the Finite to the Infinite, of the human mind as the recipient, and of the Divine Spirit as the source of truth, are old problems indeed; and while watching their appearance in different countries, and their treatment under varying circumstances, we shall be able, I believe, to profit ourselves, both by the errors which others committed before us, and by the truth which they discovered. We shall know the rocks that threaten every religion in this changing and shifting world of ours, and having watched many a storm of religious controversy and many a shipwreck in distant seas, we shall face with greater calmness and prudence the troubled waters at home.

If there is one thing which a comparative study of religions places in the clearest light, it is the inevitable decay to which every religion is exposed. It may seem almost like a truism, that no religion can continue to be what it was during the lifetime of its founder and its first apostles. Yet it is but seldom borne in mind that without constant reformation, *i.e.* without a constant return to its fountain-head, every religion, even the most perfect, nay the most perfect on account of its very perfection, more even than others, suffers from its contact with the world, as the purest air suffers from the mere fact of its being breathed.

Whenever we can trace back a religion to its first beginnings, we find it free from many of the blemishes that offend us in its later phases. The founders of the ancient religions of the world, as far as we can judge, were minds of a high stamp, full of noble aspirations, yearning for truth, devoted to the welfare of their neighbors, examples of purity and unselfishness. What they desired to found upon earth was but seldom realized, and their sayings, if preserved in their original form, offer often a strange contrast to the practice of those who profess to be their disciples. As soon as a religion is established, and more particularly when it has become the religion of a powerful state, the foreign and worldly elements encroach more and more on the original foundation, and human interests mar the simplicity and purity of the plan which the founder had conceived in his own heart, and matured in his communings with his God. [...]

If missionaries could show to the Brahmans, the Buddhists, the Zoroastrians, nay, even to the Mohammedans, how much their present faith differs from the faith of their forefathers and founders; if they could place in their hands and read with them in a kindly spirit the original documents on which these various religions profess to be founded, and enable them to distinguish between the doctrines of their own sacred books and the additions of later ages; an important advantage would be gained, and the choice between Christ and other Masters would be rendered far more easy to many a truth seeking soul. But for that purpose it is necessary that we too should see the beam in our own eyes, and learn to distinguish between the Christianity of the nineteenth century and the religion of Christ. If we find that the Christianity of the nineteenth century does not win as many hearts in India and China as it ought, let us remember that it was the Christianity of the first century in all its dogmatic simplicity, but with its overpowering love of God and man, that conquered the world and superseded religions and philosophies, more difficult to conquer than the religious and philosophical systems of Hindus and Buddhists.

(From F. Max Müller, *Chips from a German Workshop: Volume 1 Essays on the Science of Religion*, 1869, reprinted Chico (CA), Scholars Press, 1985, pp. xxi–iii and xxiv–v)

(B)   FRIEDRICH MAX MÜLLER ON MISSIONARIES, 1887

This is an extract from a speech by F. Max Müller given at a missionary meeting in St John's College, Oxford, in 1887. The text of the speech was cited by Müller's wife and biographer as providing a clear account of Müller's views about Christian mission to other religions.

After a long experience in life, I have been led to divide all my friends, missionaries included, into two classes—those who seem to have eyes for all that is good, and those who seem to have eyes for all that is bad. Well, you all know the men I mean. If you go with them to a concert, they will speak of nothing but the wrong notes. If you go with them to church, the first they tell you is what the preacher ought not to have said. I have been a guide through Oxford for many years, and in watching my friends from every part of the globe, I found they fell into two classes, what I call the *bright-eyed* and the *dark-eyed*. The *dark-eyed* tell you that the Oxford buildings are all in rags, that the stone decays and is hideous. They point out incongruities in architectural style, they are scandalized at the attire of the undergraduates coming home in crowds from football, and they wonder whether all University lectures are given in the Park, because they see undergraduates nowhere else. But there are others, whom I call my *bright-eyed* friends, who admire the effects of light and shade on the crumbling old stones, who read history in the incongruities of architectural style, who approve of the bones and sinews of our athletes, and who express real regret that they could have heard only one of Professor Palgrave's lectures, or one of the Bishop of Ripon's sermons. Now I need not tell you which of these two classes I like best, and I may add that I generally find that the really great artists and scholars and statesmen are bright-eyed, the smaller artists, scholars, and statesmen dark-eyed. [...]

We need not wonder, therefore, if missionaries too are dark-eyed and bright-eyed. Some see only the darkness of the night, others the brightness of the stars, even if so dim that ordinary eyes can hardly perceive them. I shall to-night appeal to Dr. Codrington and Mr. Cousins to tell us something, however little it may be, of the bright side, something of what St. Augustine meant when he said that there is no religion which does not contain some truth. They have been so long among heathens that they must have seen more than the mere surface of their religion. They must surely have met some God-fearing men, some pure-minded women, some human creatures to prove that St. Paul was right in saying that God never left Himself without witness, and that St. Peter perceived a great truth when he boldly declared that in every nation he that feareth God and worketh righteousness is accepted with God.

(From G. A. Müller (ed.) *The Life and Letters of the Right Honourable Friedrich Max Müller Edited by his Wife*, Volume II, New York, London and Bombay, Longmans, Green, 1902, pp. 480–1)

(C)   FRIEDRICH MAX MÜLLER ON THE TERMS FOR CONVERSION TO CHRISTIANITY, 1899

The extract is taken from a letter written by F. Max Müller to P. C. Mozoomdar, a leading light in the Hindu theistic movement, the Brahma Samaj, with whom Müller developed a close friendship. In this letter, Müller makes explicit the terms on which he expects Hindu admirers of Jesus to be able to make a profession of Christian faith.

Now it seems to me that the first thing you have to do is to try to remove the differences that still exist among yourselves, and to settle how much of your ancient religion you are willing to give up, if not as utterly false, still as antiquated. You have given up a great deal, polytheism, idolatry, and your elaborate sacrificial worship. You have surrendered also, as far as I can judge, the claim of divine revelation which had been so carefully formulated by your ancient theologians in support of the truth of the *Vedas*. These were great sacrifices, for whatever may be thought of your ancient traditions, to give up what we have been taught by our fathers and mothers, requires a very strong conviction, and a very strong will. But though this surrender has brought you much nearer to us, there still remain many minor points on which you differ among yourselves in your various *samdjes* or congregations. Allow me to say that these differences seem to me to have little to do with real religion; still they must be removed, because they prevent united action on your part. ... If you are once united among yourselves, you need no longer trouble about this or that missionary, whether he come from London, Rome, Geneva, or Moscow. They all profess to bring you the Gospel of Christ. Take then the New Testament and read it for yourselves, and judge for yourselves whether the words of Christ, as contained in it, satisfy you or not.

I know that you yourself, as well as Rammohun Roy and Keshub Chunder Sen, have done that. I know one countryman of yours who wrote a searching criticism on the Old and New Testaments, and then joined the Christian Church, as established in England, because there was something in the teaching and life of Christ which he could not withstand. I know this is not an argument, yet it is something to reflect on.

Christ comes to you as He comes to us in the only trustworthy records preserved of Him in the Gospels. We have not even the right to dictate our interpretation of these Gospels to you, particularly if we consider how differently we interpret them ourselves. If you accept His teachings, as there recorded, you are a Christian. There is no necessity whatever of your being formally received into the membership of one or the other sect of the Christian Church, whether reformed or unreformed. That will only delay the growth of Christianity in India. All that has grown up in the Church after the death of Christ, or the Apostles, does not concern you. You will want, no doubt, some kind of constitution, some government, some Church or Somâj. Have a baptism, or *Upanayana*, if you please, as an outward sign of the new life which baptism signified among the early Christians, and which was well known also to your great teachers of old. Remember, before all things, that you can be followers of Christ, without being Roman Catholics, Anglo-Catholics, or Greek Orthodox Catholics, without assuming the names and fashions of Presbyterians, Congrega-tionalists, Unitarians, or any other Dissenters. Keep aloof of all of them, they have proved only stumbling-blocks in the progress of Christianity. Keshub Chunder Sen used to say that, after all, Christ was in many respects an Oriental, and was better understood by Orientals than by Occidentals. Whether this be true or not, you have, at all events, as much right to constitute and regulate your own Church, your own Parishads, your own Samgha, as the Greeks, in their time, had at Alexandria, or the Romans at Rome. You have nothing to do with popes, bishops, priests, ministers, *et hoc genus omne,* unless for some reason or other you wish, besides being Christians, to belong to one of the historical associations also that have sprung up. ... I do not like to appear sailing under false colours. I am, myself, a devoted member of the English Church, because I think its members enjoy greater freedom and more immunity from priestcraft than those of any other Church. There are, no doubt, many things in that Church also, which still require reformation. But though we are not altogether free from the evils that seem inseparable from the establishment of any priesthood, we have thrown off many of the hideous accretions which nearly took the life out of Christianity during the long night of the dark ages. The real Church, you should remember, before you take any steps towards framing a constitution of your own, consists of the laity alone. It was the laity that appointed its ministers, but these original ministers—such is human nature—have almost invariably become the masters of their masters. The English Church, however, though it has sometimes forgotten the supreme and indefeasible rights of the laity, has never surrendered them formally and altogether; and the highest seat of authority, in matters of faith as well as of public worship, has always remained with the laity and the civil powers, and has never been surrendered formally to the clergy. ... Try whether you cannot join the Church of England as lay members, but have nothing to do with their ecclesiastical constitutions, and keep aloof of all discussions on so-called orders or their validity. Lay members of the English Church are perfectly free, and I have never repented having joined it. ...

Only remember, that there is no reason whatever, why you, in forming your own Christian Church, should join any of the European Churches. That idea is what has delayed your progress so long.

(From G. A. Müller (ed.) *The Life and Letters of the Right Honourable Friedrich Max Müller Edited by his Wife,* Volume II, New York, London and Bombay, Longmans, Green, 1902, pp. 412–14)

(D) MONIER WILLIAMS'S AND FRIEDRICH MAX MÜLLER'S SUBMISSIONS TO THE MEMBERS OF CONVOCATION OF THE UNIVERSITY OF OXFORD, 1860

In their submissions to the Convocation of the University of Oxford during 1860, Monier Williams and F. Max Müller set forth their respective claims to become the next Boden Professor in Sanskrit at the University. Both attempted to demonstrate the relevance of their scholarly achievements to date. Whereas Müller pointed to his international reputation as a translator of Vedic Sanskrit, Monier Williams stressed his close personal connections with India and his experience as a teacher of Sanskrit. Although both committed themselves to promoting the cause of Christianity in India, it was Monier Williams who committed himself explicitly and more wholeheartedly to fulfilling the conditions laid down by the Founder of the Boden Chair.

GENTLEMEN,

In offering myself as a Candidate for the Boden Professorship of Sanskrit, now vacant, I respectfully lay before you a few particulars which bear upon my fitness for that office.

Having been born in India (the son of the late Lieutenant-Colonel Monier Williams, Surveyor-General of Bombay), my earliest thoughts and studies were directed towards the East. I was presented to an Indian writership in 1840, and was therefore compelled to leave Balliol College, Oxford, (where I had resided for a year and a half,) to proceed as a student to the East India College, Haileybury, where I gained the first prizes in all the Oriental subjects. In consequence of the death of a brother in one of the battles of India, I resigned my writership in 1841, and returned to Oxford, where I became a member of University College and took my Degree in 1844.

During my second residence at Oxford my attention continued to be directed to Oriental studies, and in 1843 I was elected to one of the Boden Scholarships.

In 1844 I was appointed to an Oriental Professorship at Haileybury College, where I remained for about 14 years, till the abolition of that Institution. In the first year of my appointment my duties were to lecture in Sanskrit, Persian and Hindústání. In the last 13 years I was employed exclusively in the Sanskrit department.

As Haileybury College usually numbered from 80 to 100 students, and as every student was compelled to pass a prescribed test in Sanskrit, an amount of experience has been gained by me in teaching the Sanskrit language, which could not have been acquired at any other place of education. From the first moment of my appointment to the Haileybury Professorship, the one idea of my life has been to make myself thoroughly conversant with Sanskrit, and by every means in my power to facilitate the study of its literature.

With this view I have published a Grammar, a Dictionary (the former of which was brought out under the patronage of the Delegates of the

Oxford Press, and the latter under that of the East India Company,) and various other Oriental works, a list of which is annexed.

In 1855, when the new system of competition for the Indian Civil Service was introduced, I was selected by the Government to examine in Sanskrit, and I have held the appointment of Sanskrit Examiner for five years consecutively.

Having commenced my career as a Scholar on the foundation of Colonel Boden, I owe a deep debt of gratitude to the munificent benefactor, who provided for the perpetual study of Sanskrit in the University of Oxford, and if I am elected to the Boden Professorship, my utmost energies shall be devoted to the one object which its Founder had in view;—namely, "*The promotion of a more general and critical knowledge of the Sanskrit Language, as a means of enabling Englishmen to proceed in the conversion of the natives of India to the Christian religion.*"

I have the honour to be,

Gentlemen,

Your faithful Servant,

MONIER WILLIAMS.

(From M. Monier-Williams, Miscellaneous papers, press cuttings and articles covering the life and work of Sir M. Monier-Williams and especially the foundation and early history of the Indian Institute, Oxford (on microfilm in the Indian Institute Library, University of Oxford))

To the Members of Convocation

I beg most respectfully to offer myself as a Candidate for the Boden Professorship of Sanskrit, vacant by the lamented death of Professor H.H.W.

During the last thirteen years I have been employed by the East India Company in editing, for the first time, the text and commentary of the Rig-Veda, "the oldest authority," according to Professor Wilson, "for the religious and social institutions of the Hindus." That work is described by the Minute of the Court of Directors as "in a peculiar manner deserving of the patronage of the East India Company, connected as it is with the early religion, history and language of the great body of their Indian subjects," The Veda is, in fact, to the Hindus what the Koran is to the Mohammedans.

Considering that without this work a complete knowledge of the religious teaching of the Brahmans could not be acquired, and that the want of it has hitherto proved a serious bar to Missionary exertions, I may perhaps be permitted to think that I have spent the principal part of my life in promoting the object of the Founder of the Chair of Sanskrit. Three volumes of my edition of the Rig-Veda have appeared; three more remain to be published. Professor Wilson has been at the same time preparing from my text an English translation, of which three volumes have been printed.

I am likewise engaged in the Catalogue of the large collection of Vedic Sanskrit MSS. at the Bodleian Library, which will demand much time and labour for many years. A list of my other works will be found below.

In seeking this Chair my wish is to devote myself entirely, as I did before my appointment to the Taylorian Professorship of Modern Languages and Literature, to the study of Sanskrit, and the completion of works connected with it.

I shall lose no time in collecting Testimonials from the most eminent Sanskrit scholars in Europe and India, and submitting them to Members of Convocation. I shall likewise submit Testimonials from Missionaries in India, explaining the assistance they have derived from my publications in their endeavours to overthrow the ancient systems of idolatry still prevalent in that country, and to establish the truths of Christianity among the believers of the Veda.

MAX MÜLLER, FELLOW OF ALL SOULS COLLEGE,
M.A. CHRIST CHURCH

ALL SOULS COLLEGE
May 16 1860
(From F. Max Müller, The Papers of Friedrich Max Müller (1823–1900). Testimonials and letters relating to the election of the Boden Professorship of Sanskrit at Oxford, 1860–1 (98 leaves:MS.Eng.c.2807, Bodleian Library, University of Oxford))

6   ISLAM AND SOUTH ASIAN RELIGIONS IN VICTORIAN BRITAIN

(A)   J. SALTER ON THE ASIATIC IN ENGLAND, 1873

This account is taken from Joseph Salter's description of Muslim prayer being performed by a retainer of the Nawab of Surat. Salter visited the London residence of the Nawab on several occasions in his role as a Christian missionary to Asians visiting Britain and also to receive instruction in Hindustani. He died in 1899.

To this strange group may be added Mishameeram, the old man who attended to the door. He was of a very religious spirit, and seemed to pray for the whole suite. His prayers were most earnest and rapid, and very frequent; for he was mostly praying, especially after supper. I never heard any other in this suite pray. He used to place a small form in an eastern direction, and then cover it with an ornamented green cloth; then, minus his slippers, but adorned with his white turban, he would mount the form, and, with his face eastward, would commence his incantations by three invocations of Mohammed. His prayers would be performed in various attitudes, sometimes standing erect with his arms straight down, at other times he would sit on his heels, with his hands on his thighs, and in his prostrations his forehead, knees, and toes would sustain the weight of the rest of his body. His articulations were so excessively quick, sometimes only a mumble, that I never could catch a word he said. If the company wished to ask him a question, he had not objection to suspend his prayer for a minute to answer it; or if he wished to ask a question himself on any subject that had just occurred to his mind, he would rather make the inquiry in the midst of his prayer than run the risk of forgetting it. Should, however, a knock come to the door, or anything required to be done that did not require his tongue to perform it, he lost no time, for he would descend from his form and discontinue his prayers till he returned again. He was quite satisfied if he were but permitted to begin and terminate his prayers on his sacerdotal form. Such was the singular scene in the Nawab's kitchen nearly every night. My own presence, perhaps, in such an unusual group, might complete the scene. Generally I occupied one end of a long table, capable of seating about fifteen persons, Mohammed Shah would be at my side, while the opposite end was occupied by the card-players, the interval being usually filled up by tea and coffee drinkers and smokers. Sometimes the riot and the fumes were so intolerable that I could not get on with my reading, nor could Mishameeram proceed with his prayers, and I was compelled to retire into an adjacent room with my pupil.

(From J. Salter, *The Asiatic in England: Sketches of Sixteen Years' Work Among Orientals*, London, Seeley, Jackson & Halliday, 1873, pp. 48–9)

(B)   SISTER NIVEDITA ON 'HOW AND WHY I ADOPTED THE HINDU RELIGION', 1902

Sister Nivedita (Margaret Noble, b. 1867) was an Irish educationalist who adopted the Hindu religious philosophy of Swami Vivekananda whom she heard speak in London in 1896. Before following him to India, she was one of a small knot of British disciples who tried to keep Swami Vivekananda's message alive in Britain. In this extract and the following one, she explains to Hindu audiences how she came to reject Christianity in favour of the Hindu religious philosophy of Swami Vivekananda.

I am a born and bred English woman and unto the age of eighteen, I was trained and educated as English girls are. Christian religious doctrines were of course early instilled into me. I was even from my girlhood inclined to venerate all religious teachings and I devotedly worshipped the child Jesus and loved Him with my whole heart for the self-sacrifices He always willingly underwent, while I felt I could not worship Him enough for His crucifying Himself to bestow salvation on the human race. But after the age of eighteen, I began to harbour doubts as to the truth of the Christian doctrines. Many of them began to seem to me false and incompatible with truth. These doubts grew stronger and stronger and at the same time my faith in Christianity tottered more and more. For seven years I was in this wavering state of mind, very unhappy, and yet, very very eager to seek the Truth. I shunned going to Church and yet sometimes my longing to bring restfulness to my spirit impelled me to rush into Church and be absorbed in the service to feel at peace within, as I had hitherto done, and as others around me were doing. But alas! no peace, no rest was there for my troubled soul all eager to know the truth.

During the seven years of wavering it occurred to me that in the study of natural science I should surely find the truth I was seeking. So, ardently I began to study how this world was created and all things in it and I discovered that in the laws of Nature at least there was consistency, but it made the doctrines of the Christian religion seem all the more inconsistent. Just then I happened to get a life of Buddha and in it I found that here, alas, also was there a child who lived ever so many centuries before the child Christ, but whose sacrifices were no less self-abnegating than those of the other. This dear child Gautama took a strong hold on me and for three more years I plunged myself into the study of the religion of Buddha, and I became more and more convinced that the salvation he preached was decidedly more consistent with the truth than the preachings of the Christian religion.

And now came the turning point for my faith. A cousin of your great Viceroy Lord Ripon invited me to have tea with him and to meet there a great Swami from India who, he said, might perhaps help the search my soul was longing for. The Swami I met here was none other than Swami Vivekananda who afterwards became my Guru and whose teachings have given relief my doubting spirit had been longing for so long. Yet it was not during one visit or two that my doubts were dispelled. Oh no! I had several warm discussions with him and I pondered on his teachings for more than a year. Then he asked me to visit India, to see the Yogis and to study the subject in the very country of its birth, and I found, at last, a faith I could lean upon and obtain my Mukti through the uplifting of the spirit till it is merged into Ananda. Now I have told you how and why I have adopted this religion of yours. If you care to hear more, I would gladly go on.

(From Sister Nivedita, *The Complete Works*, Volume 2, Calcutta, Rama-krishna Sarada Mission Sister Nivedita's Girls School, 2nd edn, 1972, pp. 460–1)

(C) SISTER NIVEDITA ON VEDANTA MISSIONARY WORK, 1897

To not a few of us the words of Swami Vivekananda came as living water to men perishing of thirst. Many of us had been conscious for years past of that growing uncertainty and despair, with regard to Religion, which has beset the intellectual life of Europe for half a century. Belief in the dogmas of Christianity has become impossible to us, and we had no tool, such as we now hold, by which to cut away the doctrinal shell from the kernel of Reality in our Faith. To these, the Vedanta has given intellectual conformation and philosophical expression of their own mistrusted intuitions. "The peoples that walked in darkness have seen a great light." So that, if it had done no more, merely by enlargement of our religious culture, this system of thought would have been of incalculable benefit to us. But it has done much more.

We have not all shared that spirit of doubt and negation which is certainly the characteristic thought mood of cultured Europe today. Many gentle souls are able to adapt the religious instruction of childhood to their own mental growth, and these, without any anguished sense of rupture from truths and associations, gain a generous outlook, and a readiness to get truth from whatever quarter of the horizon it may hail. To these (the two classes are not of course entirely distinct), it has not been the intellectual basis of Belief as a whole, but special ideas, that have come as great inspirations, throwing light upon all previous experience, and opening the door to the acceptance of Vedantic doctrine as a whole.

(From Sister Nivedita, *The Complete Works*, Volume 2, Calcutta, Ramakrishna Sarada Mission Sister Nivedita's Girls School, 2nd edn, 1972, pp. 389–90; reproduced from *Brahmavadin*, 15 September 1897)

(D)   ABDULLAH QUILLIAM, 'MINUTES OF AGM', 1896

This reading is taken from the report of the Annual General Meeting of the Liverpool Muslim Institute in 1896 as published in the Institute's own journal. In this extract, Abdullah (formerly William) Quilliam (b. 1856), a Manx convert to Islam and the founder of the Muslim Institute, responds vigorously to Christian prejudice against Islam. He argues that the unity of Islam will ensure its ultimate supremacy. In this context, as leader of British Muslims (Sheikh-ul-Islam of the British Isles), he justifies his fatwa *(Islamic legal judgement), in which he condemned all who abetted the British government in deploying Egyptian Muslim soldiers against fellow Muslims in the Sudan during the campaign to pacify the Sudan after the Mahdi's uprising.*

The first efforts to establish Islam in this country were regarded and stigmatised by them [Christian clerics] as the foolish efforts of a lunatic, and I was regarded as a fit subject for a straight jacket and incarceration in a cell in an asylum for imbeciles. The simple existence of a Muslim Society in England mainly composed of Englishmen, however, focussed attention upon the principles of the religion. It caused enquiries to be made, and then the consistent and regular progress of Islam throughout the world began to be noted, and enquirers discovered that things were not as they had been represented, that Islam was a living faith, standing on the vantage ground of simplicity and truth (applause). The clerics no longer laugh at us. They now see that their craft is in danger, and one of the leading Christian ecclesiastics of the present day—no less a personage than the Archbishop of Canterbury, the head of the Anglican church—has on several recent occasions spoken strongly on this matter. His last important utterance upon the subject was at a recent meeting of the Society for the Propagation of the Gospel, when he solemnly and seriously warned his auditors about the power and spirit of Islam. "All," said he, "that has been said of the extreme difficulty of making the slightest impression upon the rock of Islamism has been verified a thousand-fold. It is a rock beneath which are volcanic forces of the most terrible kind, as has been seen in the almost complete wiping out, if we are correctly informed, of one of the most ancient Christian churches." His Grace was referring here, of course, to the Armenians. "In Mohammedanism," the Archbishop declared, "there lies a double difficulty. There is its thorough belief in extermination, and also a very high degree of cultivation, for the culture of its leaders is as marvellous as the fanaticism of its rank and file." This last utterance was doubtless a revelation to many of the Archbishop's auditors. Not a few good Christian simpletons mistakenly look upon all Muslims as semi-savage, untutored folk (laughter). They are, indeed, vastly mistaken. To use a Koranical quotation, we may say—"The likeness of these people is like unto an ass laden with books" (renewed laughter). But by far the most impressive words spoken by his Grace of Canterbury at this meeting were the following, which I feel I must quote to you in all their naked and tremendous forcefulness:—"I hope, " he exclaimed, "that interest of the church will be more and more concentrated on this question, *for unless Christianity can make an impression on Mahomedanism, Christianity is destined to see Christ's promise fail, that the gates of hell shall not prevail against it.*" Very strong language for an Archbishop, but then "desperate diseases always require desperate remedies" (applause). I fear that our Muslim brethren throughout the world do not thoroughly appreciate their own strength. It is high time they did so. We are numerically and socially the most compact religious body in the world. United under a trusted leader we could bid defiance to any combination of Christian sects or countries. They talk of the union of Christendom. It is a good phrase, but will never be ought else. But the union of Islam might easily become an accomplished fact. The differences of our schools of thought are so slight that they should soon be smoothed over and adjusted. [...] Islam teaches that in things essential there must be unity, and every Muslim [... agrees] that God is one and Mahomed is His Prophet. In things doubtful Islam gives liberty of thought, and in all things it inculcates charity and forbearance. "Let there be no violence in religion," are the inspired words of the Koran, luminously standing forward as though they were written in letters of living light upon the pages of the sacred volume (applause). I call upon our brethren throughout the world to promote such an union! The Muslim's first duty is to God and Islam. The first thing necessary in order to bring about the crowning victory of Islam in the world is to carry out in its absolute entirety and in its fullest sense the immortal truth, "Verily the True Believers are brethren." Let no Muslim be even a consenting, much less an assisting, party to the injury of another Muslim by a stranger to the faith. This is Muslim law; let it be equally Muslim practice (applause). We have a lamentable example before us at the present time of the evils of disunion. I allude to the position of affairs in Egypt and the Soudan. The Khalifa, who has expressed his willingness to conform to the ruling of his suzerain lord, the Sultan of Turkey and Caliph of the Faithful, as represented by the authority of his representative, the Khedive, is being attacked by the Muslim soldiers of Egypt, not by the desire either of the Egyptian *de jure* rulers or people, but at the command of interlopers and strangers, aliens by birth, race and creed, but who are nevertheless the *de facto* rulers of *Dar-ul-Misr*. My attention was officially called to this matter, and I deemed it to be my duty to issue the following proclamation upon the subject:—

In the name of Allah, most merciful, most compassionate!

Peace to all True Believers to whom this shall come!

Know ye, O Muslims, that the British Government has decided to commence military and warlike operations against the Muslims of the Soudan, who have taken up arms to defend their country and their faith. And it is in contemplation to employ Muslim soldiers to fight against these Muslims of the Soudan.

For any True Believer to take up arms and fight against another Muslim who is not in revolt against the Khalif is contrary to the Shariat, and against the law of God and His holy Prophet.

I warn every True Believer that if he gives the slightest assistance in this projected expedition against the Muslims of the Soudan, even to the extent of carrying a parcel, or giving a bite of bread or a drink of water to any person taking part in the expedition against these Muslims, that he thereby helps the Giaour against the Muslim, and his name will be unworthy to be continued on the roll of the faithful.

Signed at the Mosque in Liverpool, England, this 10th day of Shawall, 1313 (which Christians erroneously in their ignorance call the 24th day of March, 1896),

W. H. Abdullah Quilliam, Sheikh-ul-Islam of the British Isles.

The publication of this proclamation caused considerable interest, especially abroad. Within a fortnight of its having been issued I received letters from Muslims in Bulgaria, France, Greece, and Crete congratulating me upon the declaration thus made. The Islamic press in many countries translated and republished the document. Three of the Paris newspapers devoted leading articles to the subject, and many of the English papers also alluded to it. From no Muslim country or individual True-Believer was there a dissenting word or an antagonistic word, save in India. The press of that country, which was under the control of Europeans and Christians, naturally shrieked and tore their passion to tatters. This might of course be expected. According to some of them, "Only my very insignificance saved me from being prosecuted for high treason," while one of the Hindoo papers suggested that a sound flogging and a long imprisonment with a diet of bread and water might be found a wholesome corrective. [...]

However, three of the Indian Muslim papers also took up the chorus, and with a desire to parade their own loyalty, at once announced that they washed their hands of the whole affair, and disclaimed any sympathy with the terms of the proclamation. [...] They considered—doubtless, honestly thought—that I had committed a strategical error in making my patriotism subservient to my religious convictions. I think otherwise, and I am confirmed in my opinion by the recollection that the Prophet said—"Moslems are brothers in religion; and they must not oppress one another, nor abandon assisting each other, nor hold one another in contempt. The seat of righteousness is the heart; therefore that heart which is righteous does not hold a Moslem in contempt; and it is wicked to hold a Moslem in contempt; and all things of one Moslem are unlawful to another, his blood, property, and reputation; he must not act or speak that by which the blood of a Moslem might be spilt, and his property destroyed and his reputation lost." (Applause.) In Islam we are each entitled to enjoy our own opinion and to reasonably express it. Time, that great revealer of secrets, will yet show which of us was correct in our judgement. I await the issue with patience (applause). [...]

Notwithstanding these few Indian press strictures, it is a remarkable fact that, while I have received numerous letters from India approving of my action in this matter, I have not received one condemning it, and only one which advised me "to leave politics alone and confine myself simply to preaching Islam." This is not and has never been a question of politics with me. It is purely and solely a question of religion. I decline to stand dumb and see Muslim set against Muslim in fratricidal strife, embroiled in a quarrel for which there is no cause, at the bidding of any *Giaour* or nation of *Giaours*. The person who would cowardly hold his peace on such an occasion I regard as unworthy of the name of a man and a True-Believer. I believe in the complete union of Islam, and of all Muslim peoples; for this I pray, for this I work, and this I believe will yet be accomplished. In England we enjoy the blessed privilege of a free press, with liberty to express our thoughts in a reasonable way, and this advantageous position can be used for the purpose of promoting the entire re-union of Muslim peoples. The True-Believers are scattered all over the world, in the ice-bound land of the white Czar, as well as under the burning sun at the Equator. In the Islands of the West Indies and in British Guiana, in the sandy deserts of Western Australia or the fertile valley of the Nile, the Negro, the Arab, the Indian, the warlike African, brave Turk, polite Persian, and the Moor all join in the Fatheha, and turn their face Mecca wards five times each twenty-four hours. From Liverpool our steamers and trading vessels journey to each part of the world, and here within the walls of this Institution who knows but that the scattered cords may not be able to be gathered together and woven into a strong rope, *Al-Habbulmateen*, of fraternal union.

> "There's a light about to glow,
> There's a fount about to flow,
> There's a midnight blackness changing into grey;
> Men of thought and men of action clear the way."

This is no idle dream on my part; it is a feasible project, which only requires unity of purpose and effort on the part of True Muslims to be made an accomplished fact. Here in Liverpool, brethren, let us do our part to bring about this glorious consummation of our hopes. 'Tis true that it is not in mortals to command success, but all can work so as to deserve it (applause). Let your fixed determination be to work shoulder to shoulder—

> "Hand to hand united,
> Heart to heart as one"—

Always pressing forwards, undaunted by obstacles, not discouraged by no immediate success, working and praying, working and waiting, but always working and striving, having your eyes fixed upon the ultimate goal of your endeavours, THE WORLD FOR ISLAM.

(From *Islamic World*, Vol. IV, No. 39, July 1896, pp. 84–90)

(E)   ABDULLAH QUILLIAM, 'HYMN FOR THE PROPHET'S BIRTHDAY'

Members of the Liverpool Muslim Institute gathered for prayer according to Islamic custom but also held open meetings designed to appeal to individuals more familiar with Christianity. In presenting the teaching of Islam at these open meetings, hymns were used that had either been specially composed or suitably adapted from well-known Christian hymns. Abdullah Quilliam, the founder of the Muslim Institute, was responsible for several of these 'Muslim hymns'. This example and the following one are taken from the Institute's journal, the Islamic World.

> The people that in darkness sat
> A glorious light have seen;
> God's prophet now to them hath come—
> Muhamed, Al Emin.
>
> We hail thee, Allah's prophet true,
> Of prophecy the seal!
> We read with reverence the book
> Thou wast sent to reveal.
>
> For thou the burden did'st remove,
> Idolatry's fell rod;
> And in thy day the idols fell
> Before the sword of God.
>
> To bless Arabia and the world,
> Most surely thou wast raised:
> We'll sing thy praises evermore,
> Our Mustapha, the praised.
>
> We watch with gentle, fostering care
> The seed that thou hast sown;
> And trust to hear the world declare
> God's prophet as its own.
>
> We laugh with scorn at those who say
> That God has had a son;
> With confidence we do declare
> "La Allah," God is One.

1st Rabia-al-awal, 1314

This hymn is so arranged that it can be sung to 'Horsley' or any common metre tune.

(From *Islamic World*, Vol. IV, No. 40, August 1896, p. 128)

(F)   J. L. M. GOUGH, 'MOSLEM MORNING HYMN'

Soul of the Worlds! To Thee we turn our gaze,
Bask in Thy smile, and worship in its rays:
Before Thee, God, how small doth seem a creed!
Lord of the Worlds! 'Tis Thee alone we need!

Teach us, O Allah, Thine own perfect way;
Al-Latif, lead us, that we may not stray;
Our erring footsteps guide Thou e'er aright,
Our Tower of Strength be Thou in our life's fight.

Compassionate and Merciful! To Thee,
Without another succour, lo we flee:
Teach us to bend our stubborn wills to Thine;
Teach us the gold that doth in Patience shine!

King on the Day of Judgment! Lo, we bow
In adoration 'neath Thine august brow;
Yet for Thy Chosen One's, Muhammed's sake,
Deign our poor off'ring graciously to take!

12 January 1897

(From *Islamic World*, Vol. IV, No. 46, February 1897, p. 320)

(G)   MOSLEMISM IN LIVERPOOL: QUILLIAM, FATHER AND SON, 1891

The following extract from the Liverpool Review *illustrates something of the antagonism that the Liverpool Muslim Institute faced within the city during the 1890s. It should be noted, however, that this article is itself a comment on an earlier article published by the* Liverpool Post, *which is taken to task for being too tolerant of the public practice of Islam in the city.*

ENGLAND is a free country where any man may pursue his peculiar tastes and fancies with impunity, so long as they do not bring him into conflict with the law, which is very elastic on such points, or with his neighbour, who is generally very forbearing. But there is a limit to all things, even in England, though much latitude may be allowed before that limit is reached.

There is a limit to the patience of *D. P.* [*Daily Post*] readers, who find too much prominence given, periodically, to the Mohammedan tastes and doings of certain persons who have elected to join the "faithful believers" [...] If anyone chooses to make himself conspicuous by espousing an un-English religion, why should the *D. P.* give prominence to his journeyings, interviews, ways and doings? [...]

The latest picture presented is that of "Mr Quilliam's little son," kneeling at his devotions during a violent attack on the Moslem Temple in Liverpool, a fortnight ago, when fireworks and "bucketsful of missiles" were thrown by the crowd. In alluding to this outbreak, the *D. P.* lost sight of causes in denouncing effects, [...]. To make matters quite clear, it should be explained that certain persons have thought fit to establish a Moslem Temple in Liverpool, which they are entitled to do. The name sounds big, but the quarters are only an ordinary house and garden in Brougham Terrace, not far from Hengler's Circus. In this "Temple," according to the *D. P.*, a service is held at seven o'clock on Sunday evenings for' all-comers, Mahommedan or Christian, but later another service is held—making two "shows" in one night—open to the "faithful" only. This latter function is preceded by what was probably the cause of the violent proceedings of the crowd—the "Muezzin" shouting the call to prayer, in Eastern fashion, from the balcony of the house. This was doubtless the red rag that aroused the mob's active antagonism, for such a glaring advertisement in England, by the outside showman of the performance inside, cannot escape ridicule, and naturally tempts thoughtless and excitable opponents to resort to practical joking and violence. [...] In the East untold horrors and cruelty have been suffered by Christians, however weak and inoffensive their ways, but here, it is not the private and inoffensive worship of Mohammed that is objectionable, but the public advertisement of him. Travellers in the East expect to hear the "Muezzin" call the faithful to their devotions, for there is nothing unusual or incongruous in the custom there, but the warning voice that fitly sounds from the midst of Eastern minarets and mosque towers is ridiculous from the balcony of a three-storey house in Brougham Terrace. Here it is most incongruous, unusual, silly and unwelcome, and the man who stands howling on a first floor balcony in such a fashion is certain to collect a ribald crowd, anxious to offer him a copper to go into the next street, or even ready to respond to his invitation with something more forcible than jeers. Such things cannot be done with impunity, for they may be expected to interfere with the ways and beliefs of the vast majority, more than one can expect a Catholic band to go scatheless through an Orange district, or an Orange band through a Catholic neighbourhood. It is all very well to preach that the law upholds what people have a *right* to do, but we are governed by custom as well as by law, and if prevailing customs are not sensibly respected, hard knocks are the inevitable consequence, and should arouse little sympathy.

Evidently Liverpool at large does not want any dealings with Moslemism. Let Mr. Quilliam and his fellow-believers in the Prophet do as they like inside their own quarters, but suppress the balcony business. In the east the "Faithful" hear their call to prayer and respect it as they please; here, the few "Faithful" sojourners in the city, with any enthusiastic converts, will doubtless wend their way to Brougham Terrace Temple, if they like, without any bidding, but the cry of the "Muezzin" has no serious meaning for the hundreds within sound of it, who are not of Mohammed's followers and detest his creed. Western folk do not believe in the Eastern humbug. We regard his creed—and history proves it true—as hand-and-glove with cruelty, murder, moral and imperial decay, and barbarous ferocity. England hates the creed which has done its utmost to make itself hated by its ways and actions. There has been a standing feud between Christianity and Moslemism since the days of the Crusaders, and it is not likely that one of the false prophet's followers can emerge upon a balcony, and advertise his creed aggressively into Western ears, without causing irritation, because the Western fixed belief is that Mohammedanism lives and moves in an atmosphere of darkness, bloodshed and cruelty. How, then, can any Mohammedan, however earnest or enthusiastic, *dare* to force his objectionable creed upon the notice of a mixed crowd in a Christian country? When such efforts are made no wonder opposition is aroused. Lawlessness and disorder, as a rule, are reprehensible, but are sometimes—like all extremes—necessary and defensible. Let the infatuated believers in Mohammed refrain from publicly advertising their creed, and the English public will, no doubt, willingly allow them to stand on their heads, or play any antics they choose, inside their makeshift Temple in Brougham Terrace. But the showman on the balcony-rostrum cannot fail to arouse antagonism and riot.

(From *Liverpool Review*, 28 November 1891, p. 14)

(H)   SUNDAY IN LIVERPOOL: WITH THE MOSLEMS, 1896

Another example of public comment on the conduct of the Liverpool Muslim Institute is provided by the following extract from an issue of the Liverpool periodical, Sunday at Home, *published in 1896. Apart from the insights that this account provides into the style of worship practised in the mosque, it is also noteworthy that the account strives to be purely factual and offers no judgement on the presence of Islam in Liverpool.*

Greek and Oriental Liverpool

The variety of peoples, races and tongues in Liverpool, with their corresponding Sunday observances, has already come before us. It would be easy to add to the number. In Prince's Avenue, we shall find the chief sacred building of the Hellenic community in Liverpool—the Greek Church, a picturesque and oriental-looking edifice, with walls of red brick, semi-cupolas, and Romanesque arches, a copy of the famous Church of the Theotokas at Constantinople. The Greek settlers in Liverpool, though not numerous, are influential. Sunday service is held in the morning only.

In the same fashionable thoroughfare is the Jewish synagogue of the Ashkenazi branch of the community, its gabled front flanked with lofty Moorish turrets and Moorish arches.

The Mussulmans in Liverpool

We shall also find a Mohammedan population in Liverpool, with a special building devoted to the religion of Islam. Liverpool is the only seaport in England which possesses a Mosque and Moslem Institute, with an appointed Sheikh and Emâm, and religious services on the sacred day.

The Liverpool Mosque is situate not, as might be imagined, among the nautical riverside population, but on the farther side of the city, in the West Derby Road. At Brougham Terrace, the visitors will find a house bearing conspicuously on its front the Mohammedan symbols—the golden star and crescent. Here daily at noon, the Emâm of the mosque calls the followers of the Prophet to prayers, using the balcony instead of a minaret to deliver the summons.

Within are the peculiar arrangements characteristic of Moslem worship. Entering beneath a Moorish arch the visitor sees at the east end the *mihrab* or niche, indicating the *Kibla* or direction of Mecca; the *mimbar* or pulpit for the sermon, and a raised platform from which the Koran is recited.

Prayer and meditations are the devotions to which the Liverpool Moslems are called on Sunday mornings. In the evening at seven o'clock the proceedings are of a more congregational character, and an address is delivered.

But Friday and not Sunday is the Mussulman's sacred day. Congregational service is held, and hymns (in English) are sung.

Their Hymns

A collection entitled "Hymns suitable for English-speaking Moslem congregations," has been compiled, and finds much acceptance with the worshippers. To the Christian visitor it is at first sight startling to see that nearly all the hymns are taken from English Evangelical poets and divines. He hears the congregation singing with fervour and evident familiarity, hymns by Wesley, Watts, Doddridge, Cowper, and Bonar. Only on a further inspection does he see the selections are confined to those which denote the unity of the Godhead, some of them being altered and adapted for the purpose. With English-speaking Moslems, as well as with Christians, the hymn "My God, my Father, whilst I stray," is, we are told, a favourite. So is the hymn, "Abide with me," in which the last verse has been adapted for Moslem worship:

> "Abide with me when close these mortal eyes!
> Shine through the gloom, and point me to the skies!
> Heaven's morning breaks, and earth's vain shadows flee;
> In life, in death, Allah abide with me!"

Such is the influence which Christian surroundings are exercising upon the religion of Mohammed in Liverpool, in the hands of leaders remarkably susceptible to western and Christian culture.

The Liverpool mosque, humble as it is at present in its externals, stands high in the esteem and expectancy of Moslems abroad, and is frequently visited by distinguished Asiatics during their temporary stay in England. It has recently received an endowment from the Shahzada of Afghanistan.

There are now upwards of one hundred members, besides children, connected with the Moslem congregation. The leaders are evidently earnest men, and sanguine of the future of their work. An extension of the premises is in progress, and a space will be appropriated to a Khan in which Moslem visitors can be received during their stay in Liverpool.

(From *Sunday at Home* (New Series) Part 19, May 1896, pp. 33–4)

INDEX